T0389655

Emerging Trends in Learning Analytics

Contemporary Approaches to Research in Learning Innovations

The titles published in this series are listed at *brill.com/carl*

Emerging Trends in Learning Analytics

Leveraging the Power of Education Data

Edited by

Myint Swe Khine

BRILL

SENSE

LEIDEN | BOSTON

All chapters in this book have undergone peer review.

Library of Congress Cataloging-in-Publication Data

Names: Khine, Myint Swe, editor.
Title: Emerging trends in learning analytics : leveraging the power of
  education data / edited by Myint Swe Khine.
Description: Leiden ; Boston : Brill Sense, [2019] | Series: Contemporary
  approaches to research in learning innovations 12 | Includes
  bibliographical references.
Identifiers: LCCN 2019005549 (print) | LCCN 2019007409 (ebook) | ISBN
  9789004399273 (ebook) | ISBN 9789004399266 (pbk. : alk. paper) | ISBN
  9789004396616 (hardback)
Subjects: LCSH: Education--Research--Statistical methods. | Education--Data
  processing. | Learning--Evaluation. | Educational evaluation.
Classification: LCC LB1028.43 (ebook) | LCC LB1028.43 .E448 2019 (print) |
  DDC 370.72--dc23
LC record available at https://lccn.loc.gov/2019005549

Typeface for the Latin, Greek, and Cyrillic scripts: "Brill". See and download: brill.com/brill-typeface.

ISSN 2542-8756
ISBN 978-90-04-39926-6 (paperback)
ISBN 978-90-04-39661-6 (hardback)
ISBN 978-90-04-39927-3 (e-book)

Contents

Figures and Tables

Figures

Tables

Notes on Contributors

Arif Altun
is a professor of computer education and instructional technologies at Hacettepe University, Ankara, Turkey. His current research areas include cognitive issues in learning with hypertext, designing personalized e-learning environments, computerizing neuro-psychological tests, and developing educational ontologies.

Alexander Amigud
received his PhD degree in Network and Information Technologies from Universitat Oberta de Catalunya. His current research interests include: learning analytics, ethical issues in technology, academic integrity, behavioural biometrics, and learning technology. He is a member of the IEEE and a member of the Project Management Institute.

Dongwook An
is a graduate student in Learning Technologies program at UT-Austin. His research interest includes the impact of emerging technologies such as machine learning and block chain on education, as well as how to teach their philosophy, implication, and social impact.

Mirella Atherton
has a special interest in vulnerability and how vulnerable consumers interact with institutions and modern business models within Australia. In the past, Mirella has researched confidence and uncertainty levels of individuals who have experienced barriers to education using the third person effect and emerging trend analytics.

Leigh Blackall
is Education Developer at RMIT University in Australia. His professional focus is on educational research and development, networked learning and flexible teaching and assessment. He primarily works in the tertiary education, training and communication sectors, offering professional development, consultation services and project leadership.

Robert Carpenter
is Associate Provost for Analytics and Institutional Assessment, Professor of Economics and Public Policy and also Deputy Chief Information Officer

(CIO) in the Division of Information Technology (DoIT) at the University of Maryland, Baltimore County.

He also advises several technology firms on the development of their higher education analytics platforms, and currently serves as a member of the executive committee for the APLU Commission on Information, Measurement, and Analysis (CIMA).

Martin Ebner

is the Head of the Department Educational Technology at Graz University of Technology, Austria, and responsible for all university wide e-learning activities. He holds an Adjunct Professor position on media informatics and also works at the Institute for Interactive Systems and Data Science as senior researcher.

John Fritz

is Associate Vice President for Instructional Technology in University of Maryland, Baltimore County. John holds a PhD in Language, Literacy and Culture from UMBC, an MA in English from the University of Maryland, a BA in English and religion from Columbia Union College in Takoma Park, Maryland.

Yoshiko Goda

is an associate professor at Research Center for Instructional Systems, Kumamoto University, Japan. She received her PhD (Science Education) at Florida Institute of Technology (FIT) with partial support of a Fulbright scholarship. Her current research interests include self-regulated learning for e-learning, instructional and learning design, online education program evaluation, and innovative community for global education.

Yasemin Gulbahar

is a Professor at the Department of Informatics at Ankara University. She has also been the Director of the university's Distance Education Center and a researcher of e-learning for a number of years.

Junko Handa

is an adjunct faculty member at Saitama Institute Technology, and a visiting associate professor at Polytechnic University of Japan. She is also a visiting researcher at Meiji University. She received a Doctor of Education (EdD) in Instructional Technology at Towson University in Maryland, USA. Her research interests are language education, instructional and learning design, and learning with media.

Dirk Ifenthaler

is Professor and Chair of Learning, Design and Technology at University of Mannheim, Germany and Adjunct Professor at Deakin University, Australia. His research focuses on the intersection of cognitive psychology, educational technology, data analytics, and organisational learning. He is the Editor-in-Chief of the Springer journal *Technology, Knowledge and Learning*.

Yumi Ishige

is a professor in the Faculty of Modern Social Studies at Otemae University, Japan. She received her MA from Ryukoku University, Japan, and PhD from Durham University, the United Kingdom. Her current research project focuses on the system of learning support in higher education, and the nationwide survey on current situation of the learning support centers.

Il-Hyun Jo

is a professor in the Department of Educational Technology, Ewha Womans University, Seoul, Korea. He earned his PhD from the Florida State University, USA and specializes in curriculum theory, teacher education, teaching methods and learning analytics.

Kosuke Kaneko

is an associate professor of Cybersecurity Center in Kyushu University, Japan. He received his PhD (Computer Science) from Kyushu University. His current research interests include cybersecurity, network/communication, robotics and learning analytics.

Myint Swe Khine

is a Professor of Education at Emirates College for Advanced Education, United Arab Emirates and Adjunct Professor at Curtin University, Australia. He publishes widely in international refereed journals and edited several books. His recent book *International Trends in Educational Assessment* was published by Brill in the Netherlands in 2019.

Selcan Kilis

is an Assistant Professor at Giresun University, Turkey, she is also Deputy Manager of the university's Distance Education Research and Application Center. She attained her PhD from the Computer Education and Instructional Technology department of the Middle East Technical University.

Daniel Klasen

is a postdoctoral researcher in Learning, Design and Technology at the University of Mannheim, Germany. He holds a doctoral degree in computer science. Daniel's current interests are situated in the research fields of learning analytics and educational data mining.

Mehmet Kokoç

is currently a researcher at Center for Research and Application in Distance Education, Karadeniz Technical University. Dr. Kokoç received his PhD in Computer Education and Instructional Technology from Hacettepe University. His academic interest areas are learning analytics, educational data mining, open and distance learning, social media in education and video-based learning.

Shin'ichi Konomi

is a Professor at Faculty of Arts and Science, Kyushu University. He is also a Director of Learning Analytics Center in Kyushu University.

Philipp Leitner

is currently working at the Department of Educational Technology at Graz University of Technology, Austria, and completing his doctorate on Learning Analytics. His research focuses on technology enhanced learning, learning analytics, data privacy and recommender systems.

Chenglu Li

is a doctoral student in Learning Technologies Program and has a strong interest in educational games and educational data mining.

Min Liu

is a Professor of Learning Technologies at the University of Texas at Austin. Her teaching and research interests center on educational uses of new media and other emerging technologies, particularly the impact of such technologies on teaching and learning; and the design of new media enriched interactive learning environments for learners at all age levels. She also serves on a number of editorial boards for research journals in educational technology.

Karin Maier

is currently pursuing a Master's degree in Computer Science at the Department of Educational Technology at Graz University of Technology, Austria. She specializes in knowledge technologies and IT security and is interested in bringing these two together in the field of education.

Jon Mason

is a senior lecturer at Charles Darwin University in Australia where he leads research into digital education futures. He also holds adjunct positions as a Professor within the Department of e-Learning at Korea National Open University, a Professor of Educational Technology at East China Normal University, and as a Project Consultant for the Advanced Innovation Center for Future Education at Beijing Normal University.

Misato Oi

is a Research Fellow at Faculty of Arts and Science, Kyushu University. Her research includes educational psychology and learning analytics.

Fumiya Okubo

is an Assistant Professor at Faculty of Arts and Science, Kyushu University, Japan. He received his PhD in Science from Waseda University. His research interests focus on theoretical computer science, automata theory and computation theory. He also works at Learning Analytics Center in Kyushu University to research educational data mining.

Xin Pan

is currently a second-year doctoral student in Learning Technologies at UT-Austin. Her interests in educational technology include MOOCs, game-based learning, enhancing science literacy with simulations and animations, and integrating technologies into informal spaces such as museums.

Zilong Pan

is a doctoral student in the Learning Technologies program at The University of Texas at Austin. He earned his master's degree in Middle School Education from the University of Georgia. He had taught in middle schools in Atlanta area as a science and math teacher for two years. His research interests include learning analytics and integrating learning technology into STEM education.

Stefan Popenici

is a scholar with over 20 years of experience in teaching, research and leadership in higher education with universities in Europe, North America, South East Asia, New Zealand and Australia. He is currently working at Charles Darwin University. He was a senior advisor of the Minister of Education in Romania on educational reform and research, senior consultant of the President of De La Salle University Philippines. For his work and strategic leadership in education he was awarded a knighthood by the President of Romania, the Order 'Merit of Education.'

Clara Schumacher

is a research assistant at the chair of Economic and Business Education – Learning, Design and Technology at the University of Mannheim. Her research interests focus on educational technology, learning analytics, self-regulated and informal learning.

Peter Shaw

is a Senior Lecturer at Charles Darwin University in Australia. Dr Shaw is currently researching in parameterized complexity and has recently published a number of papers in the area of algorithmic techniques for FPT kernelization including: iterative compression, greedy localization, crown-rules and LDP problem dual kernelization. Dr Shaw received his PhD in Computer Science at Newcastle University Australia.

Yi Shi

is a doctoral student in the Learning Technologies program at UT. With a background in education, she is interested in how technologies could be used to enhance the process of teaching and learning.

Atsushi Shimada

is an Associate Professor at Faculty of Information Science and Electrical Engineering, Kyushu University. His research interests mainly focus on image processing, pattern recognition, machine learning and their application to learning analytics.

Yuta Taniguchi

is an Assistant Professor at Faculty of Information Science and Electrical Engineering, Kyushu University. His research includes text mining and educational data mining.

Billy Tak-Ming Wong

is Research Coordinator at the Open University of Hong Kong. He has widely published in the areas of technology-enhanced education, research capacity development, and computational linguistics, besides having obtained paper awards in various academic conferences.

Masanori Yamada

is an associate professor in Faculty of Arts and Science, Learning Analytics Center and Graduate School of Human-Environment Studies at Kyushu University. He is currently engaged in research and development of computer-mediated communication systems for project-based learning, and learning support system based on learning analytics and self-regulated learning.

Wenting Zou

is currently a doctoral student in Learning Technologies program at The University of Texas at Austin. She is interested in using learning analytics to understand learners' behaviours across different e-learning platforms.

PART 1

Introduction

∵

CHAPTER 1

Big Data Analytics in Education for Dynamic Personalised Learning Design

Myint Swe Khine

1 Introduction[1]

The term Learning Analytics is defined as the measurement, collection, analysis, and reporting of information about learners and their contexts for the purposes of understanding and optimizing learning. In recent years learning analytics has emerged as a promising area of research that trails the digital footprint of the learners and extract useful knowledge from educational databases to understand students' progress and success. With the availability of increased amount of data, potential benefits of learning analytics can be far reaching to all stakeholders in education including students, teachers, leaders, and policy-makers. Educators firmly believe that if properly harnessed, learning analytics will be an indispensable tool to enhance the teaching-learning process, narrow the achievement gap and improve the quality of education.

2 Contributions of Learning Analytics

In recent years, the contributions of learning analytics have been discussed in the educational research community. Most educators agree that learning analytics can facilitate evaluation of the effectiveness of pedagogies and instructional practices. Some suggest that learning analytics has the potential to contribute to the quality of teaching and learning by designing innovative and adaptive lessons to suit the individual students' cognitive abilities. The Learning Management Systems (LMSs) that combine content delivery, discussion forums, and quiz and assessment allows to monitor students' learning activities, and from the analysis, the instructor can detect the students at risk and undesirable behaviors. Once the issues are identified, the instructor can provide remedial solutions to support the students and help increase the level of achievement.

According to Hwang et al. (2017) learning analytics can assist in identifying the status of students' learning and the problems they face in the learning process. They also note that instructors will have a comprehensive view of students' interaction with the course materials, peers and instructors. This information may contain raising questions, clarifying concepts, seeking advice, making observations and providing alternative views and so on. By analyzing these learning behaviors and the interactions with the content, it will be possible to design personalized and adaptive learning contents, practices and user interfaces to maximize the learning of individual students.

The learning analytics can be an indispensable tool for supporting informed decision making in course design and development. The information and analyses generated from the data can assist the instructor to improve the course contents and instructional resources regularly. It is the responsibility of instructors to know the behaviors of their students. By analyzing the source of data, the patterns can be established to understand the interactions between students, resources, and peers within the course. Providing timely feedback is a key feature in the learning process and crucial for both learners and instructors (Brookhart, 2017). The results from learning analytics can indicate when to provide feedback to specific learners. Many studies have been reported the positive contributions of learning analytics. The encouraging results confirm that if properly used, learning analytics can help instructors to identify the learning gaps, implement intervention strategies, increase students' engagement and improve the learning outcomes (Merceron et al., 2015).

3 Applying Learning Analytics to Improve Education Process

From the citation database of peer-reviewed literature, Wong (2017) identifies case studies that report empirical findings on the application of learning analytics in higher education. A total of 43 research papers were selected for in-depth analysis to discover the objectives, approaches and major outcomes from the studies. Wong (2017) classifies six aspects that learning analytics can support to improve the education process. These are (i) improving student retention, (ii) supporting informed decision making, (iii) increasing cost-effectiveness, (iv) understanding students' learning behavior, (v) arranging personalized assistance to students, and (vi) providing timely feedback and intervention. These aspects are not to consider in a separate entity but are inextricably linked (see also Chapter 5 in this book).

3.1 *Student Retention*
In educational settings detecting early warning signs for students who are coping with their study can be an advantage for the instructors. The issues and problems

that students are facing may vary from social and emotional issues to academic matters or other factors that may lead to giving-up from the study. Those students can be provided with remedial instructions to overcome some of the problems. For example, Star and Collette (2010) report that knowing the circumstance and understanding the causes, an instructor can increase the interaction with the students to provide personal interventions. As a result, the students showed better academic performance and significantly increase the retention rate. In a similar study Sclater et al. (2016) describe that increase interactions with students promote a sense of belonging to the learner community and learning motivations. It was found that in the process the students' attrition rate dropped from 18 to 12%.

3.2   *Informed Decision Making*

The results from learning analytics can also be used to support informed decision making. A study by Toetenel and Rienties (2016) at the Open University in the UK involves analyzing the learning designs of 157 courses taken by over 60,000 students and identify the common pedagogical patterns among the courses. The authors suggest that educators should take note of activity types and workload when designing a course and such information will be useful in the decision making of specific learning design. However, the authors conclude that further studies are needed to find out whether particular learning design decisions result in better student outcomes.

3.3   *Cost-Effectiveness*

With the funding cut and raising expenditure, cost-effective has become the key indicator of sustainability in the education sector. One of the effective ways is to take advantage of the learning management systems that not only deliver the course materials, also keep track of the learners' activities. Instructors can analyze the activities and report the progress to the students and other stakeholders in a cost-effective manner. As Sclater et al. (2016) note, after conducting the analysis, notifications were automatically generated and send to students and their parents on students' performance.

3.4   *Students' Learning Behavior*

To better understand the students' learning behavior, instructors can explore the data collected from the learning management systems and social media networks. Instructors can examine the relationships between students' utilization of resources, learning patterns and preferences and learning outcomes. This approach has been adopted by Gewerc et al. (2014) when attempted to examine the collaboration and social networking in a subject for education degree course. The study analyzes the intensity and relevance of the student's contribution to the collaborative framework by using social network analysis and information extraction. The authors concluded that findings from the study help to understand more clearly how students behave during the course.

3.5   *Personalized Assistance to Students*

Given the advantages of data mining techniques and algorithms that are used in business and manufacturing industry, learning analytics has emerged as educational data mining of students and the courses they study. An investigation into the application of such technique in education domain was conducted by Karkhanis and Dumbre (2015) to discover the insightful information about the students and interaction with the course. They report that after analyzing the students' study results, demographics and social data, instructors can identify who needs assistant most to provide individual counseling.

3.6   *Timely Feedback and Intervention*

Providing feedback to students is a central role of teachers in any educational settings. This process enables students to learn from their action and can have a significant impact on the motivation of the learners. The quality and timeliness of feedback are crucial in the learning process. From the learning analytics, teachers can identify students who are in need of assistance and provide appropriate intervention to the specific students. Dodge et al. (2015) report that interventions through emails to the students work best and found that such approach impact on student achievement.

Similar to business forecast, ability to predict students' success can be a powerful practice in all levels of education. Daud et al. (2017) highlight that there is such a possibility to predict student performance with the use of advanced learning analytics. In their study, a wide-ranging background and personal data that includes students' household family expenditure, family income, students' personal information such as gender, marital and employment status and the family assets, are collected. By using discriminative and generative classification models, the authors can predict whether a student will be able to complete the course.

4   Privacy Concerns in Learning Analytics

While learning analytics can delve into the students' interaction data with instructors and course materials, identifying and using their behaviors and personal preferences to predict their success may amount to breaching privacy and confidentiality. Such concerns have been raised by Lawson et al. (2016)

and describe that identification of at-risk students using analytics and providing them intervention strategies raise an ethical dilemma for the educators. However, they contend that possible ways to resolve the issue are that the institutions could obtain consent from the students at different levels and increase the transparency of the process to avoid any missteps.

Given the importance of the ethical and legal considerations surrounding the use of data from learning analytics, educators find ways to overcome the issues while still providing feedback that will benefit them. Sclater (2016) draws attention to the Code of Practice for Learning Analytics developed by the Joint Information Systems Committee (JISC). The Code covers the main issues that educational institutions need to address to progress ethically and legally in this area. The process results in a taxonomy of ethical, legal and logistical issues for learning analytics that is grouped into distinct areas. These include ownership and control, consent, transparency, privacy, validity, access, action, adverse impact, and stewardship. Each area is identified whether it is an ethical, legal or logistical concern and the person responsible for dealing with it. With such clear guidelines and procedures, educators can comfortably proceed with the practice in learning analytics.

From the students' point of view, they are conservative in sharing data and expect learning analytics systems to include elaborate adaptive and personalized dashboards. This was found by Ifenthaler and Schumacher (2016) when the authors conduct a study with 330 university students. The authors suggest that learning analytics should be aligned with organizational principles and values and include all stakeholders in collecting and use of data. They further suggest that data should be analyzed transparently and free of bias for the benefits of all stakeholders.

5   Advancing and Moving Forward

The educational community is witnessing remarkable progress in theory development, research design and technical advancement in learning analytics over the past decade. With the increase capabilities in data mining techniques and power statistics, educators can exploit the information retrieved from the students' learning experience and transform into a model that can suggest remedial actions for the learners and predict the students' success (Gasevic & Pechenizkiy, 2016). Several studies are reported to describe the future of learning analytics in improving teaching and learning. In this regards, Strang (2017) demonstrated that by using the student attributes and their online activities, key learning engagement factors can be identified and able to develop a General Linear Model to predict the students learning outcomes. His study involves 228 university students, and students' engagement data was collected from the learning management system logs.

There has been much discussion about the advantages of personalized and adaptive instruction in education in the past. However, cost-effectiveness is a hindrance in implementing across educational institutions. With the use of technology and learning analytics, the adaptive instruction may become a reality in large scale. Liu et al. (2017) attempted to use the data to understand the behavior patterns of the learner and design an adaptive instruction for a group of 128 pharmacy students in a university. The study involves a commercially available system that uses an adaptive algorithm and semantic analytics engine to take various input data from the students and generates personalized learning paths based on students' performance. The authors suggest that in designing adaptive learning, students' non-cognitive factors such as motivation and goal orientation should also be considered. Mavroudi et al. (2017) conducted a systematic review of twenty-one studies to better understand the nature of adaptive learning analytics with the research questions ranging from the context, objectives and when and where adaptive learning is applied and facilitated. They report that more insightful models of complex student behaviors can be developed to create constructive-collaborative environment in the future.

6   Organization of the Book

This book is organized in four parts. An introductory chapter in Part 1 examines the recent attempts to conduct systematic and multidisciplinary research in learning analytics. The chapters in Part 2 describe trends in learning analytics and Amingud in Chapter 2 explores how data and information technology transform learning environments. In Chapter 3 Liu and her team reviewed the literature from 2015 to present and report the use of analytics for educational purposes in different settings. Kilis and Gulbahar also conducted a systematic review of research on learning analytics in Chapter 4. In the open and distance education contexts Billy Wong reviewed and provides the evidence on the benefits of learning analytics in Chapter 5.

Part 3 of the book covers pedagogical applications of learning analytics and in Chapter 6, Mason, Shaw and Khan from Charles Darwin University in Australia elaborate the new smarts in teaching and learning based on learning analytics. Arif Altun and Mehmet Kokoç in Chapter 7 present how to profile learners and visualize the learning process for building better learning experiences. In Chapter 8 Atherton presents analytical indicators for profiling and improving engagement and success of vulnerable participants. From the University of Maryland, John Fritz and Robert Carpenter in Chapter 9 introduce a unique approach in triangulating student engagement with "Built & Bought" learning analytics.

Part 4 of the book introduces research and development works and innovative approaches in the learning analytics. In Chapter 10, Schumacher, Schon, and Ifenthaler shared their experiences in the implementation of a learning analytics system in a productive higher education environment in Germany. This chapter is followed by the work by Yamada and his team in Japan (Chapter 11) concerning discourse analysis visualization based on community of inquiry framework. In Chapter 12, Okubo and her research team present their findings on experimenting learning support systems based on cohesive learning analytics. Professor Jo from Ewha Womans University in Korea (Chapter 13) describes the learning analytics and flipped problem-based for toll-design learning. Finally, in Chapter 14 Maier, Leitner, and Ebner in Graz University in Austria demonstrate how learning analytics cockpit for MOOC platforms can be built.

Many investigations have been conducted and disseminated in the literature and studies related to learning analytics are growing exponentially. This book documents recent attempts to carry out systematic, prodigious and multidisciplinary research in learning analytics and present their findings and identify areas for further research and development. The contributors in this book share the distinguished and exemplary works in the field highlighting the current trends, privacy and ethical issues, creative and unique approaches, innovative methods, frameworks, and theoretical and practical aspects of learning analytics. It is hope that the book will be a catalyst for future research and inspires cutting-edge research in this area.

Note

1 Part of this chapter was presented at the European Conference on Education, Brighton, United Kingdom in July 2018.

References

Brookhart, S. M. (2017). *How to give effective feedback to your students*. Alexandria, VA: ASCD.

Daud, A., Aljohani, N. R., Abbasi, R. A., Lytras, M. D., Abbas, F., & Alowibdi, J. S. (2017, April). Predicting student performance using advanced learning analytics. In

Proceedings of the 26th International Conference on World Wide Web Companion, International World Wide Web Conferences Steering Committee (pp. 415–421).

Dodge, B., Whitmer, J., & Frazee, J. P. (2015, March). Improving undergraduate student achievement in large blended courses through data-driven interventions. In *Proceedings of the Fifth International Conference on Learning Analytics and Knowledge* (pp. 412–413). New York, NY: ACM.

Gasevic, D., & Pechenizkiy, M. (2016). Let's grow together: Tutorials on learning analytics methods. *Journal of Learning Analytics, 3*(3), 5–8.

Gewerc, A., Montero, L., & Lama, M. (2014). Collaboration and social networking in higher education. *Media Education Research Journal, 42*, 55–63.

Hwang, G. J., Chu, H. C., & Yin, C. (2017). Objectives, methodologies and research issues of learning analytics. *Interactive Learning Environments, 25*(2), 143–146.

Ifenthaler, D., & Schumacher, C. (2016). Student perceptions of privacy principles for learning analytics. *Educational Technology Research and Development, 64*(5), 923–938.

Karkhanis, S. P., & Dumbre, S. S. (2015). A study of application of data mining and analytics in education domain. *International Journal of Computer Applications, 120*(22).

Lawson, C., Beer, C., Rossi, D., Moore, T., & Fleming, J. (2016). Identification of 'at risk' students using learning analytics: The ethical dilemmas of intervention strategies in a higher education institution. *Educational Technology Research and Development, 64*(5), 957–968.

Liu, M., Kang, J., Zou, W., Lee, H., Pan, Z., & Corliss, S. (2017). Using data to understand how to better design adaptive learning. *Technology, Knowledge and Learning, 22*(3), 271–298.

Mavroudi, A., Giannakos, M., &Krogstie, J. (2017). Supporting adaptive learning pathways through the use of learning analytics: Developments, challenges, and future opportunities. *Interactive Learning Environments, 26*(2), 206–220.

Merceron, A., Blikstein, P., & Siemens, G. (2015). Learning analytics: From big data to meaningful data. *Journal of Learning Analytics, 2*(3), 4–8.

Sclater, N. (2016). Developing a code of practice for learning analytics. *Journal of Learning Analytics, 3*(1), 16–42.

Star, M., & Collette, L. (2010). GPS: Shaping student success one conversation at a time. *Educause Quarterly, 33*(4), n4.

Strang, K. D. (2017). Beyond engagement analytics: Which online mixed-data factors predict student learning outcomes? *Education and Information Technologies, 22*(3), 917–937.

Toetenel, L., & Rienties, B. (2016). Analysing 157 learning designs using learning analytic approaches as a means to evaluate the impact of pedagogical decision making. *British Journal of Educational Technology, 47*(5), 981–992.

Wong, B. T. M. (2017). Learning analytics in higher education: An analysis of case studies. *Asian Association of Open Universities Journal, 12*(1), 21–40.

PART 2

Trends in Learning Analytics

∵

Post-Traditional Learning Analytics: How Data and Information Technology Transform Learning Environment

Alexander Amigud

1 Introduction

The educational environment can be delineated into two paradigms—traditional with its brick and mortar schools, and post-traditional, where communication technologies bridge the physical gap between learners and academic service providers. The traditional paradigm contains a strong element of control, standardization, and institutional centralism. Learning is tailored to suit the standard student whose performance was assessed on a standardized scale within the standard curriculum. Data and data-driven decision-making are instrumental in serving a quality control function such as identifying and mitigating risks of student failure that do not reflect well on institutional reports. It is far more efficient to weed out students early on, at the admissions or the exam stage, than provide individual interventions. Hence, the extensive body of research dedicated to performance indicators and predictors of student achievement. Openness and accessibility are not design considerations in the traditional paradigm which has high control and power over learning and teaching resources. For example, assessment proctoring is a staple of the traditional paradigm, where the learning environment is physically controlled to maintain test integrity. Assessment tasks generally involve solving a problem in a certain way. On the one hand, the institutional-centric approach hindered the development of student autonomy, as they followed a prescribed plan; on the other hand, this entailed inherent guidance and structure built into the learning process. It does not require much contemplation on the part of students as to what they should do next.

As information and communication technologies became more accessible, they were eagerly adopted by institutions offering distance learning. One of the key features of e-learning is flexibility—a key requirement for post-traditional learners (Soares, 2013). In addition to the digitization of educational resources, institutions were making administrative and support services, such as admissions, tutoring, assessments, and libraries available online, yielding a greater level of accessibility and convenience to students and more efficient resource management for the institutions. To minimize the costs associated with the production of learning materials, including licensing, printing and mailing out thousands of course kits every semester, schools started to explore the open-access alternatives and electronic production and distribution of learning materials. It may appear that the post-traditional paradigm was engineered as a means to improve the traditional approach through the use of technology that enables accessibility and convenience. However, carrying over processes and services from the brick and mortar environment to the distributed one turned out to be a non-trivial endeavor as many processes were not readily translatable. This prompted a need to design new processes that work around technical and contextual constraints of distributed learning.

The pioneers of the technology-mediated learning were forced—due to legal, technical, and pedagogical constraints, among others—to compromise, experiment, and innovate, which led to the development of new pedagogies, approaches, and learning technologies. Communities of inquiry (Garrison, Anderson, & Archer, 1999), the teaching and learning of creativity (Loveless, 2002), the emergence of the maker education (Halverson & Sheridan, 2014; Wang, Zhou, & Wu, 2016), and the philosophy of students as partners (Healey, Flint, & Harrington, 2016) among others, are products of overcoming gaps and constraints of existing at the time tools, policies, and instructional approaches. The post-traditional approach, as it exists now, emerged out of necessity to address constraints imposed by the technical, pedagogical, social, and legal frameworks. There was a need to secure exams, to engage learners, and to distribute course content in a way that does not infringe on intellectual property rights. The last was addressed through open access (Schwabach, 2014; Yiotis, 2005). Furthermore, maintaining integrity of assessments in a distributed learning environment proved to be rather challenging, as instructors had no control over the remote learning environment. To address this limitation, many of the schools adhered to traditional proctoring for online courses, which undermined the promise of anytime and anyplace learning. Some schools decreased the number of high stakes assessments due to logistical challenges, and adopted authentic assessments such as portfolios and projects (Bailie & Jortberg, 2009).

With a shift towards accessibility and openness, resulting in a greater than ever volume of learning resources, the post-traditional paradigm opened doors to opportunities for students who would generally be left behind by the traditional system, not only in terms of access convenience, but also in terms of variety and cost. The post-traditional learning environment offers more choices than ever before, from course materials to tutoring services to assessment formats. This would not have been possible without technologies that facilitate support for providing learning and teaching. But getting in the driver's seat and having the freedom to chart their own path to learning requires students to develop new skills such as self-engagement, initiative, and resourcefulness. It also requires new tools for students, academic practitioners, and developers to monitor quality of learning, provide support, deliver services, and engage students. One of these tools is learning analytics, which is increasingly becoming geared towards supporting students in their quest to become autonomous learners. The interest in learning and institutional analytics is gaining traction because it provides a quantitative view of the learning environment and the ability to conditionally trigger interventions, automating and expediting delivery of academic services. It also constitutes a type of learning technology that facilitates exploration of real world problems through data.

Before we get into examples of the latest analytics-driven applications, it is important to review how analytics, being a computational approach, evolved. We then take a closer look at how institutions strategically utilize data to manage learning and teaching processes, and discuss emerging trends that will further shape the educational landscape.

2   A Change in Centricity

The use of data for decision making is not new—admissions criteria and success factors, the cost of tuition, student performance, faculty remuneration, and government funding were tabulated and computed before personal computers entered the academic offices. What is peculiar to the current temporal phase is the variety, breadth, and depth of analyses and tools. Learning and institutional analytics are terms that describe the application of computational techniques to data generated by academic institutions. Unlike mobile learning and social media for education (Gikas & Grant, 2013), the two preceding trends that were aimed at addressing the respective issues of accessibility, support, and engagement—analytics has a much wider range of application. It should be considered a set of problem-solving techniques conducted to address issues raised by stakeholders.

The traditional application of analytics in the academic environment serves two purposes: first, to provide information about the state of learning and teaching, and second, to benchmark operational performance. For example, identifying students who struggle to meet learning objectives would fall under learning analytics, and discovering trends in marketing performance would fall under institutional analytics. This chapter focuses on the former type, which is defined by the Society for Learning Analytics Research as: "the measurement, collection, analysis and reporting of data about learners and their contexts, for purposes of understanding and optimizing learning and the environments in which it occurs" (Siemens, 2012). This definition assumes that analytics is designed for and operated by anyone other than students, which limits the scope of its applications. As we will discuss later, student facing analytics renders this definition incomplete and this chapter proposes a broader definition of analytics as techniques for analyzing academic data. This expands its scope from being a strictly administrative tool that serves instructors and administrators to a learning aid, designed for and used by students.

Analytics is not an abstract task, but an application of computational techniques with a well defined scope. Analytics should be viewed as a sum of parts, whose performance needs to be continually assessed, and if needed, readjusted to keep up with dynamic changes in the environment. Analytics itself may serve as a catalyst for change; thus, it requires a continuous feedback loop. Given the context-specific nature of the data analysis tasks the one-size-fits-all approach may not be the most beneficial option to use (Gašević, Dawson, Rogers, & Gasevic, 2016; Larose, 2005). Strategies that worked well at one institution may not necessarily work at another, therefore avoiding a temptation to use out-of-the-box solutions would save a lot of resources in the long run. Furthermore, results of the data analyses—which often involve hypothesis testing—are prone to errors and subject to interpretation. Considering that much of the data represents constructs such as disengaged behavior or various emotional states, and output from the analyses serve as inputs to decision making processes, validity is of paramount importance. Evidence-based indicators should be used as much as possible, because the off-the shelf analytics software makes it easy to cherry pick data points that could lead to reaffirmed bias. Analytics should not be viewed as an end in itself; the insights are as useful as the institutional commitment to act upon them.

Learning analytics may be divided into two approaches: institution-centric and learner-centric. The former approach—reminiscent of the traditional paradigm—places instructors at the helm, to arbitrate knowledge and strive to attain institutional strategic goals. Analytics serves as a means to control the learning process raising attention to issues that present challenges for institutional stakeholders. Analytics, within the traditional paradigm, merely provides a new means to do what is already being done, for example reporting performance and managing risks. It aims to answers such questions as: How many students participated in a learning activity?; Is there a difference between midterm and final exams?; and How well can past student performance predict the future performance? (Ross et al., 2017).

Thus, the change that analytics introduced to institutions operating within a traditional model can be characterized as a technological one, rather than a philosophical one.

In contrast, the student-centric approach considers students as principal stakeholders in the learning process. The role of analytics here is not to control, but to transform the learning environment to improve learning experiences in order to make learning more accessible, engaging, and convenient. Technological advances are channeled towards putting students in the driver's seat, towards helping them become autonomous explorers of information, partners and creators of knowledge. This approach promotes learner autonomy, marking a departure from unequivocal subordination and passive consumption of information to participation and knowledge creation. Data not only provides the necessary support structure, but expands the scope of learning. The growing number of applications consider students as key actors in the learning process—what Bodily and Verbert (2017) described as "student-facing learning analytics" or Ferguson et al. (2017) labeled as "student-led analytics" highlight just that.

The next section discusses analytics-based applications congruent with the post-traditional paradigm.

3 Post-Traditional Learning Analytics

Instructors and teaching assistants provide students with feedback and support, identify content students find challenging, and suggest future directions, among performing other functions. With increasing adaptation of intelligent technologies, a number of human-performed tasks are being outsourced to computational systems that provide tutoring (Wetzel et al., 2017; Zhuhadar, Marklin, Thrasher, & Lytras, 2016), provide assessment and feedback (Khan et al. 2017; Xi, 2010), offer recommendations (Aly, Eskaf, & Selim, 2017; Krauss, 2016), and generate performance reports (Bodily & Verbert, 2017; Verbert, Duval, Klerkx, Govaerts, & Santos, 2013). These are examples of analytics applications. As much as it may be perceived as threatening to have a machine replace a human in certain tasks, automation has its benefits. For one, it sets instructors free to pursue other matters. Unlike the face to face mode of education, distributed learning allows content to be delivered electronically, shared, and reused. Automation adds convenience and minimizes wait time for making decisions or receiving a service. The benefit that automation brings to students is that it minimizes dependence on instructors' availability and the benefit for instructors is that routine tasks are automated, and their roles are becoming more focused on quality control and facilitation of learning.

Two areas where analytics improves convenience and efficiency is tutoring and student assessment. For example, a system that analyzes human interactions and provides feedback, proposed by Khan et al. (2017), can serve as a teaching aid for learning language and communication skills. Another system, called OnTask, provides automated personalized feedback. It allows instructors to define conditions under which the feedback is provided. The system is customizable and should fit the requirements of different learning activities and learning platforms (Kennedy, Corrin, & De Barba, 2017). A more specialized application called Knowledge Building Discourse Explorer (KBDeX) is designed to analyze social and temporal networks, using textual data of learner discourse, and visualize how individual learners and groups contribute to knowledge creation (Ma, Matsuzawa, Chen, & Scardamalia, 2016; Oshima, Oshima, & Matsuzawa, 2012). The tool was employed in a study by Lee, Tan, and Chee (2016) that enabled instructors to track emerging ideas, and promote creativity and engagement.

The time and space gap in the distributed learning environment presents a challenge for the integrity of learner assessment. As such, the assessment components more often than not follow the traditional protocols, particularly for high stakes exams. In spite of e-learning being promoted as an anytime and anyplace activity, much of the assessment retains the traditional form. This has implications for operations, costs, and convenience. The problem stems from the fact that the traditional approach to academic integrity relies on human observation and control over the learning environment, which in turn negates the benefits of anytime, anyplace learning. Remote proctoring services allow for taking exams in the convenience of one's own home; however, they often require installation of monitoring software that performs screen captures, and key logging, and restricts features of the operating system, in addition to monitoring students through the assessment session via a webcam. Proctoring-based strategies are generally invasive. Less invasive approaches such as plagiarism detection tools do not provide identity assurance and have blind spots (Fiedler & Kaner, 2010; Heather, 2010), therefore, they only partly address the issue of academic integrity.

Analytics-based methods have been recently applied to address academic integrity challenges in the distributed environment (Amigud, Arnedo-Moreno, Daradoumis, & Guerrero-Roldan, 2017b). This strategy takes advantage of the readily-available student-produced content. Instead of trying to control the remote learning environment, which more often than not is a futile exercise, it analyzes patterns in student produced artifacts in order to align identity and authorship. The rationale behind this approach is that by virtue of participation in learning activities, students create academic artifacts that are expected to be more stylistically similar to each other than to that of other students. Analytics provides insights into how the students learn, as opposed to how they cheat. This strategy has several advantages over traditional methods. First, the strategy relies on computational techniques to extract patterns from student artifacts; therefore, can be performed in the background. Analytics-based academic integrity strategies provide a convenient non-intrusive, and privacy preserving means for concurrent verification of student identities and validation of authorship of the submitted work. This minimizes the need for making scheduling arrangements, travelling to secure test centers, employing human proctors, providing third parties with access to personal computers, and being watched throughout the assessment session. In the post-traditional learning environment, where students seek the flexibility and convenience of learning (Soares, 2013), the delivery model should reflect student expectations; it is unreasonable to run distributed learning services in the traditional way, particularly when technologies that support flexibility and convenience are available.

Another area where analytics is transforming the learning landscape is the pedagogy and design of learning activities. For example, "Knowledge Community and Inquiry (KCI) is an approach that combines automated guidance with support for learning in a knowledge-building community" (Ferguson et al., 2017, p. 39). Analytics is the technology that has been used to provide both of these functions. Analytics is a means to achieve agility and flexibility of learning processes, which can be introduced, monitored, and modified on the fly. It may also serve as an instructional technique that allows students to explore real world uncertainty by using data as a learning aid. Traditional learning strives for standardization; students are expected to solve a specific problem in a certain way. In contrast, post-traditional learning does not shy away from fuzzy tasks and authentic assessments. By building learning activities around real world problems, represented by data, students engage with content and problems that are meaningful to them. Data analysis tools "can be used to encourage exploration, play, and puzzlement" (Ferguson et al., 2017, p. 35). There are a number of data sets and analysis tools available to instructors to be integrated in learning activities and available to students to explore and experiment outside of the classroom (McNamara, 2016). For example, Common Online Data Analysis Platform (CODAP) is a free web based platform that allows data exploration without a need for writing computer code (Erickson, 2016; Frischemeier, Biehler, & Engel, 2016). ThemeTrack is an algorithm for thematic and structural visualization of written content that makes structural comparisons between texts (Amigud, Arnedo-Moreno, Daradoumis, & Guerrero-Roldan, 2017a). It can be used as a language learning/teaching tool that depicts user-defined structures in textual data, and also as a literature review tool, that identifies and summarizes main themes. The code is openly available on Github. Even if the instructional strategy does not include the use of analytics as learning aids, students can obtain and use these tools on their own. Many analytics software and online services are aimed at novice users and provide intuitive interfaces. For students who want to expand their data literacy skills there are a number of resources available, such as massive open online courses (MOOCs), Q&A communities, video tutorials on popular video sites, and open code repositories.

Ferguson et al. (2017) note that "Data education is highly experiential; it is a practised art and a developed skill. Students need to encounter purposeful project-based, real-world applications with real data to build their conceptual understanding" (p. 33). This notion is also found in the 2016 Guidelines for Assessment and Instruction in Statistics Education (GAISE) college report that underlines a need to "foster active learning...use technology to explore concepts and analyze data...integrate real data with a context and purpose... give students experience with multivariable thinking" (Carver et al., 2016). The environment where data—which represents an array of real world events ranging from human behavior to astrophysical phenomena—is the object of examination. Instructors may assign fuzzy tasks such as providing new interpretations of the results through exploration and finding new relationships in data. This approach contrasts with the traditional assessment tasks that require a problem to be solved using a standard protocol.

Through interaction with data, students learn to apply computational methods and develop alternative interpretations of the results; and by doing so they build the necessary data literacy skills which is a value added benefit for their professional careers. Ferguson et al. (2017) argued that "People should no longer be passive recipients of data-based reports. They need to become active data explorers who can plan for, acquire, manage, analyse, and infer from data" (p. 5). Loveless (2002) asserted that ICT makes "a distinctive contribution to creative processes of developing ideas, making connections, creating and making, collaboration and communication for audiences" (p. 2). Analytics tools constitute knowledge-building technology that enables exploration, visualization, pattern discovery, simulation and modeling, something that would fall under the notion of creative activities (Cybulski, Keller, Nguyen, & Saundage, 2015). As students engage with technologies and use them to produce artifacts, analytics can also provide insights for understanding creativity. It is a multi-purpose tool that can be adapted to a variety of contexts, and problem scenarios.

4   Discussion

The previous section provided examples of student-facing analytics applications and introduced the notion of analytics as learning aids. This section discusses the implications of these developments for students and academic service providers.

Along with the shift in balance of control over the learning environment came a change in ownership of learning resources and student roles. Students have access to a variety of community and commercial alternatives to learning resources provided within a course and in certain domains can even create their own learning aids, particularly through the use of data tools. This precipitates a transformation in pedagogical approaches and learning activities that put greater emphasis on exploration (Ferguson et al., 2017). The departure from passive receiving of prepackaged learning content to exploration and construction of new knowledge entails participation in the investigation process. The traditional model where students enroll in school to learn a new skill contingent for securing a job is being challenged, because learning occurs in classrooms as much as outside of the school walls and students have the potential to contribute to knowledge creation. Because students have access to many of the same computational tools that institutions are using to analyze their data, the divide between in-class learning and out-of-class learning experiences is narrowed. This places the post-traditional learners in the category of academic partners. The notion of students as partners is gaining interest not only because it addresses the ever-present issue of student engagement, but also because it fits into the post traditional paradigm where technological constraints and pursuit of convenience and flexibility forced students to learn to be self-regulated and independent agents. Autonomy, independence, and choice were argued to be the prerequisites for partnership (Healey et al., 2016), and these are the characteristics that are inherent to the post-traditional learners.

Accessibility and ubiquity of technology made academic institutions lose their monopolistic edge in knowledge production. For example, high powered computing, electronic components, and 3D printing technology have become accessible at the consumer level. The open-data and maker movement—growing social trends—denote this trend. Technology provides the means to learn informally, through hands-on activities and online sources, including networking with like-minded groups, and create knowledge outside of academia. Like the learning process itself, the process of knowledge creation is a distributed one. Even the process of documenting knowledge creation is being conducted informally, through blogs, social media, and online communities. This goes in parallel with scholarly publications, and often the two overlap. Post-traditional learners have exposure to a vast volume of information and the means of its dissemination, which, coupled with the opportunity for hands on experience in areas that schools may not yet provide, forms the basis for establishing the necessity of academic partnerships. This is being acknowledged and adopted by schools who provide maker-spaces (Julian & Parrott, 2017) and foster non-informal learning, and by open data initiatives (Molloy, 2011) that promote transparency, integrity, and efficiency of scientific inquiry.

5 Conclusion

The ultimate aim of analytics research is to embed findings into practice. However, much of the literature discusses theoretical perspectives. The transformation of theory into pragmatic solutions has been sporadic; it depends on multidisciplinary research to define metrics and map data to actions. It also puts an onus on instructors to adopt technology-enhanced pedagogies, and on institutions to reevaluate the role of students in the learning process, and reconceive service delivery options. This chapter illustrated that analytics made an impact and has the power to transform the learning environment by enhancing convenience, providing support, and serving as an instructional device. One should anticipate greater inclusion of students in the use of analytics in the future, however, the rate of adoption of student-facing learning analytics, and analytics as learning aids, as any other technology, will vary among institutions, instructors, and students. The student-centered approach is not yet a mainstream position among academic service providers but considering the blurring divide between formal and informal learning the traditional paradigm will give way to the one that acknowledges students as main stakeholders.

For every new technological development in ICT, the learning technology community is eager to apply it ad-hoc to solve immediate problems. A quick look at the roster of accepted papers of any education technology related conference or journal in education shows spikes in interest that coincide with every new technological or social trend. For instance, interactive videos, social media, and mobile devices are some of the past trends that drew high interest, but have since started losing their appeal. Today, data-based technologies appear to be the next big thing, but unlike the earlier trends it is likely to gain further interest as schools continue generating vast volumes of data and increasingly rely on ICT for managing their operations. One reason why analytics will retain momentum within research and practitioner communities is that it advances the evolution of learning towards a more open state. It allows students to be placed in the center of the learning process, to deliver academic services in a more convenient fashion, to offer new instructional methods, to provide on-demand support and assessment, and to maintain service quality, while enabling institutions to maintain a grip on its operations. Whether institutions embrace the post-traditional paradigm of learning or defy it, neither can escape the call to use data since analysis is part of the academic process.

References

Aly, W. M., Eskaf, K. A., & Selim, A. S. (2017). *Fuzzy mobile expert system for academic advising*. Paper presented at the 30th IEEE Canadian Conference on Electrical and Computer Engineering (CCECE). IEEE.

Amigud, A., Arnedo-Moreno, J., Daradoumis, T., & Guerrero-Roldan, A.-E. (2017a). *A method for thematic and structural visualization of academic content*. Paper presented at the 17th IEEE International Conference on Advanced Learning Technologies (ICALT). IEEE.

Amigud, A., Arnedo-Moreno, J., Daradoumis, T., & Guerrero-Roldan, A.-E. (2017b). Using learning analytics for preserving academic integrity. *The International Review of Research in Open and Distributed Learning, 18*(5).

Bailie, J. L., & Jortberg, M. A. (2009). Online learner authentication: Verifying the identity of online users. *Journal of Online Learning and Teaching, 5*(2), 197.

Bodily, R., & Verbert, K. (2017). Review of research on student-facing learning analytics dashboards and educational recommender systems. *IEEE Transactions on Learning Technologies, 10*(4), 405–418.

Carver, R., Everson, M., Gabrosek, J., Horton, N., Lock, R., Mocko, M., Rossman, A., Holmes Rowell, G., Velleman, P., Witmer, J., & Wood, B. (2016). *Guidelines for assessment and instruction in statistics education: College report 2016*. Retrieved from http://www.amstat.org/asa/education/Guidelines-for-Assessment-and-Instruction-in-Statistics-Education-Reports.aspx

Cybulski, J. L., Keller, S., Nguyen, L., & Saundage, D. (2015). Creative problem solving in digital space using visual analytics. *Computers in Human Behavior, 42*, 20–35.

Erickson, T. (2016). *Practical public online data: Introducing TUVA and CODAP*. IASE 2016 Roundtable Workshop.

Ferguson, R., Barzilai, S., Ben-Zvi, D., Chinn, C. A., Herodotou, C., Hod, Y., Kali, Y., Kukulska-Hulme, A., Kupermintz, H., McAndrew, P., Rienties, B., Sagy, O., Scanlon, E., Sharples, M., Weller, M., & Whitelock, D. (2017). *Innovating pedagogy 2017: Innovation report 6*. Milton Keynes: The Open University.

Fiedler, R. L., & Kaner, C. (2010). Plagiarism-detection services: How well do they actually perform? *Technology and Society Magazine, IEEE, 29*(4), 37–43.

Frischemeier, D., Biehler, R., & Engel, J. (2016). *Competencies and dispositions for exploring micro data with digital tools.* Presented at the IASE Roundtable Conference.

Garrison, D. R., Anderson, T., & Archer, W. (1999). Critical inquiry in a text-based environment: Computer conferencing in higher education. *The Internet and Higher Education, 2*(2), 87–105.

Gašević, D., Dawson, S., Rogers, T., & Gasevic, D. (2016). Learning analytics should not promote one size fits all: The effects of instructional conditions in predicting academic success. *The Internet and Higher Education, 28*, 68–84.

Gikas, J., & Grant, M. M. (2013). Mobile computing devices in higher education: Student perspectives on learning with cellphones, smartphones & social media. *The Internet and Higher Education, 19*, 18–26.

Halverson, E. R., & Sheridan, K. (2014). The maker movement in education. *Harvard Educational Review, 84*(4), 495–504.

Healey, M., Flint, A., & Harrington, K. (2016). Students as partners: Reflections on a conceptual model. *Teaching & Learning Inquiry, 4*(2), 1–13.

Heather, J. (2010). Turnitoff: Identifying and fixing a hole in current plagiarism detection software. *Assessment & Evaluation in Higher Education, 35*(6), 647–660.

Julian, K. D., & Parrott, D. J. (2017). Makerspaces in the library: Science in a student's hands. *Journal of Learning Spaces, 6*(2), 13–21.

Kennedy, G., Corrin, L., & de Barba, P. (2017). Analytics of what? Negotiating the seduction of big data and learning analytics. In R. James, S. French, & P. Kelly (Eds.), *Visions for Australian tertiary education* (pp. 67–76). Melbourne, Australia: Melbourne Centre for the Study of Higher Education.

Khan, S., Suendermann-Oeft, D., Evanini, K., Williamson, D., Paris, S., Qian, Y., Huang, Y., Bosch, P., D'Mello, S., Loukina, A., & Davis, L. (2017, March 13–17). MAP: Multimodal assessment platform for interactive communication competency. In S. Shehata & J. P.-L. Tan (Eds.), *Practitioner track Proceedings of the 7th International Learning Analytics & Knowledge Conference (LAK17)* (pp. 6–12). Vancouver, Canada. SoLAR, Simon Fraser University.

Krauss, C. (2016). *Smart learning: Time-dependent context-aware learning object recommendations.* Paper presented at the FLAIRS Conference.

Larose, D. T. (2005). An introduction to data mining. *Traduction et Adaptation de Thierry Vallaud.*

Lee, A. V. Y., Tan, S. C., & Chee, K. J. K. (2016). Idea identification and Analysis (I2A): A search for sustainable promising ideas within knowledge-building discourse. In C. K. Looi, J. Polman, U. Cress, & P. Reimann (Eds.), *Transforming learning, empowering learners: The International Conference of the Learning Sciences (ICLS) 2016* (Vol. 1, pp. 90–97). Singapore: International Society of the Learning Sciences.

Loveless, A. (2002). *Literature review in creativity, new technologies and learning.* A NESTA.

Ma, L., Matsuzawa, Y., Chen, B., & Scardamalia, M. (2016). *Community knowledge, collective responsibility: The emergence of rotating leadership in three knowledge building communities*. Singapore: International Society of the Learning Sciences.

McNamara, A. (2016). On the state of computing in statistics education: Tools for learning and for doing. *ArXiv Preprint ArXiv:1610.00984*.

Molloy, J. C. (2011). The open knowledge foundation: Open data means better science. *PLoS Biology, 9*(12), e1001195.

Oshima, J., Oshima, R., & Matsuzawa, Y. (2012). Knowledge building discourse explorer: A social network analysis application for knowledge building discourse. *Educational Technology Research and Development, 60*(5), 903–921.

Ross, T., Chang, T.-W., Ives, C., Parker, N., Han, A., & Graf, S. (2017). The academic analytics tool: Workflow and use cases. In *Innovations in smart learning* (pp. 231–236). Springer.

Schwabach, A. (2014). *Internet and the law: Technology, society, and compromises: Technology, society, and compromises*. Santa Barbara, CA: ABC-CLIO.

Siemens, G. (2012). *Learning analytics: Envisioning a research discipline and a domain of practice*. Paper presented at the Proceedings of the 2nd International Conference on Learning Analytics and Knowledge, ACM.

Soares, L. (2013). *Post-traditional learners and the transformation of postsecondary education: A manifesto for college leaders*. Retrieved from http://www.acenet.edu/newsroom/Pages/Post-traditional Learners-and-the-Transformation-of-Postsecondary-Ed

Verbert, K., Duval, E., Klerkx, J., Govaerts, S., & Santos, J. L. (2013). Learning analytics dashboard applications. *American Behavioral Scientist, 57*(10), 1500–1509.

Wang, H., Zhou, C., & Wu, Y. (2016). *Smart cup, wisdom creation: A project-based learning initiative for maker education*. Paper presented at the Advanced IEEE 16th International Conference on Advance Learning Technologies (ICALT). IEEE.

Wetzel, J., VanLehn, K., Butler, D., Chaudhari, P., Desai, A., Feng, J., Grover, S., Joiner, R., Kong-Sivert, M., Samala, R., Tiwari, M., van de Sande, B., & Patade, V. (2017). The design and development of the Dragoon intelligent tutoring system for model construction: Lessons learned. *Interactive Learning Environments, 25*(3), 361–381.

Xi, X. (2010). Automated scoring and feedback systems: Where are we and where are we heading? *Language Testing, 27*, 291–300.

Yiotis, K. (2005). The open access initiative: A new paradigm for scholarly communications. *Information Technology and Libraries, 24*(4), 157.

Zhuhadar, L., Marklin, S., Thrasher, E., & Lytras, M. D. (2016). Is there a gender difference in interacting with intelligent tutoring system? Can Bayesian knowledge tracing and learning curve analysis models answer this question? *Computers in Human Behavior, 61*, 198–204.

CHAPTER 3

The Use of Analytics for Educational Purposes: A Review of Literature from 2015 to Present

Min Liu, Zilong Pan, Xin Pan, Dongwook An, Wenting Zou, Chenglu Li and Yi Shi

1 Introduction

Learning analytics refers to "the measurement, collection, analysis and reporting of data about learners and their contexts, for purposes of understanding and optimizing learning and the environments in which it occurs" (Long & Siemens, 2011, p. 34). As an emerging field, learning analytics increasingly are being used in various educational settings for educators to examine user data for making decisions to support teaching and learning. Researchers believe analytics can help improve student performance through adaptive learning, predictive modeling, and social network analysis (Siemens, 2012).

Due to the increasing interests on the topic, more studies have been published in recent years. The purpose of this study was to conduct a systematic review of literature on the most recent empirical studies about using analytics in education. A literature review on this topic should provide much-needed perspectives and updates to educators and researchers about the current state of learning analytics research thus to provide useful insights to all interested in the topic. Our research questions are:

1. What research studies in learning analytics for educational purposes have been published from 2015 to present?
2. What factors are investigated in these research studies in connection to learning?

2 Method

2.1 *Article Selection Criteria*

We reviewed empirical research published from 2015 to present that involved the usage of learning analytics in educational settings. We followed the selection criteria used in our previous research of literature reviews (Liu, Kang, Liu, Zou, & Hodson, 2017), but focused on learning analytics in education as the

© KONINKLIJKE BRILL NV, LEIDEN, 2019 | DOI: 10.1163/9789004399273_003 topic of this study. The following four criteria guided our selection: (a) research published in refereed journals only (not including conference proceedings or book chapters), (b) research published between 2015 and February 2018, when the analysis of this review began, (c) research that are data-based empirical studies, not including literature review, descriptions of constructing or optimizing certain algorithms or the articles merely discussing benefits and/or limitations, and finally (d) excluding those studies that did not include log data or the ones that did not describe the analytic techniques used.

2.2   *Article Selection Process*
Using the criteria above, researchers went through several steps in refining and verifying our data sources—articles for inclusion in the review. First, the research team went through the articles (n = 103) that have been collecting on the topic in past several years (Liu et al., 2017; Liu, Lee, Kang, & Liu, 2016). Then we conducted a preliminary selection based on criterion a and criterion b and created a list of potential journals (n = 28). Each inclusion or elimination of an article was verified and discussed by at least two researchers until consensus was reached. Then the research team reviewed the references of each of these articles and created a list of journals (n = 12) in which possible relevant articles were published. Each member of the research team then browsed the abstract of these journals from 2015 to February 2018, the timeframe of this review) using the four criteria. The team also did a search using "analytics," education," and "educational analytics" as keywords to ensure all relevant articles were included. After this process, we selected a total of 39 articles for further analysis.

The research team then started an in-depth analysis of these 39 articles based on the four criteria. In this step, we eliminated those articles that appeared to have met the criteria given the abstract but actually did not. Again, the inclusion or elimination of an article was double-checked by at least two or more researchers for verification. After this deliberative process of selecting, checking, refining, and verifying, a total of 26 articles were included in our final review (see Table 3.1).

3   Findings and Discussion

Our research questions for this review of literature were: (1) what research studies have been published from 2015 to present and (2) what factors are investigated in these research studies about using analytics in education? To address these two research questions, we have categorized the 26 studies into the following categories: technologies involved, analytic techniques and data

TABLE 3.1   Articles reviewed and the journals these articles were published in

Author (Year)	Journal
Angeli, C., Howard, S. K., Ma, J., Yang, J., and Kirschner, P. A. (2017)	*Computers & Education*
Cagiltay, N. E., Ozcelik, E., and Ozcelik, N. S. (2015)	*Computers & Education*
Chang, C., Chang, M., Liu, C., Chiu, B., Fan Chiang, S., Wen, C., ... Chai, C. (2017)	*Journal of Computer Assisted Learning*
Cheng, M. T., Lin, Y. W., and She, H. C. (2015)	*Computers & Education*
Cheng, M. T., Rosenheck, L., Lin, C. Y., and Klopfer, E. (2017)	*Computers & Education*
de Barba, P. G., Kennedy, G. E., and Ainley, M. D. (2016)	*Journal of Computer Assisted Learning*
de Kock, W., and Harskamp, E. (2016)	*Journal of Computer Assisted Learning*
Gauthier, A., Corrin, M., and Jenkinson, J. (2015)	*Computers & Education*
Giannakos, M. N., Jaccheri, L., and Krogstie, J. (2016)	*British Journal of Educational Technology*
Goggins, S., and Xing, W. (2016)	*Computers & Education*
Kerr, D. (2015)	*Journal of Educational Data Mining*
Liu, M., Lee, J., Kang, J., and Liu, S. (2016)	*Technology, Knowledge and Learning*
Loh, C. S., Sheng, Y., and Li, I. H. (2015)	*Computers in Human Behavior*
Marbouti, F., Diefes-Dux, H. A., and Madhavan, K. (2016)	*Computers & Education*
Martin, F., and Whitmer, J. C. (2016)	*Technology, Knowledge and Learning*
Ornelas, F., and Ordonez, C. (2017)	*Technology, Knowledge and Learning*
Pursel, B. K., Zhang, L., Jablokow, K. W., Choi, G. W., and Velegol, D. (2016)	*Journal of Computer Assisted Learning*
San Pedro, M. O. Z., Baker, R. S., and Heffernan, N. T. (2017)	*Technology, Knowledge and Learning*
Sipiyaruk, K., Gallagher, J. E., Hatzipanagos, S., and Reynolds, P. A. (2017)	*Technology, Knowledge and Learning*
Snow, E. L., Allen, L. K., Jacovina, M. E., and McNamara, D. S. (2015)	*Computers & Education*

(cont.)

TABLE 3.1   Articles reviewed and the journals these articles were published in (*cont.*)

Author (Year)	Journal
Strang, K. D. (2017)	*Education and Information Technologies*
Van Horne, S., Curran, M., Smith, A., VanBuren, J., Zahrieh, D., Larsen, R., and Miller, R. (2018)	*Technology, Knowledge and Learning*
Van Laer, S., and Elen, J. (2018)	*Technology, Knowledge and Learning*
Van Leeuwen, A., Janssen, J., Erkens, G., and Brekelmans, M. (2015)	*Computers & Education*
Yang, X., Li, J., and Xing, B. (2018)	*The Internet and Higher Education*
Zhang, X., Meng, Y., Ordóñez de Pablos, P., and Sun, Y. (2019)	*Computers in Human Behavior*

used, types of research designs, subject matter areas and education levels, and their connections to learning. The findings and the discussion are presented below.

3.1   *Research Studies Published from 2015 to Present*
We examined the technologies involved, types of analytic techniques and data, types of research designs, subject matter areas as well as education levels.

3.1.1   Technologies Involved
Learning analytics has been widely applied to investigate human-computer interactions in recent years. Among the 26 papers that we examined, the types of technologies used included simulations and games, online instruction using learning management systems (LMS), and technical tools/systems, in addition to traditional face-to-face settings. Some of them were conducted in the context of computer games and simulations ($n = 11$, 42%, see Figure 3.1), and most of these included computer games or simulations developed by the researchers for data collection (Angeli, Howard, Ma, Yang, & Kirschner, 2017; Cagiltay, Ozcelik, & Ozcelik, 2015; Cheng, Rosenheck, Lin, & Klopfer, 2017; Liu et al., 2016). Angeli et al. (2017) specifically developed a glass-box simulation and asked participants to solve a problem about the immigration policy. Other studies used games that were developed by other people or organizations. For example, Sipiyaruk, Gallagher, Hatzipanagos,

and Reynolds (2017) adopted a serious game designed for dental public health in their research.

Online instruction (38%, *n* = 10), including Massive Open Online Courses (MOOCs), was a common technology platform where researchers used students' log data in online platforms to investigate their behaviors in order to make predictions (de Barba, Kennedy, & Ainley, 2016; Giannakos, Jaccheri, & Krogstie, 2016). The various learning management systems used by these studies included Coursera (de Barba et al., 2016), Moodle (Strang, 2017; Van Laer & Elen, 2018) and Rio Learn (Ornelas & Ordonez, 2017).

Four studies (15%) investigated the use of web-based tools or systems in the process of teaching and learning (Gauthier, Corrin, & Jenkinson, 2015; San Pedro, Baker, & Heffernan, 2017; Van Leeuwen, Janssen, Erkens, & Brekelmans, 2015; Zhang, Meng, Ordóñez de Pablos, & Sun, 2019). The study by Gauthier et al. (2015), for example, used click-stream data in a game study aid group and a non-game study aid group, and investigated the influence of game design on students' learning behavior and outcome. In addition, learning analytics was also used in conventional face-to-face (F2F) classrooms (*n* = 2, 8%) (Angeli et al., 2017; Marbouti, Diefes-Dux, & Madhavan, 2016). In their study, Marbouti et al. (2016) used students' scores and other classroom performance data to predict students' learning behaviors.

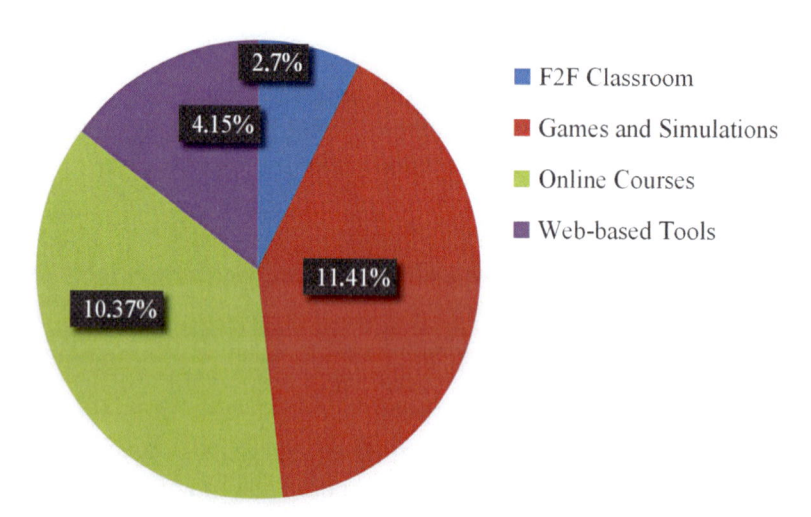

FIGURE 3.1   Frequency of technologies involved

3.1.2   Types of Analytic Techniques and Data

The studies reviewed utilized multiple types of data and various techniques in their research using analytics. Some researchers analyzed different types of

TABLE 3.2   Types of data collected in the reviewed research

Data type	Frequency
Learner activities generated by the system (e.g. game logs, MOOC logs)	23
Questionnaires/surveys/interviews	14
Assessments (e.g. tests, quizzes)	12
Learner activities coded by researchers, e.g. discourse	5
Secondary data (e.g. national data)	3

data in one study, such as system-generated data and self-reported data, and adopted multiple analytic techniques at the same time. Table 3.2 shows the five types of data collected in these 26 studies.

As shown in Table 3.2, the most frequently used type in these 26 studies was system-generated data (n = 23). Such data were collected through MOOC platforms and educational games. The study by Pursel, Zhang, Jablokow, Choi, and Velegol (2016) examined such analytics as students' views of course videos and readings per week in MOOC courses. To investigate students' participation specifically in the discussion forums, Goggins and Xing (2016) used automatically generated data including messages posted or messages read. Similarly, game logs such as clickstream data and attempted tasks were utilized to evaluate learner performance. For example, Cheng, Lin, and She (2015) collected data on students' behaviors in a game, such as the number of in-game characters being used and the total number of views of information. Sipiyaruk et al. (2017) also analyzed data including time and duration each student logged into a game, the number of times the answers submitted, and the answers they submitted.

The second frequently used data type is user self-reported data (n = 14), such as student reflections, surveys, and interview responses. In these reviewed studies, self-reported data were analyzed together with log data to gain further understanding of the relationships between students' attitudes and learning performances. In the study by Strang (2017), students were asked to evaluate their own performance based on the course objectives. Researchers then conducted the text analysis to identify the relationship between their reflection and learning outcome. Cagiltay et al. (2015) used a Turkish version of the instructional materials motivation survey (IMMS) to assess students' motivation towards the game. The result revealed that competitions in the game enhanced motivation of the participants, as these participants spent more time on answering questions in the game than the control group.

Assessments (n = 12), such as knowledge tests and quizzes, were often used to evaluate learners' understanding of related concepts and knowledge. The study by Chang et al. (2017) collected data from tests which included multiple choice questions on science concepts in order to examine what the students learned and students' ability to apply the knowledge in other situations. Similarly, Kerr (2015) conducted research in two classes where one class of students were playing the original version of a video game and the other class were using the revised version. Students were given a test at the beginning of the program and an immediate post-test and a delayed post-test as assessments. The results showed learners' performance improved after using the revised version of the game.

Other types of data, such as discourse data and observation notes, were also used in some studies (n = 5). In these studies, students' discourse data or observation notes were coded by researchers. For example, in Chang et al.'s study (2017), discourse data were analyzed and sorted into different categories based on the purpose of the collaborative learning tasks under investigation, such as understanding and representing. San Pedro et al. (2017) conducted observations on students' emotions and engagement and analyzed the field notes in accordance with the Baker Rodrigo Ocumpaugh Monitoring Protocol.

Besides the data directly collected from research experiments, some studies used secondary data which were drawn from large-scale datasets to evaluate learner performance (n = 3). For example, Angeli et al. (2017) used large-scale datasets from national programs like Australian Digital Educational Revolution in New South Wales (DER-NSW) and Australian National Assessment Program Literacy and Numeracy (NAPLAN) assessments. These datasets provided researchers an overview of student performance nationwide. San Pedro et al. (2017) used the college enrollment data from the National Student Clearinghouse as their data source.

Table 3.3 presents the types of analytic methods used in these 26 studies. The most commonly used methods include statistical analyses such as t-test, ANOVA, and correlation. These techniques were used to analyze the differences between and among groups or to measure the relationships between variables. Of the 26 studies in this review, seven (23.3%) used this method. For example, Giannakos et al. (2016) used the t-test to distinguish video lecture usage patterns between two different student groups. Cagiltay el al. (2015) used t-test, two-way ANOVA, and correlation analysis to compare the outcomes between the control group and the experimental group.

The second most prevalent method used was clustering (n = 6, 20.0%). Other common methods included regression (n = 5, 16.7%), structural equation modeling (SEM) (n = 4, 13.3%), and classification (n = 4, 13.3%).

TABLE 3.3   Types of analytics techniques used

Technique	Frequency	Percentage (%)
Statistics (t-test, ANOVA, and correlation)	7	23.3
Clustering	6	20.0
Regression	5	16.7
Structural Equation Modeling	4	13.3
Classification	4	13.3
Sequential Analysis	2	6.7
Association Rules Mining	1	3.3
Propensity Score Matching	1	3.3

Regression refers to linear regression including multivariate linear regression and hierarchical linear regression. SEM includes partial least squares and path analysis techniques. Less commonly used techniques included two data mining techniques: Sequential analysis or Sequential Pattern Mining ($n = 2$, 6.7%), association rules mining ($n = 1$, 3.4%), and propensity score matching ($n = 1$, 3.3%).

Many researchers utilized more than one analytic techniques such as clustering and regression at the same time or clustering and classification at the same time to address their research questions. For example, Cheng et al. (2015) used clustering and linear regression to discover behavior patterns in a serious game. Marbouti et al. (2016) utilized clustering and a variety of classification algorithms such as support vector machine, Naive Bayes, logistics regression, decision tree, and artificial neural network to construct a prediction model. In a study on motivation in a MOOC, de Barba et al. (2016) used SEM and other statistical methods such as Mann–Whitney U Test and Spearman Correlations to build a model to analyze the relationships of motivation constructs and student performance. It is worth noting that some analytic techniques were used due to the types of data in the studies. For example, to analyze text data like student discussions in the forum and conversations between students in the text chatroom, Chang et al. (2017) used lag sequential analysis, a technique for discourse analysis.

The findings showed that about half of the total of 26 studies used both system-generated data and qualitative data like surveys on prior knowledge or student motivation. Researchers also frequently used traditional analytical methods such as statistics along with data mining techniques in order to address a variety of research questions.

3.1.3 Types of Research Designs

In these 26 articles, the findings showed that quantitative research design was the most frequently used (n = 16, see Figure 3.2). It also appeared mixed methods research design was also getting popular for learning analytics research (n = 10). No qualitative research design was used in these articles, which was expected.

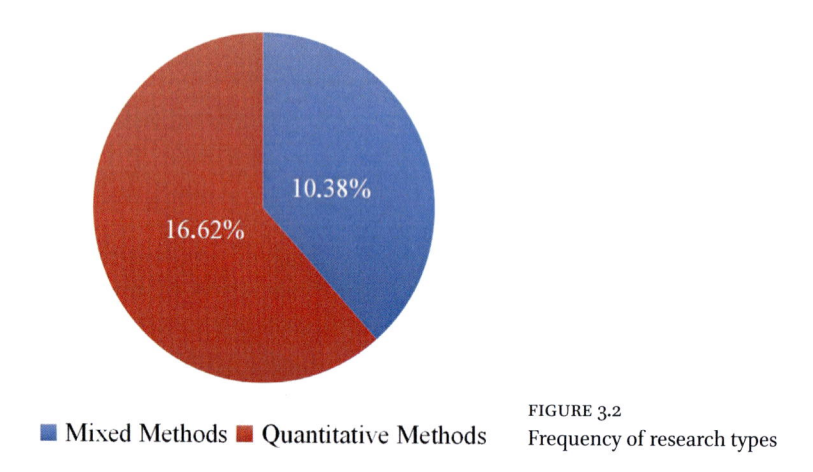

■ Mixed Methods ■ Quantitative Methods

FIGURE 3.2
Frequency of research types

3.1.4 Subject Matter Areas and Education Levels

Figure 3.3 shows the distribution of the studies by the subject matter areas with corresponding the education level at which the research was conducted. The results revealed that science (n = 6), engineering (n = 3), and mathematics (n = 3) were the most popular subjects of the 26 studies. In addition, science was the only subject that was covered in all the educational contexts of the 26 studies. Other less common subject matter areas included business (n = 2), instructional technology (n = 2), medical field (n = 2), multidisciplinary (n = 2), and other topics (n = 2) which included non-specified subjects, but more generic skills, such as strategic thinking. The least commonly researched subject matter areas included economics (n = 1), language (n = 1), pre-service teacher training (n = 1), and social studies (n = 1). Interestingly, the most common subject matter areas were all from STEM, which suggests that it was easier to generate and collect log data in these areas.

Figure 3.3 also shows the majority of learning analytics research was conducted with the participants from higher education (n = 18, 69%). Other studies included participants from middle school (n = 5, 19%), high school (n = 2, 8%), and adult education (n = 1, 4%). It is interesting to note that there were no studies at the elementary school level. The fact the majority of the studies occurred at higher education level suggests the convenience of conducting such research with higher education students as they probably were more readily accessible to researchers.

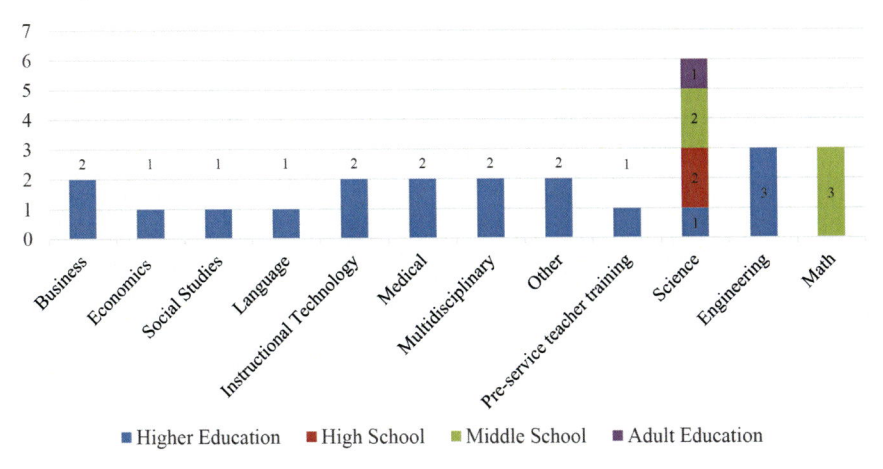

FIGURE 3.3 Frequency of subject matters at different educational levels

3.2 *Factors Investigated in the Research Studies in Connection to Learning*

We were particularly interested in how analytics was used in each study to support learning. After reviewing the 26 articles, we synthesized the findings and presented them in the following three categories: (a) predicting learning performances, (b) detecting behaviors and learning patterns, and (c) facilitating learning experiences.

3.2.1 Predicting Learning Performances

Research has shown learning analytics mainly served two roles in predicting students' learning performances and outcomes. The first role was to help instructors identify performance indicators or predictors across various platforms including MOOCs (de Barba et al., 2016; Pursel et al., 2016), learning forums (Goggins & Xing, 2016), serious games (Gauthier et al., 2015), and learning management systems such as Moodle (Strang, 2017). The second role was to create certain prediction models in order to help educators identify at-risk students (Marbouti et al., 2016; Ornelas & Ordonez, 2017), classify novice and expert learners (Loh, Sheng, & Li, 2015), and predict students' future college attendance (San Pedro et al., 2017).

In the study by de Barba et al. (2016), learner's participation data were measured by video hits and quiz attempts in a MOOC course. These two factors were identified as predictors of students' final performance and their levels of motivation. Students' participation as a vital predictor of learning performance was also revealed in a MOOC (Pursel et al., 2016). In this study, video views, which was considered as an important indicator of learner participation level, was shown to be a strong predictor of course completion rate, so did forum engagement. Moreover, aiming to gain more insights about students' participation in online courses, Goggins and Xing (2016) focused on discussion forums, and proposed that instead of only relying on a number of posts, the time dimension of students' behaviors such as the time spent in reading posts should also be considered. In addition, various techniques using learning analytics also helped researchers identify other predictors. For example, course login counts and quiz scores were shown to be important learning indicators in a Moodle course (Strang, 2017) and tasks completion rate was also found as a significant predictor of post-test in a study about games (Gauthier et al., 2015).

Learning analytics was also used to construct prediction models. Ornelas and Ordonez (2017) built a model using students' log data and their performance scores from eleven courses based on Naive Bayes algorithm to classify at-risk and successful students. Their model showed accuracy over 90%. Another study by Marbouti et al. (2016) aimed to identify at-risk students using analytics. Based on students' performance data such as in-class quizzes and team participation, the researchers developed a model consisting of Naive Bayes, Support Vector Machine and K-Nearest Neighbors, which was shown to achieve a high accuracy. In addition, learning analytics was also used in building models to predict college enrollment. In a study by San Pedro et al. (2017), the researchers used linear regression based on student data from the online system and assessed their learning experience in terms of knowledge, academic emotions, and engaged and disengaged behaviors. Their results showed that high school course selection and college attendance were related to students' performance and engagement at the middle school level. Furthermore, learning analytics was used in studying serious games to predict expert–novice performances (Loh et al., 2015). In this study, the researchers coded players' action sequences by tracking the path they had traversed in the game to differentiate and compare expert and novice players. The results showed the efficiency of incorporating tile-based action sequence coding approach in a serious games analytic model.

The findings of these studies in using analytics to identify learning performance predictors and create prediction model construction can help instructors and researchers across various subjects and platforms to better design learning environments so as to enhance students' learning.

3.2.2 Detecting Behaviors and Learning Patterns

Learning analytics was also used by researchers and educators to detect learning patterns across various educational platforms including serious games (Cagiltay et al., 2015; Cheng et al., 2015; Cheng et al., 2017; Gauthier et al., 2015; Kerr, 2015), simulations (Angeli et al., 2017; Chang et al., 2017), learning management systems (Giannakos et al., 2016; Yang, Li, & Xing, 2018), collaboration platforms (Zhang, Meng, Ordóñez de Pablos, & Sun, 2019) and blended learning environments (Van Laer & Elen, 2018). The findings of these studies were discussed in the following sections.

3.2.2.1 *Learning Patterns in Serious Games*

A study from Cheng et al. (2015) examined the effects of a serious game for 7th-grade biology and the interplay of student concept learning, gaming performance, and in-game behaviors. Analysis showed that students' in-game behaviors, such as frequencies and duration of viewing specific content in the game, were significantly correlated with their game performance which subsequently influenced their learning outcomes. Moreover, cluster analysis revealed three groups of learners featuring low learning outcomes/low gaming performance, high learning outcomes, and high gaming performance. The study by Cagiltay et al. (2015) also used similar descriptors such as duration of viewing concept explanations, total response time to questions and accuracy (game performance) to understand students' in-game behavioral patterns in relation to their motivation and post-test scores. The results of this study showed that learners' motivation and post-test scores in a game environment with competition settings were significantly higher than those who played the non-competition game.

Cheng et al. (2017) collected log data from high school students as they played a Massively Multiplayer Online Game (MMOG) for science learning. Data from a specific genetics quest in the game were analyzed by using data mining techniques to examine the relationship between tool use and quest completion status, how the use of certain tools may influence content-related game choices, and the multiple pathways available to players in the game. The study identified that in this particular quest, learners' use of two tools, the "trait examiner" and "trait decoder," was more likely to lead to success.

Gauthier et al. (2015) investigated the educational impact of a serious game for studying human vascular anatomy versus a similar non-game study aid and how it related to the participants' demographic traits and voluntary use over a 35-day period. Their analyses suggested that game mechanics encouraged more specific problem-solving strategies than the non-game study aid did, leading to greater predictability of learning outcomes. However, there was no significant difference in frequencies of tool-use between the experimental and control groups. It also appeared that students' studying habits had the greatest influence on the level of engagement indicated by frequencies of tool-use.

Kerr and Chung's study (2012) on a 6th-grade math game found that (a) it was common for students to pass certain levels using incorrect mathematical strategies and (b) throughout the game, a large number of students used order-based strategies to solve problems rather than strategies based on mathematics. Based on this study, Kerr's (2015) modified this game and randomly assigned students to play either the original version or the revised version. The study examining the effect on student performance used two in-game measures of performance (the number of attempts per level and the percentage of first attempts that were solutions) and two paper-based measures of performance (immediate post-test score and delayed post-test score). The results showed that students who played the revised version significantly reduced the use of incorrect mathematical strategies and order-based strategies than students who played the original version.

3.2.2.2   *Learning Patterns in Simulations*
Chang et al. (2017) studied students' different behavioral patterns while solving physics problems in both individual-based and collaborative simulations. Lag sequential analysis revealed that students' learning patterns in these two simulations were different significantly. Students in collaborative simulations, although they presented a higher level of collaborative activity, did not transform discussions into suitable problem-solving activities, while students in the individual-based simulation completed individual learning by exploring independently before heading towards group reflection. Angeli et al. (2017) conducted a similar study, but instead of dividing learners into two simulations, the researchers separated learners based on their cognitive styles (i.e. field-dependent and field-independent) by using educational data mining techniques. The results showed that learners with different cognitive styles exerted different patterns of interactions in the same simulation during the problem-solving process. These two studies illustrated how learning analytics was used in a simulation to detect students' interaction patterns.

3.2.2.3   *Learning Patterns in Learning Management Systems*
Giannakos et al. (2016) analyzed learner's usage patterns such as watching period, platforms used, and video duration in an online video-assisted software

engineering course and found out that these patterns were related to students' attitudes while learning and interacting on this platform. Thus, this research provided a new direction of analyzing learner attitudes via behaviors patterns. Moreover, behavior patterns discovered by learning analytics were also used to identify students' levels of knowledge construction and engagement. Yang et al. (2018) conducted a study on students' knowledge construction in translation activities using log data. The analysis from the lag sequential analysis showed that knowledge co-construction behaviors occurred more continually and frequently in the higher-engagement group.

3.2.2.4   *Learning Patterns in Collaboration Tools/Blended Learning*

Zhang et al. (2019) examined students' collaboration patterns on a group collaborative platform—Slack. The results using partial least squares revealed that students' interaction patterns involving social influence, mutual trust, as well as social and academic reward valence had positive influences on students' teamwork engagement. Van Laer and Elen (2018) analyzed log data from a Moodle course using K-means cluster analysis, one-way ANOVA, and MANOVA, and three clusters were found. The cluster with the highest standardized scores showed that the frequency of a learners' sequential pattern such as from "course module viewed" to "discussion made" was much higher than the other two groups, while the cluster with the lowest scores had higher frequency of the sequential pattern from "discussion made" to "test made." These findings based on learning analytics revealed important self-regulatory behaviors patterns in a blended learning environment.

In summary, the studies in this category mainly focused on two aspects of learning when analyzing the log data: learners' engagement and strategies. To measure learners' engagement, the researchers often calculated the duration and frequency of performing specific tasks or accessing specific tools (Cagiltay et al., 2015; Cheng et al., 2015; Gauthier et al., 2015; Sipiyaruk et al., 2017; Van Laer & Elen, 2018). In contrast, to investigate learners' strategies, the researchers mainly examined learners' choices of using certain tools/performing certain actions, or the sequence of performing different tasks/actions (Angeli et al., 2017; Chang, et al., 2017; Cheng et al., 2017; Gauthier et al., 2015; Kerr, 2015; Yang et al., 2018). In some cases, both engagement and strategies were analyzed in order to present a more comprehensive view of learners' behaviors in certain platforms (Chang et al., 2017; Cheng et al., 2017).

It is also noteworthy that, instead of discussing learning patterns in isolation, many studies attempted to understand the causes and implications of diverse learning patterns. In this regard, researchers often examined the correlation between learning patterns and other elements, such as different system settings that may trigger varied behaviors (Cagiltay et al., 2015; Chang et al., 2017; Gauthier et al., 2015), learning outcomes associated with certain learning patterns (Cagiltay et al., 2015; Cheng et al., 2015; Cheng et al., 2017; Kerr, 2015; Snow, Allen, Jacovina, & McNamara, 2015), learners' motivations (Cagiltay et al., 2015; Giannakos et al., 2016) and cognitive/learning styles (Angeli et al., 2017; Van Horne et al., 2018).

3.2.3   Facilitating Learning Experiences

Previous research found learning analytics had played a crucial role in facilitating learning by adapting to individual needs (Martin & Whitmer, 2016; Van Horne et al., 2018; Van Leeuwen et al., 2015) and by optimizing learning platforms (Angeli et al., 2017; de Kock & Harskamp, 2016; Giannakos et al., 2016; Kerr, 2015). Learning analytics offers new opportunities to adapt learning, such as using analytics to create dashboards which can not only improve students' engagement levels and performances (Horn et al., 2017; Martin & Whitmer, 2016), but also facilitate teachers to monitor student learning progress (Van Leeuwen et al., 2015). In a study by Van Horne et al. (2018), researchers created a dashboard that can provide students real-time learning progress, assessments scores, and learning suggestions, using the data generated from students' log activities as well as their learning profiles such as their high school GPAs. The result revealed that users with higher frequencies of accessing the dashboard obtained significantly higher grades than those who had lower frequencies. Van Leeuwen et al. (2015) used a dashboard to assist teachers to diagnose students' learning obstacles thus to intervene accordingly during a computer-supported collaborative writing activity. Their result showed that using the dashboard encouraged teachers to intervene more often in general and especially with targeted groups who were experiencing difficulties.

Learning analytics techniques also enabled educators to optimize educational platforms to further improve students' learning performances. Kerr (2015) modified their educational game based on data mining results so as to reduce construction of irrelevant behaviors in the game. This modification also led to more positive perceptions of the game compared with the original setting. In another research conducted by de Kock and Harskamp (2016), the researchers applied learning analytics techniques to compare the effects of two types of hints on student performance during mathematical word problem-solving activities in a learning management system. Researchers used pre- and post-tests to examine the differences in problem-solving skills and collected log files. They found that procedural-content hints could better facilitate students' problem-solving skills than procedural only hints, which led to an enhanced approach for this learning platform by incorporating more procedural-content hints. Moreover, Giannakos et al. (2016) analyzed students' learning patterns and discovered that the patterns were related to students' attitudes towards the lectures. The finding offered designers useful insights for improving video-based lectures to fulfill their teaching objectives. These findings demonstrated the potentials of using analytics to improve and enhance learning environments and cultivate more positive learning behaviors and attitudes.

Although we discussed the recent research on learning analytics' role to support students' learning in three categories, these categories are not isolated from each other. In fact, they are interrelated. The capability of a learning analytic method to predict students' learning performance was also determined by how well this method can detect students' behavior patterns (de Barba et al., 2016; Strang, 2017) such as access frequencies in an LMS (de Kock & Harskamp, 2016; Giannakos et al., 2016). Instructors could gather and interpret the data to give feedback accordingly (Van Leeuwen et al., 2015). Moreover, in order to better optimize a learning platform such as a serious game, researchers would need to analysis how learners' behavioral patterns had changed (Cagiltay et al., 2015; Cheng et al., 2015) and whether learning performance had improved (Cheng et al., 2017; Gauthier et al., 2015) thus to evaluate a modification (Kerr, 2015). The research has shown the efficacy of using analytics as performance predictors and learning behavior detectors to facilitate teaching and learning and improve the designs of learning environments.

4   Summary and Conclusion

This review of literature presented a systematic review of how learning analytics has been used in different educational settings from 2015 to present and identified factors that were related to learning in these studies. A total of 26 peer-reviewed studies were included in this review. The discussion focused on technologies involved, analytic techniques and data used, types of research designs, subject matter areas, and educational levels. Importantly, the use of analytics in connection to learning was analyzed. The findings showed that the most common categories as emerged in these studies included predicting learning performances, detecting behaviors and learning patterns, and facilitating learning experiences. Specifically, learning analytics was used to build predictive models in order to predict student performance so as to help instructors provide more effective interventions to assist students' learning. Studies have shown by identifying the learning patterns, learning analytics provided useful insights into ways to motivate and engage learners and stimulate a deeper understanding of knowledge. Many studies also utilized more than two data sources as well as various analytic techniques in one study to address research questions. User logs and survey data were the two most frequently used data types and analytic techniques such as t-test, ANOVA, and cluster analysis were more frequently used to discover user behavior patterns. We hope the findings of this literature review on most recent literature in learning analytics for educational purposes will provide useful information and insights to researchers interested in the topic and inform educational practices.

References

Note: * indicates articles included in this literature review

*Angeli, C., Howard, S. K., Ma, J., Yang, J., & Kirschner, P. A. (2017). Data mining in educational technology classroom research: Can it make a contribution? *Computers and Education, 113*, 226–242. Retrieved from https://doi.org/10.1016/j.compedu.2017.05.021

*Cagiltay, N. E., Ozcelik, E., & Ozcelik, N. S. (2015). The effect of competition on learning in games. *Computers and Education, 87*, 35–41. Retrieved from https://doi.org/10.1016/j.compedu.2015.04.001

*Chang, C. J., Chang, M. H., Liu, C. C., Chiu, B. C., Fan Chiang, S. H., Wen, C. T., Hwang, F.-K., Chao, P.-Y., Chen, Y.-L., & Chai, C. S. (2017). An analysis of collaborative problem-solving activities mediated by individual-based and collaborative computer simulations. *Journal of Computer Assisted Learning, 33*(6), 649–662. Retrieved from https://doi.org/10.1111/jcal.12208

*Cheng, M. T., Lin, Y. W., & She, H. C. (2015). Learning through playing virtual age: Exploring the interactions among student concept learning, gaming performance, in-game behaviors, and the use of in-game characters. *Computers and Education, 86*, 18–29. Retrieved from https://doi.org/10.1016/j.compedu.2015.03.007

*Cheng, M. T., Rosenheck, L., Lin, C. Y., & Klopfer, E. (2017). Analyzing gameplay data to inform feedback loops in the radix endeavor. *Computers and Education, 111*, 60–73. Retrieved from https://doi.org/10.1016/j.compedu.2017.03.015

*de Barba, P. G., Kennedy, G. E., & Ainley, M. D. (2016). The role of students' motivation and participation in predicting performance in a MOOC. *Journal of Computer Assisted Learning, 32*(3), 218–231. Retrieved from https://doi.org/10.1111/jcal.12130

*de Kock, W. D., & Harskamp, E. G. (2016). Procedural versus content-related hints for word problem solving: An exploratory study. *Journal of Computer Assisted Learning, 32*(5), 481–493. Retrieved from https://doi.org/10.1111/jcal.12148

*Gauthier, A., Corrin, M., & Jenkinson, J. (2015). Exploring the influence of game design on learning and voluntary use in an online vascular anatomy study aid. *Computers and Education, 87*, 24–34. Retrieved from https://doi.org/10.1016/j.compedu.2015.03.017

*Giannakos, M. N., Jaccheri, L., & Krogstie, J. (2016). Exploring the relationship between video lecture usage patterns and students' attitudes. *British Journal of Educational Technology, 47*(6), 1259–1275. Retrieved from https://doi.org/10.1111/bjet.12313

*Goggins, S., & Xing, W. (2016). Building models explaining student participation behavior in asynchronous online discussion. *Computers and Education, 94*, 241–251. Retrieved form https://doi.org/10.1016/j.compedu.2015.11.002

*Kerr, D. (2015). Using data mining results to improve educational video game design. *Journal of Educational Data Mining, 7*(3), 1–17.

Kerr, D., & Chung, G. K. (2012). Identifying key features of student performance in educational video games and simulations through cluster analysis. *Journal of Educational Data Mining, 4*(1), 144–182.

Liu, M., Kang, J., Liu, S., Zou, W., & Hodson, J. (2017). Learning analytics as an assessment tool in serious games: A review of literature. In *Serious games and edutainment applications: Volume II* (pp. 537–563). Retrieved from https://doi.org/10.1007/978-3-319-51645-5_24

*Liu, M., Lee, J., Kang, J., & Liu, S. (2016). What we can learn from the data: A multiple-case study examining behavior patterns by students with different characteristics in using a serious game. *Technology, Knowledge and Learning, 21*(1), 33–57. Retrieved from https://doi.org/10.1007/s10758-015-9263-7

*Loh, C. S., Sheng, Y., & Li, I. H. (2015). Predicting expert-novice performance as serious games analytics with objective-oriented and navigational action sequences. *Computers in Human Behavior, 49*, 147–155. Retrieved from https://doi.org/10.1016/j.chb.2015.02.053

Long, P., & Siemens, G. (2011). Penetrating the fog: Analytics in learning and education. *EDUCAUSE Review, 46*, 30–32. Retrieved from https://doi.org/10.1145/2330601.2330605

*Marbouti, F., Diefes-Dux, H. A., & Madhavan, K. (2016). Models for early prediction of at-risk students in a course using standards-based grading. *Computers and Education, 103*, 1–15. Retrieved from https://doi.org/10.1016/j.compedu.2016.09.005

*Martin, F., & Whitmer, J. C. (2016). Applying learning analytics to investigate timed release in online learning. *Technology, Knowledge and Learning, 21*(1), 59–74. Retrieved from https://doi.org/10.1007/s10758-015-9261-9

*Ornelas, F., & Ordonez, C. (2017). Predicting student success: A naïve bayesian application to community college data. *Technology, Knowledge and Learning, 22*(3), 299–315. Retrieved from https://doi.org/10.1007/s10758-017-9334-z

*Pursel, B. K., Zhang, L., Jablokow, K. W., Choi, G. W., & Velegol, D. (2016). Understanding MOOC students: Motivations and behaviours indicative of MOOC completion.

Journal of Computer Assisted Learning, 32(3), 202–217. Retrieved from https://doi.org/10.1111/jcal.12131

*San Pedro, M. O. Z., Baker, R. S., & Heffernan, N. T. (2017). An integrated look at middle school engagement and learning in digital environments as precursors to college attendance. *Technology, Knowledge and Learning, 22*(3), 243–270. Retrieved from https://doi.org/10.1007/s10758-017-9318-z

Siemens, G. (2012). *Learning analytics: Envisioning a research discipline and a domain of practice* (pp. 4–8). Paper presented at the 2nd International Conference on Learning Analytics & Knowledge. Retrieved from https://doi.org/10.1145/2330601.2330605

*Sipiyaruk, K., Gallagher, J. E., Hatzipanagos, S., & Reynolds, P. A. (2017). Acquiring critical thinking and decision-making skills: An evaluation of a serious game used by undergraduate dental students in dental public health. *Technology, Knowledge and Learning, 22*(2), 209–218. Retrieved from https://doi.org/10.1007/s10758-016-9296-6

*Snow, E. L., Allen, L. K., Jacovina, M. E., & McNamara, D. S. (2015). Does agency matter? Exploring the impact of controlled behaviors within a game-based environment. *Computers and Education, 82*, 378–392. Retrieved from https://doi.org/10.1016/j.compedu.2014.12.011

*Strang, K. D. (2017). Beyond engagement analytics: Which online mixed-data factors predict student learning outcomes? *Education and Information Technologies, 22*(3), 917–937. Retrieved from https://doi.org/10.1007/s10639-016-9464-2

*Van Horne, S., Curran, M., Smith, A., VanBuren, J., Zahrieh, D., Larsen, R., & Miller, R. (2018). Facilitating student success in introductory chemistry with feedback in an online platform. *Technology, Knowledge and Learning, 23*(1), 21–40.

*Van Laer, S., & Elen, J. (2018). Adults' self-regulatory behaviour profiles in blended learning environments and their implications for design. *Technology, Knowledge and Learning*, 1–31. Retrieved from https://doi.org/10.1007/s10758-017-9351-y

*Van Leeuwen, A., Janssen, J., Erkens, G., & Brekelmans, M. (2015). Teacher regulation of cognitive activities during student collaboration: Effects of learning analytics. *Computers and Education, 90*, 80–94. Retrieved from https://doi.org/10.1016/j.compedu.2015.09.006

*Yang, X., Li, J., & Xing, B. (2018). Behavioral patterns of knowledge construction in online cooperative translation activities. *Internet and Higher Education, 36*, 13–21. Retrieved from https://doi.org/10.1016/j.iheduc.2017.08.003

*Zhang, X., Meng, Y., Ordóñez de Pablos, P., & Sun, Y. (2019). Learning analytics in collaborative learning supported by Slack: From the perspective of engagement. *Computers in Human Behavior, 92*, 625–633. Retrieved from https://doi.org/10.1016/j.chb.2017.08.012

CHAPTER 4

A Snapshot of Research on Learning Analytics: A Systematic Review

Selcan Kilis and Yasemin Gulbahar

1 Introduction

The recent emergence of *learning analytics* and data mining has gained importance as a significant role in many fields, including commerce. Data mining, the analysis of 'big data' and smart systems learning from such data is of vital importance, with Eynon declaring that 'big data represents a paradigm shift in the ways we understand and study our world' (2013, p. 237). Whilst big data is incredibly bold, it is still relatively unexplored (Long & Siemens, 2011; Lyon, 2014; Watters, 2013).

A huge amount of data is recorded in the digital world and the use of such data for various purposes is of significant value and can generate vast commercial profit. Similarly, in the field of education, there is a significant amount of data recorded via learning management systems (LMSs), the Internet, and through Massive Open Online Courses (MOOC). This educational data can be used in order to understand and optimise learning and the environments in which it occurs (Long & Siemens, 2011), improving student success and retention (Arnold, 2010; Clow, 2013), identifying at-risk students (Marbouti, Diefes-Dux, & Madhavan, 2016), building machine learning models in order to predict leaners' needs for special support to avoid dropout, to alleviate existing difficulties or eliminate misconceptions (Pardo, Jovanovic, Dawson, Gašević, & Mirriahi, 2017), assessing the nature and patterns of online interactions (Manca, Delfino, & Mazzonit, 2008; Stahl, 2006; Wegerif, 2006; Zhu, 2006), and understanding learners' psychological characteristics, such as an interest in a particular topic (Woolf, Burleson, Arroyo, Dragon, Cooper, & Picard, 2009).

Data analytics is essential in ensuring that learners receive the highest quality of learning and the best possible supporting personalised service in order to achieve according to their capability and enter the workforce ready to compete on the global stage (De Freitas, Gibson, Du Plessis, Halloran, Williams, Ambrose, Dunwell, & Arnab, 2015). However, there is still need for further research in order to direct the recently emerging field of learning analytics. Especially, it is very important for research on how to conduct the process of investigating variables and the interpretation of findings based on scientific evidence. With regards to this issue, the current study aims to draw a roadmap for learning analytics research in order to reveal the current position in terms of what has already been achieved to date and what studies could be undertaken in the future by conducting a systematic review of the existing literature. With this aim, the research questions that guide this study are as follows.

1. What demographic information is known about previous learning analytics research studies?
2. What were the sample/data sizes, research design type, study aim/s, and research variables on previous learning analytics research studies?
3. What were the participants' grade level, data collection method/instrument, and data analysis method on previous learning analytics research studies?

2 Methodology

This research adopts a method of systematic review, also known as research synthesis, in order to provide an impartial review that delivers a comprehensive overview of research undertaken to date on learning analytics (Gough, Oliver, & Thomas, 2012). It is basically defined as a process of selecting, identifying, and synthesising primary research studies so as to provide a thorough representation of the issue being reviewed (Oakley, 2012). This type of research design, as Petticrew and Roberts (2008) state, guides researchers in their future research by providing hints, an overview, and documenting gaps in the existing research (Gough et al., 2012). In the current study, the topic or issue of review is learning analytics. According to Gough et al. (2012), systematic review includes three main activities: (1) identification and describing of relevant research, (2) critical appraisal of research reports in a systematic manner, and (3) synthesising research findings into a coherent statement. Of the two types of systematic review, namely aggregative and configurative (Gough et al., 2012), the current study specifically adopts a configurative design which configures data from the sampled research in order to answer specific research (or review) questions. The detailed steps applied in the methodology of the current study are presented as follows.

2.1 Search Strategy

For the sample research of the current study, the first step is identifying existing studies through a detailed search using Google Scholar. Of the journals included in Google Scholar, the top ten ranked[1] educational technology journals were selected based on their five-year h-index and h-median metrics. The identified top-five ranked journals were selected in accordance with the highest h-5 index, and then h-5 median.

TABLE 4.1   Rank and title of journal included in literature search

Rank	Title of the journal	h-5 index	h-5 median
1.	*Computers & Education (C&E)*	94	137
2.	*British Journal of Educational Technology (BJET)*	53	78
3.	*Journal of Educational Technology and Society (JET&S)*	49	72
4.	*The Internet and Higher Education (I&HE)*	46	97
5.	*The International Review of Research in Open and Distributed Learning (IRRODL)*	41	68

From the top five journals, an electronic search was conducted using the search term 'learning analytics.' The 'learning analytics' search term was selected because it refers to all studies of data analytics in educational settings including online learning, blended learning, face-to-face settings, and mobile learning. The criteria used in selecting published research from these five journals are explained in the following section.

2.2 *Criteria for Selection of Published Research*

From the top five ranked educational technology journals selected, a search was conducted using certain criteria in order to select the published research items. The inclusion and exclusion criteria for the synthesis was as follows;

- match to the search term,
- within predefined publication years,
- being a journal article,
- not being a colloquium or editorial note,
- not being a review study, which also means a reflection paper rather than empirical research, and
- not being a research study out of scope.

At the first stage, the first criteria is matching the search term of 'learning analytics.' A search was conducted against each of the selected journals for the term 'learning analytics' in the title, keywords, or abstract, in order to access the best results. The second criteria used in the search was publication year, which refers to the time limitation of the performed search. Only articles published within the past five years (2013–2017) were included so as to retrieve only the latest developments and innovations in the field of study, and thereby to draw better conclusions from the retrieved studies as the latest developments in the field of learning analytics. The third criteria was being a journal article, rather than a chapter, report or a conference paper published in proceedings.

TABLE 4.2   Search results for included and excluded articles

Journal title	Numbers of articles		
	1st stage	2nd stage	3rd stage
Computers & Education	12	12	11
British Journal of Educational Technology	13	10	8
Journal of Educational Technology and Society	11	10	5
The Internet and Higher Education	9	9	7
The International Review of Research in Open and Distributed Learning	13	13	8
Total	58	54	39

The search results for each stage, including the title of the journal and the number of articles retrieved are provided in Table 4.2. As can be seen, a total of 58 articles were accessed in the first stage of the search.

In the second stage, from the articles selected in the first stage (n = 58), those which are a type of colloquium (n = 1) or editorial notes (n = 3) were then excluded. A total of 54 articles remained after the second stage (see Table 4.2).

In the third stage, those articles which were review studies and not empirical research (n = 6), reflection papers (n = 3), or research studies out of scope (n = 6) were excluded from the 54 articles from the second stage. A total of 39 articles remained after the third stage (see Table 4.2).

Numbers of articles found for each stage for each journal are presented in Table 4.2. Overall, a total of 39 journal articles were included in the current study. Those are marked with asterisk in the reference list.

Of the 39 journal articles included in the synthesis, most were published in 2017 (n = 14, 36%), followed by 2015 (n = 12, 31%), 2016 (n = 8, 21%), 2014 (n = 4, 10%), and 2013 (n = 1, 3%).

2.3   Analysis Framework

A total of nine criteria based on the three research questions were employed for the analysis: (1) number of authors, (2) country or geographic area of study, (3) sample/data size, (4) research design, (5) study aim/s, (6) research variables, (7) participants' grade level, (8) data collection method/instrument, and (9) data analysis method. The first two criteria were used to answer the first research question, whereas criteria items 3, 4, 5, and 6 were used to answer the second research question. Finally, criteria items 7, 8, and 9 were used to answer the third research question.

2.4 *Coding*

Descriptive codes or keywords are applied to each study included in a systematic review according to various characteristics, and is termed as the analysis framework. This enables the researcher/s to describe or map the size and nature of the literature (Gough et al., 2012, p. 125). In the current study, this equates to the research design, study aim/s, research variables, etc. which are the nine criteria used in the analysis, It is important to note that in this type of research, coding differs from the primary research data because it is conducted with the interpretation of both the participant data and author analysis (Britten, Campbell, Pope, Donovan, Morgan, & Pill, 2002, 2002; Gough et al., 2012). In the current study, codes were generated independently by the two researchers and then reviewed together. The following section presents the findings of the study following the coding exercise and the interpretations of the researchers.

3 Results

The findings of the current study are presented and organised in accordance with the three research questions.

3.1 *Research Question One: What Demographic Information Is Known About Previous Learning Analytics Research Studies?*

The first research question was analysed and its findings presented in the following two sub-sections regarding the number of authors and the country or geographic area of study, which refer to the demographic information for the studies examined on learning analytics.

3.1.1 Number of Authors

Figure 4.1 illustrates the number of authors that conducted the selected published studies. As can be seen, most of the studies were conducted by three or four authors, whilst only a few were conducted by either one or more than five authors.

Data for the number of authors shows that most research in the field of learning analytics is conducted with small team of researchers.

3.1.2 Country or Geographic Area of Study

Of the 39 research articles studied, with regard to the country or geographic area of study only three articles (8%) were conducted on solely one country, whereas the vast majority (n = 36, 92%) were conducted across more than one country. The distribution of country or geographic area of study is illustrated

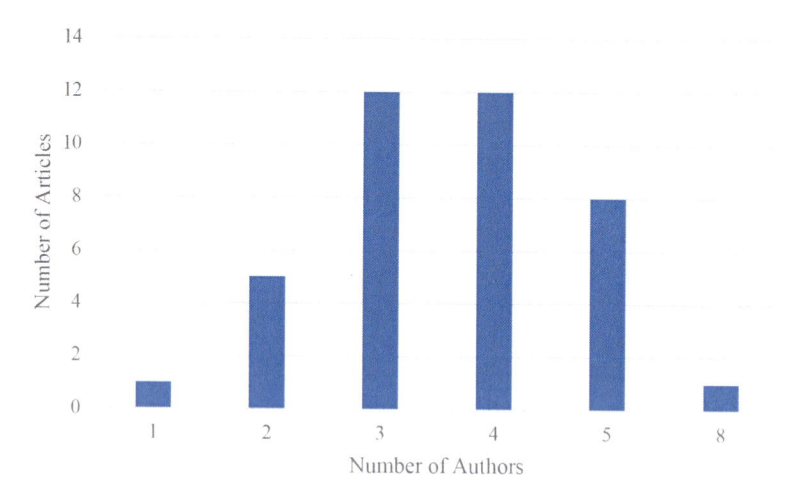

FIGURE 4.1   Number of authors per selected article

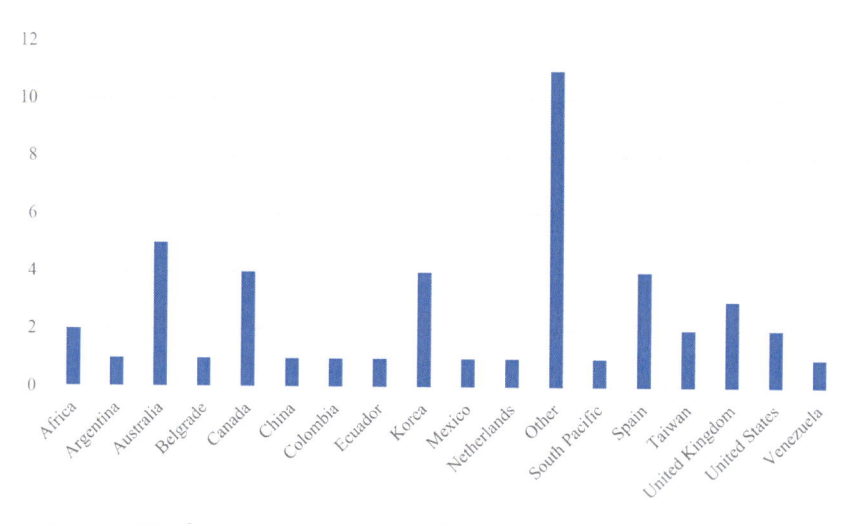

FIGURE 4.2   Distribution of country or geographic area of study

in Figure 4.2. In should be noted that some of the examined studies did not declare a country or countries of study, and some conducted research with data extracted from online learning programmes which included students from numerous countries worldwide. Studies where the country of study was not discernible were classed as 'Other.'

Figure 4.2 shows us that studies in the field of learning analytics have been conducted across many countries worldwide. Overall, the highest percentage of studies were in Korea, Australia, Canada, and Spain, respectively.

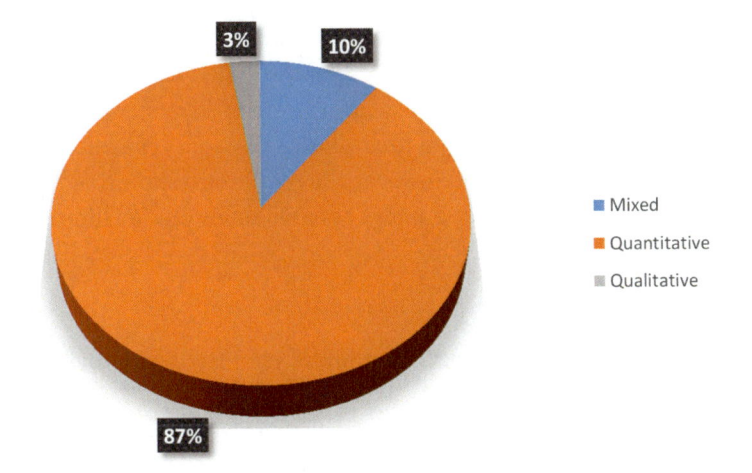

FIGURE 4.3   Distribution of research design

3.2   *Research Question Two: What Were the Sample/Data Sizes, Research Design Type, Study Aim/s, and Research Variables on Previous Learning Analytics Research Studies?*

The second research question was analysed and its findings are presented in the subsequent four sub-sections of sample/data size, research design, study aim/s, and research variables.

3.2.1   Sample/Data Size

With regard to the sample size or data size of the selected articles, the findings indicate that the sample or data size was mostly in the range of 0–100 (38%), followed by 100–500 (23%), then 500–1,000 (10%), 1,000–5,000 (18%), and the remainder (n = 4, 10%) with more than 5,000. The smallest sample size was just five, whereas the largest was 60,000. The average sample size of all the 39 articles studied was 5,120; however, some studies had a really small sample size. The reason for the high average sample or data size was due to a few articles having a very large sample or data size, such as the study by Teo, Johri, and Lohani (2017) with a data size of 31,219 and the study conducted by De Freitas et al. (2015) with an even larger data size of 51,181. When sample/data size is examined, it can be seen that sample size is usually very high. It can therefore be inferred that learning analytics facilitates studying with large sample sizes, thanks mostly to the features of platforms that record log files.

3.2.2   Research Design

In terms of type of research applied in the selected articles, the analysis showed (see Figure 4.3) that most of the studies, as expected, had employed a quantitative research design (n = 34, 87%), followed by a mixed research method design (n = 4, 10%). Only one of the studies (3%) had adopted a pure qualitative design.

As expected, most research adopted a quantitative research type because of the large volumes of collected data. However, the results also show that it is possible to perform research on learning analytics based solely on a qualitative design.

3.2.3   Study Aims

With regard to the aim of the selected articles, the analysis results are provided in Table 4.3.

There is a considerable variety seen between the research aims of the selected articles (see Table 4.3). Mostly, the articles aimed to develop a framework or a model and assess its efficiency; explore learners' interaction and interaction types, instructor-related issues such as guiding and supporting instructors about learners, supporting them also in providing feedback, etc., and learners' achievement or overall course performance. It can therefore be inferred that the field of learning analytics and data mining have already started to change direction, focusing on other concepts in education including self-regulated learning skills, feedback, knowledge creation, and cognitive issues, rather than merely achievement, interaction patterns, and/or supporting and informing instructors about learner behaviours and performance. This change in research focus for the field of learning analytics and data mining could return much increased profits by enhancing the scope, objectives and variables of studies and therefore providing deeper and meaningful analysis and understanding.

3.2.4   Research Variables

One of the most important points may be the variables which were the focus of the research studies selected in the scope of the current study. Analysis of the research variables across the selected 39 articles concluded the following.

- achievement/performance (n = 16)
- interaction (n = 7)
- cognitive load (n = 3)
- feedback/feedback quality (n = 3)
- self-regulation (n = 3)
- time management strategies (n = 3)
- learning experience (n = 2)
- learning strategies (n = 2)

TABLE 4.3   Aim of selected articles

Aim of articles (*Note*: articles may or may not be multi-purposed)	# of indicators	% of indicators
Academic dishonesty	1	3
Assessing efficiency of a tool	4	10
Developing a framework or model and assessing its efficiency	5	13
Examining the effect of feedback	2	5
Exploring knowledge creation	1	3
Exploring learners' cognitive issues (cognitive load/style)	2	5
Exploring learners' interaction and defining its types	5	13
Exploring learning experience	4	10
Exploring self-regulated learning skills	4	10
Exploring time management strategies	2	5
Instructor-related issues (guiding, efficiency, support)	5	13
Predicting and modelling course selection	1	3
Predicting learners' achievement/success/ overall performance	5	13
Other	7	18

- participation in discussion (n = 2)
- course selection (n = 1)
- demographics (n = 1)
- dropout (n = 1)
- inquiry/teacher inquiry (n = 1)
- knowledge creation (n = 1)
- motivation (n = 1)
- satisfaction (n = 1)
- teacher inquiry (n = 1)

Of the 39 empirical research studies, the most focus (n = 16, 41%) was given to the evaluation of learners' achievement or success. The next most focused upon variables were interaction (n = 7, 18%), time management strategies (n = 3, 8%), self-regulated learning skills (n = 3, 8%), cognitive load (n = 3, 8%), and feedback or feedback quality (n = 3, 8%). Other variables were course selection, dropout, inquiry, satisfaction, learning experience, knowledge crea-

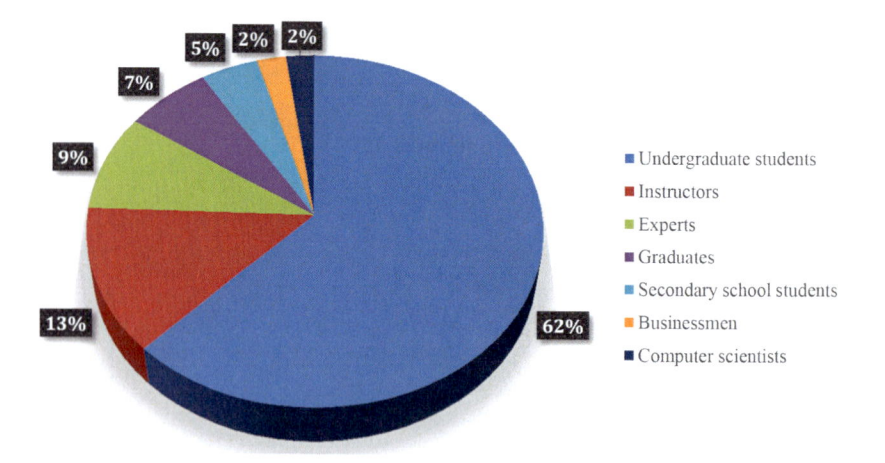

FIGURE 4.4   Distribution of participants' grade level

tion, learning strategies, motivation, participation in discussion, overall experience, and perceived usefulness of a tool.

3.3   *Research Question Three: What were the Participants' Grade Level, Data Collection Method/Instrument, and Data Analysis Method on Previous Learning Analytics Research Studies?*

The third research question was analysed and its findings are explained in
the following three sub-sections of participants' grade level, data collection
method/instrument, and data analysis method.

3.3.1   Participants' Grade Level
When looking at the research subjects for the selected studies, it can be clearly
seen from Figure 4.4 that the majority of the research was on undergraduate
students studying for their bachelor's degree (n = 28, 62%). Other categories of
subject were dramatically lower and varied, including instructors (n = 6, 13%),
experts (n = 4, 9%), graduates (n = 3, 7%), secondary schools students (n = 2,
5%), and computer scientists (n = 1, 2%).

The distribution of subjects indicates a variety, which was as to be expected.

3.3.2   Data Collection Method/Instrument
When the data collection method and instruments of the selected studies were
analysed, the findings revealed that in general, both log data or interaction
data is collected as well as data collected through another instrument such
as survey, interview, or observation. Only two of the research studies did not

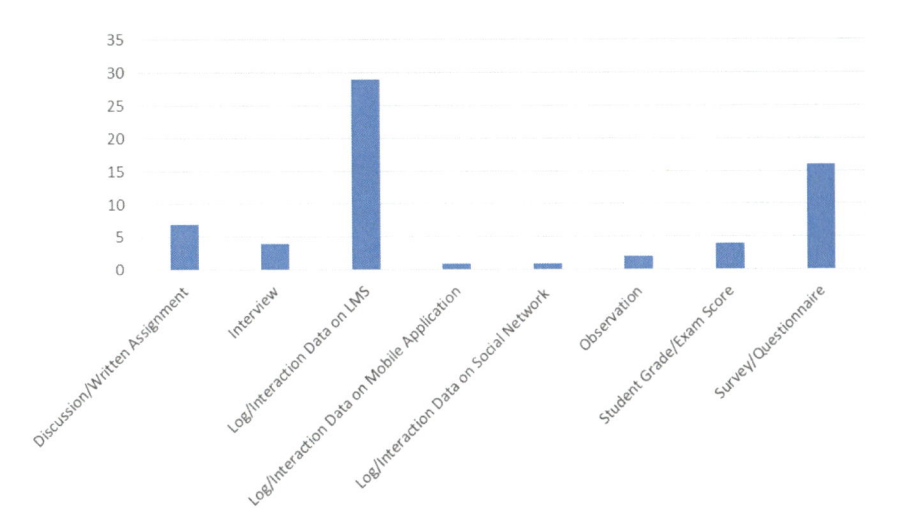

FIGURE 4.5   Distribution of data collection types

include information about how the data was collected. Of the 37 studies that did specify the data collection method, more than half (n = 20, 54%) used only one type of data, while the others (n = 17, 46%) collected more than one type of data. Most of the studies (n = 31, 84%) collected data from both log/ interaction data on LMS and an online platform like social media or mobile application. Also, most (n = 33, 89%) collected other types of data including survey data, discussion posts, interview, etc. More details can be seen as illustrated in Figure 4.5.

As Figure 4.5 indicates, although the majority of research studies collected data from web-based platforms (log data and/or interaction data) as well as surveys, other data types were also collected and evaluated. It also shows that written assignments, discussion posts, interviews or observations could be studied and therefore beneficial to studies of this field. It is arguable that research in this field that focuses on these data types would provide more accurate and meaningful results. Learners' footprints, after being analysed through data mining approaches and learning analytics, could be expanded with qualitative data and therefore provide an increased level of information about learners' behaviours. Similarly, teachers' observations about their learners could also provide much more meaningful and detailed information.

3.3.3   Data Analysis Method

Figure 4.6 illustrates the variety of data analysis methods employed in the selected studies. Most of the studies applied more than one data analysis

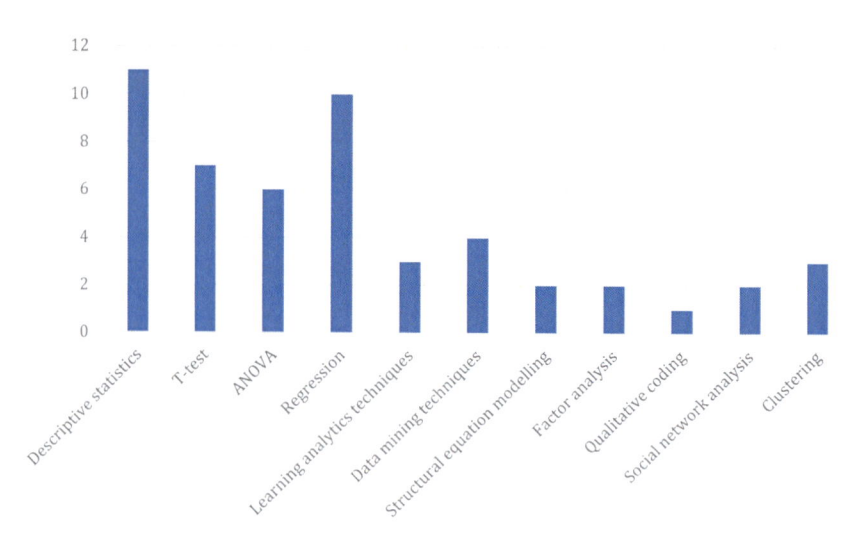

FIGURE 4.6   Distribution of employed data analysis method

method. At the parent-level, only one study adopted qualitative data analysis methodology (3%), whilst all others were conducted as quantitative data analysis (n = 38, 97%). Of the 38 quantitative data analysis studies, most (n = 23, 61%) conducted inferential statistical analysis (e.g. *t*-test, correlation, regression), whereas nearly one-third (n = 11, 29%) conducted descriptive statistics (e.g. mean, standard deviation, frequency). Other techniques including specific data mining techniques, learning analytics approach or social network analysis were used by almost one-third of the studies (n = 12, 32%). Figure 4.6 indicates each specific type of data analysis employed, together with the numbers of studies.

As can be seen in Figure 4.6, the data analysis type used in the selected studies that were examined in the scope of current study vary, and include descriptive statistics (n = 11, 28%), regression (n = 10, 26%), *t*-test (n = 7, 18%), ANOVA (n = 6, 15%), data mining techniques (n = 4, 10%), learning analytics techniques (n = 3, 8%), clustering (n = 3, 8%), structural equation modelling (n = 2, 5%), factor analysis (n = 2, 5%), and qualitative coding (n = 1, 3%). Besides the specific data analysis methods employed, when the software used in data analysis is examined, the findings indicated that most studies (n = 33, 85%) did not declare which software was used, whereas the others indicated SPSS (5%), SAS (n = 1, 3%), AMOS (n = 1, 3%), ORA (n = 1, 3%), and NVivo (n = 1, 3%). Although most of the studies did not mention the software used in the data analysis, they did specify the analysis type.

4   Discussion and Conclusion

This study performed a systematic synthesis of the existing literature on learning analytics which was conducted with 39 journal articles from 58 selected from the top-five ranked educational technology journals from 2013 to 2017 with the aim of producing a comprehensive overview and impartial synthesis of research carried out to date in this field. A configurative systematic review was conducted with an analysis framework including nine criteria; (1) number of authors, (2) country or geographic area of study, (3) sample/data size, (4) research design, (5) study aim/s, (6) research variables, (7) participants' grade level, (8) data collection method/instrument, and (9) data analysis methods. Analysis was conducted after excluding studies that were in fact editorial notes, colloquium, review or reflection papers, or other studies deemed as out of scope. The codes used in the analysis were generated by the current study's two authors and then reviewed together.

Results were reported in accordance with the study's three research questions. For the first research question, the findings indicated that research was usually conducted with a team of three to five researchers people, and that Korea, Australia, Canada and Spain are the countries where most research has been conducted.

In regard to the second research question, the findings revealed that contrary to other primary research, sample size or data size for learning analytics research, as expectedly high due to data sourced from web platforms that recorded user footprints. Although some studies used a small sample (e.g. Amigud, Arnedo-Moreno, Daradoumis, & Guerrero-Roldan, 2017; Chen & Yeh, 2017; Avramides, Hunter, Oliver, & Luckin, 2015), most studies were conducted with a large sample or data size (e.g. De Freitas et al., 2015; Teo et al., 2017). In a usual primary research, conducting research with a very large sample of 20,000 to 40,000 or more may be extremely challenging or even impossible in many instances; but is achievable thanks to learning analytics and data-mining approaches, as well as web platforms recording log data or the interaction data of users. Moreover, the research design employed in the selected articles showed that quantitative studies were mostly conducted; having started with research in this field based solely on interaction data or log data. However, research has recently started to employ either mixed or qualitative types of design, which could in turn provide a better understanding of the issue or phenomenon (Creswell, 2002; Fraenkel, Hyun, & Wallen, 2012). In addition, analysis of the research aims of the selected articles showed a promising variety with recent research examining issues including time management strategies, self-regulated skills, cognitive load, feedback knowledge creation, etc. rather than merely behavioural or interaction types. This advance in the aims of research into learning analytics is a significant development for the field. Conducting research employing mixed or qualitative designs with the aim of examining new issues or phenomena rather than interaction style, behavioural intent, course selection or dropouts, by focusing on other variables such as cognitive load, satisfaction, self-regulation brings new insights to the field. It also potentially provides a better and more in-depth understanding of the field and opens up new directions for future research.

With regards to the third research question, there was a variety seen in terms of the participants' grade level, data collection method or instruments, and data analysis method. For the grade level of participants, through heterogeneity, further research could better focus on other samples such as students and/or teachers in primary schools, students and/or teachers in secondary schools, instructional designers, and systems developers. As for data collection methods or instruments, research has already started to collect data through written assignments, discussion posts, interviews, etc. (e.g. Amigud et al., 2017; Avramides et al., 2015; McKenney & Mor, 2015), in addition to data recorded on web platforms. For example, measuring self-regulated learning skills and behaviours or cognitive load is not possible under normal conditions from footprints of learners in a usual LMS. However, it could be possible from self-evaluation reports, self-observations, teachers' observations, etc.

On this basis, focusing on new add-ons or platforms with more features that track data about learners' behaviours during the learning process is therefore of significant importance and could be the focus of system developers and computer scientists. Especially for platforms with many users such as Udemy, EdX, Open University, etc. with the education programmes they offer, would provide opportunity for empowerment in a relatively short period of time. Efficiency, quality, and satisfaction of learners in education, and also from the platforms or tools they use, could be improved. This could open up new directions for a better understanding of the field through access to more detailed information. Furthermore, the introduction of learning analytics, social network analysis, and data-mining approaches to analyse the collected data has recently changed and been enriched with other statistical analysis methods including inferential statistics like regression, correlation, etc., structural equation modelling, and path analysis. Based on these advancements, online educators and instructors can also improve their course designs in accordance with learners' requirements.

The overall findings of the current study forms a roadmap (see Figure 4.7) to guide researchers and other interested parties for the future of learning analytics research in light of these issues.

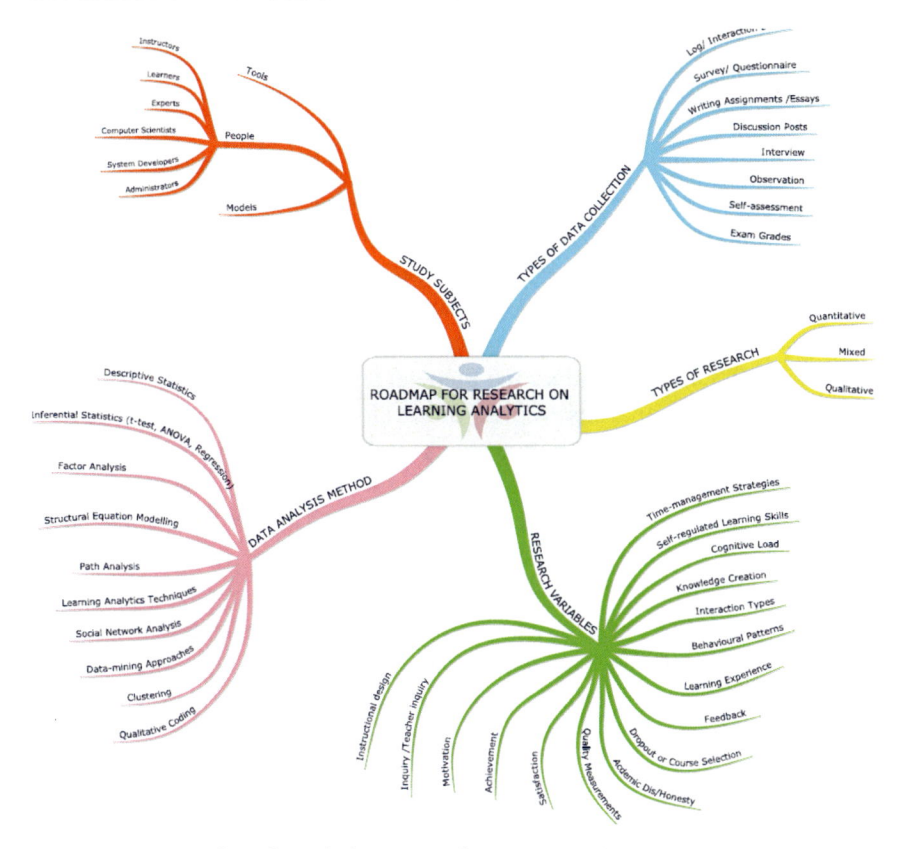

FIGURE 4.7 Research roadmap for learning analytics

As can be seen from the research roadmap for learning analytics in Figure 4.7, the framework includes five primary dimensions: study subjects, types of data collection, types of research, and research variables, and data analysis method.

The 'study subjects' dimension includes three sub-components: tools, people, and models, and refers to the potential samples for any research as not only people, as in learners, instructors, system developers, etc., but also learning tools or models could be the subject of study.

The 'types of data collection' and 'type of research' dimensions in the roadmap describe how research can be designed, and what data can be collected through which instruments. As can be seen from the 'types of research' dimension, studies can be designed as a purely qualitative research or as a mixed-type, providing a more detailed understanding and thereby potentially more accurate findings (Creswell, 2002, p. 535; Fraenkel et al., 2012, p. 558) than pure quantitative measures.

The 'research variables' dimension indicates the variables to be investigated and has the potential to be expanded in future research to elaborate the field of learning analytics. For example, variables such as achievement, interaction types, learning experience, and dropout or course selection have already been the focus of many research studies. However, other variables such as cognitive load, self-regulated learning skills, inquiry or teacher inquiry, and academic dishonesty were first introduced in the articles examined under the current study. It should be noted that some variables have only recently been examined in just a few research studies or settings, and therefore their findings cannot be generalised at this point. As the authors of those studies recommended, such variables should be made the focus of further research studies (Amigud et al., 2017; Ellis, Han, & Pardo, 2017; Toetenel & Rienties, 2016).

Finally, the 'data analysis method' dimension in the roadmap details various statistical analysis or other methods like qualitative coding, path analysis, etc. besides learning analytics techniques and data-mining approaches.

In summary, as Tabuenca, Kalz, Drachsler, and Specht (2015) declared, 'indeed, the more customised the learning analytics are, the more relevant will be for the student' (p. 55). The research roadmap generated by the current study (see Figure 4.7) for learning analytics has been achieved following a systematic review of 39 journal articles selected from the top-five ranking educational technology journals. The roadmap is expected to guide and support researchers and other stakeholders interested in the field of learning analytics research. By detailing potential dimensions for future research studies, the researchers of the current study aim to bring about a better understanding of learning analytics as a field of academic study, and thereby provide much improved academic benefit for the field.

Note

1   Google Scholar search performed using: https://scholar.google.com/citations?view_op=top_venues&hl=en&vq=soc_educationaltechnology

References

Note: References marked with an asterisk indicate studies included in the systematic review.

*Alexandron, G., Ruipérez-Valiente, J. A., Chen, Z., Muñoz-Merino, P. J., & Pritchard, D. E. (2017). Copying@ scale: Using harvesting accounts for collecting correct answers in a MOOC. *Computers & Education, 108*, 96–114.

*Ali, L., Asadi, M., Gašević, D., Jovanović, J., & Hatala, M. (2013). Factors influencing beliefs for adoption of a learning analytics tool: An empirical study. *Computers & Education, 62*, 130–148.

*Amigud, A., Arnedo-Moreno, J., Daradoumis, T., & Guerrero-Roldan, A.-E. (2017). Using learning analytics for preserving academic integrity. *The International Review of Research in Open and Distributed Learning, 18*(5), 192–210.

*Archer, E., & Barnes, G. (2017). Revisiting sensemaking: The case of the Digital Decision Network Application (DigitalDNA). *The International Review of Research in Open and Distributed Learning, 18*(5), 249–276.

Arnold, K. E. (2010). Signals: Applying academic analytics. *Educause Quarterly, 33*(1), n1.

*Avramides, K., Hunter, J., Oliver, M., & Luckin, R. (2015). A method for teacher inquiry in cross-curricular projects: Lessons from a case study. *British Journal of Educational Technology, 46*(2), 249–264.

*Bodily, R., Nyland, R., & Wiley, D. (2017). The RISE framework: Using learning analytics to automatically identify open educational resources for continuous improvement. *The International Review of Research in Open and Distributed Learning, 18*(2), 103–122.

Britten, N., Campbell, R., Pope, C., Donovan, J., Morgan, M., & Pill, R. (2002). Using meta-ethnography to synthesis of qualitative research: A worked example. *Journal of Health Services Research & Policy, 7*(4), 209–215.

*Brooks, C., Erickson, G., Greer, J., & Gutwin, C. (2014). Modelling and quantifying the behaviours of students in lecture capture environments. *Computers & Education, 75*, 282–292.

*Chen, S. Y., & Yeh, C. C. (2017). The effects of cognitive styles on the use of hints in academic English: A learning analytics approach. *Journal of Educational Technology & Society, 20*(2), 251–264.

Clow, D. (2013). An overview of learning analytics. *Teaching in Higher Education, 18*(6), 683–695.

Creswell, J. W. (2002). *Educational research: Planning, conducting, and evaluating quantitative research* (4th ed.). Boston, MA: Pearson Education.

*De Freitas, S., Gibson, D., Du Plessis, C., Halloran, P., Williams, E., Ambrose, M., Dunwell, I., & Arnab, S. (2015). Foundations of dynamic learning analytics: Using university student data to increase retention. *British Journal of Educational Technology, 46*(6), 1175–1188.

*De Lima, M., & Zorrilla, M. E. (2017). Social networks and the building of learning communities: An experimental study of a social MOOC. *The International Review of Research in Open and Distributed Learning, 18*(1), 40–64.

*Ellis, R. A., Han, F., & Pardo, A. (2017). Improving learning analytics – Combining observational and self-report data on student learning. *Journal of Educational Technology & Society, 20*(3), 158–169.

Eynon, R. (2013). The rise of big data: what does it mean for education, technology, and media research? *Learning, Media and Technology, 38*(3), 237–240.

Fraenkel, J. R., Hyun, H. H., & Wallen, N. E. (2012). *How to design and evaluate research in education* (8th ed.). New York, NY: McGraw Hill.

*Gašević, D., Dawson, S., Rogers, T., & Gasevic, D. (2016). Learning analytics should not promote one size fits all: The effects of instructional conditions in predicting academic success. *The Internet and Higher Education, 28*, 68–84.

*Gil-Jaurena, I., Callejo-Gallego, J., & Agudo, Y. (2017). Evaluation of the UNED MOOCs implementation: Demographics, learners' opinions and completion rates. *The International Review of Research in Open and Distributed Learning, 18*(7), 141–168.

Gough, D., Oliver, S., & Thomas, J. (Eds.). (2017). *An introduction to systematic reviews.* London: Sage Publications.

*Jo, I.-H., Kim, D., & Yoon, M. (2015). Constructing proxy variables to measure adult learners' time management strategies in LMS. *Journal of Educational Technology & Society, 18*(3), 214–225.

*Jo, I.-H., Park, Y., Yoon, M., & Sung, H. (2016). Evaluation of online log variables that estimate learners' time management in a Korean online learning context. *The International Review of Research in Open and Distributed Learning, 17*(1), 195–213.

*Joksimović, S., Gašević, D., Loughin, T. M., Kovanović, V., & Hatala, M. (2015). Learning at distance: Effects of interaction traces on academic achievement. *Computers & Education, 87*, 204–217.

*Jovanović, J., Gašević, D., Dawson, S., Pardo, A., & Mirriahi, N. (2017). Learning analytics to unveil learning strategies in a flipped classroom. *The Internet and Higher Education, 33*, 74–85.

*Kim, D., Park, Y., Yoon, M., & Jo, I.-H. (2016). Toward evidence-based learning analytics: Using proxy variables to improve asynchronous online discussion environments. *The Internet and Higher Education, 30*, 30–43.

*Kizilcec, R. F., Pérez-Sanagustín, M., & Maldonado, J. J. (2017). Self-regulated learning strategies predict learner behavior and goal attainment in massive open online courses. *Computers & Education, 104*, 18–33.

Long, P., & Siemens, G. (2011). Penetrating the fog: Analytics in learning and education. *Educause Review, 46*(5), 30–40.

Lyon, D. (2014). Surveillance, Snowden, and big data: Capacities, consequences, critique. *Big Data & Society, 1*(2), 1–13. doi:10.1177/2053951714541861

*Ma, J., Han, X., Yang, J., & Cheng, J. (2015). Examining the necessary condition for engagement in an online learning environment based on learning analytics approach: The role of the instructor. *The Internet and Higher Education, 24*, 26–34.

Manca, S., Delfino, M., & Mazzonit, E. (2008). Coding procedures to analyze interaction patterns in education web forums. *Journal of Computer Assisted Learning, 25*(2), 189–200.

*Marbouti, F., Diefes-Dux, H. A., & Madhavan, K. (2016). Models for early prediction of at-risk students in a course using standards-based grading. *Computers & Education, 103*, 1–15.

*McKenney, S., & Mor, Y. (2015). Supporting teachers in data-informed educational design. *British Journal of Educational Technology, 46*(2), 265–279.

*Melero, J., Hernández-Leo, D., Sun, J., Santos, P., & Blat, J. (2015). How was the activity? A visualization support for a case of location-based learning design. *British Journal of Educational Technology, 46*(2), 317–329.

*Montgomery, A. P., Mousavi, A., Carbonaro, M., Hayward, D. V., & Dunn, W. (2017). Using learning analytics to explore self-regulated learning in flipped blended learning music teacher education. *British Journal of Educational Technology*.

Oakley, A. (2012). Foreword. In D. Gough, S. Oliver, & J. Thomas (Eds.), *An introduction to systematic reviews* (pp. vii–x). London: Sage Publications.

*Ognjanovic, I., Gasevic, D., & Dawson, S. (2016). Using institutional data to predict student course selections in higher education. *The Internet and Higher Education, 29*, 49–62.

*Pardo, A., Jovanovic, J., Dawson, S., Gašević, D., & Mirriahi, N. (2017). Using learning analytics to scale the provision of personalised feedback. *British Journal of Educational Technology*. doi:10.1111/bjet.12590

Petticrew, M., & Roberts, H. (2008). *Systematic reviews in the social sciences: A practical guide*. Malden, MA: John Wiley & Sons.

*Prasad, D., Totaram, R., & Usagawa, T. (2016). Development of open textbooks learning analytics system. *The International Review of Research in Open and Distributed Learning, 17*(5), 215–234.

*Rodríguez-Triana, M. J., Martínez-Monés, A., Asensio-Pérez, J. I., & Dimitriadis, Y. (2015). Scripting and monitoring meet each other: Aligning learning analytics and learning design to support teachers in orchestrating CSCL situations. *British Journal of Educational Technology, 46*(2), 330–343.

*Scheffel, M., Drachsler, H., Stoyanov, S., & Specht, M. (2014). Quality indicators for learning analytics. *Journal of Educational Technology & Society, 17*(4), 117–132.

Stahl, G. (2006). *Group cognition: Computer support for building collaborative knowledge*. Cambridge, MA: The MIT Press.

*Tabuenca, B., Kalz, M., Drachsler, H., & Specht, M. (2015). Time will tell: The role of mobile learning analytics in self-regulated learning. *Computers & Education, 89*, 53–74.

*Teo, H. J., Johri, A., & Lohani, V. (2017). Analytics and patterns of knowledge creation: Experts at work in an online engineering community. *Computers & Education, 112*, 18–36.

*Timmers, C. F., Walraven, A., & Veldkamp, B. P. (2015). The effect of regulation feedback in a computer-based formative assessment on information problem solving. *Computers & Education, 87*, 1–9.

*Toetenel, L., & Rienties, B. (2016). Analysing 157 learning designs using learning analytic approaches as a means to evaluate the impact of pedagogical decision making. *British Journal of Educational Technology, 47*(5), 981–992.

*Van Leeuwen, A., Janssen, J., Erkens, G., & Brekelmans, M. (2014). Supporting teachers in guiding collaborating students: Effects of learning analytics in CSCL. *Computers & Education, 79*, 28–39.

*Van Leeuwen, A., Janssen, J., Erkens, G., & Brekelmans, M. (2015). Teacher regulation of cognitive activities during student collaboration: Effects of learning analytics. *Computers & Education, 90*, 80–94.

Watters, A. (2013, October 13). *Student data is the new oil: MOOCs, metaphor, and money* [blog post]. Retrieved from https://academiccommons.columbia.edu/catalog/ac:177768

Wegerif, R. (2006). A dialogic understanding of the relationship between CSCL and teaching thinking skills. *International Journal of Computer-Supported Collaborative Learning, 1*(1), 143–157.

Woolf, B., Burleson, W., Arroyo, I., Dragon, T., Cooper, D., & Picard, R. (2009). Affect-aware tutors: Recognising and responding to student affect. *International Journal of Learning Technology, 4*(3–4), 129–164.

*Xie, K., Yu, C., & Bradshaw, A. C. (2014). Impacts of role assignment and participation in asynchronous discussions in college-level online classes. *The Internet and Higher Education, 20*, 10–19.

*Yang, D., Wen, M., Kumar, A., Xing, E. P., & Rose, C. P. (2014). Towards an integration of text and graph clustering methods as a lens for studying social interaction in MOOCs. *The International Review of Research in Open and Distributed Learning, 15*(5), 214–234.

*Yen, C.-H., Chen, I.-C., Lai, S.-C., & Chuang, Y.-R. (2015). An analytics-based approach to managing cognitive load by using log data of learning management systems and footprints of social media. *Journal of Educational Technology & Society, 18*(4), 141–158.

*You, J. W. (2016). Identifying significant indicators using LMS data to predict course achievement in online learning. *The Internet and Higher Education, 29*, 23–30.

Zhu, E. (2006). Interaction and cognitive engagement: An analysis of four asynchronous online discussions. *Instructional Science, 34*(6), 451–480.

CHAPTER 5

The Benefits of Learning Analytics in Open and Distance Education: A Review of the Evidence

Billy Tak-Ming Wong

1   Introduction

Learning analytics refers to the collection, measurement, analysis and reporting of data on learners and learning contexts in order to understand and improve students' learning and the learning environments (Siemens, 2011). It is regarded as a sub-type of academic analytics, which is defined as the analysis and evaluation of organizational information obtained from higher education institutions for reporting and making decisions (Campbell, DeBlois, & Oblinger, 2007). By analyzing the big data from learners, learning analytics can enhance understanding of learning behaviors, and help educational institutions to improve their performance and decision-making in educational delivery. ODL presents an ideal context for the use of learning analytics. Because of its openness and distance learning mode, ODL courses usually attract a large number of students with diverse backgrounds who participate in the learning activities on online and mobile platforms. There is therefore a very considerable amount of data available which can be analyzed with learning analytics.

In ODL institutions, the application of learning analytics has become increasingly prevalent in recent years—a similar trend as in conventional face-to-face institutions. Various tools, systems and methods have been employed to support the processing of data. As Baker and Siemens (2014) explained, the data are usually collected from the learning management systems and online discussion platforms. They are then analyzed by a variety of statistical methods (e.g. prediction modeling for anticipating students' drop-out rates and learning achievements); social network analysis (for identifying the relationship between individuals, groups and organizations); and relationship mining techniques (for discovering the connections and patterns between data sets), as well as human judgement (e.g. data visualization for empowering instructors to provide students with timely feedback and improve pedagogy). The results of analysis can facilitate the achievements of educational goals, such as understanding students' learning behaviors, enhancing the curriculum design, personalizing assistance to students, and designing learning interventions.

In view of the mounting research on and practice of learning analytics in the context of ODL, this paper presents a systematic literature review in this area. It aims to give an overview of this emerging field and provide a foundation for further exploration of this topic. Specifically, it covers the objectives of learning analysis practices by ODL institutions; the analytic approaches employed; and the outcomes obtained.

2   Literature Review

The benefits of learning analytics in ODL have been reported in the literature. For example, Scanlon, McAndrew, and O'Shea (2015) showed how it can help in understanding the mutual influence of technology and education in learning design. They found that alternative ways to assist learning at a distance had been offered in open education, and students who had been underserved (e.g. the disabled) by conventional institutions benefited from open educational resources. Calvert (2014) revealed that, by resorting to predictive analytical techniques, it is possible to predict students' success (i.e. how many students can pass in a course) based on relatively small sets of data collected at different points of time throughout the students' learning journey. Rosewell and Jansen (2014) developed a benchmark process for the evaluation and monitoring of an e-learning course, and demonstrated the effectiveness of the process in helping students to feel reassured about their learning experience. Subotzky and Prinsloo (2011) developed a socio-critical model and a framework for a better understanding of student learning behaviors, predicting student success and improving student performance. Their work was shown to be able to inform and improve the academic performance of an institution and the provision of assistance to students, in order to maximize their success and satisfaction. Also, Archer, Chetty, and Prinsloo (2014) presented an academic-business collaboration approach to figure out students' habits and learning behaviors, using a tool employed in business settings, which contribute to student success and retention.

There are different aspects of ODL that have a high potential to be addressed by the use of learning analytics. According to Ojo and Olakulehin (2006), there is usually very little or even no face-to-face exchange between students and instructors in distance learning. Self-motivating, learner-oriented course materials are provided for students, but only some ODL institutions offer tutorial sessions; and extra assistance from instructors will often be given only on a needs basis. Minnaar (2013) stated that academic support is essential and important for ODL students. Nevertheless, due to the high cost of providing academic support to the large number of students in the ODL institutions, there is a pressing need to work out a more cost-effective approach to academic support via technology (McKay & Makhanya, 2008). Finally, Slade and Prinsloo (2015) investigated how an ODL university can apply learning analytics to provide timely and appropriate assistance to students more cost-effectively, and the ways to assist students proactively in order to help them achieve the learning objectives.

In sum, the literature on learning analytics in ODL has already covered a broad range of areas—such as the illustration of analytics approaches and methods; the investigation of benefits from using of data-driven analytics; the development of tools and platforms; and the identification of factors which contribute to student success. The key achievements of learning analytics practices have also been reported—such as the methods for predicting student success; the early identification of at-risk students who may give up a course or terminate their studies; and the provision of personalized assistance and specific academic support drawing on the data analysis results. There is therefore a need to review and summarize the existing work so as to reveal the present situation in this field.

3   Methodology

This study aims to investigate how learning analytics has been adopted in open and distance education and the benefits obtained. Relevant case studies were collected from Google Scholar using the keywords 'learning analytics' and 'university' in combination with 'distance learning,' 'open education,' 'open distance learning' and 'ODL.' The studies were selected based on the following criteria:

1. The study involved one or more empirical cases of the adoption of learning analytics.
2. The institution offered open and distance learning.
3. The article reporting the case(s) contained the objectives of using learning analytics, a description of analytics, research methods, and outcomes of the adoption of analytics.

A total of 21 articles which fulfilled all the above criteria were selected for further analysis. Relevant information was retrieved from the articles and categorized in terms of the objectives, analytical approaches and benefits.

4   Results

4.1   *Objectives and Analytical Approaches*

Table 5.1 summarizes the objectives of the learning analytics practices and the analytical approaches adopted by the ODL institutions. The objectives covered various areas, such as the prediction of learners' performance, understanding of interaction and collaboration patterns, and enhancement of learner engagement. The approaches included the collection of data from existing systems such as LMS/VLE and MOOC, and data analysis using techniques such as predictive statistics, social network analysis and data visualization.

It is also notable that the institutions included, in addition to those primarily offering ODL courses, conventional face-to-face institutions (e.g. the University of Maryland) offering distance learning courses, particularly MOOCs. The institutions spread over different parts of the world—Africa: South Africa; Asia: India, Pakistan, the Philippines; Europe: Greece, Spain, the UK; North America: Canada, the USA; South America: Brazil; Australia—showing that learning analytics has been widely practiced.

4.2   *Benefits for Institutions, Staff and Students*

4.2.1   Improve Student Retention

Table 5.2 summarizes the outcome of the learning analytics practices in terms of improving student retention. By monitoring the cases where students were successful and persistent, factors promoting students' tendencies on course enrollment and completion could be identified and more effective student retention strategies could be formulated. The outcome also showed the differences between students who were likely and unlikely to complete courses. In addition to course completion, the willingness of students to take another course in the institution was also investigated, which provided institutions and staff with information on the way students obtain success, satisfaction and experience in completing the courses in which they had enrolled.

4.2.2   Predict at-Risk Students and Student Failure

Table 5.3 shows the benefits of learning analytics in predicting students at risk of failure in their studies. By the use of predictive analytical techniques, such as a predictive model, individuals or groups of student who are likely to fail in a course could be identified early. For example, Yasmin (2013) found that employed and married students were more likely to be at risk. The results can help staff to adjust the course and/or provide students with appropriate assistance to enhance their pass rate and lower the dropout rate.

Institution	Objective	Approach	*Source*
Allama Iqbal Open University, Pakistan	Provide educational and administrative support to the large numbers of students	Development of an online support system using open-source technologies for data analysis and quick response	Mir (2016)
Athabasca University, Canada	Investigate how emergent technologies can bring impact to the design of learning environments	Adoption of analytics tools to visualize complex networks between students studying in MOOCs	Kop, Fournier, and Mak (2011)
Federal University of Pelotas, Brazil	Investigate the relation between guidance given by professors and students' study performance	Examining the association between (1) the number of interactions between students and professor and (2) the students' performance	Cechinel (2014)
Hellenic Open University, Greece	Examine the interaction and collaboration among students and instructors in a learning management system	Employment of social network analysis	Koulocheri, Soumplis, and Xenos (2012)
Murdoch University, Australia	Build measures concerning the success of MOOCs and scalable open online courses (SOOCS)	Measures derived from the characteristics of open online courses, ODL institutes, students, student motivation and data analytics	Klobas (2014)

(cont.)

Institution	Objective	Approach	*Source*
The UK Open University	1. Investigate how predictive analytics can be applied to generate a model of student success and retention 2. Predict students' success 3. Identify students who are potentially at-risk of failure in their studies 4. Personalize timely assistance to individual students and improve retention 5. Assist students through their studies and optimize their chances of achieving learning objectives	Use of a predictive analytical model	Calvert (2014); Prinsloo, Slade, and Galpin (2012); Slade and Prinsloo (2015); Wolff, Zdrahal, Nikolov, and Pantucek (2013)
	Explore factors affecting student enrolment and completion of massive open online courses (MOOCs)	Drawing together a variety of publicly available sources of data online to aggregate information about enrolment and completion of MOOCs	Jordan (2014)
The University of South Africa, South Africa	1. Examine the state of student data at the university and their potentials in learning analytics practices 2. Develop a model for the understanding, prediction, and enhancement of student success	Development of an analytics model	Prinsloo, Archer, Barnes, Chetty, and Zyl (2015); Subotzky and Prinsloo (2011)
	3. Identify possible factors impacting student success 4. Develop guidelines for facilitating student success in ODL		

(*cont.*)

TABLE 5.1 Learning analytics objectives and approaches for ODL institutions (cont.)

Institution	Objective	Approach	Source
	1. Understand student success and retention 2. Benchmark successful students' habits and learning behaviors	Monitoring student data using an analytical model	Archer, Chetty, and Prinsloo (2014)
	1. Explore an alternative approach to data visualization and dashboard design 2. Develop an enriched database which involves key indicators from different data sources for dashboards	A case study illustrating various views of stakeholders	Archer and Barnes (2015)
Universidad Politécnica de Madrid, Spain	Predict student academic performance	Using multiple linear regression to find relationships between student interactions on the virtual learning environment (VLE) and academic performance	Agudo-Peregrina, Hernández-García, and Iglesias-Pradas (2012)
University of Maryland, USA	1. Provide more participatory modes of education production and delivery 2. Illustrate how data is embedded in different courses and can be used to track course development and engagement 3. Enhance understanding of a MOOC platform ecosystem and identify new areas for research 4. Explore factors related to learners' participation in online courses	Using descriptive analytics to analyze the log data from the Peer 2 Peer University (P2PU) platform	Ahn, Butler, Alam, and Webster (2013a); Ahn, Weng, and Butler (2013b)

(cont.)

TABLE 5.1   Learning analytics objectives and approaches for ODL institutions (*cont.*)

Institution	Objective	Approach	*Source*
University of North Bengal, India	1. Select predictors for student dropout in ODL 2. Provide input for counselors and faculty members to offer assistance to at-risk learners	Using a data mining approach to identify the predictive relationships between pre-entry variables of learners and their dropout behaviors	Yasmin (2013)
University of the Philippines Open University, the Philippines	1. Evaluate the acceptability of an open source online curriculum mapping system in distributed curriculum development 2. Collect instructional and curricular design data	Using an online curriculum mapping system for curriculum design and data collection	Cantada (2014)
University of Phoenix, USA	Identify students who are likely to fail in a course	Development of a predictive model with data from the LMS and financial aid system	Barber and Sharkey (2012)

TABLE 5.2   Benefits of learning analytics: improve student retention

Institution	Major outcome	Source
Athabasca University	Developed pedagogy to support students in their learning journey via the learning platforms and resources	Kop et al. (2011)
The UK Open University	Provided a precise view of the trends in the development as well as the student enrolment in and completion of MOOCs	Jordan (2014)
	Kept student information updated and discovered student experience	Slade and Prinsloo (2014)
The University of South Africa	Developed a context-appropriate socio-critical model for understanding, prediction, and enhancement of student success	Subotzky and Prinsloo (2011)
	1. Developed a new approach to identify at-risk students 2. Examined successful students' habits and behaviors that contributed to their success	Archer et al. (2014)
University of North Bengal	Identified the pre-entry demographic variables that distinguish between learners who are likely and unlikely to complete courses	Yasmin (2013)

4.2.3   Deepen Understanding of Student Behaviors

Table 5.4 presents the outcome of learning analytics in understanding student behaviors. Through the investigation of student data, learning analytics allows educators to have a deeper understanding of students' behaviors and needs so as to design and modify the courses and learning materials to address them. For example, Koulocheri et al. (2012) reported that, when students find a course too easy, this could result in their getting a high grade but a low level of course participation.

4.2.4   Enhance Support to Students

As shown in Table 5.5, students can benefit from the improvement of student support informed by learning analytics. The learning analytics practices involved analyzing existing data and developing new student support systems. As ODL students do not, or only infrequently, have face-to-face interaction with staff in an institution, timely identification of student problems and a prompt response to their needs are key to their success in learning. The

TABLE 5.3   Benefits of learning analytics: predict at-risk student and student failure

Institution	Major outcome	Source
The UK Open University	1. Identified the data related to student success 2. Predicted the probability of students who can pass the course and the total number of students who can pass 3. Predicted student failure via the observation of students' activities in the virtual learning environment and students' behaviors	Calvert (2014); Wolff et al. (2013)
Universidad Politécnica de Madrid	Predicted students' academic performance via interaction typologies	Agudo-Peregrina et al. (2012)
University of North Bengal	Identified variables leading to learners at-risk, e.g. employed and married	Yasmin (2013)

improvement of student support was shown to enhance student learning experience and satisfaction, reduce student drop-out, and serve better specific learner groups (e.g. the disabled) who were underserved in conventional education.

4.2.5   Enhance Student Participation

Table 5.6 summarizes the use of learning analytics for enhancing student participation. Student participation in learning activities has for long been identified as one of the major factors affecting their academic performance. It was investigated by learning analytics usually through the traces students left on LMS/VLE in order to analyze their learning experience. It supports the exploration of the forms of participation and the interaction between students and teachers.

4.2.6   Provide Feedback and Intervention

Table 5.7 shows the benefits of learning analytics in offering appropriate feedback and intervention in order to enhance student success. Personalized assistance can be provided to students who need extra support. Academic support teams also benefited from the results of learning analytics practices by prioritizing students for intervention and referral to additional resources.

TABLE 5.4   Benefits of learning analytics: deepen understanding of student behaviors

Institution	Major outcome	Source
Allama Iqbal Open University	Being able to analyze the nature and category of student queries based on interrelated parameters	Mir (2016)
Hellenic Open University	Identified the reason why students with high grades tend to have a lower level of activity— namely lack of interest in finding a course too easy.	Koulocheri et al. (2012)
Murdoch University	Enabled quantitative analysis of learners, their learning journeys and their use of learning resources from the massive amount of MOOC data	Klobas (2014)
The UK Open University	Allowed investigation of student data, so as to impact and shape the approaches to student needs	Prinsloo et al. (2012); Slade and Prinsloo (2016)
The University of South Africa	Revealed the potential of using big data in ODL where students were found to have a preference for working independently or with a group of people they did not know	Pilkington and Sanders (2014); Prinsloo et al. (2015)
University of Maryland	Understood learner engagement and participation, which facilitated course development, assessment design, fellow learner recruitment, and learning environment sustainability	Ahn et al. (2013a)

5   Discussion and Conclusion

This study reviews the practices of learning analytics in ODL institutions and summarizes the benefits for the institutions. The results revealed that learning analytics has been practiced by ODL institutions in different parts of the world. The benefits revolved around improving student retention; predicting at-risk students and student failure; deepening understanding of student behaviors; strengthening student support; enhancing student participation; and providing appropriate feedback and intervention. The approaches and benefits of learning analytics for ODL institutions are similar to those for face-to-face institutions (Li, Ye, & Wong, 2018; Wong, 2017; Wong, Li, & Choi, 2018), despite the significant difference between them in terms of student profiles and learning environments (Li, Wong, & Wong, 2015).

TABLE 5.5   Benefits of learning analytics: enhance support to students

Institution	Major outcome	Source
Allama Iqbal Open University	1. Being able to handling queries coming from different sources, e.g. website, email and telephone 2. Improved the quality of response to students' queries, e.g. sending automatic emails and SMS to students	Mir (2016)
Athabasca University	Addressed gaps in student understanding which had been identified as being particularly problematic, e.g. algebraic reasoning	Yan and Law (2013)
Federal University of Pelotas	Helped to plan new support services for students based on data from student support experience	Cechinel (2014)
The UK Open University	Benefited groups who were underserved in conventional face-to-face education, such as the disabled, and helped to develop various ODL ways for students' needs	Rosewell and Jansen (2014); Scanlon et al. (2015)
The University of South Africa	Informed and improved academic and student support practices to enhance student satisfaction and success	Subotzky and Prinsloo (2011)
	Discovered embedded tensions and assumptions at the institution, such as perceptions concerning academic demands	Archer et al. (2014)
	Identified how open online education could suit different student needs	Pilkington and Sanders (2014)

Many of the learning analytics practices remained at an early stage in the ODL institutions, such as predicting students' study performance and identifying those who are at risk; and only a few practices focused on taking remedial actions for students as the last stage of the learning analytics cycle (Clow, 2012). As emphasized in Gašević, Dawson, Rogers, and Gašević (2016), the development of a data-informed culture has been recognized as a major challenge ahead of higher education institutions for them to benefit from learning analytics. Li et al. (2018) also showed that some institutions are still facing the obstacle of a lack of institutional culture or even resistance to change from their senior management. With the publication of more empirical evidence

TABLE 5.6   Benefits of learning analytics: enhance student participation

Institution	Major outcome	Source
The UK Open University	Reassured students about their experience in learning activities	Rosewell and Jansen (2014)
	Showed how students reacted to the emerging uses of their personal and academic data, and how educators facilitated a more considered and informed response to them	Slade and Prinsloo (2014)
The University of South Africa	Supported learners in identifying and exploring areas which needed further drills, and developed their ability to drill themselves extensively	Archer and Barnes (2015)
Universidad Politécnica de Madrid	Assisted students to evaluate themselves and interact with other students and teachers, which had an effective impact on student performance	Agudo-Peregrina et al. (2012)
University of Maryland	Developed alternative, participatory forms of educational production and delivery, with the support of social platforms	Ahn et al. (2013a)
	1. Enabled students to learn from other students who shared similar fields of study	Ahn et al. (2013b)
	2. Enabled researchers to initiate new questions concerning how student participate, collaborate, and learn in the online platforms	

on the outcomes and cost-effectiveness analysis of practicing learning analytics (e.g. Choi, Lam, Li, & Wong, 2018; Wong, 2017; Wong, Li, & Choi, 2018), it is expected that better informed decisions on the adoption of learning analytics can be made by the institutions.

The results of this review also suggest the potentials of learning analytics which are yet to be fully realized in ODL. The continuous development of ODL, particularly in developing regions with a growing population, remains an advantage for learning analytics as data can be collected on a large scale (Wong & Wong, 2018). Features of ODL, such as open admission and the distance learning mode, allow a wide range and a large number of students to study the same course with very limited face-to-face interaction. Sharing similar characteristics, MOOCs also feature a massive and diverse student base studying in an online learning environment (Wong, 2015). The current learning analytics implementation has yet to address such features. Hence, learning

TABLE 5.7   Benefits of learning analytics – provide feedback and intervention

Institution	Major outcome	Source
The UK Open University	1. Informed student support teams with the development of intervention strategies 2. Established student support and intervention services	Slade and Prinsloo (2015)
University of Phoenix	Helped to prioritize students for intervention and referral to additional resources	Barber and Sharkey (2012)

analytics solutions that have been shown to be effective in conventional face-to-face education institutions may not work equally well in the ODL context. For example, giving personalized consultation as intervention to individual at-risk students would be too costly for an ODL course or MOOC with thousands, or even tens of thousands, of students (Choi et al., 2018).

Future work should therefore explore further specific factors related to the ODL setting to identify plausible approaches for the practice of learning analytics. As emphasized in Gašević et al. (2016), learning analytics should not target a one-size-fits-all solution. Tailoring the practice for the specific needs of institutions, staff and students should be the direction for learning analytics to flourish in ODL.

References

Agudo-Peregrina, A. F., Hernández-García, A., & Iglesias-Pradas, S. (2012). Predicting academic performance with learning analytics in virtual learning environments: A comparative study of three interaction classifications. In *Proceedings of the 2012 International Symposium on Computers in Education (SIIE)* (pp. 1–6). Andorra la Vella, Andorra.

Ahn, J., Butler, B. S., Alam, A., & Webster, S. A. (2013a). Learner participation and engagement in open online courses: Insights from the peer 2 peer university. *MERLOT Journal of Online Learning and Teaching, 9*(2), 160–171.

Ahn, J., Weng, C., & Butler, B. S. (2013b). *The dynamics of open, peer-to-peer learning: What factors influence participation in the P2P university?* Paper presented at the 2013 46th Hawaii International Conference on System Sciences. Retrieved from http://ieeexplore.ieee.org/document/6480217/

Archer, E., & Barnes, G. (2015). *Re-examining dashboard development: Putting the horse back in front of the cart.* Paper presented at the EAIR 37th Annual Forum. Retrieved from http://uir.unisa.ac.za/bitstream/handle/10500/19044/EAIR%20-%20 Archer%20and%20Barnes%20%28Track%203%29.pdf?sequence=1&isAllowed

Archer, E., Chetty, Y. B., & Prinsloo, P. (2014). Benchmarking the habits and behaviours of successful students: A case study of academic-business collaboration. *The International Review of Research in Open and Distributed Learning, 15*(1). Retrieved from http://www.irrodl.org/index.php/irrodl/article/view/1617/2810

Baker, R., & Siemens, G. (2014). Educational data mining and learning analytics. In R. K. Sawyer (Ed.), *Cambridge handbook of the learning sciences* (2nd ed., pp. 253–274). Cambridge: Cambridge University Press.

Barber, R., & Sharkey, M. (2012). *Course correction.* In Proceedings of the 2nd International Conference on Learning Analytics and Knowledge – LAK '12 (pp. 259–262). New York, NY: ACM. Retrieved from https://dl.acm.org/citation.cfm?id=2330664

Calvert, C. E. (2014). Developing a model and applications for probabilities of student success: A case study of predictive analytics. *Open Learning, 29*(2), 160–173.

Campbell, J. P., DeBlois, P. B., & Oblinger, D. G. (2007). Academic analytics. *EDUCAUSE Review, 42*(4), 40–57.

Cantada, R. (2014). Online curriculum mapping as a learning analytic tool for collaborative distributed curriculum development: Implications for open and distance learning. In K. C. Li & K. S. Yuen (Eds.), *Studies and practices for advancement in open and distance education* (pp. 236–250). Hong Kong: Open University of Hong Kong Press.

Cechinel, C. (2014). Quantitative aspects about the interactions of professors in the learning management system during a final undergraduate project distance discipline. *Interdisciplinary Journal of E-Learning and Learning Objects, 10*, 269–283.

Choi, S. P. M., Lam, S. S., Li, K. C., & Wong, B. T. M. (2018). Learning analytics at low cost: At-risk student prediction with clicker data and systematic proactive interventions. *Educational Technology & Society, 21*(2), 273–290.

Clow, D. (2012). The learning analytics cycle: Closing the loop effectively. In *Proceedings of the 2nd International Conference on Learning Analytics and Knowledge* (pp. 134–138). New York, NY: ACM.

Gašević, D., Dawson, S., Rogers, T., & Gašević, D. (2016). Learning analytics should not promote one size fits all: The effects of instructional conditions in predicting academic success. *The Internet and Higher Education, 28*, 68–84.

Jordan, K. (2014). Initial trends in enrolment and completion of massive open online courses. *The International Review of Research in Open and Distributed Learning, 15*(1). Retrieved from http://www.irrodl.org/index.php/irrodl/article/view/1651

Klobas, J. E. (2014). Measuring the success of scaleable open online courses. *Performance Measurement and Metrics, 15*(3), 145–162.

Kop, R., Fournier, H., & Mak, J. S. (2011). A pedagogy of abundance or a pedagogy to support human beings? Participant support on massive open online courses. *The International Review of Research in Open and Distributed Learning, 12*(7). Retrieved from http://www.irrodl.org/index.php/irrodl/article/view/1041/2025

Koulocheri, E., Soumplis, A., & Xenos, M. (2012). *Applying learning analytics in an open personal learning environment: A quantitative approach.* Paper presented at the 2012 16th Panhellenic Conference on Informatics. Retrieved from http://ieeexplore.ieee.org/document/6377407/

Li, K. C., Wong, B. T. M., & Wong, B. Y. Y. (2015). *Catering for diverse needs for student support: Differences between face-to-face and distance-learning students.* Paper presented at the 29th Annual Conference of the Asian Association of Open Universities, Kuala Lumpur, Malaysia.

Li, K. C., Ye, C. J., & Wong, B. T. M. (2018). Status of learning analytics in Asia: Perspectives of higher education stakeholders. In S. K. S. Cheung, J. Lam, K. C. Li, O. Au, W. W. K. Ma, & W.-S. Ho (Eds.), *Technology in education: Innovative solutions and practices* (pp. 267–275). Singapore: Springer.

McKay, V., & Makhanya, M. (2008). Making it work for the South: Using open and distance learning in the context of development. In T. Evans, M. Haughey, & D. Murphy (Eds.), *International handbook of distance education* (pp. 29–48). Bingley: Emerald.

Minnaar, A. (2013). Challenges for successful planning of Open and Distance Learning (ODL): A template analysis. *The International Review of Research in Open and Distributed Learning, 14*(3). Retrieved from http://www.irrodl.org/index.php/irrodl/article/view/1387

Mir, K. (2016). Design and development of online student support system. *Pakistan Journal of Distance Education & Online Learning, 3*(1). Retrieved from http://pjdol.aiou.edu.pk/ojs/files/journals/1/articles/46/public/46-121-1-PB.pdf

Ojo, D. O., & Olakulehin, F. K. (2006). Attitudes and perceptions of students to open and distance learning in Nigeria. *The International Review of Research in Open and Distributed Learning, 7*(1). Retrieved from http://www.irrodl.org/index.php/irrodl/article/view/313

Pilkington, C., & Sanders, I. (2014). An online collaborative document creation exercise in an ODL research project module. *Computers & Education, 77*, 116–124.

Prinsloo, P., Archer, E., Barnes, G., Chetty, Y., & Zyl, D. V. (2015). Big(ger) data as better data in open distance learning. *The International Review of Research in Open and Distributed Learning, 16*(1). Retrieved from http://www.irrodl.org/index.php/irrodl/article/view/1948

Prinsloo, P., Slade, S., & Galpin, F. (2012). *Learning analytics: Challenges, paradoxes and opportunities for mega open distance learning institutions.* In Proceedings of the 2nd International Conference on Learning Analytics and Knowledge (pp. 130–133), Vancouver, Canada.

Rosewell, J., & Jansen, D. (2014). The OpenupEd quality label: Benchmarks for MOOCs. *The International Journal for Innovation and Quality in Learning, 2*(3), 88–100.

Scanlon, E., McAndrew, P., & O'Shea, T. (2015). Designing for educational technology to enhance the experience of learners in distance education: How open educational resources, learning design and MOOCs are influencing learning. *Journal of Interactive Media in Education, 2015*(1). Retrieved from https://jime.open.ac.uk/articles/10.5334/jime.al/

Siemens, G. (2011). *Learning and academic analytics.* Retrieved from http://www.learninganalytics.net/?p=131

Slade, S., & Prinsloo, P. (2014). Student perspectives on the use of their data: Between intrusion, surveillance and care. *European Journal of Open, Distance and E-learning, 18*(1). Retrieved from http://www.eurodl.org/index.php?p=special&sp=articles&inum=6&abstract=672&article=679

Slade, S., & Prinsloo, P. (2015). *Stemming the flow: Improving retention for distance learning students.* Paper presented at the EDEN 2015 Annual Conference Proceedings, Barcelona, Spain. Retrieved from http://oro.open.ac.uk/44537/

Slade, S., & Prinsloo, P. (2016). Student vulnerability, agency, and learning analytics: An exploration. *Journal of Learning Analytics, 3*(1), 159–182.

Subotzky, G., & Prinsloo, P. (2011). Turning the tide: A socio-critical model and framework for improving student success in open distance learning at the university of South Africa. *Distance Education, 32*(2), 177–193.

Wolff, A., Zdrahal, Z., Nikolov, A., & Pantucek, M. (2013). *Improving retention: Predicting at-risk students by analysing clicking behaviour in a virtual learning environment.* Paper presented at the Third Conference on Learning Analytics and Knowledge, Leuven, Belgium. Retrieved from http://oro.open.ac.uk/36936/

Wong, B. T. M. (2015). Pedagogic orientations of MOOC platforms: Influence on course delivery. *Asian Association of Open Universities Journal, 10*(2), 49–66.

Wong, B. T. M. (2017). Learning analytics in higher education: An analysis of case studies. *Asian Association of Open Universities Journal, 12*(1), 21–40.

Wong, B. T. M., Li, K. C., & Choi, S. P. M. (2018). Trends in learning analytics practices: A review of higher education institutions. *Interactive Technology and Smart Education, 15*(2), 132–154.

Wong, B. Y. Y., & Wong, B. T. M. (2018). Open and distance learning in Asia: Status and strengths. In K. C. Li, Y. S. Yuen, & B. T. M. Wong (Eds.), *Innovations in open and flexible education* (pp. 61–72). Singapore: Springer.

Yan, H., & Law, S. (2013). Designing an interactive OER course development at Athabasca university based on ODL principles. *Open Praxis, 5*(4). Retrieved from https://openpraxis.org/index.php/OpenPraxis/article/view/96

Yasmin, D. (2013). Application of the classification tree model in predicting learner dropout behaviour in open and distance learning. *Distance Education, 34*(2), 218–231.

PART 3

Pedagogical Applications of Learning Analytics

∵

CHAPTER 6

The New Smarts in Teaching and Learning

Jon Mason, Stefan Popenici, Leigh Blackall and Peter Shaw

1 Introduction

Data presented as 'analytics' has (or have)[1] been around for over a decade so it might be reasonable to assume that some maturity is evident in this field. In some ways, however, this term is really a re-branding because making use of log files and 'hit counters' emerged not long after the web was first invented. The use of 'likes' in social media soon followed. Initially, the promise of analytics was all about monitoring and optimizing website engagement through better understanding the behaviours of users or customers with a view to growing market share. Mouse-clicks on the web had already been monetized and 'analytics' emerged as a new term to describe a new trend and a new future. Prior to the business community recognising the power of analytics researchers like Michael Rappa had been advocating as early as 1999 for the formation of institutes dedicated to focused research and development in this new field (Booker, 2013). While the Web Analytics Association had been formed in 2004 even corporations such as Google were not active in this space until 2008 when it established Google Analytics as a 'freemium' web service. Of course, it is now a dominant player. And, in education, analytics was initially seen as the key to fine-tuning performance and streamlining its measurement and identifying ways of improving student retention (Daniel, 2015; Norris, Baer, Leonard, Pugliese, & Lefrere, 2008).

About this time, there was also another significant development taking place. The smartphone had achieved market presence that its forerunners such as various iterations of the Palm and Newton could only dream of. The mobile revolution was underway. As was an early trend toward ideas about 'smart education' and 'smart learning' (Hoel & Mason, 2018).

With data analytics established as a new market it did not take long for offshoots such as learning analytics to emerge (Buckingham Shum & Ferguson, 2012; Greller & Drachsler, 2012; Siemens, 2010). And, in more recent years, teaching analytics is also becoming a focus area (Sergis & Sampson, 2016). Knight and Buckingham Shum (2017) summarise the sentiment that many researchers in the field of learning analytics now subscribe to: 'education, as both a research field and as a professional practice, is on the threshold of a data-intensive revolution analogous to that experienced by other fields' (p. 18). Looking to the near future the development of the Internet of Things will likely add a new dimension to data analytics.

In summarising a key milestone that characterises the emerging data-driven era 28 years after he invented the web, however, Tim Berners-Lee has bemoaned that 'we've lost control of our personal data' (Berners-Lee, 2017). Other observers have documented this trend in terms of the rise of 'surveillance capitalism' and emergence of 'big other' (Zuboff, 1988, 2015). This reality presents a significant issue for all educators. For certain, education has lost control of most data associated with its users, as corporate solutions are almost uniformly adopted by schools and universities. Even social media platforms such as Facebook and Twitter and Google products are now routinely used in schools and universities. All data collected and aggregated by anti-plagiarism software or the big-5 corporations (Facebook, Google, Apple, Microsoft and Amazon) is collected, aggregated and used beyond the control or knowledge of universities or educators. A challenge for the future for universities to develop their own software solutions to regain control over data. Perhaps more importantly, universities need to update their policies and procedures to reflect mature awareness of this stark reality. While such a challenge may now seem futile given that the start has long been lost and the gap may now be insurmountable, the General Data Protection Regulation[2] implemented as law in Europe during 2018 demonstrates that legislative instruments can achieve far-reaching reform in terms of maintaining privacy through data protection. Reform can take place at the level of public policy.

1.1 Terminology

While the 'new' has been driving the edge of innovation for centuries it is a preoccupation or distinguishing feature of the discourses associated with e-learning and educational technology. Kalantzis and Cope (2012) even use it to describe the field as 'new learning,' while others speak of 'new power' (Heimans & Timms, 2018). In the context of this chapter, we identify two other terms as important to scrutinise: *privacy* and *smart*. Of course, there are others that are prominent in public discourse such as 'post-truth' and 'fake news' but we think that the semantics associated with privacy and smart warrant closer investigation because they represent common words that have been appropriated largely because of their high utility—but appropriated in a range of ways.

1.1.1 Privacy

Where data is collected and used for the automated observation and intervention on people's options, behaviour and preferences, 'privacy' is a common term used to represent a range of concerns and considerations. Everyday usage of this term indicates a certain level of common understanding as to its meaning and implications and has become a primary ethical consideration in the popular conception around the governance of data and related development (Slade & Prinsloo, 2013).

When we turn our attention to the idea that data about personal preferences is being used to make recommendations to both the generators of that data as well as third parties, a fuzzy boundary appears in terms of whether that data exists reasonably in the public domain or whether it is private. In the context of teaching and learning taking place within the confines of a learning management system, perhaps the case may not be so fuzzy; however, it is increasingly the case that online learning within universities involves the use of multiple systems, personal and institutional. Consequently, a new frontier concerning data governance must be considered and this is where *privacy* becomes implicated with notions of *power*, a sort of power that Shoshana Zuboff has termed, 'surveillance capitalism' (Zuboff, 2015). In time, it is not difficult to imagine a waiver being signed by students at enrolment making it explicit that the university will gather their learning habits as a way to improve their learning; however, a deidentified version of this data will also be used for research.

1.1.2   Smart

In recent work by Hoel and Mason (2018), 'smart' is examined from a perspective of international standardization while grappling with a proliferation of journals and research into this space. Widespread adoption of this term—as in smart phones, smart cities, smart education, and smart learning environments—is presented as a problem for the field of e-learning standardization because it is used to describe almost anything at the frontier of digital innovation, including artificial intelligence, data analytics, ubiquitous computing, and the Internet of Things. On the one hand, this term has been successfully adopted as evidenced by its market traction; on the other hand, this adoption mixes ambiguous and sometimes muddled semantics and this presents a problem for standardization. Adding to this picture is use of the term 'smarts,' as we have done in coining a title for this chapter in line with contemporary reports concerned with identifying plausible futures in the workplace and learning (Foundation for Young Australians, 2017). In the context of this book, we do this advisedly because we think that we need to bring into focus the challenge of developing human 'smarts' in this super-charged technological environment.

Together with these two terms we also see artificial intelligence (AI) as a pivotal field in the context of emerging technology trends in education—it also brings with it an array of new terminology. Semantically, it sits comfortably within the discourse on *smart technologies*. AI can be defined as a set of human-like behaviours that are recreated by algorithms used by computing systems on complex processes such as memory, reasoning, evaluating, communicating, learning, adapting, designing, synthesizing, self-correction and the use of data for complex processing tasks able to create new solutions (Popenici & Kerr, 2017). However, AI is also dependent—at least to a certain extent—on algorithms created by human programmers and is unable to replicate the unpredictability and creativity of the human mind; these two aspects carry various implications. Such current limitations are not dissimilar to the halting problem in computer science (the unknowability of whether certain computer programs will finish or run forever) and Gödel's incompleteness theorems in mathematics which posit that new questions will always arise probing the boundaries of knowability (Nagel & Newman, 2001; Davis, 1958).

Because of human input, AI solutions are susceptible to replicate biases and prejudices in its programmers and, as DeDeo (2015, p. 1) notes, '[algorithms] may be mathematically optimal but ethically problematic.' Determined by human specifications, AI solutions remain opaque in terms of transparency of data processing and The White House's Office of Science and Technology Policy noted that this aspect presents a threat to the foundation of democracy's civil rights, privacy and individual rights, warning about the 'potential of encoding discrimination in automated decisions' (Executive Office of the President, 2016, p. 45). There is vast literature on the fact that AI solutions are just as good as people who design them (Knight, 2017), and the troubling idea that the bias maintained in the AI algorithms created by various IT corporations may influence decisions on students' evaluations, tests, rankings and their futures. For example, the recent case of teachers in Houston who had won the legal case in 2017 after they were wrongly ranked by a flawed obscure and "very complex" algorithmic model that impacted directly on their employment (U.S. Government Publishing Office, 2017) stand as a warning of risks ahead for education. There have been many similar events such as the racist and sexist tendencies in one of Google's AI platforms.

The second problem raised by our definition of AI is linked to the difference between algorithmic solutions and human creativity and capacity for unpredictable ideas. This also helps distinguish a key difference between AI and machine learning—in machine learning the reasoning behind the decision-making is known whereas outputs from AI often remain a mystery because the processes have been through a 'black-box.' These are openings that stand vital for innovation and very complex problem-solving. This difference is important for a nuanced and well-calibrated approach of a rethink of learning and teaching in the era of artificial intelligence, and the use of AI solutions in higher education. So how might we best understand the systems boundaries of learning analytics?

1.2 Anomalies from the Frontline

One of the most prominent groups providing lead advocacy for design and deployment of learning analytics systems is the Society for Learning Analytics Research (SOLAR). While this has been around for some years, as of March 2018 nowhere on its website is there any indication about its history—just a vision statement and profile of membership. Given the decades of work done in the field of metadata for the web, this blind spot seems somewhat ironic and it does not bode well for the rigour required in consolidating a new field of research and practice. Analytics would not exist without metadata. This blind spot in web documentation is not uncommon and signals a deficit characteristic of our era that arises from preoccupation with the immediacy of social media and the next shiny device. In a way, Google and Facebook have schooled us into a fast-food culture of inquiry and connection. The metaphor is not fortuitous, as the fast food industry is a cause of an epidemic of diabetes and associated diseases with poor diet habits, with vast costs for governments and taxpayers. In the same way, the monopoly over data and cultural influences of the 'big-five' is already causing vast personal and society imbalances: the manipulation of news and facts, of elections and civic choices, screen addictions, cultural hegemony and hindering of knowledge production and innovation. It is interesting to note the relationship of China to the 'big-five' in its own attempts to maintain its cultural integrity.

1.3 Trends and Tensions

A key feature of contemporary educational settings is the design and implementation of digital infrastructure that meets current needs while also aiming to develop 'readiness' for the future. This process is ongoing, with routine updates of software and new technology innovations becoming available. In terms of strategic planning needs, it is useful to identify trends, challenges and opportunities within the broader environment. Imagining various plausible futures is not so difficult; however, making informed decisions about likely futures is another matter. Numerous innovations in digital technologies have often been a catalyst for unpredicted and profound change. SMS is a classic example. In discerning what trends are important some form of environmental scanning is necessary to identify tensions where trends often incubate. Examples of the kinds of tensions involved is depicted in Figure 6.1. Annual reports, such as the *Horizon Report* published by the New Media Consortium and *Inno-*

vating Pedagogy published by the Open University aim to address the requirement of identifying trends to assist in this process (Adams Becker et al., 2017; Sharples et al., 2016; Wong et al., 2017). It is arguably more instructive, however, to consider the tensions which give rise to trends because doing so compels one to think carefully about plausible futures. Thus, while learning analytics is clearly on the map with a prominent trajectory it is not yet clear what kind of futures will coalesce as a result. As an emergent field, many questions arise (Mason, Chen, & Hoel, 2016); however, this new field is also emerging within a very complex environment where many other tensions can be identified which are already incubating unforeseen futures. For us, identifying these tensions are critical to the process of formulating ongoing research questions.

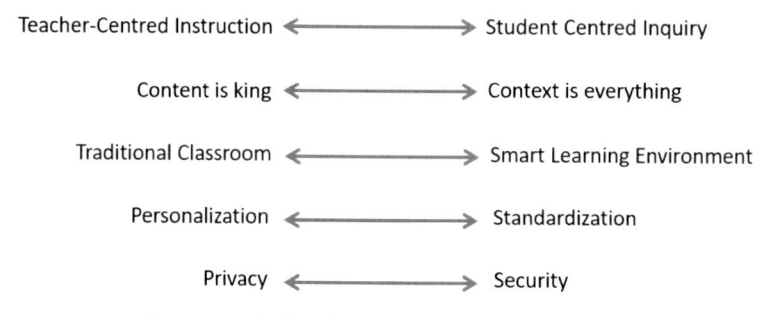

FIGURE 6.1   Tensions in the digital environment

The expanding interest for learning analytics solutions and the use of Big Data in higher education is now associated with new ethical and practical challenges, which are impacting directly all aspects of life of academics, students, and the future of citizens. The recent scandal involving Facebook, as it was discovered that the company worked with Cambridge Analytica to manipulate millions of voters through the 'psychographic-profiling method, which 'scraped' Facebook profiles in order to develop unique voter-targeting models' (Persily, 2017) serves as a warning[3] of unethical practices that impact on privacy, the structure of our society and our common prospects. With over 87 million Facebook users affected by this breach of trust in using personal data, it was revealed that the practice of collecting and aggregating data without users' knowledge allowed the creation of extremely detailed personal profiles that were used against individuals' interests. The extent of this breach reportedly altered the result of the Brexit referendum in the UK and election results in United States. Some commentators have sounded the alarm bells arguing that this represents a *de facto* end of our democratic systems, with a substantial alteration of election processes and an end of basic privacy for individuals.

While alarm bells always ring in the media, this event stands relevant for education in significant ways. Firstly, in terms of organisational change, universities are increasingly interlinked with corporations that are also specialised in data mining, data collection, analytics and complex software, including artificial intelligence solutions, often with an equally obscure process of using and securing data or the design of algorithmic solutions. Secondly, the traditions of 'academic autonomy' and freedom of thought may now be on the precipice of a very new fight. Thirdly, the boundary between data collection activities associated with teaching and research needs to be re-examined. The dystopian nature of possibilities for data use is not limited to the obscure manipulation of personal data with complex software and web-trackers—it also impacts on millions of citizens on one of the most powerful economies in the world. Reuters reported in March 2018 that China will begin applying its 'social credit system' to stop people with a bad score to board flights and trains and extend to many other domains such as housing loans (Reuters, 2018). Based on the idea 'once untrustworthy, always restricted,' the Social Credit System for Chinese citizens integrates Big Data, collecting data from public and online spaces, CCTV cameras and online activities, aggregating all for a score that determine the individuals' position in society. It seems that a trial of this scoring system is already applied in China, as numerous citizens were banned based on the social media scores and 'credit system' to board trains and planes. This unprecedented social experiment, that will ultimately change one of the social interactions in one of most populous countries in the world, is an invitation for a serious reflection on the importance of securing extreme privacy of data for students and those who work in education. The rise of populist movements in Europe and across the world opens the possibility of a future where Big Data can be misused by various decision makers for 'social scores' that determine employment, social and physical mobility. Universities have the social responsibility to treat students' data as one of the most important assets under their control. The increasing use of Big Data and learning analytics, complex software for plagiarism detection and data mapping in learning and teaching stand commonly associated with loose and superficially understood requirement of consent for data use from our students. The need to inform students on all implications and secure their consent is now paramount for their future and for universities' social responsibility requirements; it also secures institutions to avoid future scandals similar with that facing Cambridge Analytica in 2018.

The application of Big data in education systems is perhaps even more worrying. We need students to express their thoughts. Even when they are wrong or misguided a good teacher can help the student and class to critically reflect on their argument; however, with social biased monitoring, students are likely to just repeat party lines making learning complex. Many Chinese and Indian students will feel they are expected to plagiarize to avoid persecution—it goes without saying that this cultural gap is set to collide with western academic traditions.

We now consider a range of scenarios that represent innovations in the way that learning is now taking place, both informally and formally. These scenarios provide real-world context for discerning the questions that then must guide the *how* and *why* of smart technology adoption and the *how* and *why* of smart teaching and learning.

1.4   A New World of the Quantified Self

In Defining Networked Learning, Blackall (2014) described a method for quantifying learning outcomes from a timeline that referenced his own distributed and networked learning data. While it was primarily associated to the ideas of informal learning webs (Illich, 1971; Brown, 2008) and situated participatory learning (Lave & Wenger, 1991), it also happens to be an example of 'Quantified Self'—a term that emanates from a computing and internet subculture where people generally engage in the generation and collection of data about themselves, to analyse for insight, and also referred to as overt 'self-tracking' to distinguish it from 'covert surveillance' (Lupton, 2016). Blackall's method was to recount a narrative of informal learning and link in available data to help build out a narrative of learning with evidence of outcome.

Hayes (2013) describes this approach of the learner as the quantified self to the 2013 IEEE International Symposium on Technology and Society (ISTAS). Hayes used the example among others to propose that data generation and publishing is itself an act of research with value in the academic publishing tradition. Likewise, Blackall was arguing that data can be used to validate informal learning toward assessment practices within formal education.

The notion of quantified self came to broader attention in 2007–2008, as the large-scale effect of socially networked media was becoming clearer (Hesse, 2008; Wolf, 2010). Of course, there were threads to this movement reaching back well before 2007. An ontology approximately encompassing transhumanism, sousveillance and open data for example, and these domains connect to broader discourses of collectivism and connectivism. A quantified self approach to learning analytics carries within it principles of user agency and control. Such principles might be distilled to the concern of power, and through such consideration, different and perhaps better formed ideas for learning analytics can be made. That's a 'maybe' because it is arguably the case that notions of individual agency are themselves being impacted by the ubiquity of systems that harvest and process data about us.

Such innovations open a new frontier to the use of personal data that naturally also trigger new questions such as, *in what ways can the quantified self inform a 'quantified public'?* And, *how many selves can be depicted?* We can tell many stories about the 'self' because our identities are formed through diverse experiences and roles and datasets that we might collect will typically have interruptions. This can also present an issue in relation to what has been termed 'broken data' because of the 'the incompleteness, inaccuracy and dispersed nature of personal self-tracking data' (Pink, Ruckenstein, Willim, & Duque, 2018).

1.5 *Teaching Machines to Teach? A Case Study*

During 2016–2017 a small group within a School of Fashion and Textiles at RMIT University in Australia were exploring the possibilities of learning through the links and recommendations made by YouTube's algorithms. In short, they were wanting to teach YouTube how to teach. Some initial months were spent working with a teacher to set up a YouTube channel into which instructional videos were uploaded, supported by playlists and subscriptions to a range of other channels. Students were then asked to participate in some usability testing and be observed. The students were asked to load YouTube and note any recommendations being made before creating an account. They were then asked them to create a new account and return to the YouTube home page to see if anything in the recommendations and search seemed different. They were then asked to find the teacher's channel and subscribe to it and again notice the differences. They were instructed how to reject recommendations, and accept others, consciously customising their new YouTube account into specific subject areas and notably improving the recommendations and search results that YouTube was making. By extension then, the same methods could be applied in Facebook and Google search.

What did they find? Not surprisingly, a marked improvement was observed in the search results, recommendations, and associations being made by the algorithm. This then led the team to consider what else could be achieved with more time and with a larger network.

After the YouTube experiment, Leigh Blackall (one of the researchers involved in the experiment) decided to test similar methods on ResearchGate, a social media platform dedicated to academics. After setting up his profile, making some connections, and establishing some basic presence on the platform he posed a question, *'Can we teach the machine to teach—using algorithms as a learning resource?'* Quite quickly, responses from other ResearchGate users started coming in, noticeably from new connections and Leigh found himself in stimulating discussion with others offering interesting perspectives and greater experience. For Leigh, however, the experience of how the algo-rithms behind the scene were facilitating connections was entirely new. *Were these new connections simply arising from shared mutual interests? How was ResearchGate calibrated to do this?* For Leigh, someone very experienced in social media, these new interactions were short lived despite his best efforts to honour the responses offered. While trying to sustain collaborative inquiry his experience was that the platform does not yet successfully alert responders in ways that nurture ongoing interaction.

From a broader perspective that considers the evolution of artificial intel-ligence since it first appeared as a field with computer science over 50 years ago, certain questions have persisted. *'Can a machine think?'* is a prominent one and an audit of informed answers to it reveals positions that offer either a binary yes/no response to those that offer deeper analysis into specific con-texts. Moreover, questions concerning the nature of intelligence also arise and this has been a characteristic 'moving feast' of AI. During the 1990s, computer applications such as voice recognition were very much considered to be within the scope of AI; today, our smartphones easily handle this task to the extent that the novelty of 'smartness' wears off fairly quickly—and is sometimes irri-tating in the form of smart text! While a machine can certainly process data and information and even encode some aspects of knowledge, the preceding scenario demonstrates that certain aspects of teaching can be taught. So then, what is it exactly that we mean when we are asking questions about machines thinking?

1.6   *Black Boxes, Algorithms, and Human Sensibility*

There is an important question that now clearly challenges educators from early childhood to higher education: *How do we balance the affordances of innovations in digital technology with the human 'smarts' we need to learn and teach?* Numerous questions follow—among them, questions arising from the field of education that speak to deeply human potential *not* mediated by any form of technology—*how do we nurture a growth mindset in our educational systems?* (Dweck, 2017). Related questions arise that query what the nature of human sensibility is and how we make sense of the world in the age of the algorithm—*what are people for?* (Madsbjerg, 2017). And then there are the age-old questions concerning the amount of 'screen' technology in young people's lives—*how can we re-calibrate our teaching to reclaim student critical thinking abilities and focus?* (Clement & Miles, 2018).

The field of Learning Analytics has in many ways helped to foreground this situation in higher education through deepening what can now be described as a *fault line* between research and teaching—a fault line in the sense of divergent practice and double standards. In social and educational research, consent is mandatory though arguably overdone. Within teaching and learning, explicit consent hardly even exists in data collection principally because doing so is rationalised as part and parcel of evaluation. And, this divergence is not just about data associated with learners—the practice of gathering data from teachers also exists without explicit consent. In the latter case, however, such data collection is the fine print of the employment contract in which performance requires measurement.

While *fuzzy logic* had been developed by Lotfi Zadeh (1965) it was not really until the 1990s that its utility was recognised (Kosko, 1993). The impact of this breakthrough is still being realised in fields such as artificial intelligence and machine learning today. As we probe the opportunities and pitfalls associated with learning analytics it would seem there will be new opportunities for us to interact with digital systems that also learn how to effectively and optimally with us.

While much of this discussion has been focused on emergent technologies it can be instructive to look back at theoretical models in education that have persisted and evolved over time—a prominent example is Bloom's taxonomy of educational objectives (Bloom et al., 1956). Whether you agree with such models or not is beside the point—which in this case is that the foundation of the cognitive domain rests on fact-based knowledge. Computer systems are essentially the same and, metaphorically speaking, AI and data analytics are at this base. Higher order thinking skills are not yet the domain of AI, even though the media and the film industry like to portray such scenarios.

1.7   *Conclusion—Some Lingering Questions*

To be optimistic about the future in education it may well be that AI, machine learning, Big Data, data analytics systems, and the Internet of Things will enable many previously proposed and desirable teaching practices that otherwise would be beyond imagination. When imagining the future, we may worry about what jobs will be taken over by AI technologies. But, if we consider earlier technology revolutions then who would want to claim back many of the basic administrative jobs such as typists?

At the outset our discussion has been one of inquiry. There are numerous 'bigger pictures' and narratives concerning the role of analytics for teaching and learning and the range of plausible future scenarios involving this new field in education include both triumphant and dystopian options. We therefore conclude this discussion by aggregating a list questions arising from our discussion that might guide further inquiry.

– What does it mean to *learn* in our times?

- Are standardised methods of e-testing sophisticated enough to measure the nuances and scope of non-standard learning today?
- Can learning analytics systems be effectively calibrated to identify students at risk in ways that also guarantee fairness students?
- What do we mean when we are asking questions about machines thinking?
- In what ways might universities address the deepening fault line between data handling practices in teaching and research?
- How do we balance the affordances of innovations in digital technology with the human 'smarts' we need to learn and teach?
- How do we nurture a growth mindset in our educational systems?
- How do we enact a transformative approach to teaching and learning, maintaining a critical edge to our thinking and practice?
- In environments influenced by artificial intelligence, machine learning, and the Internet of Things what are people for?
- How can we re-calibrate our teaching to reclaim student critical thinking abilities and focus?
- What new things can we do and automate with the assistance of digital technology?
- What new jobs can we imagine?

Notes

1   Academic pedantry may deem that the 'correct' form must be 'data are' but such a position is misguided in terms of the evolution of language and contemporary usage. Like 'sheep,' the term 'analytics' is a similar noun where analytics *is* and analytics *are* both represent acceptable expressions.
2   https://www.eugdpr.org/
3   Arguably, this scandal also masks the naivety if not wilful prejudice of news services that somehow overlook the fact that related practices have been pervasive for a long time, and by all parties.

References

Adams Becker, S., Cummins, M., Davis, A., Freeman, A., Hall Giesinger, C., & Ananthanarayanan, V. (2017). *NMC horizon report, 2017 higher education edition*. Austin, TX: The New Media Consortium. Retrieved from http://cdn.nmc.org/media/2017-nmc-horizon-report-he-EN.pdf

Berners-Lee, T. (2017). *Three challenges for the web: An open letter to the web foundation.* Retrieved from http://webfoundation.org/2017/03/web-turns-28-letter/

Blackall, L. (2014). Defining networked learning. *Wikiversity.*

Bloom, B. S., Engelhart, M. D., Furst, E. J., Hill, W. H., & Krathwohl, D. R. (1956). *Taxonomy of educational objectives: The classification of educational goals. Handbook I: Cognitive domain.* New York, NY: David McKay Company.

Booker, E. (2013). Big data profile: Michael Rappa, institute for advanced analytics. *Information Week.* Retrieved from https://www.informationweek.com/big-data/big-data-analytics/big-data-profile-michael-rappa-institute-for-advanced-analytics/d/d-id/1111295

Brown, S. (2008). From VLEs to learning webs: The implications of web 2.0 for learning and teaching. *Interactive Learning Environments, 18*(1), 1–10.

Buckingham Shum, S., & Ferguson, R. (2012). Social learning analytics. *Educational Technology & Society (Special Issue: Learning & Knowledge Analytics), 15*(3), 3–26.

Clement, J., & Miles, M. (2018). *Screen schooled.* Carlton: Black Inc.

Cope, B., & Kalantzis, M. (2014). *Big data comes to school: Reconceptualizing evidence and research in the era of technology-mediated learning* (pp. 1–35). Retrieved from http://kc-test.cg-creator.com/_uploads/Big_Data_Comes_to_School.pdf

Daniel, B. (2015). Big data and analytics in higher education: Opportunities and challenges. *British Journal of Educational Technology, 46*(5), 904–920.

Davis, M. (1958). *Computability and unsolvability.* New York, NY: McGraw-Hill.

Dawson, S., Gašević, D., Siemens, G., & Joksimovic, S. (2014). Current state and future trends: A citation network analysis of the learning analytics field. In *Proceedings of the 4th International Conference on Learning Analytics and Knowledge (LAK 14)* (pp. 231–240). New York, NY: ACM. doi:10.1145/2567574.2567585

DeDeo, S. (2015). *Wrong side of the tracks: Big data and protected categories.* Ithaca, NY: Cornell University Library. Retrieved from https://arxiv.org/pdf/1412.4643v2.pdf

Dweck, C. (2017). *Mindset: Changing the way you think to fulfil your potential.* London: Robinson.

Executive Office of the President. (2014). *Big data: Seizing opportunities, preserving values.* Washington, DC: The White House. Retrieved from https://obamawhitehouse.archives.gov/sites/default/files/docs/big_data_privacy_report_may_1_2014.pdf

Foundation for Young Australians. (2017). *The new work smarts: Thriving in the new work order.* Retrieved from https://www.fya.org.au/wp-content/uploads/2017/07/FYA_TheNewWorkSmarts_July2017.pdf

Gillard, C. (2017). Pedagogy and the logic of platforms. *EDUCAUSE Review, 52*(4), 64–65.

Greller, W., & Drachsler, H. (2012). Translating learning into numbers: Toward a generic framework for learning analytics. *Educational Technology & Society, 15*(3), 42–57.

Hayes, A. (2013). *Identity awareness and re-use of research data in veillance and social computing.* Paper presented at the 2013 IEEE International Symposium on Technology and Society (ISTAS).

Heimans, J., & Timms, H. (2018). *How power works in our hyperconnected world: And how to make it work for you.* New York, NY: Doubleday.

Hoel, T., & Mason, J. (2018). Standards for smart education: Towards a development framework. *Smart Learning Environments, 5*(3), 1–25.

Illich, I. (1978). Disabling professions. *India International Centre Quarterly, 5*(1), 23–32.

Kalantzis, M., & Cope, B. (2012). *New learning: Elements of a science of education.* Port Melbourne: Cambridge University Press.

Knight, M. (2017, July 12). Biased algorithms are everywhere, and no one seems to care. *MIT Technology Review.* Retrieved from https://www.technologyreview.com/s/608248/biased-algorithms-are-everywhere-and-no-one-seems-to-care/

Knight, S., & Buckingham Shum, S. (2017). Theory and learning analytics. In C. Lang, G. Siemens, A. Wise, & D. Gašević (Eds.), *The handbook of learning analytics: Society for learning analytics research.* doi:10.18608/hla17

Kosko, B. (1993). *Fuzzy thinking: The new science of fuzzy logic.* New York, NY: Hyperion.

Lang, C., Siemens, G., Wise, A., & Gašević, D. (Eds.). (2017). *The handbook of learning analytics: Society for learning analytics research.* doi:10.18608/hla17

Lupton, D. (2016). *The quantified self: A sociology of self-tracking cultures.* Cambridge, MA: Polity Press.

Madsbjerg, C. (2017). *Sensemaking: The power of the humanities in the age of the algorithm.* New York, NY: Hachette Books.

Mason, J., Chen, W., & Hoel, T. (2016). Questions as data: Illuminating the potential of learning analytics through questioning an emergent field. *Research and Practice in Technology Enhanced Learning, 11*(12), 1–14.

Nagel, E., & Newman, J. R. (2001). *Gödel's proof.* New York, NY: New York University Press.

Norris, D., Baer, L., Leonard, J., Pugliese, L., & Lefrere, P. (2008). Action analytics: Measuring and improving performance that matters in higher education. *EDUCAUSE Review, 43*(1), 42–67.

Persily, N. (2017). The 2016 U.S. election: Can democracy survive the internet? *Journal of Democracy, 28*(2), 63–76. doi:10.1353/jod.2017.0025

Pink, S., Ruckenstein, M., Willim, R., & Duque, M. (2018). Broken data: Conceptualising data in an emerging world. *Big Data & Society, 5*(1), 205395171775322.

Popenici, S., & Kerr, S. (2017). Exploring the impact of artificial intelligence on teaching and learning in higher education. *Research and Practice in Technology Enhanced Learning, 12*(1), 12–22.

Reuters. (2018, March 16). *China to bar people with bad 'social credit' from planes, trains.* Retrieved from https://www.reuters.com/article/us-china-credit/china-to-bar-people-with-bad-social-credit-from-planes-trains-idUSKCN1GS10S

Sergis, S., & Sampson, D. (2016). Towards a teaching analytics tool for supporting reflective educational (re) design in inquiry-based STEM education. In *Proceedings, IEEE 16th International Conference on Advanced Learning Technologies (ICALT)* (pp. 314–318).

Sharples, M., de Roock, R., Ferguson, R., Gaved, M., Herodotou, C., Koh, E., Kukulska-Hulme, A., Looi, C.-K., McAndrew, P., Rienties, B., Weller, M., & Wong, L. H. (2016). *Innovating pedagogy 2016: Open university innovation report 5.* Milton Keynes: The Open University.

Siemens, G. (2010, August 25). What are learning analytics? *Elearnspace.* Retrieved from http://www.elearnspace.org/blog/2010/08/25/what-are-learning-analytics/

Slade, S., & Prinsloo, P. (2013). Learning analytics: Ethical issues and dilemmas. *American Behavioral Scientist, 57*(10), 1509–1528.

U.S. Government Publishing Office. (2017, May 4). *14-1189 - Houston federation of teachers local 2415 et al v. Houston independent school district.* Retrieved from https://www.gpo.gov/fdsys/pkg/USCOURTS-txsd-4_14-cv-01189

Uskov, V. L., Howlett, R. J., & Jain, L. C. (Eds.). (2015). *Smart education and smart e-learning: Smart innovation, systems, and technologies.* London: Springer.

Wong, L.-H., Sharples, M., Gao, Y., Mason, J., & Looi, C.-K. (2017). Meta-synthesis and trends reports of educational technologies and pedagogies: What is their value proposition? In *Proceedings of the 25th International Conference on Computers in Education, Asia-Pacific Society for Computers in Education* (pp. i35–i39). Taiwan: Asia Pacific Society for Computers in Education (APSCE)

Zadeh, L. A. (1965). Fuzzy sets. *Information and Control, 8*, 338–353.

Zuboff, S. (1988). *In the age of the smart machine: The future of work and power.* New York, NY: Basic Books.

Zuboff, S. (2015). Big other: Surveillance capitalism and the prospects of an information civilization. *Journal of Information Technology, 30*, 75–89.

CHAPTER 7

Following the Learners' Traces: Profiling Learners and Visualizing the Learning Process for Building Better Learning Experiences

Arif Altun and Mehmet Kokoç

1 Introduction[1]

Learning can be explained as a complex and collaborative process, which can change depending on individuals or contexts in formal or informal environments (Robinson, Molenda, & Rezabek, 2008). Supporting learners and improving learning performance are main goals of educational technologies (AECT, 2018). To mediate learning process, researchers primarily have to perform; (1) basic research for exploring what variables affect learning process, (2) operationally define the role of instructional technologies in learning process, and (3) investigate learning experiences by using multiple and rich data collecting from different data sources in detail. The key issue here is to what extent we understand the learning processes of learners. Understanding individualized or collaborative learning process could be supported by huge amount of user data which are created as a result of interaction between instructional technologies or online tools and individual (Gasevic, Dawson, & Siemens, 2015). For this purpose, educational data mining techniques and learning analytics tools have significant contribution to our understanding of online learning processes (Peña-Ayala, 2014; Siemens & Gasevic, 2012; Spector, 2013; Vandewaetere & Clarebout, 2014).

The development of e-learning technologies has contributed to the advancement of educational data mining and learning analytics literature as well (Siemens, 2013). Existing e-learning environments and content/learning management systems provide extensive data derived from a large community of learners to educational data mining researchers to develop and test new educational data mining techniques (Vandewaetere & Clarebout, 2014). Learning management systems, therefore, offer suitable and accessible environments for researchers and practitioners to collect data and test their applications. Furthermore, latent behavior patterns of learners can be extracted by analyzing interaction data to improve both learning performance and learning environments (Gasevic, Dawson, & Siemens, 2015).

2 Comprehensive Overview of Learning Analytics

The fields of learning analytics and educational data mining share similar goals of employing data mining techniques for predicting and analyzing learning performances. As an emerging discipline, educational data mining researchers are interested in developing methods for exploring the unique types of educational data sets, latent learner profiles and student models to improve education by improving assessment and deliver proper intervention (Baker & Yacef, 2009; Siemens & Baker, 2012). Romero and Ventura (2013) defines educational data mining as an interdisciplinary area combining three main areas including computer science, statistics, and education. Educational data mining and learning analytics refer to analyzing large-scale data extracted from educational settings, but only learning analytics emphasize the optimization of learning processes and learning environments by real-time modeling (Ifenthaler & Widanapathirana, 2014). It can be stated that main point of using learner interaction data is to record and process learners' data appropriately about where, when, and how they interact with other learners and course contents. The growing number of previous studies have reported that learners' interaction data can be used to predict academic performance of learners (Akçapınar, Altun, & Aşkar, 2015; You, 2016), model relationship between cognitive traits and learning styles of learners (Graf et al., 2009), build open social student model (Brusilovsky et al., 2015), explore meaningful patterns of learning experiences (Kokoç & Altun, 2016), visualize patterns of learners behavior (Park & Jo, 2015), develop learning analytics tools and modules (Ali, Hatala, Gasevic, & Jovanovic, 2012; Bayrak & Yurdugül, 2016), provide real-time social network visualizations of interaction activities (Dawson, Bakharia, & Heathcote, 2010; Hernández-García, González-González, Jiménez-Zarco, & Chaparro-Peláeza, 2015), and profiling learners across their learning behaviors (Cerezo, Sánchez-Santillán, Paule-Ruiz, & Núñeza, 2016; Li & Tsai, 2017) by applying data mining techniques.

Research results based on learner interaction data in educational context are expected to inform teachers and/or learners about actionable knowledge and to provide insightful information about learning processes and learning designs. In terms of implementation, learning analytics tools are increasingly recognized as emerging technologies that support informed decision making for learners and teachers by analyzing and visualizing interaction data. To start with, it will be useful to describe the scope of learning analytics and the related concepts.

In the first Learning Analytics and Knowledge Conference, Siemens and Long (2011) proposed the following definition: learning analytics is *"the measurement, collection, analysis and reporting of data about learners and their contexts, for the purposes of understanding and optimizing learning and the environments in which it occurs.*" The basic assumption of learning analytics field is that learners' traces representing their online interaction data and the emerged knowledge extracted from these data are advantageous for instructors, individuals, and educational managers (Dyckhoff et al., 2012; Slade & Prinsloo, 2013). Learning analytics focuses on comprehensive understanding and optimizing learning and learning context. It can be said that the main objective of the learning analytics studies is to improve learners' performance and effectiveness of learning process by analyzing user interaction and personal data derived from learners' traces in e-learning environments.

Learning analytics process has a multi-phased complex structure (Siemens, 2013). Despite there are different frameworks proposed by researchers on learning analytics process in the literature, the learning analytics process proposed by Lal (2014) has been applied in this study and presented in Figure 7.1. The stages can be represented as follows: (1) Capture data, (2) Structure and aggregate data, (3) Analyze, (4) Representation and visualization, (5) Action, (6) Refine.

FIGURE 7.1   Learning analytics process

In the phase of *Capture Data*, important questions need to be answered in terms of learning analytics process as follows: (1) Why should we collect learner data, (2) Which data can provide meaningful insights? This phase helps to determine the boundaries of the data collection and the goal of the learning analytics in educational context. Firstly, we decide which learner data will be collected from various sources. Following this, we determine how to collect learner data and how frequently learner data are updated.

In the phase of *Structure and Aggregate Data*, interaction data collected from various sources are loaded to a data warehouse, which integrates data and makes it available for educational data mining (Lal, 2014). Open and distance learning systems like learning management systems trace and register learner interaction data with timestamp and course information for each action. Data transformation is needed to make it available for analysis. Learning analytics tools can process raw interaction data to derive data structures that will be used for provide meaningful representation and generating intervention.

During the Analysis phase, it is first decided which educational data mining technique such as clustering, classification, text mining etc. will be used. This decision may differ depending on features of collected data, nature of the learning context, purpose of the learning analytics research and possible implications. In this phase, what is important is to reveal useful insights about the learning process and represent the meaningful patterns of relationship between interaction data and learning outcomes. Different statistical techniques can be applied to explore learner data for discovering hidden interaction patterns (Chatti, Dyckhoff, Schroeder, & Thüs, 2012).

In the phase of *Representation and Visualization*, data visualization techniques are employed to visualize the obtained results from interaction data. Learning analytics tools display online learning patterns through visual elements like graphs, charts, tables, social networks using any visualization API. Learning dashboards as learning analytic tools are widely used in visualizing large amount of learner data (Duval, 2011). It is expected that learning dashboards can allow learners to compare their performance with other peers and to visualize real-time and valid information and analysis results about learners to improve learning conditions.

Actions play vital role in learning analytics process. In the phase of *Action*, learning dashboards generate actionable knowledge about learning process as a result of analysis and visualization of learner interaction data. Using actionable knowledge, personalized timely feedback and early alert message can be provided to learners to be encouraged to engage more in online learning activities (Wong, 2017). Learning dashboards aims to support learners improving their learning strategies and to help teachers building accurate learner profiles and decision-making.

In the last phase of learning analytics process, *Refine*, the impact of the learning dashboards is monitored to see whether employed statistical and mining models need to be updated and if so, to what extent personalized intervention is effective on learning performance (Lal, 2014). In addition, post-processing process is conducted to continuous improvement of learning dashboards. Post-processing data involves collecting new data from new data sources, determining new attributes, identifying new metrics for learner model and choosing a new analytics method, if needed (Chatti, Dyckhoff, Schroeder, & Thüs, 2012).

Learning analytics process aims to support learners learning process and to improve learning performance by analyzing and making intervention in real time. There are various research topics in terms of application, implementation and theoretical aspects in the learning analytics field. One of these topics is visualizing the learning process for building better learning experiences. Educational data visualization plays an important role in representation learner profiles and visualizing online learning behavior in personalized learning environment. Considering the using maps, drawings and graphics in education, it can surely be asserted that visualization techniques in learning is not a new phenomenon (Klerkx, Verbert, & Duval, 2014). In recent years, processing trace data of learners in e-learning environments put forward that data visualization studies need to be conducted in the context of learning analytics (Papamitsiou & Economides, 2014). The contributions of data visualization studies to the learners demonstrate the importance of using learning dashboards in e-learning environments.

The term of learning dashboard can be classified as a learning analytics tool, which provide monitoring online learning experience with performance indicators using data visualization techniques. Verbert et al. (2013) describe learning dashboard as the applications based on visualizing the traces to support learners. Schwendimann et al. (2016) uses the term "learning dashboard" to refer to a single display that aggregates different indicators about learners, learning process and learning context into one or multiple visualizations. This concept is based on the movement of "quantified-self" that has an emerging technology in recent years with the contribution of learning analytics in applications. Quantified self, which can be defined as tracking data relevant to daily activities with technology, has shown among popular technologies during next years (Horizon Report, 2014). RescueTime (https://www.rescuetime.com/) which tracks time spent on applications and web sites as a time management tool can be considered as an example of quantified-self technologies. The importance of performance and time management systems for organizations and willingness to track all activities numerically increase the interest of quantified-self movement (Duval, 2011). Verbert et al. (2014) emphasize that basic idea of quantified self-technologies is to provide self-analysis and comparison with other users by tracking numerical and/or visualized data collected from their activity traces. Considering affordances of quantified self on learning, the main goal of this movement is monitoring learners' learning performances and enabling awareness of learning process using learning dashboards in e-learning environments.

Sample interfaces of these learning dashboards are displayed in Figure 7.2. On the right side is the interface of a course titled Course Signal to provide early alerts to learners in Purdue University (Pistilli & Arnold, 2012). On the left is an example of the interface of LOCO-Analyst learning dashboard developed for teachers (Ali, Hatala, Gasevic, & Jovanovic, 2012).

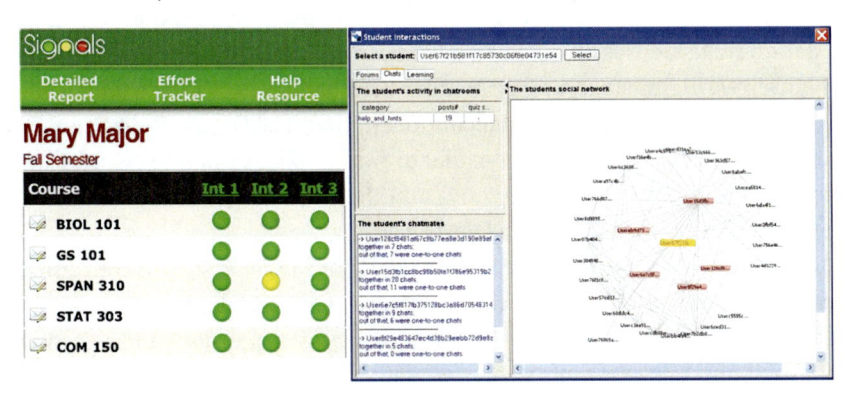

FIGURE 7.2   Samples of learning dashboards

Learning dashboards can be classified into three groups as follows; (1) dashboards that support traditional face-to-face lectures, (2) dashboards that support face-to-face group work and 3) dashboards that support awareness, reflection, sense-making and behavior change in online or blended learning (Verbert et al., 2014). To better understand the affordances of learning analytics process and its implications, Daniel (2015) and Sampson (2016) classified learning dashboards into three distinct types as follows descriptive analytics, predictive analytics and prescriptive analytics. Additionally, it is noticed that design and evaluation approaches of learning dashboards differ depending on their visual and technical features. A well-known example of these approaches is principals of data visualization explained by Few (2009). Another example of what have been used as evaluation approaches of learning dashboards is Kirkpatrick model including four simple levels as follows reaction, learning, behavior, and results (Kirkpatrick & Kirkpatrick, 2014).

Monitoring and tracking performances of learners can be explained with learning analytics process model (Verbert et al., 2013) and stage-based model of personal informatics systems (Li, Dey, & Forlizzi, 2010).

The Stage-Based Model of Personal Informatics Systems includes a series of five iterative stages as follows: (1) Preparation, (2) collection, (3) integration, (4) reflection, and (5) action. The preparation stage is concerned with users' motivation to collect personal information, how they determine what kind of information they will record. This stage is conducted before collecting personal information. The collection stage focuses on obtaining personal information about users such as behavior, interaction, thoughts and environment. The integration stage is concerned with preparing, combining and transforming the information collected for users to reflect on. In the reflection stage, users interact with information visualizations, aware of performances about themselves and reflects on their personal information in the short term or in the long term. The action stage focuses on deciding what users will do with their new insights of themselves. In this stage, users can tailor their behaviors to match their goals depending on personal alerts and recommendations (Li, Dey, & Forlizzi, 2010).

Learning analytics process model that draws on ideas from information foraging theory proposed by Piroli (2007) and the personal informatics systems consists of four stages as stated in Figure 7.3.

According to learning analytics process model, "awareness" stage is concerned with just learner data that can be visualized using data visualization techniques. (Self-)Reflection stage emphasizes importance of asking questions and assessing how useful and relevant their visualized data are. Sense-making stage focuses on learners' answering the questions asked in the previous stage and creation of new insights. Impact stage is concerned with inducing new meaning or insights gained from these visualizations as a goal of the process (Verbert et al., 2013, 2014).

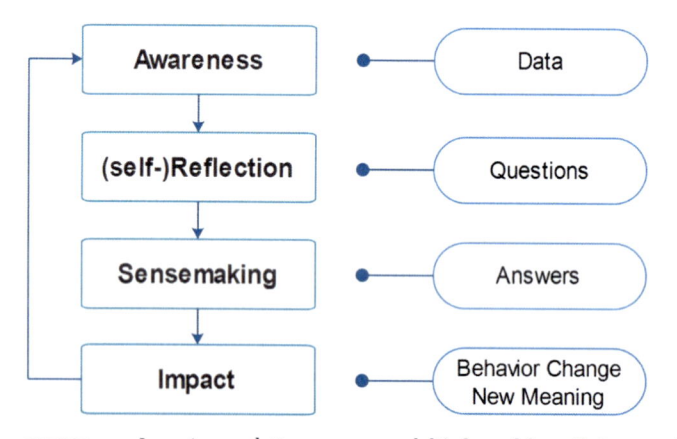

FIGURE 7.3   Learning analytics process model (adapted from Verbert et al., 2013)

The steps in the models explained above point out that learners can benefit more from learning dashboards since they provide awareness so that learners can act on their own behavioral and cognitive performances. Similarly, it can be said that the overall objective of using learning dashboards in real educational context is to improve learning performance for building better learning experiences based on meaningful behavior pattern of learners. At this point, a critical question could be raised about how to improve learning process by employing learning dashboards. Possible answers to this question bring to our mind the concepts of "actionable knowledge" and "intervention."

Actionable knowledge in learning analytics can facilitate teachers to translate the information into concrete learner support of some kind (van Leeuwen, Wermeskerken, Erkens, & Rummel, 2017; Lockyer, Heathcote, & Dawson, 2013). Learning dashboards can provide meaningful intervention that enable learners tailor their learning behavior by using automatically generated actionable knowledge. Goal of the provided intervention for learners is to build effective online learning experiences (Pardo & Dawson, 2016).

There has been an increase in learning analytics field in recent years (Verbert et al., 2014; Yoo, Lee, Jo, & Park, 2015). In this study, a prescriptive learning dashboard (PLD) as a learning analytics tool was developed. The essential features of the PLD are reporting and visualizing online learning traces of learners including learning analytics indicators such as resource usage, social interaction; cognitive performances and helping learners improve their learning performances through personalized recommendation.

3   A Prescriptive Learning Dashboards (PLDs)

Prescriptive learning analytics can be defined as a tool, which generates reports on learner's performance results and recommend teaching and learning actions to either the teacher or learner (Sampson, 2016). In developing PLDs, information dashboard design principles (Few, 2013) and information visualization principles (Mazza, 2009) were taken as reference while designing and developing the PLDs. Figure 7.4 shows the abstract architecture of the PLDs we have built.

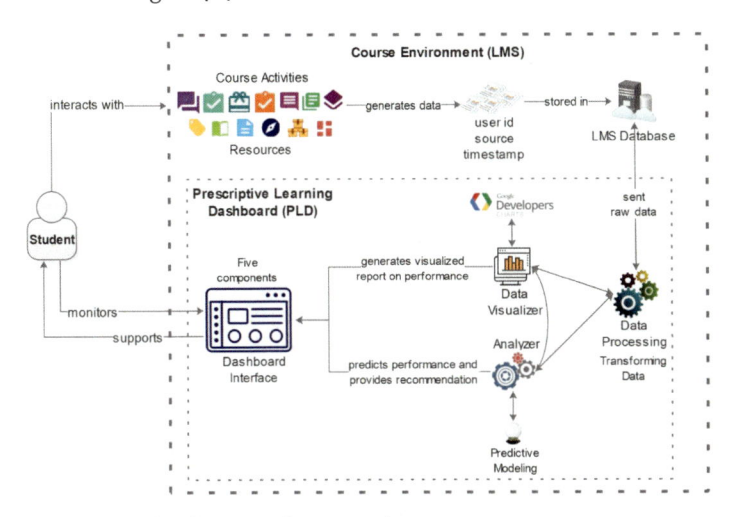

FIGURE 7.4   The abstract architecture of PLDS

The main idea of the PLDs is to monitor and show online learning traces of learners including predictive learning analytics indicators such as resource usage, social interaction (in discussion activities), cognitive performances (quiz results) and help learners improve their learning performances through personalized recommendations. The PLDs track interaction data from Moodle and transform log data into numbers. Also, the PLDs visualize learning analytics indicators that were found as predictor of learners' academic performance applying several visualization techniques as bar charts, line charts, column charts, gauge and risk chart for learners dynamically. Target users of PLDs are students. The essential features of the PLD are reporting and visualizing online learning traces of learners including learning analytics indicators such as resource usage, social interaction; cognitive performances and helping learners improve their learning performances through personalized recommendation.

The interface of the PLDs is divided into five tabs: Basic Usage (PLD_1), Learning Objects (PLD_2), Discussion Activities (PLD_3), Assessment (PLD_4) and Recommendations (PLD_5). These tabs can be opened in the same window of the PLDs when clicked any tab button. Features of each PLDs tabs are explained as follows with their screenshots.

FIGURE 7.5   The PLD1 tab: A=The button named Open/Close PLD; B=Profile Info; C=The tab named Basic Usage; D=Titles of Indicators; E=Individual Performance; F=Class Means

PLD1 represents the Basic Usage. In the opening page, learners' log in numbers, total time they spend in the whole e-learning environment and total navigation time in the course activities was presented both individually and as class average. The data were visualized on a bar chart. Learning analytics indicators visualized in the PLD₁ tab are listed as follows:

– Learners' log in numbers
– Total time spent in the whole e-learning environment
– Total number of clicks that the learner performs on course activities

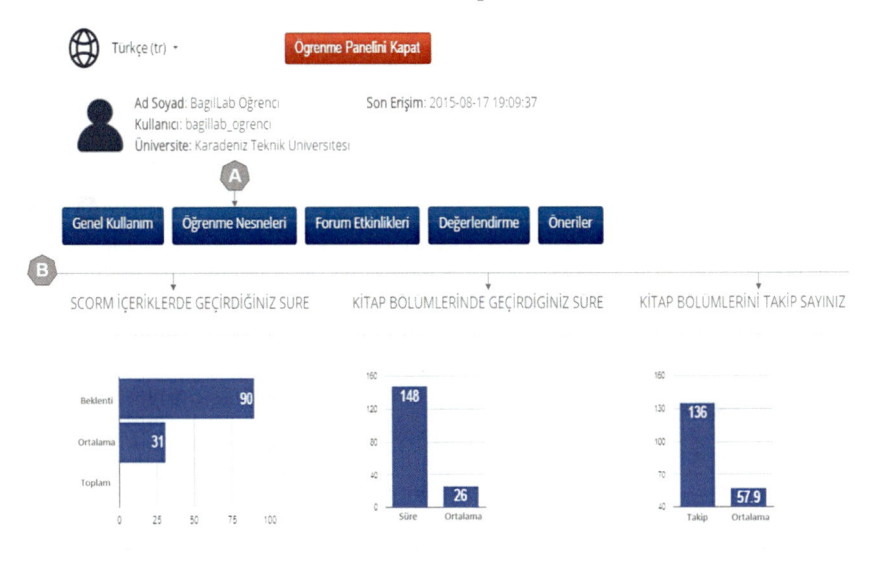

FIGURE 7.6   The PLD2 tab: A=The tab named Learning Objects; B=Titles of Indicators

The second section, PLD2, refers to the Learning Objects. In this section of the PLD, times spent on learning objects with SCORM packages and the number of times navigated to learning objects were visualized as individual performance and class averages in the same graphs. The graphs drawn were a line chart and two column charts. Learning analytics indicators visualized in the PLD₂ tab are listed below:

– Total time spent on learning objects
– Total time spent on books
– Total number of clicks that the learner performs on learning objects and books

PLD₃ is Discussion Activities as seen in Figure 7.7. The number of messages learners posted to the instructor, the number of replies learners debated, numbers in the forums, number of their response in the debates, number of their responses to the instructor and time they spent in the forum are visualized in the PLD₃ tab. The data were visualized with a bar chart both individually and as class average. Learning analytics indicators visualized in the PLD₃ tab are listed as follows:

– Number of created discussion topic
– Number of reply posts to peers

FIGURE 7.7   The PLD3 tab: A=The tab named Discussion Activities; B=Titles of Indicators

FIGURE 7.8   The PLD4 tab: A=The tab named Assessment; B=Titles of Indicators

– Number of reply posted to instructor
– Total time spent on discussion forums

In Figure 7.8, quiz numbers that learners completed, results they had in these quizzes, class averages for each quiz and instructors' expectation and the quiz averages are presented in the PLD$_4$ tab. The data were visualized with a gauge grouping column graphic and a single column graphic. The learning analytics indicators visualized in the PLD$_4$ tab are listed below:

– Average mean of the exam scores
– Exam scores
– Number of completed exams
– Total number of quizzes completed

In Figure 7.9, PLD5 shows the learning materials, forum facilities, dashboard in which learners observed their performances under evaluation and general success criteria. In this dashboard, suggestions were provided to learners about their performances, including their current performances and risk fac-

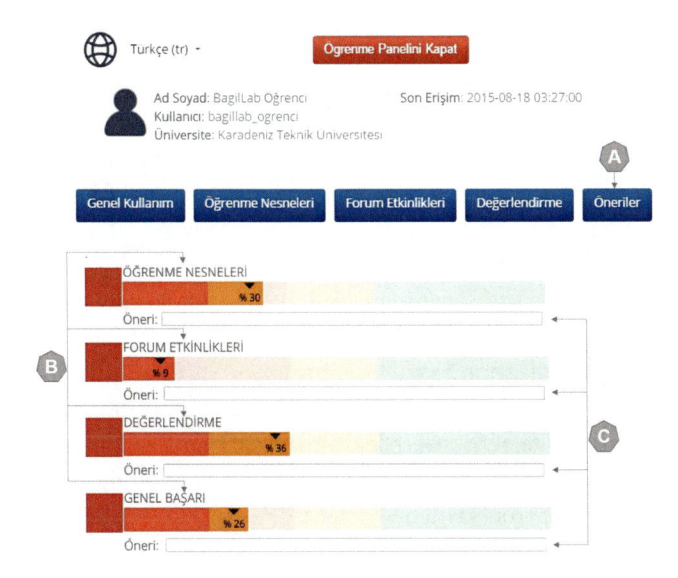

FIGURE 7.9   The PLD5 tab: A=The tab named Recommendations; B=Titles of Indicators;
C=Recommendation Messages

tors, if any. Learner performances were visualized as percentages. In addition,
suggestions were offered to learners by using previously formed success prediction models. For example, under overall success tab, learners' interaction
data in PLD_1, PLD_2, and PLD_3 were analyzed with success prediction model
and supporting suggestions were offered to learners about learning process.

The learning analytics indicators visualized in the PLD_5 tab are listed as follows successively.

– Risk status on Learning Resources
– Risk status on Social Interaction
– Risk status on Assessment Scores
– Risk status on Total Performance

As an important feature, the PLD allows learners to compare their performance
with the mean performance of the class based on the learning analytics indicators. The PLD predicts future performance trends in learner progress through run-
ning regression modelling algorithms using student learning model generated by
Ozgur (2015) and learning analytics indicators of learners automatically. The PLD
visualizes predicted academic performance as a risk status. It uses color cues to
present the extent to which a student is performing to be successful in the course.
Moreover, it generates personalized recommendations for learners as an actionable knowledge about further possible learning actions to be taken. The personalized recommendations were given as text info, relevant to resource usage,
social interaction, assessment activities and predicted final grade separately. As

an example, if a student spent less time viewing learning objects and viewing learning objects was a need for her to be successful based on automated predictive modelling analysis, s/he can see a recommendation on PLD_5 below the titles of resource usage in a text form as follows: "Too risky! You have to increase your effort. Study more with learning objects to be successful." Personalized recommendations were created for each of possible risk status and actual performance to support learners by improving their learning performances.

Research on learning dashboards have increased in the last decade exponentially. The PLD is one of the learning dashboards which provide recommendation with multiple visualization based learning experiences of learners. Along with this growth in learning dashboards studies, a systematic literature review investigating current state of the art in learning dashboards can be beneficial to shed light on future research studies. In the following section, a current review of learning analytics tools will be presented.

4   Review on Learning Analytics Tools

This section presents a systematic review in the field of learning analytics. The purpose of the study is to better understand design and pedagogical features of the learning dashboards as learning analytics tools in the literature. The main reason to employ systematic review method is clearly to present an overview of the learning dashboards involving the use of data visualization, learning analytics indicators and learning context. Figure 7.10 shows our searching strategy and employed during the review process.

Firstly, the following key subject terms were identified to retrieve relevant papers: "Learning Analytics," "Learning Dashboards," "Personalized Learning," and "Educational Data Visualization." The search was conducted using the Web of Science, ScienceDirect, Scopus, Springer, Taylor & Francis, JSTOR and ERIC databases. Search queries were created in the databases through a combination of the key subject terms. A number of selection criteria were specified to review the papers, including research papers that explained design, development and/ or application process of any learning dashboard in a learning context. The papers are considered as eligible for inclusion in the systematic review if they were peer-reviewed articles or conference papers published since 2006 to 2016.

The search on the online academic databases resulted in a total of 108 papers. We selected one article if duplicate papers from multiple academic databases were detected. Reading the full text of the papers, we selected 42 paper for final inclusion. We grouped the papers into two clusters as follows: (1) design and development of the tool and (2) application of the tool. In the papers on design and development tool, it was determined that design and

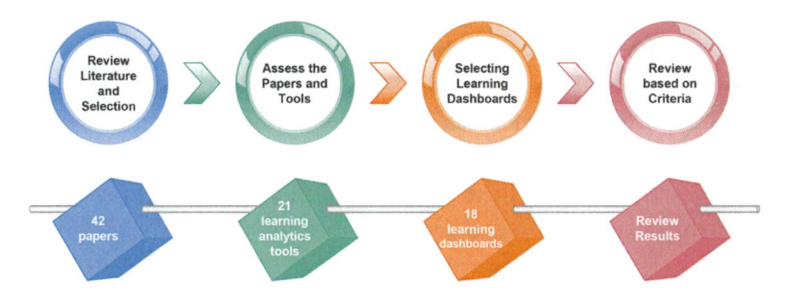

FIGURE 7.10   Employed process for systematic review

development process of a learning dashboard are explained clearly. Other papers present research findings related to implementation of learning dashboard in learning context. Reviewing all the papers, we found that a total of 21 learning dashboard with different design and pedagogical features have been developed. Three learning dashboard with not data visualization feature were excluded in the review. The papers were reviewed in terms of its features and functions. Two researchers examined the learning dashboards in detail based on target users, educational level, learning analytics indicators, visualization techniques, working platform and recommendation mechanism. The researchers coded the learning dashboards using an electronic spreadsheet software. The researchers conducted a new coding session to ensure the validity of the coding. The findings of the study are presented in terms of target users, educational level, learning analytics indicators, visualization techniques, working platform and recommendation mechanism.

Distribution of the learning dashboards in terms of target users (teacher and learner) is presented in Figure 7.11.

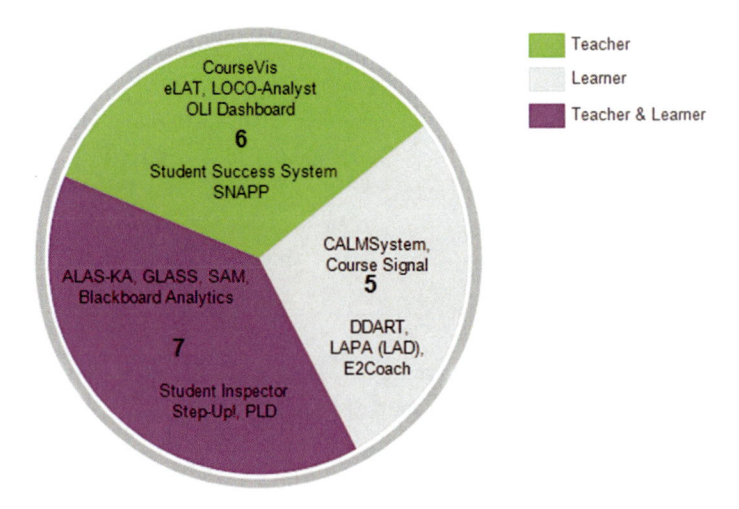

FIGURE 7.11   Distribution of learning dashboards across educational levels by target users

Figure 7.11 shows that only a small number of learning dashboards were developed for teachers or learners, although the distribution of learning dashboards according to target users seems balanced. Learning dashboards can be developed as integral to a learning management system without making educational levels explicit. Figure 7.12 shows the numbers of learning dashboards that were implemented in higher education, primary education and all educational levels.

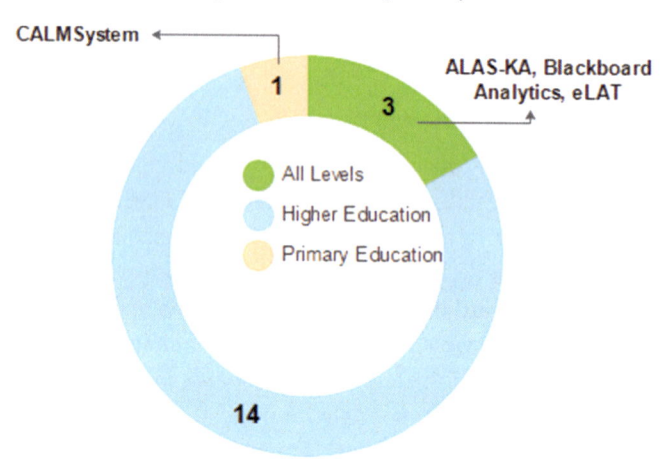

FIGURE 7.12   Distribution of learning dashboards by educational levels

TABLE 7.1   Learning analytics indicators and data visualization techniques used in learning dashboards

Dashboard	Learning analytics indicators	Visualization techniques
ALAS-KA	Access, cognitive performance, time spent, resource usage, badges, affective state	Pie chart, line chart, bar chart, candlestick chart
Blackboard Analytics	Access, performance results, resource usage, social network	Bar chart, scatterplot, line chart, win-lose chart
CALMSystem	Time spent, learners' knowledge levels, confidence beliefs	Visual icons
Course Signal	Access, performance results, time on task, resource usage, risk level	Traffic signals
CourseVis	Follow-ups and threads in discussions, cognitive performances, access and participation to resources and activities	Histogram, matrix, 2D metric space, 3D scatterplot

(cont.)

TABLE 7.1   Learning analytics indicators and data visualization techniques used in learning
dashboards *(cont.)*

Dashboard	Learning analytics indicators	Visualization techniques
DDART	Social interaction performances, resources usage, participation	Social networks, tree map, many charts: Pie, bar, line, gauge, scatter, area, combo
eLAT	Access, resources usage, social performance, user activities, assessment performance	Bar chart, line chart
GLASS	Access, performance results, resources usage, time spent	Bar chart, timeline
LAPA (LAD)	Access, participation, time spent, resources usage	Bar chart, scatter chart, column chart, combo chart
LOCO-Analyst	Access, performance results, resources usage, social interaction	Table matrix, bar chart, pie chart, tag cloud
OLI Dashboard	Self-assessment activities, resources usage, time spent, artifacts produced, predicted mastery level	Traffic signals, bar chart
SAM	Access, time spent, resources usage, performance results	Line chart, parallel coordinates, bar chart, tag cloud
Student Inspector	Performance results, resources usage	Bar chart, pie chart
Student Success System	Performance results, social networks, risk level	Risk quadrant, scatterplot, win-lose chart, sociogram
SNAPP	Social interactions, resources usage	Sociogram
StepUp!	Access, social interaction performances, resources usage, time spent	Bar chart, table matrix, line chart
PLD	Access, social interaction, time spent, resource usage, quiz results, peer performances	Bar chart, line chart, gauge, win-lose chart
E2Coach	Performance results	Colored messages

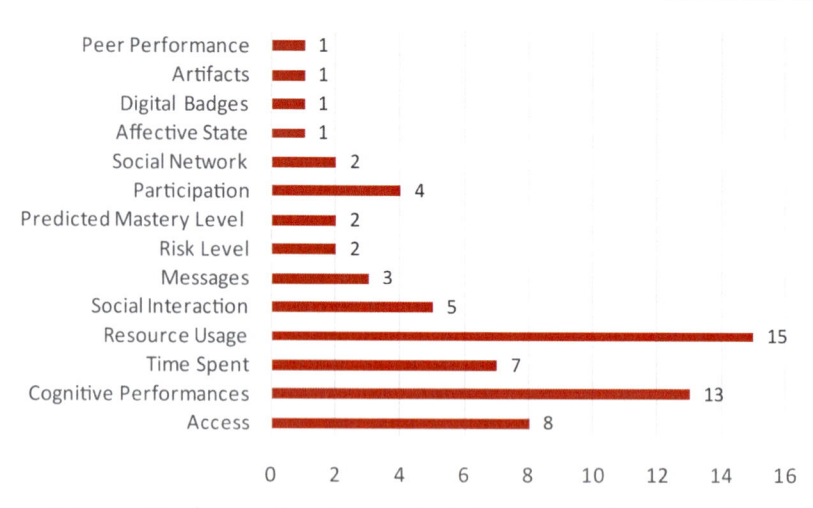

FIGURE 7.13   Distribution of learning analytics indicators used in learning dashboards

The most of the learning dashboards were implemented in universities at higher education levels as seen in Figure 7.12. Only a dashboard titled CALMSytem was applied at primary school and other three dashboards integrated in learning management system or course platforms were applied in all educational levels. Learning analytics indicators presented in learning dashboards and the visualization techniques applied are summarized in Table 7.1.

What stands out in Table 7.1 is using multiple data visualization techniques to illustrate learning analytics indicator in a learning dashboard. The results indicated that line chart, bar chart, pie chart, and scatter diagrams are often used while gauge, tag clouds, sociogram, tree maps, and affective visuals are used at low levels in learning dashboards. Figure 7.13 provides an overview of learning analytics indicators used in learning dashboards.

As represented in Figure 7.13, the most preferred learning analytics indicators illustrated in the learning dashboards are action-related indicators (usage of resources such as videos and content) and result-related indicators (cognitive performance results, average grade etc.). In addition, it was found that time spent on learning environment and access frequency are more employed in learning dashboards comparing other learning analytics indicators. The least visualized learning analytics indicators were found to be peer performances, digital badges, artifacts produced and affective status.

Considering working platform of learning dashboards, it was revealed that two learning dashboards are compatible to mobile devices and its operating systems. This is a rather surprising result, since it is known that most of learners use mobile devices commonly for learning purposes. In addition, we found that three learning dashboards (SAM, E2Coach, and PLD) have recommendation mechanism for learners.

5 Conclusion and Future Directions

Monitoring, processing and modeling of all actions and activities of learners in e-learning environments could contribute to a better understanding of online learning experiences. In addition, visualizing learners' traces via learning dashboards could increase learners' awareness of their learning process with its trigger role. Using learners' traces, more research in learning analytics field is needed to demonstrate benefits and to provide implications for building better online learning experience. This chapter presented the current state of the art of learning dashboards as learning analytics tools in terms of design and pedagogical features.

The results from our analysis indicated that there were a wide range of designs in learning dashboards that visualize action-related indicators and results-related indicators to be used by teachers. A rich variety of learning analytics indicators have been used to build learning dashboards. However, it is remarkable that these learning analytics indicators heavily reflect behavioral and cognitive engagement of learners in e-learning environments. In future studies, physical sensors may be used to track learner data for learning dashboards and learning dashboards may visualize comparative cognitive performances and affective states reflecting emotional engagement of learners.

Another interesting result is that social network analysis and win-lose chart indicating predicted risk level are rarely used in learning dashboards whilst basic visualizing techniques such as line chart, bar chart and pie chart are employed to visualize learners' traces. We can infer from this result that learning dashboards use a specific visualization technique or visual metaphor for a learning analytics indicator. Future learning dashboards may enable learners to choose visualization technique for monitoring their learning traces by using multiple kinds of visualizations. We can suggest that learning analytics researchers may refer to principles of data visualization when choosing kinds of visualization for specific behavioral indicator, especially relational and comparative learner data. There are limited learning dashboards that provide suggestions to learners as an actionable knowledge and present peer-performances of leaners in the literature. It is therefore suggested that future studies can focus on designing goal-oriented learning dashboards that have intervention and/or early alert mechanism to provide actionable personalized feedback based on personalized learning paradigm (Altun, 2016;

Verbert et al., 2014). Learning dashboards may offer automatic suggestions about learners' online learning experience by modelling learner data and help teachers to make informed decision based on learning performances of learners in real-time. Considering increasing usage of mobile devices for leaners, there is need for more design of learning dashboards with compatible mobile devices and mobile software. It can also be argued that future learning dashboard studies that focus on the development of conceptual frameworks and design rules for learning dashboards design can guide researchers in learning analytics field.

Note

1   This chapter is a part of the second author's PhD thesis done under the supervision of the first author as an extended version of a paper presented at the 4th International Instructional Technologies & Teacher Education Symposium.

References

AECT. (2018, January 15). *The definition and terminology committee.* Retrieved from https://www.aect.org/#

Akçapınar, G., Altun, A., & Aşkar, P. (2015). Modeling students' academic performance based on their interactions in an online learning environment. *Elementary Education Online, 14*(3), 815–824. doi:10.17051/io.2015.03160

Ali, L., Hatala, M., Gašević, D., & Jovanović, J. (2012). A qualitative evaluation of evolution of a learning analytics tool. *Computers & Education, 58*(1), 470–489. doi:10.1016/j.compedu.2011.08.030

Altun, A. (2016). Understanding cognitive profiles in designing personalized learning environments. In B. Gros, Kinshuk, & M. Maina (Eds.), *The future of ubiquitous learning* (pp. 259–271). Berlin/Heidelberg: Springer.

Arnold, K. E., & Pistilli, M. D. (2012). *Course signals at Purdue: Using learning analytics to increase student success.* Paper presented at the Proceedings of the 2nd International Conference on Learning Analytics and Knowledge, Vancouver, British Columbia, Canada.

Baker, R. S. J. d. (2010). Data mining for education. In B. McGaw, P. Peterson, & E. Baker (Eds.), *International encyclopedia of education* (Vol. 7, pp. 112–118). Oxford: Elsevier.

Baker, R. S. J. d., & Yacef, K. (2009). The state of educational data mining in 2009: A review and future visions. *Journal of Educational Data Mining, 1*(1), 3–17.

Bayrak, F., & Yurdugül, H. (2016). Learning analytics module for web based self-assessment system. *Educational Technology Theory and Practice, 6*(2), 85–99.

Brusilovsky, P., Somyürek, S., Guerra, J., Hosseini, R., Zadorozhny, V., & Durlach, P. J. (2016). Open social student modeling for personalized learning. *IEEE Transactions on Emerging Topics in Computing, 4*(3), 450–461.

Cerezo, R., Sánchez-Santillán, M., Paule-Ruiz, M. P., & Núñez, J. C. (2016). Students' LMS interaction patterns and their relationship with achievement: A case study in higher education. *Computers & Education, 96*, 42–54.

Chatti, M. A., Dyckhoff, A. L., Schroeder, U., & Thüs, H. (2012). A reference model for learning analytics. *International Journal of Technology Enhanced Learning, 4*(5–6), 318–331.

Duval, E. (2011). Attention please! Learning analytics for visualization and recommendation. In *Proceedings of the 1st International Conference on Learning Analytics and Knowledge* (pp. 9–17). LAK '11, New York, NY: ACM.

Dyckhoff, A. L., Zielke, D., Bültmann, M., Chatti, M. A., & Schroeder, U. (2012). Design and implementation of a learning analytics toolkit for teachers. *Journal of Educational Technology & Society, 15*(3), 58–76.

Few, S. (2009). *Now you see it: Simple visualization techniques for quantitative analysis.* Oakland, CA: Analytics Press.

Few, S. (2013). *Information dashboard design: Displaying data for at-a-glance monitoring* (2nd ed.). Burlingame, CA: Analytics Press.

Gašević, D., Dawson, S., & Siemens, G. (2015). Let's not forget: Learning analytics are about learning. *TechTrends, 59*(1), 64–71.

Graf, S., Liu, T.-C., Kinshuk, Chen, N.-S., & Yang, S. J. H. (2009). Learning styles and cognitive traits: Their relationship and its benefits in web-based educational systems. *Computers in Human Behavior, 25*(6), 1280–1289.

Hernández-García, Á., González-González, I., Jiménez-Zarco, A. I., & Chaparro-Peláez, J. (2015). Applying social learning analytics to message boards in online distance learning: A case study. *Computers in Human Behavior, 47*, 68–80.

Ifenthaler, D., & Widanapathirana, C. (2014). Development and validation of a learning analytics framework: Two case studies using support vector machines. *Technology, Knowledge and Learning, 19*(1–2), 221–240. doi:10.1007/s10758-014-9226-4

Klerkx, J., Verbert, K., & Duval, E. (2014). Enhancing learning with visualization techniques. In J. M. Spector, M. D. Merrill, J. Elen, & M. J. Bishop (Eds.), *Handbook of research on educational communications and technology* (pp. 791–807). New York, NY: Springer.

Kokoç, M., & Altun, A. (2016). Building a learning experience: What do learners' online interaction data imply?. In *Proceedings of 13th International Conference on Cognition and Exploratory Learning in Digital Age 2016* (pp. 253–260). Mannheim, Germany. Retrieved from https://files.eric.ed.gov/fulltext/ED571420.pdf

Lal, P. (2014). Designing online learning strategies through analytics. In F. J. García-Peñalvo & A. M. S. Pardo (Eds.), *Online tutor 2.0: Methodologies and case studies for successful learning: Methodologies and case studies for successful learning* (pp. 1–15). IGI Global.

Li, I., Dey, A., & Forlizzi, J. (2010). A stage-based model of personal informatics systems. In *Proceedings of CHI10, 28th International Conference on Human Factors in Computing Systems* (pp. 557–566). New York, NY.

Li, L.-Y., & Tsai, C.-C. (2017). Accessing online learning material: Quantitative behavior patterns and their effects on motivation and learning performance. *Computers & Education, 114*, 286–297.

Lockyer, L., Heathcote, E., & Dawson, S. (2013). Informing pedagogical action: Aligning learning analytics with learning design. *American Behavioral Scientist, 57*(10), 1439–1459. doi:10.1177/0002764213479367

Macfadyen, L. P., & Dawson, S. (2010). Mining LMS data to develop an "early warning system" for educators: A proof of concept. *Computers & Education, 54*(2), 588–599.

Mazza, R. (2009). *Introduction to information visualization*. London: Springer.

Özgur, A. (2015). *The investigation of learner-assessment interaction in learning management systems* (Unpublished master thesis). Hacettepe University, Ankara.

Papamitsiou, Z., & Economides, A. (2014). Learning analytics and educational data mining in practice: A systematic literature review of empirical evidence. *Educational Technology & Society, 17*(4), 49–64.

Park, Y., & Jo, I.-H. (2015). Development of the learning analytics dashboard to support students' learning performance. *Journal of Universal Computer Science, 21*(1), 110–133. doi:10.3217/jucs-021-01-0110

Peña-Ayala, A. (2014). Educational data mining: A survey and a data mining-based analysis of recent works. *Expert Systems with Applications, 41*, 1432–1462. doi:10.1016/j.eswa.2013.08.042

Robinson, R., Molenda, M., & Rezabek, L. (2008). Facilitating learning. In A. Januszewski & M. Molenda (Eds.), *Educational technology: A definition with commentary* (pp. 15–48). New York, NY: Lawrence Erlbaum Associates.

Romero, C., & Ventura, S. (2013). Data mining in education. *Wiley Interdisciplinary Reviews: Data Mining and Knowledge Discovery, 3*(1), 12–27.

Sampson, D. (2016, January 05). *Learning analytics: Analyze your lesson to discover more about your students*. Retrieved from https://elearningindustry.com/learning-analytics-analyze-lesson

Siemens, G. (2013). Learning analytics: The emergence of a discipline. *American Behavioral Scientist, 57*(10), 1380–1400.

Siemens, G., & Baker, R. S. J. d. (2012). Learning analytics and educational data mining: Towards communication and collaboration. In *Proceedings of the 2nd Inter-*

national Conference on Learning Analytics and Knowledge (pp. 252–254). New York, NY: ACM.

Siemens, G., & Gasevic, D. (2012). Guest editorial: Learning and knowledge analytics. *Educational Technology & Society, 15*(3), 1–2.

Siemens, G., & Long, P. (2011). Penetrating the fog: Analytics in learning and education. *EDUCAUSE Review, 46*(5), 30.

Slade, S., & Prinsloo, P. (2013). Learning analytics: Ethical issues and dilemmas. *American Behavioral Scientist, 57*(1), 1509–1528.

Spector, J. M. (2013). Emerging educational technologies and research directions. *Educational Technology & Society, 16*(2), 21–30.

Vandewaetere, M., & Clarebout, G. (2014). Advanced technologies for personalized learning, instruction, and performance. In J. M. Spector, M. D. Merrill, J. Elen, & M. J. Bishop (Eds.), *Handbook of research on educational communications and technology* (pp. 425–437). New York, NY: Springer.

van Leeuwen, A., van Wermeskerken, M., Erkens, G., & Rummel, N. (2017). Measuring teacher sense making strategies of learning analytics: A case study. *Learning: Research and Practice, 3*(1), 42–58.

Verbert, K., Govaerts, S., Duval, E., Santos, J., Van Assche, F., Parra, G., & Klerkx, J. (2014). Learning dashboards: An overview and future research opportunities. *Personal and Ubiquitous Computing, 18*(6), 1499–1514. doi:10.1007/s00779-013-0751-2

Yoo, Y., Lee, H., Jo, I.-H., & Park, Y. (2015). Educational dashboards for smart learning: Review of case studies. In G. Chen, V. Kumar, Kinshuk, R. Huang, & S. C. Kong (Eds.), *Emerging issues in smart learning* (pp. 145–155). Berlin/Heidelberg: Springer.

CHAPTER 8

Analytical Indicators for Profiling and Improving Engagement and Success of Vulnerable Participants

Mirella Atherton

1 Introduction

Increasing numbers of students who have been vulnerable or disadvantaged in the past are accessing higher education in Australia. Some of these students will continue to be categorised as vulnerable as they interact with their chosen university. Since vulnerability can be transient, some students may be at risk at some stage as they progress on their learning journey. Government policies on widening participation and individual aspiration to attain university education are playing key roles in growth, diversity and student participation. As institutions continue to seek opportunities to spread their offerings there are concerns emerging about academic standards, academic outcomes and the overall quality of educational delivery by different kinds of educational institutions in Australia. These institutions are challenged to develop robust quality assurance frameworks which raise equity aspiration whilst maintaining standards and outcomes. The increasing use of technology in learning has produced valuable data through learning platforms. Institutions are now looking to gain insights about individual students and their engagement with learning technologies. Intelligent use of the sophisticated data could enable institutions to predict academic risks and successes by using a range of metrics such as: profile, background, barriers, expectations, access to important services, use of online technology, use of resources, attendance and performance. Data has become a valuable asset in education. Statistical indicators, statistical information, and statistical evidence are becoming respected tools for profiling and improving trends in student engagement and success, particularly those emerging that relate to vulnerable students.

2 Accessing Higher Education in Australia

Learning analytics, also referred to as 'LA,' has been considered an instructional technology that began with the advent of the learning management system 'LMS' (Brown, 2011). Learning analytics has been one of the leading trends in the study of tertiary education (Johnson, Becker, & Freeman, 2013). This form of analytics originated from the idea that student learning, academic progress, and teaching practice can be enhanced by analysing the data taken from normal administrative, teaching, or learning activities (Wright, McKay, Hershock, Miller, & Tritz, 2014). Lias and Elias (2011) considered learning analytics as an emerging field in which sophisticated analytic tools are used to improve learning and education. Analytical tools provide statistical evaluation of rich data sources to discern patterns that can help individuals at companies, educational institutions, or governments make more informed decisions. In the teaching and learning contexts, the effectiveness of analytics depends largely on the features of the faculty and the student use. At least, analytical tools can help to confirm a program's strengths or weaknesses and can determine a shortage in resources (EDUCAUSE, 2010).

A highly involved student is one who devotes considerable energy to studying; spends much time on campus; actively participates in student organizations and interacts frequently with faculty members and other students (Astin, 1999). Student engagement is considered as students' initiation of action, effort and persistence as well as ambient emotional states during learning activities (Sharma & Bhaumik, 2013; Skinner et al., 1990). Marks (2000) conceptualised engagement as a psychological process, specifically, the attention, interest, investment and effort students expend in the work of learning. Student engagement has been refered to as an optimal experience or 'flow,' a state of mind brought on by a combination of three common facets of 'flow' experiences and optimal motivation to learn including: concentration, interest and enjoyment (Shernoff, 2002). Kuh (2003) described student engagement as the time and energy students devote to educationally sound activities inside and outside of the classroom, and the policies and practices that institutions use to induce students to take part in these activities (also see Kuh, 2001) which have empirical link to desired academic outcomes (Kuh, 2009a).

The study of student engagement had its origin from Pace's (1982) who measured quality of effort, Kuh et al. (1989, 1991) and Astin's (1984, 1985) theory of involvement (Lawson & Masyn, 2015; Pike & Kuh, 2005). Astin (1984) defined engagement as the amount of physical and psychological energy that the student devotes to the academic experience. His theory of student engagement was based on five tenets: engagement refers to the investment of physical and psychological energy; engagement occurs along a continuum; engagement has both quantitative and qualitative features; the amount of student learning and development associated with an educational program is directly related to the quality and quantity of student engagement in that program; and the effectiveness of any educational practice is directly related to the ability of that practice to increase student engagement (Junco, 2012, p. 163).

Student engagement also represents how higher education institutions allocate their human and other resources as well as how they organise learning opportunities and services to encourage students to participate and benefit from involvement in activities (Manning, Kinzie, & Schuh, 2006). As such, engagement consists of various factors, including the investment in the academic experience, interactions with faculty, involvement in co-curricular activities, and interaction with peers (Kuh, 2009; Pascarella & Terenzini, 2005). Kuh (2009) also listed two major aspects that are important to student success in educational activities encompassing in-class or academic engagement and out-of-class engagement in educationally relevant or co- curricular activities. According to Lee (2014), student engagement is a multifaceted concept, and several components of student engagement are identified such as behavioral, emotional/psychological, cognitive, academic (Appleton, Christenson, & Furlong, 2008; Fredricks et al., 2004; Finn & Zimmer, 2012; Reeve, 2012). Despite having no consensus on which of these above mentioned components is important, most studies have included behavioral and emotional components (Lee, 2014).

Overall, academic success of students and the success of the institution are key aims of studying analytics. The academic success of students in university courses is highly dependent on their transition to the university from school, workplace, or in many cases the gap between high school and university education due to caring responsibilities. Data from students in courses indicates risk due to factors such as low academic achievement in high school, being first in the family to access university education, low level of confidence, financial difficulties, range of learning difficulties, mental health issues, disability, caring responsibilities, employment commitments, lack of motivation and others (Shah et al., 2014). These risk factors can be analysed to establish trends for effective transition to university with the aim to improve engagement in all facets of learning. Key literature from Australia, New Zealand, the United Kingdom and North America has indicated that Australia should avoid adopting either a deficit conception of students from low socio-economic backgrounds or a deficit conception of the institutions into which they will move (Devlin, 2013). Rather than it being the primary responsibility of the student or of the institution to change to ensure the success of enabling students, it was argued that the adjustments necessary to ensure achievement for students from low socio-economic backgrounds in Australian higher education would be most usefully thought of as a 'joint venture' between students and university.

3   Widening Diversity and Participation for Students in All Courses

Vulnerability is an important concept to consider and is an especially important aspect in learning analytics. Students are consumers of the institutions educational offerings. If students experience vulnerability then there is a risk of withdrawl or failure. There is a high degree of consistency in the literature in the United States (US), Europe and Australia relating to the categories associated with potential vulnerability which include: (1) age (2) low income (3) those who do not work (4) long term disabled (5) those with lower educational attainment (6) rural dwellers and (7) ethnic minorities. While acknowledging the consensus of several academics that there are situations where all consumers may be at risk of vulnerability, others view vulnerability as a multidimensional concept and one focused on individual characteristics or where the external markets impact on consumers to make them vulnerable. Ascertaining the elements that contribute to vulnerability using data analytics will lead to key progress in the future.

Higher education institutions are experiencing many changes. Notable changes include the growing diversity of students and increased innovation in the way courses are delivered to meet the demands of different cohorts of students (Dias, 2015; Gaskell & Mills, 2014; Shah et al., 2014). In all continents of the world, increased numbers of students who have been disadvantaged in the past are participating in higher education. Government policies on widening participation and individual aspiration to attain university education are playing a key role in the growth of student participation. As student participation diversifies and grows, there are concerns about the quality of education delivery by different kinds of institutions and academic outcomes of students (Harman & Meek, 2000; Shah et al., 2011; Shah & Nair, 2011). As institutions continue to seek opportunities to spread their offerings (Edwards, Crosling, & Edwards, 2010), concerns are emerging about academic standards and the extent to which different kinds of courses are preparing students for success in undergraduate education (Anderson, 2006; Edwards, Crosling, & Edwards, 2010).

Thomas (2002) examined some of the issues surrounding student retention in higher education based on the case study of a modern university in England that had good performance indicators of both widening participation and student retention. The two-fold nature of this success is significant, as it has been asserted that greater diversity will lead to an increase in student withdrawal. At least an opportunity to study at University level is provided. The changes to student funding in the UK has put greater financial pressures and stress on students, especially those from low-income groups. Nevertheless, many students cope with poverty, high levels of debt and significant burdens of paid work to successfully complete their courses of study (Thomas, 2002). Drawing on the work of Reay et al. (2001), Thomas (2002) adopted and explored the term 'institutional habitus,' and attempted to provide a conceptual and empirical understanding of the ways in which the values and practices of a higher education institution impact on student retention. Student retention across every discipline is still very much a topic of discussion within academic circles.

Coates (2005) reviewed current possibilities for determining the quality of university education in Australia and exposed limitations of quality assurance systems that fail to take account of student data. O'Shea and Vincent (2011) argue that coaching commencing students provides them with early exposure to the university culture and thus with a more realistic perception of the teaching and learning environment. This in turn improves their engagement and experience (Grebennikov & Shah, 2012). Academic relevancy and intrinsic motivation have been associated with student engagement. Students who found a connection between learning materials and their lives were also interested in learning for learning's sake and were more likely to listen carefully, pay attention and participate in class discussions (Crumpton & Gregory, 2011). Other research highlights the need to facilitate transition by developing resilience, institutional responsiveness and policy driven transformative and innovative education (Abbott-Chapman, 2011).

While Puzziferro (2008) found that there was no correlation between online technology self-efficacy scores and student performance, Hostager (2014) revealed that a greater use of online resources can fully offset the effects of gender and partially offset the effects of Grade Point Average (GPA) on the grades that students earn in blended courses combining face-to-face and online components. Robinson and Hullinger (2008) identified a difference in online and on campus student engagement in their study of three universities. Engaging students online has been explored in a number of subject areas with the aim of academic improvement; these have included pre and post-tests (Yang, 2011). Most recently, a report on first year experience in higher education in Australia showed high level of student engagement in online learning. As time goes on, the studies show increased engagement of students in using recorded lectures, and use of social networking for study purposes (Baik et al., 2015, p. 7). These insights have been revealed by analytics.

Diversity in the student population has created opportunities for students to interact and engage with a diverse range of ideas (Denson & Bowman, 2013). Increased diversification of the higher education students has prompted consideration of the characteristics and specific needs of students to better facilitate access, participation and engagement (Budge, 2010; Thomas, 2013; Thomas &

Heath, 2014; Devine, Brady, Moody, Wilson, Liu, Medland, & Lightbody 2016). An important aspect of encouraging diversity is to make sure that all students have the skills to succeed in their chosen academic pursuit. Factors such as integration, commitment, satisfaction, finances, prospective careers, support and psychology have been identified as important factors determining performance (McKenzie, Kirsten, & Schweitzer, 2001). It is known that a belief that one will perform successfully in a given course can predict actual successful performance in that course (McKenzie, Kirsten, & Schweitzer, 2001).

4   The Increasing Use of Technology

The increased use of technology in learning in the form of resources and platforms has provided opportunities for institutions to gain insights about individual students and their engagement with learning technologies. Intelligent use of sophisticated data could enable institutions to predict academic risks and success by using a range of metrics such as: profile, background, barriers, expectations, important services, use of online technology, use of resources, attendance and performance. The use of these analytical indicators are becoming valuable tools for profiling and improving emerging trends in engagement a particularly with most vulnerable students.

Understanding the student experience through learning analytics can assist managing transitions to University study and retaining students (Krause, 2005). The student experience is important in setting up the educational foundations for academic success (Kuh et al., 2005; Upcraft et al., 1989). Krause and Coates (2008) argue the need to monitor engagement using a combination of quantitative and qualitative measures as there is still a lack of knowledge about how to be a successful student in a tertiary environment (Whannell, Whannell, & Allen, 2012). For example, the value of Science, Technology, Engineering, Mathmatics (and Medicine) (STEM or STEMM) skills in shaping the future Australian workforce and economy has been highlighted in recent years (Office of the Chief Scientist, 2014; Australian Government, 2015; Education Council, 2015). The challenge is that as demand for high-quality STEMM graduates is anticipated to increase, there is a decline in both the participation and proficiency in maths and science at the secondary school level (Engineers Australia, 2015; King & Cattlin, 2014; Kennedy, Lyons, & Quinn, 2014). The implication of these findings is that future STEMM graduates are embarking on degrees that they may not be best equipped to successfully complete. (Budge, 2010; Thomas, 2013; Thomas & Heath, 2014; Devine, Brady, Moody, Wilson, Liu, Medland, & Lightbody 2016).

In Australia, Indigenous student school completion rates and transition to university statistics particularly in STEMM related programs, remain significantly lower than for their non-Indigenous peers. Indigenous student enrolments in fields requiring strong mathematics and scientific literacy are low in relation to other disciplines (Paige, Hattam, Rigney, Osborne and Morrison). Likewise, gender differences in skills, behaviours and achievement in STEMM areas are showing significant disparity. Olsen, Burgess, and Sharma 2015, presented the key finding from a study of the academic performance of 338,000 full-time students at 22 Australian universities. Female students passed 91.7% of courses attempted while male students passed 86.4% of courses. International female students passed 90.9% of courses attempted while international males passed 86.8%. Put simply, the females did better than the males.

According to some studies, females feel less confident than males in pursuing University courses (Dryburgh, 2000; Hancock, Davies, & McGrenere, 2002; Harrell, 1998; Todman, 2000; Wilson, 2002). A study by Stoilescu and McDougall (2011), specifically explored factors that alienate undergraduate female students and exacerbate gender disparities in confidence, performance, attitudes, and experience in undergraduate education. Women can face unique barriers that include negative stereotypes, negative influences and discrimination. In the past women have been faced with a lack of role models, lack of encouragement and insufficient opportunities to succeed in the areas of maths and science (Cordero, Porter, Israel, & Brown, 2010). Several reasons for such an occurrence have been postulated in the literature and include real and perceived challenges associated with balancing work and family life (Alpay, Hari, Kambouri, & Ahearn, 2010). There is growing literature that men are more confident than women in exam situations (Claes, Persson, & Willenhag, 2005). It is known that students who repeatedly underestimate their performance can lose motivation for learning due to a lack of self-confidence. Students who over estimate their performance may be at a disadvantage as their over confidence may impede their motivation to learn new techniques (Stankov, Morony, & Lee, 2014).

Evidence of hardwired sex differences in the brain have been measured within the field of neuroscience and has shown the brain to be adaptable and influenced by an individual's environment (Buckley, 2016). In psychological research, where gender differences in cognitive skills have been found, there has been evidence that some of these differences can be reduced through training. Along with educational research, psychology has also demonstrated that motivational factors, such as value, competence beliefs, sense of belonging and anxiety, have a large impact on mathematical achievement and attitudes towards future learning in mathematics (Buckley, 2016). The compelling message is that the principles of plasticity apply in relation to neurodevelopment and students' engagement and therefore approaches designed to target any underrepresented group should be multifaceted (Buckley, 2016). Efforts to increase students' interest, enjoyment or intrinsic value, improve confidence in students' perceptions of their competence in STEMM and promote the value of STEMM areas for future educational and career aspirations could be positive. The more STEMM is perceived as an area that is useful, enjoyable and attainable by all, irrespective of background the more likely that the gap in comprehension will start to close (Buckley, 2016).

There are approaches that describe the conceptual steps students pass through to achieve learning, for example Piaget's (1977) developmental stage approach or Von Glaserfeld's (1995) research on stages of learning. Another approach focuses on tasks in the process required to scaffold learning (Simon's et al., 2010). There are also hybrid approaches based on elements of the two previous approaches, for example, Harel and Koichi (2010, p. 118) argued that "learning is a continuum of disequilibrium–equilibrium phases manifested by (a) intellectual and psychological needs that instigate or result from these phases and (b) ways of understanding or ways of thinking that are utilized and newly constructed during these phases." This results in a constant framing and reframing of what is learned and how to behave with such knowledge (Bowles & Hattie, 2016). Understanding students conceptions of learning is important as they provide a means of understanding how students conceive of learning and how these concepts might be carefully applied to teaching in contexts (Lonka & Lindblom-Ylanne, 1996; Richardson, 1999) and importantly to develop a set of factors to use in dialogue with students about personal learning experiences, within a range of context (Richardson, 1999; Lin, Tsai, & Liang, 2012; Vermunt & Vanrijswijk, 1988; Vermunt & Vermetten, 2004).

Students are taking more complex pathways to earning credentials than is generally assumed. They are likely to earn credits from more than one institution and to transfer among institutions. Students are different than they were 25 years ago. The students are increasingly more likely to be from a minority group and to be single parents. The characteristics of students vary greatly across disciplines, with rates of minority and female participation lowest in computer science, physics, and engineering (National Academies of Sciences, Engineering, and Medicine, 2016). Students' desire to increase their knowledge, understanding, or skills, coupled with a supportive learning environment, are major factors in guiding their level of engagement in academic tasks (Marchand & Gutierrez, 2017). Students are able to differentiate between different aspects of instructional support in graduate learning and that these different perceptions may have unique impacts on qualities of motivational beliefs and actions (Marchand & Gutierrez, 2017). Some studies have investigated growth patterns both within and between individuals have provided an indication of variable centered approaches but do not capture the different trajectories of individual change that may emerge in response to a changing context (Midgley, Feldlaufer, & Eccles, 1989).

It has been asserted that student centered analyses investigating intra-individual processes and changing trajectories may yield more-illuminating results about the dynamics among these motivational processes. Turner and Patrick (2004) suggest that student behavior in learning settings is the result of a complex interaction among actual teacher actions, student perceptions of those actions, students' personal and motivational characteristics, and student achievement. The transactions between the context and the individual over time are critical for the development of positive beliefs about the self in academic domains and adaptive patterns of action during learning activities (Sameroff, 2010; Skinner, Kindermann, Connell, & Wellborn, 2009; Marchand & Gutierrez, 2017). The importance of instructional support promoting student motivation and engagement cannot be understated (Marchand & Gutierrez, 2017). Adult students may have well-established study strategies and beliefs about the value of the subject matter, yet instructional support matters and may make a difference in the quality of student motivation. Instructors in graduate courses that students may be reluctant to take, such as required research methods or statistics, may choose to emphasise how the course material may connect to students' professional or personal lives. While this approach is likely to lead to the desired result of increased value beliefs about the material and engagement, our results suggest that even adult students respond to an instructor who seems to care about them. There is considerable research on interventions to increase instructors' use of supportive behaviors, such as provision of relevance (Cheon & Reeve, 2015; Su & Reeve, 2011; Marchand & Gutierrez, 2017).

5   Intelligent Use of Data to Predict Trends in Higher Education

Romero et al. (2008) argue that the ability to predict students' performance is important in web-based educational environments and in order to achieve this aim Data Mining 'DM' is a promising arena to take into account. Of course there are limitations when considering analytics involving data. For example using student access as an indicator for engagement with learning is fraught with problems. Engagement is a very difficult variable to measure.

Student access to online platforms could provide a "footprint" to measure success. Sets of data including the number of times each student accessed the online subject content and their corresponding assessment grades is one way to profile engagement. Students who spend more time online in the content area are more actively engaged in learning by interacting with the teaching staff which results in better academic results. Offerings may vary because of different types of students and their personal choices. While online study offered in distance courses can represent a disadvantage for some students, there is an advantage to on campus students if the quantity of online interaction is higher. Shernoff (2002), identified three main factors that can have influence on student engagement including: (1) when the students are challenged in terms of academic intensity; (2) when they can actively demonstrate their skills and (3) when they work in a group instead of listening to a lecture. Sharma and Bhaumik (2013) in their study on student engagement and its predictors used ten potential predictors. The findings then spotted that the two most highly-rated predictors are found to be academic inputs (60.7%) and helpful administration (56.7%), followed by syllabus of the courses (49.3%), computer facilities (47%) and all other factors were given low to moderate ratings ranging between 18% and 47% (Sharma & Bhaumik, 2013, p. 34).

At the institution level, analytic tools with predictive models might help to arrange resources such as tutorials, online discussions, and library assistance meets the need of students more effectively. With a slightly different view, Siemens (2010) defined learning analytics as the use of learner-produced intelligent data and analysis models to discover information and social connections and to predict and advise on learning. In 2011, Siemens and Long indicated that learning analytics is the measurement, collection, analysis and reporting of data about learners and their contexts, for purposes of understanding and optimizing learning and the environments in which it occurs. Bichsel (2012), however, defined analytics as the use of data, statistical analysis, and explanatory and predictive models to gain insights and act on complex issues. Learning analytics is also defined as the collection and analysis of usage data associated with student learning and its purpose is to observe and understand learning behaviours in order to enable appropriate interventions (Brown, 2011). Learning analytics is focused on the data students leave behind in the learning process and utilises this learner activity or 'traces' to improve success for students through provision of support or adaptive learning processes (Fisher et al., 2014). They also suggest that learning analytics provides data related to students' interaction with learning materials which can inform pedagogically sound decisions about learning design (Fisher et al., 2014, p. 9).

Verbert et al. (2012) in their study on dataset driven research to support learning analytics found that many datasets can help to predict learner performance and discover learner models (also see Romero et al., 2008). Other studies have outlined the use of learning analytics including: accessing learning resources (Verbert et al., 2011); fostering learner awareness and reflection about the learning process (Govaerts et al., 2010); enhancing learning environment (Hausmann et al., 2008; Stahl, 2009; Reffay & Chanier, 2003); detecting student unusual behaviours (Baker et al., 2006; Scheffel et al., 2011), and detecting effects on learners (also see Reffay et al., 2011; Conati & Maclaren, 2005). Elias (2011) noted that the most promising aspect of learning analytics is the power to predict patterns and trends based on historical and current data. More concisely, Macfadyen and Dawson (2010) noted that, providing data from an international research project investigating which online student activities accurately predict academic achievement (p. 588). They also discovered that learning management system data variables are significant indicators of student success in a course. Meaningful information extracted from a system and made available to educators via a dashboard-like interface that incorporates predictive models and network visualization tools can help to provide statistically significant prediction of student outcomes, like increased student engagement with peers and course material, and higher overall final grades (Macfadyen & Dawson, 2010, p. 597).

Despite being few in number, studies so far have focused on the following as the predictors of student engagement. The first predictor can be found under the name of students' personal attributes. According to Fullarton (2002), students' self-concept of ability proves to be a significant predictor. Similarly, Duran et al. (2006) in their study of undergraduate students in Spain found that emotional intelligence and self-efficacy can be considered important predictors of student engagement. Moreover, in the same study, Fullarton (2002) also recognised that the gender and parents' education has influence on the level of engagement of students. Female students tend to be more engaged than males and the level of parents' education is significantly related to engagement. Situational factors, can be looked at as another predictor of student engagement (Sharma & Bhaumik, 2013). Pike and Kuh (2005) found that the policies and practices in the institutions have impact on the level of student engagement at the campus.

6 Emerging Trends in Learning

In an environment with increased focus on quality outcomes there is a need to assess the effectiveness of university courses and the extent to which courses are preparing for student success. A recent study in Australia on first year experience suggests that students with low academic achievement in high school are less able to cope with university study, displaying lower levels of academic engagement than other students. The study also found that these students are less likely to enjoy the intellectual challenge of studying, less likely to enjoy their course, less likely to find their subjects intellectually stimulating, and find it more difficult to get motivated to study (Baik et al., 2015a). Another national study on student experience found low levels of student engagement amongst mature and indigenous students. The study found a negative association between the age of the student and the learners' engagement. Younger students (aged under 25) were much more likely to be satisfied with their level of engagement than students in the three older age groups, and students aged 40 and over (Graduate Careers Australia, 2015a).

There have been substantial changes in the economic structure in Australia such as collapse of manufacturing jobs, upsurge in service sector employment and the 'mining boom' (Connolly & Lewis, 2010), demographic behaviour such as fertility declines, rise of de facto relationships, postponement of parenthood (de Vaus, 2004), and the educational system such as improved school completion rates and increasing participation in tertiary education (Marks, Fleming, Long, & McMillan, 2000). Collectively, these structural changes have had immense impacts on the lives of young people (Tomaszewski, Perales, & Xiang, 2016). The traditional pathways from school to work on the one hand, or to University on the other, have become only two options within a growing set of available alternatives (Brzinsky-Fay, 2014). It has been documented that emerging options acting as alternatives to tertiary education have been disproportionately chosen by young people from disadvantaged backgrounds. Australian research shows that students from low socio-economic backgrounds and regional or remote areas within Australia are over-represented in the Vocational Educational and Training (VET) sector (Foley, 2007). This is important, as another body of evidence indicates that VET is not an effective pathway to University for students (Wheelahan, 2009; Tomaszewski, Perales, & Xiang, 2016).

Participation at University and the attainment of tertiary level educational qualifications are amongst the strongest predictors of subsequent success in the labour market, including the attainment of secure and continuous employment (ABS, 2015; OECD, 2006), high productivity and wage growth (Borland, 2002; Daly, Lewis, Corliss, & Heaslip, 2015), occupational standing (Hauser, Warren, Huang, & Carter, 2000; Pascarella & Terenzini, 2005), and job satisfaction (Ross & Reskin, 1992). As a result of their improved work prospects, University educated individuals are also less likely to live in households which fall below the poverty line, be dependent on income-support from the Government, and report financial difficulties (Connelly, Sullivan, & Jerrim, 2014; McLachlan, Gilfillan, & Gordon, 2013; Perales et al., 2014; Raffo et al., 2007). University qualifications are known precursors of health and wellbeing. For example, individuals with degree-level education are less likely to be in poor physical health (Ross & Van Willigen, 1997; Ross & Wu, 1995), suffer from mental disorders (Anstey & Christensen, 2000), and adopt risky health behaviours, such as smoking, drinking and substance abuse (Hill, White, & Scollo, 1998). They also have higher life expectancy and greater overall quality of life (Edgerton & von Below, 2012). In addition, degree-level education is negatively related to the probability of family breakdown (Tzeng, 1992), and positively correlated with child development and child outcomes (Wolfe & Haveman, 2001). Hence, a social system that expands University participation is desirable, and so is a system which guarantees that the benefits of University participation are not restricted to individuals from advantaged social collectives (Tomaszewski, Perales, & Xiang, 2016).

The publication of "A Fair Chance for All" report (DEET, 1990), formally identified six equity groups on the basis of underrepresentation in Higher Education. Following this, a set of Higher Education equity performance indicators were developed (Martin, 1994). More recently, the 2008 Review of Australian Higher Education (the 'Bradley Review') (Bradley, Noonan, Nugent, & Scales, 2008), and the response by the Australian Government, Transforming Australia's Higher Education System (Commonwealth of Australia, 2009), set out specific participation targets to be achieved by 2025. This resulted in the establishment of the Higher Education Participation Program (HEPP) with initiatives to promote University participation among equity-group students funded at both the institutional and system levels. Following this policy focus, educational disadvantage in the context of university participation in Australia has been typically considered with reference to the six equity groups identified in the "A Fair Chance for All" report (DEET, 1990). The six equity groups are:

(i)   Aboriginal and Torres Strait Islander Australians;
(ii)   People from low socio-economic backgrounds;
(iii) People from non-English-speaking backgrounds;
(iv)   People from regional or remote areas;
(v)   People with disability; and
(vi)   Women in non-traditional subject areas.

These groups have been the focus of policies aimed at improving University participation among people from disadvantaged backgrounds, and their performance is routinely monitored by the Australian Government using five indicators (CSHE, 2008):

(i)   Access—measured as the proportion of equity group students out of all commencing domestic students;

(ii)   Participation—measured as the proportion of equity group students out of all domestic students overall;

(iii) Retention—measured as the proportion of equity group students who re-enrol at an institution in the next year;

(iv)   Success—measured as the mean student progress rate for the previous year for students from the equity group; and

(v)   Completion—measured as the proportion of equity group students completing all the academic requirements of a course (Tomaszewski, Perales, & Xiang, 2016).

The completion rates for students who aspire to a STEMM degree remain lower than in non-STEMM fields. Completion rates are lower for students from underrepresented groups compared to their white and Asian counterparts. Many students also take longer than expected to complete their credentials. In addition, the goals of STEMM aspirants earning a degree or certificate, transferring or gaining a specific job skill and student populations vary. Factors such as student goals, course completion, credit accumulation, time to and credits to degree, retention and transfer rates, degrees awarded, range of access along with graduation rates when assessing the success of an institution are important considerations (National Academies of Sciences, Engineering, and Medicine, 2016)

It is apparent that fields requiring STEMM skills are abundant. Based on the projections reported by Giffi et al. (2015), a shortage of STEMM skilled is likely to reach two million over the next decade if there is no further intervention. Yet the number of students with interest in STEMM remains substantially low (Chen & Soldner, 2013). This seems to defy logic, given that the single most common concern students express before deciding on a major is their chances of finding a job with a degree in a given field. Past experience also shows that the more marketable a given specialty/field is, the higher the enrolments in the relevant programs, for example Nursing and Business. STEMM programs, however, are an anomaly in this regard. The majority of students who enrol in STEMM related majors do not graduate with a STEMM degree. Based on a three year study of student interviews and enrolment patterns, Correll, Seymour, and Hewitt (1997) reported that about 40% of those who enrol in engineering change their programs to non-science and non-technical majors; 50% drop out of physical and biological sciences and 60% drop out of mathematics programs (Sithole, Chiyaka, McCarthy, Mupinga, Bucklein, & Kibirige, 2017). Likewise Tai et al. (2006), reported that science programs have experienced considerable declines in the number of graduates. Despite the fact that STEMM programs have contributed immensely to our daily livelihoods, student inter-est toward these sciences remains low, worldwide. In the U.S., the physical sci-ences are among the least popular fields, attracting only about 3% of students that enrol in STEM fields (Chen & Soldner, 2013). Also, academic performance and overall success of the U.S. students was found to be lower for STEMM grad-uates when compared to those in Australia, China, England, Japan, and Russia (Sunstein, 2013; Sithole, Chiyaka, McCarthy, Mupinga, Bucklein, & Kibirige, 2017).

The two groups of students with high dropouts are under-represented minority students and female students (National Science Board, 2008). Thus, race/ethnicity and gender seem to be significant groups that require inter-vention. The overall major contributing factors to STEMM attrition have been deficiencies in analytical and mathematical skills, which are critical to suc-cess in STEMM programs (Mattern, Radunzel, & Westrick, 2015). (Sithole, Chiyaka, McCarthy, Mupinga, Bucklein, & Kibirige, 2017). According to Rogers and Ford (1997), students' dislike of STEMM programs is a result of several unpleasant experiences in science courses. These experiences may include poor teaching techniques by some instructors; lack of interest in working hard, lack of students' self-interest, social backgrounds, poor institutional support mechanisms (Cheryan, Master, & Meltzoff, 2015). To all this is added the media's negative stereotyping of STEMM related programs (Rogers & Ford, 1997) which reinforces the already culturally entrenched view that the "Sci-ences" are extra hard subjects and are suited for a very select few persons with extra intelligence.

Some STEMM instructors concentrate only on non-pedagogical research and publication, with almost no effort to improve teaching techniques and virtually no attempts to offer initiatives to improve students' interest in the courses. It seems to be taken for granted that students will naturally, somehow by "osmo-sis," or mere proximity, develop positive attitudes toward science as they take science classes (Sithole, Chiyaka, McCarthy, Mupinga, Bucklein, & Kibirige, 2017). A recent study noted that 45% of incoming students had significant prob-lems with mathematics, which is central to competencies in STEMM programs (Noel-Levitz, 2013). Other studies have shown that the majority of STEMM stu-dents would end up dropping out, fail, or change their majors to professional programs, social sciences, humanities or business (Ost, 2010). According to the 2010 National Survey on STEMM Education (STEM Market Impact, LLC, 2010), STEMM education faces a number of challenges which include insufficient funding in K-12, lack of professional development for STEMM teachers, and inadequacy of STEMM education in K-8. The disjunction between availability of opportunities in STEMM careers and the lack of enthusiasm to go into those careers is a paradox that needs to be disentangled. This must also be seen in the context of the fact that STEMM jobs are not only more available but also pay far higher salaries than jobs in other fields. Thus, the inhibiting factors against STEMM careers seem to be powerful enough to even counter the monetary rewards and social prestige that comes with being a "Scientist." In most familiar situations, this would be "a risk worth taking" but in this case it is a "risk worth avoiding" (Sithole, Chiyaka, McCarthy, Mupinga, Bucklein, & Kibirige, 2017).

High attrition, low motivation, and low entrant numbers are big challenges for STEMM education growth. Griffith (2010) found a positive association between high academic performance with low dropout and high graduation rates in STEMM programs. A survey by Chen and Soldner (2013) found that on average the STEMM grades were relatively lower than non-STEMM grades. Whether the difference in these grades is related to the inherent demand for more work due to high course loads or rigor in STEMM programs is not well known. However, there is a general concern that STEMM programs do not give students adequate time for extracurricular activities. Both these concerns and the differential in grades could be contributing factors to STEMM drop-outs or switch-outs. In addition, laboratory part of the course is often coupled with their respective courses but with little direct credit assigned to them. For example, a course in physics or chemistry can have two and a half hours of lectures three days a week in addition to two "Lab" hours a week. In this day and age where maximum rewards are expected with minimum effort, within the shortest time possible, the students' disjunction between work load and expected corresponding "rewards" seems to hold much credibility (Sithole, Chiyaka, McCarthy, Mupinga, Bucklein, & Kibirige, 2017).

Processes which include integration of curriculum with career and life goals, sharing of responsibility in monitoring progress, and referring to resources for non-academic issues and co-curricular activities have been shown to be impor-tant factors in a student's success (Berdhal, 1995). Academic advising is a com-plex process. Every student is unique and requires advising that is geared to their individual circumstances and needs. Ironically, the more variations in the stu-dent circumstances, the more the advising process needs to be organized and structured. Given all the student variations, all the more reason for the need for an advising framework which a systematic structure which we can use to address the unique situations. As it is today, however, in most institutions, there is hardly a systematic form of training for faculty advisors. It seems to be mostly a mat-ter of figuring out what courses to take when and, therefore, paving out a road-map to graduation. The implications of all this is that institutions need to have mechanisms that support faculty development in students' advising. Another dimension is to encourage frequent student professor face to face interactions.

The developmental advising model is student centered and might include helping students integrate life, career and educational goals and is believed to be more effective compared to the prescriptive advising model which uses a top-down approach (Smith & Allen, 2006). The major problem here would be lack of personnel. Most institutions are "spread thin," when it comes to faculty personnel and this involves financial implications. Ideally, however, this would be the recommendation. Various studies have indicated that blending courses could lead to better student performance, perceptions, and attitudes toward the course, and higher attendance rates (Riffell & Sibley, 2004). Computer-based technologies have been successfully incorporated into traditional classes to supplement face-to-face instruction. Such activities include class discussions and virtual pre-laboratories using computer simulated activities, among others (Sithole, Chiyaka, McCarthy, Mupinga, Bucklein, & Kibirige, 2017).

Garnham, Kaleta, and Sudzina (2003) asserted that incorporating online activities into classes could motivate students in introductory classes. In addition, a website for the classes would also be helpful. However, maintaining and operating a viable course site adds financial stress to some institutions, in addition to the considerable amount of time needed to incorporate online activities into the traditional face-to-face format. Education and learning are dynamic processes. Likewise, while facts per se may be fixed (for example, the law of gravity), knowledge itself is not static. Knowledge changes according to changes in the wider society and according to the tools available at a given time. As noted elsewhere (Sithole et al., 2016) culture shapes knowledge, including scientific knowledge. The facts may be the same but their interpretation will depend on the cultural perceptions of the people amongst whom they occur. Education, therefore, cannot be conducted as if it is frozen in time. Pedagogical approaches must meet changes as they occur. Society changes dramatically so do technological tools available, the nature of the people and students. Education is a service activity and must be responsive to the changing needs of its clientele. Knowledge must be relevant but also appealing to the generation of students served. In that regard, several pedagogical approaches have been devised to motivate students to learn, including media not usually associated with subjects like science, for example magazines/newspapers (Sithole et al., 2016; Sithole, Chiyaka, McCarthy, Mupinga, Bucklein, & Kibirige, 2017).

7 Connection between Curricula and Career

According to Dancy and Henderson (2008), most of the money has been spent on research and development but very little effort has been targeted toward understanding and improving the integration of the outcomes from research in classrooms. Chalmers (2013), identified three important themes in the outcomes of science: (a) problem-solving; (b) scientific reasoning; and (c) demand for evidence to validate claims. STEMM courses improve problem-solving skills, scientific and logical reasoning skills, and quantitative reasoning. These skills help students to develop the ability to support their conclusions using well-reasoned arguments. However, on the other side of the aisle, the scant connection between curricula and career needs in STEMM programs makes these disciplines less attractive than other programs. In STEMM there is more protracted emphasis on academic mastery of concepts than career applications and relevancy. This has led to low-paying part-time careers with no job security. Instructional practices must, therefore, be adjusted to meet these challenges.

Some of the challenges faced by students are inherently dependent on student classroom preparation, and attitude. Lack of Mathematics skills results in poor basic numerical manipulation which leads to low confidence and failure. (Sithole, Chiyaka, McCarthy, Mupinga, Bucklein, & Kibirige, 2017). According to Hewson (2011), "students who freeze at the sight of numbers or equations will most certainly underperform" in STEMM. Hewson (2011) further stated that mathematics studied independently of applications remains abstract, dull, and difficult. Mathematics is used every day in STEMM as a tool to understanding the laws of nature and other concepts in these disciplines, which are often written in mathematical language. Examples of such concepts are vectors, logarithms, complex numbers, basic algebra, and calculus, which are often used in introductory physical science courses. In upper-level courses, more complex Mathematics concepts are required. For example, quantum mechanics, statistical mechanics, analytical mechanics, and electromagnetism require higher order Mathematics proficiency to understand them. Often, the struggles with the Mathematics concepts and/or a negative attitude toward Mathematics plays crucial roles in the success or failure of students (Popham, 2005). Clearly, success in STEMM strongly depends on the knowledge and interest in analytical skills (Sithole, Chiyaka, McCarthy, Mupinga, Bucklein, & Kibirige, 2017).

Hewson (2011) agrees that some students with good grades in Mathematics may not do well in sciences, engineering, and technology because of lack of confidence and/or interest. Also, there is a high degree of variance in Mathematics proficiency needed for different courses in STEMM programs. For example, programs such as physics, chemistry, geosciences, materials science, meteorology, and astronomy, have different approaches in mathematical treatment of problems and difficulty. Various studies have shown that studying habits determine the academic performance of students (Stinebrickner &

Stinebrickner, 2007). Study habits differ across different disciplines. Understanding study habits could be the foundation to motivate students to change their attitude towards learning STEMM. Typically, studying STEMM courses requires more time of study than most courses due to laboratory course requirements and research obligations. Moreover, some courses may demand more concentration and take more time to learn than others. This is typical with learning new Mathematics concepts. While there are some habits that can be developed or changes made through coaching, others require a change of attitude and personal commitment (Sithole, Chiyaka, McCarthy, Mupinga, Bucklein, & Kibirige, 2017).

Some students require inspiration, stimulation, and challenges, while others are naturally enthusiastic about the learning process. There are two major classes of motivation based on the reasons for accomplishing any given task: intrinsic motivation and extrinsic motivation. Intrinsic motivation refers to doing something because of inherent interest. The motivation force, here, is "interest." Without interest in what students do on academic work, they do not realize them as important to try and solve. For example, students may not appreciate why determining the maximum point of a curve is important if the concept has no meaning in real life to them. Extrinsic motivation, on the other hand, refers to completing a task for a gain (Ryan & Deci, 2000). Intrinsic motivation has emerged as the favorite among educators because it leads to desirable student learning outcomes and creativity (Ryan & Deci, 2000). According to Ryan and Deci (2000), extrinsic motivation makes students "complete tasks with resentment, resistance, and disinterest or, alternatively, with an attitude of willingness that reflects an inner acceptance of the value or utility of a task" (pp. 54–67). This, they argued, was because the student feels externally propelled rather than doing it through self-motivation. Understanding these different types of motivation helps educators to identify the best methods of motivating students towards programs. According to Bandura (1978), the ability to persist in the face of aversive experiences and obstacles is dependent on the strength of personal self-efficacy. In this study, he proposed that personal self-efficacy was mostly driven by psychological state, personal accomplishments, verbal persuasion, and vicarious experience. These factors are important in enhancing motivation and performance attainment (Bandura & Locke, 2003). In addition, the level of confidence for attaining specific goals determines the ability of a student to persist (Bong & Skaalvik, 2003). (Sithole, Chiyaka, McCarthy, Mupinga, Bucklein, & Kibirige, 2017).

Studies indicate that students with high self-efficacy were likely to perform better and persist longer than their peers with lower self-efficacy (Rittmayer & Beyer, 2008). The study of confidence or self-efficacy has a long history

(Fullerton & Cattell, 1892; Henmon, 1911). Studies on first year experience and retention has shown that students who are confident in their university study have better chances of remaining and progressing compared to less confident students (Archer, Cantwell, & Bourke, 1999; Habel, 2012). This idea extends the research to the findings of Atherton and Bailey (2014) and Atherton (2015, 2017). The study of confidence and uncertainty has been carried out for a number of years and a picture has formed of the enabling students and their experience of the assessments that they encounter in university courses. Limited studies have been undertaken with vulnerable students who are thought of as disadvantaged by location; financial pressures; low academic achievement in high school; failure to complete high school; illness or other personal reasons; lack of appropriate careers advice; parental discouragement of higher education; limited university education attainment within the family; a lack of confidence in one's ability to undertake university education; parenting or carer responsibilities; mental health issues; and a variety of other social problems (Shah et al., 2014). Since vulnerability can be transient, some students may be at risk at some stage as they progress on their learning journey. The increasing use of technology in learning has produced valuable data to detect vulnerability and change the prospects of each and every student.

References

Abbott-Chapman, J. (2011). Making the most of the mosaic: Facilitating post-school transitions to higher education of disadvantaged students. *The Australian Educational Researcher, 38*, 57–71.

AITSL (Australian Institute for Teaching and School Leadership). (2013). *Engagement in Australian schools.* AITSL, Melbourne. Retrieved September 30, 2015, from http://www.aitsl.edu.au/docs/default-source/default-document-library/engagement_in_australian_schools__grattan

Alpay, E., Hari, A., Kambouri, M., & Ahearn, A. L. (2010). Gender issues in the university research environment. *European Journal of Engineering Education, 35*(2), 135–145. doi:10.1080/03043790903497302

Anderson, G. (2006). Assuring quality/resisting quality assurance: Academics' responses to 'quality' in some Australian universities. *Quality in Higher Education, 12*(2), 161–173.

Anderson, H. (2007). Bridging to the future: What works? *Australian Journal of Adult Learning, 47*(3), 453–465.

Anderson, J., & Boyle, C. (2015). Inclusive education in Australia: Rhetoric, reality and the road ahead. *Support for Learning, 30*(1), 4–22.

Appleton, J. J., Christenson, S. L., & Furlong, M. J. (2008). Student engagement with school: Critical conceptual and methodological issues of the construct. *Psychology in the Schools, 45*(5), 369–386.

Archambault, I., Janosz, M., Fallu, J. S., & Pagani, L. S. (2009). Student engagement and its relationship with early high school dropout. *Journal of Adolescence, 32*(3), 651–670.

Archer, J., Cantwell, R., & Bourke, S. (1999). Coping at university: An examination of achievement, motivation, self-regulation, confidence, and method of entry. *Higher Education Research and Development, 18*(1), 31–54.

Archer, L., Halsall, A., Hollingworth, S., & Mendick, H. (2005). *Dropping out and drifting away: An investigation of factors affecting student identities and aspirations*. London: IPSE. Retrieved from http://www.drugsandalcohol.ie/6281/1/3505-3725.pdf

Archer, L., Hollingworth, S., & Halsall, A. (2007). University's not for me—I'm a Nike person: Urban, working-class young people's negotiations of style. Identity and educational engagement. *Sociology, 41*(2), 219–237.

Arnold, K. E., & Pistilli, M. D. (2012, April). Course signals at Purdue: Using learning analytics to increase student success. In *Proceedings of the 2nd International Conference on Learning Analytics and Knowledge* (pp. 267–270). New York, NY: ACM.

Asmar, C., Page, S., & Radloff, A. (2011). *Dispelling myths: Indigenous students' engagement with university. Australian Survey of Student Engagement*. Melbourne: *Australian* Council for Educational Research (ACER).

Astin, A. W. (1984). Student involvement: A developmental theory for higher education. *Journal of College Student Personnel, 25*(4), 297–308.

Astin, A. W. (1985a). *Achieving educational excellence*. San Francisco, CA: Jossey-Bass.

Astin, A. W. (1985b). Involvement the cornerstone of excellence. *Change: The Magazine of Higher Learning, 17*(4), 35–39.

Astin, A. W. (1999). Student involvement: A developmental theory for higher education. *Journal of College Student Development, 40*(5), 518–529.

Astone, N. M., & McLanahan, S. S. (1991). Family structure, parental practices and high school completion. *American Sociological Review, 56*, 309–320.

Atherton, M. (2015). Measuring confidence levels of male and female students in open access enabling courses. *Issues in Educational Research, 25*(2), 81–98.

Atherton, M., & Bailey, A. (2014). Assessing disadvantaged student confidence in learning: A case of enabling pathway programs. *Journal of Institutional Research, 12*(2), 41–53.

Baik, C., Arkoudis, S., & Naylor, R. (2015). *The first year experience in Australian universities: Findings from two decades, 1994–2014*. Melbourne: Melbourne Centre for the Study of Higher Education.

Baik, C., Naylor, R., & Arkoudis, S. (2015). *The first year experience in Australian Universities: Findings from two decades, 1994–2014*. Melbourne: Melbourne Centre for the Study of Higher Education. Retrieved from http://www.cshe.unimelb.edu.au/research/rec_publications/FYE%202014%20FULL%20report%20-%20FINAL%20-%20web.pdf

Baker, B. M. (2007). *A conceptual framework for making knowledge actionable through capital formation* (Doctoral dissertation). University of Maryland University College, Adelphi, MD.

Baker, R. (2011). *Defamation law and social attitudes: Ordinary unreasonable people.* Cheltenham: Edward Elgar Publishing.

Baker, R. S. J., Corbett, A. T., Koedinger, K. R., Evenson, S., Roll, I., Wagner, A. Z., Naim, M., Raspat, J., Baker, D., & Beck, J. (2006). Adapting to when students game an intelligent tutoring system. In M. Ikeda, K. D. Ashley, & T. W. Chan (Eds.), *Proceedings of the 8th international conference on intelligent tutoring systems* (pp. 392–401). Berlin: Springer.

Becker, M. R., McCaleb, K., & Baker, C. (2015). Paradigm shift toward student engagement in technology mediated courses. In *Handbook of research on innovative technology integration in higher education* (p. 74). Hershey, PA: IGI Global.

Bichsel, J. (2012). *Analytics in higher education: Benefits, barriers, progress, and recommendations.* Louisville, CO: EDUCAUSE Center for Applied Research.

Biggs, J., & Tang, C. (2003). *Teaching for quality learning at university.* Maidenhead: Society for Research into Higher Education.

Booth, A. (1997). Listening to students: Experiences and expectations in the transition to a history degree. *Studies in Higher Education, 22*(2), 205–220.

Bowers-Brown, T. (2006). Widening participation in higher education amongst students from disadvantaged socio-economic groups. *Tertiary Education and Management, 12*(1), 59–74.

Bowles, T., & Hattie, J. (2016). Seven motivating conceptions of learning of tertiary students. *International Journal of Learning, Teaching and Educational Research, 15*(3).

Brown, M. (2011). Learning analytics: The coming third wave. *EDUCAUSE Learning Initiative Brief, 1,* 1–4.

Brown, S. J., White, S., Sharma, B., Wakeling, L., Naiker, M., Chandra, S., & Bilimoria, V. (2015). Attitude to the study of chemistry and its relationship with achievement in an introductory undergraduate course. *Journal of the Scholarship of Teaching and Learning, 15*(2), 33–41.

Buckley, S. (2016). *Gender and sex differences in student participation, achievement and engagement in mathematics.* Melbourne: Australian Council for Educational Research.

Burgess, C., & Relf, B. (2014). Improving academic outcomes of enabling student in undergraduate nursing. *Journal of Institutional Research in South East Asia, 12*(1), 97–108.

Business Industry Advisory Committee to the OECD. (2008). *Comments on the OECD project on trade, innovation and growth.* Paris: BAIC.

Campbell, S. (2008, September). *Assessment reform as a stimulus for quality improvement in university learning and teaching: An Australian case study.* Paper presented at the OECD Conference Outcomes of Higher Education, Quality Relevance and Impact.

Cantwell, R., Archer, J., & Bourke, S. (2001). A comparison of the academic experiences and achievement of university students entering by traditional and non-traditional means. *Assessment & Evaluation in Higher Education, 26*(3), 221–234.

Carini, R. M., Kuh, G. D., & Klein, S. P. (2006). Student engagement and student learning: Testing the linkages. *Research in Higher Education, 47*(1), 1–32.

Chalmers, D., & Gardiner, D. (2015). An evaluation framework for identifying the effectiveness and impact of academic teacher development programmes. *Studies in Educational Evaluation, 46*, 81–91.

Clifton, J., Díaz-Fuentes, D., & Fernández-Gutiérrez, M. (2013). *How consumers' socio-economic background influences satisfaction: Insights for better utility regulation.* Retrieved September 20, 2016, from https://mpra.ub.uni-muenchen.de/47271/

Clow, D. (2013). An overview of learning analytics. *Teaching in Higher Education, 18*(6), 683–695.

Coaldrake, P., & Stedman, L. (1999). *Academic work in the twenty-first century.* Canberra: Higher Education Division, Training and Youth Affairs.

Coates, H. (2005). The value of student engagement for higher education quality assurance. *Quality in Higher Education, 11*(1), 25–36.

Coates, H. (2008). *Beyond happiness: Managing engagement to enhance satisfaction and grades.* Melbourne: *Australian* Council for Educational *Research.*

Coates, H. (2009). *Engaging students for success. Australasian student engagement report. Australasian survey of student engagement.* Camberwell: Australian Council for Educational Research.

Coates, H. (2010). *Getting first-year students engaged: Research briefing: Australasian student engagement report.* Camberwell: Australian Council for Educational Research.

Coates, H., & Ransom, L. (2011). *Dropout DNA, and the genetics of effective support.* Retrieved October 12, 2015, from http://research.acer.edu.au/cgi/viewcontent.cgi?article=1000&context=ausse

Conati, C., & Maclaren, H. (2005). Data-driven refinement of a probabilistic model of user affect. In L. Ardissono, P. Brna, & A. Mitrovic (Éd.), *User modeling 2005* (Vol. 3538, pp. 40–49). Berlin: Springer.

Coombes, P., & Danaher, G. (2006). From the margins to the centre: The power of transformative learning in Australia. *Teaching and Teacher Education, 22*(7), 759–765.

Cordero, E., Porter, S., Israel, T., & Brown, M. (2010). Math and science pursuits: A self-efficacy intervention comparison study. *Journal of Career Assessment, 18*(4), 362–375. doi:10.1177/1069072710374572

Corno, L. (1993). The best-laid plans modern conceptions of volition and educational research. *Educational Researcher, 22*(2), 14–22.

Crock, M., Baker, J., & Turner-Walker, S. (2014). Open universities Australia. *Open Source Technology,* 320–335.

Crumpton, H. E., & Gregory, A. (2011). I'm not learning: The role of academic relevancy for low-achieving students. *The Journal of Educational Research, 104*(1), 42–53.

Cuthill, M., & Jansen, D. (2013). Initial results from a longitudinal impact study focusing on a higher education 'widening participation' program in Australia. *Widening Participation and Lifelong Learning, 15*(1), 7–21.

Cybela. (2002). *Engaging learners in learning checklist.* Retrieved October 12, 2015, from http://www.uwex.edu/erc/doc/ai/EngagingLearners.doc

Dawe, S. (2004). Enabling learners: Diverse outcomes. *NCVER, AVETRA 2004,* 1–10.

Devine, C., Brady, J. P., Moody, H. R., Wilson, T., Liu, Y., Medland, R., & Lightbody, I. D. (2016). *Why volunteer? What stimulates involvement in a STEM peer learning facilitation program?* Paper presented at the Australian Conference on Science and Mathematics Education, University of Queensland, Brisbane.

Devlin, M. (2013). Bridging socio-cultural incongruity: Conceptualising the success of students from low socio-economic status backgrounds in Australian higher education. *Studies in Higher Education, 38*(6), 939–949.

Devlin, M., Kift, S., Nelson, K., Smith, L., & McKay, J. (2012). *Practical advice for teaching staff.* Retrieved October 12, 2015, from http://www.lowses.edu.au/assets/Practical%20Advice%20for%20Teaching%20Staff.pdf

Denson, N., & Bowman, N. (2013). University diversity and preparation for a global society: The role of diversity in shaping intergroup attitudes and civic outcomes. *Studies in Higher Education, 38*(4), 555–570.

Dias, D. (2015). Has massification of higher education led to more equity? Clues to a reflection on Portuguese education arena. *International Journal of Inclusive Education, 19*(2), 103–120.

Dringus, L. P. (2012). Learning analytics con- sidered harmful. *Journal of Asynchronous Learning Networks, 16*(3), 87–100.

Dryburgh, H. (2000). Underrepresentation of girls and women in computer science: Classification of 1990s research. *Journal of Educational Computing Research, 23*(2), 181–202. doi:10.2190/8RYV-9JWH-XQMB-QF41

Duran, A., Extremera, N., Rey, L., Fernández-Berrocal, P., & Montalbán, F. M. (2006). Predicting academic burnout and engagement in educational settings: Assessing the incremental validity of perceived emotional intelligence beyond perceived stress and general self-efficacy. *Psicothema, 18*(Suppl.), 158–164.

Dymock, D. (2007). *Engaging adult learners: The role of non-accredited learning in language, literacy and numeracy*. Canberra: Adult Learning Australia.

EDUCAUSE. (2010). *7 Things you should know about analytics*. Retrieved November 18, 2015, from https://net.educause.edu/ir/library/pdf/ELI7059.pdf

Edwards, J., Crosling, G., & Edwards, R. (2010). Outsourcing university degrees: Implications for quality control. *Journal of Higher Education Policy and Management, 32*(3), 303–315.

Elena, C. (2011). Business intelligence. *Journal of Knowledge Management, Economics and Information Technology, 1*(2), 101–113.

Elias, T. (2011). *Learning analytics: The definitions, the processes, and the potential*. Retrieved from http://learninganalytics.net/LearningAnalyticsDefinitionsProcesses Potential.pdf

Erling, E. J., & Richardson, J. T. (2010). Measuring the academic skills of university students: Evaluation of a diagnostic procedure. *Assessing Writing, 15*(3), 177–193.

Fiaidhi, J. (2014). The next step for learning analytics. *IT Professional, 5*, 4–8.

Finn, J. D. (1993). *School engagement and students at risk*. Washington, DC: National Center for Education Statistics.

Finn, J. D., & Zimmer, K. S. (2012). Student engagement: What is it? Why does it matter? In *Handbook of research on student engagement* (pp. 97–131). New York, NY: Springer.

Fisher, J., Valenzuela, R., & Whale, S. (2014). *Learning analytics: A bottom-up approach to enhancing and evaluating students' online learning*. Retrieved from http://www.olt.gov.au/resource-library

Fleming, M. J., & Grace, D. M. (2015). Eyes on the future: The impact of a university campus experience day on students from financially disadvantaged backgrounds. *Australian Journal of Education*, 1–15. doi:10.1177/0004944114567689

Forrester, G., Motteram, G., Parkinson, G., & Slaouti, D. (2005). Going the distance: Students' experiences of induction to distance learning in higher education. *Journal of Further and Higher Education, 29*(4), 293–306.

Forsyth, A., & Furlong, A. (2003). *Socio-economic disadvantage and access to higher education*. Bristol: Policy Press.

Forsyth, R. (2013). The right to higher education: Beyond widening participation. *Widening Participation and Lifelong Learning, 15*(1), 71–73.

Fredricks, J. A., Blumenfeld, P. C., & Paris, A. H. (2004). School engagement: Potential of the concept, state of the evidence. *Review of Educational Research, 74*(1), 59–109.

Fullarton, S. (2002). *Student engagement with school: Individual and school-level influences*. Camberwell: Australian Council for Educational Research.

Fullerton, G., & Mckeen Cattell, J. (1892). *On the perception of small differences*. Philadelphia, PA: University of Pennsylvania.

Gale, T. (2011). Student equity's starring role in Australian higher education: Not yet centre field. *The Australian Educational Researcher, 38*(1), 5–23.

Gaskell, A., & Mills, P. (2014). The quality and reputation of open, distance and e-learning: What are the challenges? Open learning. *The Journal of Open, Distance and eLearning, 29*(3), 190–205.

Goldstein, P. J., & Katz, R. N. (2005). *Academic analytics: The uses of management information and technology in higher education.* Retrieved November 15, 2015, from https://net.educause.edu/ir/library/pdf/ecar_so/ers/ers0508/EKF0508.pdf

Goodenow, C. (1993). Classroom belonging among early adolescent student relationships to motivation and achievement. *The Journal of Early Adolescence, 13*(1), 21–43.

Goodenow, C., & Grady, K. E. (1993). The relationship of school belonging and friends' values to academic motivation among urban adolescent students. *The Journal of Experimental Education, 62*(1), 60–71.

Gough, D. (2014, September 18). Does 'university access for all' mean lowering standards? *The Conversation.*

Govaerts, S., Verbert, K., Klerkx, J., & Duval, E. (2010). Visualizing activities for self-reflection and awareness. In X. Luo, M. Spaniol, L. Wang, Q. Li, W. Nejdl, & W. Zhang (Eds.), *Advances in web-based learning* (pp. 91–100). Berlin: Springer.

Graduate Careers Australia (GCA). (2015a). *2014 university experience survey national report.* Melbourne: Graduate Careers Australia (GCA).

Graduate Careers Australia (GCA). (2015b). *University experience survey national report 2014.* Retrieved from http://docs.education.gov.au/system/files/doc/other/ues14_report_final_access2a.pdf

Grebennikov, L., & Shah, M. (2012). Commencing student experience: New insights and implications for action. *European Journal of Higher Education, 2*(2–3), 267–289.

Greene, T. G., Marti, C. N., & McClenney, K. (2008). The effort-outcome gap: Differences for African American and Hispanic community college students in student engagement and academic achievement. *The Journal of Higher Education, 79*(5), 513–539.

Greenland, S. J., & Moore, C. (2014). Patterns of online student enrolment and attrition in Australian open access online education: A preliminary case study. *Open Praxis, 6*(1), 45–54.

Habel, C. (2012). 'I can do it, and how!' Student experience in access and equity pathways to higher education. *Higher Education Research and Development, 31*(6), 811–825. doi:10.1080/07294360.2012.659177

Hall, L. (2015). What are the key ingredients for an effective and successful tertiary enabling program for Aboriginal and Torres Strait Islander students? An evaluation of the evolution of one program. *Australian Journal of Adult Learning, 55*(2), 244.

Hancock, M., Davies, R., & McGrenere, J. (2004). *Focus on women in computer science.* In Western Canadian Conference on Computing Education 2004. Retrieved from http://www.cs.ubc.ca/wccce/program04/Papers/mark.html

Handelsman, M. M., Briggs, W. L., Sullivan, N., & Towler, A. (2005). A measure of college student course engagement. *The Journal of Educational Research, 98*(3), 184–191.

Harman, G. S., & Meek, V. L. (2000). *Repositioning quality assurance and accreditation in Australian higher education.* Canberra: Department of Education, Training and Youth Affairs.

Harrell, W. Jr. (1998). Gender and equity issues affecting educational computer use. *Equity & Excellence in Education, 31*(3), 46–53. doi:10.1080/1066568980310307

Harvey, L., & Drew, S. (2006). *The first year experience: Briefing on induction. The higher education academy.* Retrieved October 1, 2015, from http://www.hear.ac.uk/assets/was%20York%20-%20delete%20this%20soon/documents/ourwork/research/literature_reviews/first_year_experience_briefing_on_induction.pdf

Hausmann, R. G. M., van de Sande, B., & VanLehn, K. (2008). Trialog: How peer collaboration helps remediate errors in an ITS. In *Proceedings of the 21st International FLAIRS Conference* (pp. 415–420). AAAI Press.

Haythornthwaite, C., de Laat, M., & Dawson, S. (2013). Introduction to the special issue on learning analytics. *American Behavioral Scientist, 57*(10), 1371–1379.

Heaslip, G., Donovan, P., & Cullen, J. G. (2014). Student response systems and learner engagement in large classes. *Active Learning in Higher Education, 15*(1), 11–24.

Heng, K. (2014). The relationships between student engagement and the academic achievement of first-year university students in Cambodia. *The Asia-Pacific Education Researcher, 23*(2), 179–189.

Henmon, V. A. C. (1911). The relation of the time of a judgment to its accuracy. *Psychological Review, 18*(3), 186–201. Retrieved from http://psycnet.apa.org/journals/rev/18/3/186/

Henschen, D. (2005). Web analytics. *Intelligent Enterprise, 8*(4), 15.

Hilmer, F. (2013, July 11). Higher uni participation shouldn't mean lesser quality. *The Drum.*

Hodges, B., Bedford, T., Hartley, J., Klinger, C., Murray, N., O'Rourke, J., & Schofield, N. (2013). *Enabling retention: Processes and strategies for improving student retention in university-based enabling programs.* Retrieved from http://www.olt.gov.au/system/files/resources/CG10_1697_Hodges_Report_2013.pdf

Hostager, T. J. (2014). Online learning resources do make a difference: Mediating effects of resource utilization on course grades. *Journal of Education for Business, 89*(6), 324–332.

James, R. (2012). Social inclusion in a globalised higher education environment: The issue of equitable access to university in Australia. In T. Basitand & S. Tomlinson (Eds.), *Social inclusion and higher education* (pp. 83–108). Bristol: Polity Press.

James, R., Krause, K. L., & Jennings, C. (2010). *The first year experience in Australian universities.* Canberra: Department of Education, Employment and Workplace Relations (DEEWR).

Johnson, L., Becker, S. A., & Freeman, A. (2013). *NMC horizon report: 2013 Museum edition.* Austin, TX: The New Media Consortium.

Johnson, L., Smith, R., Willis, H., Levine, A., & Haywood, K. (2011). *The 2011 horizon report*. Austin, TX: The New Media Consortium.

Johnson, M. K., Crosnoe, R., & Elder, G. H. (2001). Students' attachment and academic engagement: The role of race and ethnicity. *Sociology of Education, 74*(4), 318–340.

Jones, R. (2010). *Student retention and success, research synthesis for the higher education academy*. York: Higher Education Academy.

Junco, R. (2012). The relationship between frequency of Facebook use, participation in Facebook activities, and student engagement. *Computers & Education, 58*(1), 162–171.

Kahu, E. R. (2013). Framing student engagement in higher education. *Studies in Higher Education, 38*(5), 758–773.

Kent, M. L., Carr, B. J., Husted, R. A., & Pop, R. (2011). Learning web analytics: A tool for strategic communication. *Public Relations Review, 37*(5), 536–543.

Kift, S. (2009). *Articulating a transition pedagogy to scaffold and to enhance the first year student learning experience in Australian higher education: Final report for ALTC senior fellowship program*. Retrieved from http://www.altc.edu.au/resource-first-year-learning-experience-kift-2009

Klinger, C. M., & Murray, N. (2009, November). Enabling education: Adding value and transforming lives. In *Proceedings of the 3rd National Conference for Enabling Education*, University of Southern Queensland, Toowoomba.

Könings, K. D., Brand-Gruwel, S., van Merriënboer, J. J., & Broers, N. J. (2008). Does a new learning environment come up to students' expectations? A longitudinal study. *Journal of Educational Psychology, 100*(3), 535.

Krause, K. L. (2005). Serious thoughts about dropping out in first year: Trends, patterns and implications for higher education. *Studies in Learning, Evaluation, Innovation and Development, 2*(3), 55–68. Retrieved from http://www98.griffith.edu.au/dspace/bitstream/handle/10072/15410/45960.pdf?sequence=1

Krause, K. L., & Armitage, L. (2014). Australian student engagement, belonging, retention and success: A synthesis of the literature. *The Higher Education Academy*.

Krause, K. L., & Coates, H. (2008). Students' engagement in first year university. *Assessment and Evaluation in Higher Education, 33*(5), 493–505. Retrieved from http://www98.griffith.edu.au/dspace/bitstream/handle/10072/26304/53553_1.pdf?sequence=1

Kuh, G. D. (2001). Assessing what really matters to student learning inside the national survey of student engagement. *Change: The Magazine of Higher Learning, 33*(3), 10–17.

Kuh, G. D. (2003). What we're learning about student engagement from NSSE: Benchmarks for effective educational practices. *Change: The Magazine of Higher Learning, 35*(2), 24–32.

Kuh, G. D. (2009a). The national survey of student engagement: Conceptual and empirical foundations. *New directions for institutional research, 2009*(141), 5–20.

Kuh, G. D. (2009b). What student affairs professionals need to know about student engagement. *Journal of College Student Development, 50*(6), 683–706.

Kuh, G. D., Cruce, T. M., Shoup, R., Kinzie, J., & Gonyea, R. M. (2008). Unmasking the effects of student engagement on first-year college grades and persistence. *The Journal of Higher Education, 79*(5), 540–563.

Kuh, G. D., Gonyea, R., & Williams, J. (2005). What students expect from college and what they get. In T. Miller, B. Bender, J. Schuh, & Associates (Eds.), *Promoting reasonable expectations: Aligning student and institutional views of the college experience.* San Francisco, CA: Jossey-Bass.

Kuh, G. D., Kinzie, J., Cruce, T. M., Shoup, R., & Gonyea, R. M. (2007). *Connecting the dots: Multi-faceted analyses of the relationships between student engagement results from NSSE, and the institutional practices and conditions that foster student success.* Bloomington, IN: Indiana University Center for Postsecondary Research.

Kuh, G. D., Kinzie, J., Schuh, J., & Whitt, E. (2005). *Student success in college.* San Francisco, CA: Jossey-Bass.

Kuh, G. D., Schuh, J. H., Whitt, E. J., Andreas, R. E., Lyons, J. W., Strange, C. C., Krehbiel, L. E., & MacKay, K. A. (1991). *Involving colleges: Encouraging student learning and personal development through out-of-class experiences.* San Francisco, CA: Jossey-Bass.

Kuh, G. D., Whitt, E. J., & Strange, C. C. (1989, March 27–31). *The contributions of institutional agents to high quality out-of-class experiences for college students.* Paper presented at the Annual Meeting of the American Educational Research Association, San Francisco, CA.

Laird, T., & Cruce, T. (2009). Individual and environmental effects of part-time enrollment status on student-faculty interaction and self-reported gains. *The Journal of Higher Education, 80*(3), 290–314.

Lawson, M. A., & Masyn, K. E. (2015). Analyzing profiles, predictors, and consequences of student engagement dispositions. *Journal of School Psychology, 53*(1), 63–86.

Lee, J. S. (2014). The relationship between student engagement and academic performance: Is it a myth or reality? *The Journal of Educational Research, 107*(3), 177–185.

Leithwood, K., & Jantzi, D. (1999). The relative effects of principal and teacher sources of leadership on student engagement with school. *Educational Administration Quarterly, 35*, 679–706.

Leung, C. (2014). Researching language and communication in schooling. *Linguistics and Education, 26*, 136–144.

Lias, T. E., & Elias, T. (2011). *Learning analytics: The definitions, the processes, and the potential.* Retrieved November 15, 2015, from http://citeseerx.ist.psu.edu/viewdoc/summary?doi=10.1.1.456.7092

Littlefield, J., & Keillor, C. (2012). *Engaging adults learners with technology*. St. Paul, MN: Macalester College.

Long, M., Ferrier, F., & Heagney, M. (2006). *Stay, play or give it away? Students continuing, changing or leaving university study in first year*. Melbourne: Centre for the Economics of Education and Training, Monash University.

Long, P., & Tricker, T. (2004, September 16–18). *Do first year undergraduates find what they expect?* Paper presented at the British Educational Research Association Annual Conference, University of Manchester, Manchester.

Lysne, S. J., Miller, B. G., & Eitel, K. B. (2013). Exploring student engagement in an introductory biology course. *Journal of College Science Teaching, 43*(2), 14.

Macfadyen, L. P., & Dawson, S. (2010). Mining LMS data to develop an "early warning system" for educators: A proof of concept. *Computers & Education, 54*(2), 588–599.

Macfadyen, L. P., & Dawson, S. (2012). Numbers are not enough. Why e-learning analytics failed to inform an institutional strategic plan. *Educational Technology and Society, 15*(3), 149–163.

Manning, K., Kinzie, J., & Schuh, J. H. (2013). *One size does not fit all: Traditional and innovative models of student affairs practice*. New York, NY: Routledge.

Marchand, G. C., & Gutierrez, A. P. (2017). Processes involving perceived instructional support, task value, and engagement in graduate education. *The Journal of Experimental Education, 85*(1), 87–106.

Marks, H. M. (2000). Student engagement in instructional activity: Patterns in the elementary, middle, and high school years. *American Educational Research Journal, 37*(1), 153–184.

Mattingly, K. D., Rice, M. C., & Berge, Z. L. (2012). Learning analytics as a tool for closing the assessment loop in higher education. *Knowledge Management & E-Learning: An International Journal (KM&EL), 4*(3), 236–247.

Mavelli, L. (2014). Widening participation, the instrumentalization of knowledge and the reproduction of inequality. *Teaching in Higher Education, 19*(8), 860–869.

McInnis, C., James, R., & Hartley, R. (2000). *Trends in the first year experience in Australian universities*. Melbourne: Centre for the Study of Higher Education.

McKenzie, K., & Schweitzer, R. D. (2001). Who succeeds at university? Factors predicting academic performance in first year Australian university students. *Higher Education Research and Development, 20*(1), 21–33. doi:10.1080/07924360120043621

Moulton, B. (2008). *Kift ALTC senior fellowship: Articulating a transition pedagogy*.

Muldoon, R., O'Brien, D., Pendreigh, H., & Wijeyewardene, I. (2009, November 25–27). *The UNE pathways enabling program – A case study*. In Proceedings of the 3rd National Enabling Educators Conference: Enabling Pathways, Toowoomba.

Munro, L. (2011). 'Go boldly, dream large': The challenges confronting non-traditional students at university. *Australian Journal of Education, 55*(2), 115–131.

National Academies of Sciences, Engineering, and Medicine. (2016). *Barriers and opportunities for 2-year and 4-year STEM degrees: Systemic change to support students' diverse pathways*. Washington, DC: National Academies Press.

Nelson, K. J., & Creagh, T. A. (2013). *A good practice guide: Safeguarding student learning engagement*. Brisbane: Queensland University of Technology.

Norton, A. (2012). *Mapping Australian higher education*. Carlton: Grattan Institute.

Olama, M. M., Thakur, G., McNair, A. W., & Sukumar, S. R. (2014, May). *Predicting student success using analytics in course learning management systems* (pp. 91220M–91220M). In SPIE Sensing Technology Applications, International Society for Optics and Photonics.

Olmos, M., & Corrin, L. (2012). Learning analytics: A case study of the process of design of visualizations. *Journal of Asynchronous Learning Networks, 16*(3), 39–49.

Olsen, A. J., Burgess, Z., & Sharma, R. (2015). The comparative academic performance of international students in Australia. *International Higher Education, 42*.

Osborne, R., & Leith, H. (2000). *Evaluation of the targeted initiative on widening access for young people from socio-economically disadvantaged backgrounds*. Dublin: Higher Education Authority.

O'Shea, S., & Vincent, M. (2011). Uni-start: A peer-led orientation activity designed for the early and timely engagement of commencing university students. *The Journal of Continuing Higher Education, 59*(3), 152–160.

Pace, C. R. (1995). *From good practices to good products: Relating good practices in undergraduate education to student achievement*. Paper presented at the Association of Institutional Research, Boston, MA.

Pace, C. R. (1982). *Achievement and the quality of student effort*. Washington, DC: National Commission on Excellence in Education.

Paige, K., Hattam, R., Rigney, L. I., Osborne, S., & Morrison, A. (2016). *Strengthening indigenous participation and practice in STEM*.

Parsons, J., & Taylor, L. (2011). Improving student engagement. *Current issues in education, 14*(1).

Pascarella, E. T., Pierson, C. T., Wolniak, G. C., & Terenzini, P. T. (2004). First-generation college students: Additional evidence on college experiences and outcomes. *Journal of Higher Education, 75*(3), 249–284.

Pascarella, E. T., & Terenzini, P. T. (2005). *How college affects students: A third decade of research*. San Francisco, CA: Jossey-Bass.

Pekrun, R., & Linnenbrink-Garcia, L. (2012). Academic emotions and student engagement. In S. L. Christenson, A. L. Reschly, & C. Wylie (Eds.), *Handbook of research on student engagement* (pp. 259–282). New York, NY: Springer.

Pellas, N. (2014). The influence of computer self-efficacy, metacognitive self-regulation and self-esteem on student engagement in online learning programs: Evidence from the virtual world of second life. *Computers in Human Behavior, 35*, 157–170.

Phillips, R., Maor, D., Cumming-Potvin, W., Roberts, P., Herrington, J., Preston, G., & Perry, L. (2011). *Learning analytics and study behaviour: A pilot study*. Paper presented at Australasian Society for Computers in Learning in Tertiary Education (ASCILITE) Annual Conference.

Pike, G. R., & Kuh, G. D. (2005). A typology of student engagement for American colleges and universities. *Research in Higher Education, 46*(2), 185–209.

Pistilli, M. D., Willis III, J. E., & Campbell, J. P. (2014). Analytics through an institutional lens: Definition, theory, design, and impact. In J. A. Larusson & B. White (Eds.), *Learning analytics* (pp. 79–102). New York, NY: Springer.

Puzziferro, M. (2008). Online technologies self-efficacy and self-regulated learning as predictors of final grade and satisfaction in college-level online courses. *The American Journal of Distance Education, 22*(2), 72–89.

Quinn, J., Thomas, L., Slack, K., Casey, L., Thexton, W., & Noble, J. (2005). *From life crisis to lifelong learning. Rethinking working class 'drop out' from higher education*. York: Joseph Rowntree Foundation.

Radloff, A. (2011). *Student engagement in New Zealand's universities*. Retrieved October 12, 2015, from https://www.acer.edu.au/files/AUSSE_New_Zealand_Report_Web_Version.pdf

Radloff, A., & Coates, H. (2010). *Doing more for learning: Enhancing engagement and outcomes: Australasian survey of student engagement: Australasian student engagement report*. Camberwell: Australian Council for Educational Research (ACER).

Ream, R. K., & Rumberger, R. W. (2008). Student engagement, peer social capital, and school dropout among Mexican American and non-Latino White students. *Sociology of Education, 81*(2), 109–139.

Reay, D., Davies, J., David, M., & Ball, S. J. (2001). Choices of degree or degrees of choice? Class, race and the higher education choice process. *Sociology, 35*(4), 855–874.

Reeve, J. (2012). A self-determination theory perspective on student engagement. In S. L. Christenson, A. L. Reschly, & C. Wylie (Eds.), *Handbook of research on student engagement* (pp. 149–172). New York, NY: Springer.

Reffay, C., & Chanier, T. (2003). How social network analysis can help to measure cohesion in collaborative distance learning. In B. Wasson, S. Ludvigsen, & H. U. Hoppe (Eds.), *Computer supported collaborative learning* (pp. 1–10). Dordrecht: Kluwer.

Reffay, C., Teplovs, C., & Blondel, F.-M. (2011). Productive re-use of CSCL data and analytic tools to provide a new perspective on group cohesion. In H. Spada, G. Stahl, N. Miyake, & N. Law (Eds.), *Proceedings of CSCL 2011*. Mahwah, NJ: Lawrence Erlbaum Associates.

Report of the Project Cherub 'Other Qualifications Group'. (2004). Report presented to the academic board of Unitec New Zealand. Auckland: Unitec New Zealand.

Reyes, J. A. (2015). The skinny on big data in education: Learning analytics simplified. *TechTrends, 59*(2), 75–80.

Richardson, D. (2003). The transition to degree level study. *Higher Education Academy.*

Richardson, M., & Hunt, J. (2013). Widening access to HE-family centred summer schools. *Higher Education, Skills and Work-Based Learning, 3*(2), 118–129.

Richardson, S. (2011). *Uniting teachers and learners: Critical insights into the importance of staff-student interactions in Australian university education.* Camberwell: Australian Council for Educational Research.

Roberts, G. G. (2002). *SET for success: The supply of people with science, technology, engineering and mathematics skills: The report of Sir Gareth Roberts' review.* London: UCL Institute of Education.

Robinson, C. C., & Hullinger, H. (2008). New benchmarks in higher education: Student engagement in online learning. *Journal of Education for Business, 84*(2), 101–109.

Romero, C., Ventura, S., Espejo, P. G., & Hervs, C. (2008). Data mining algorithms to classify students. In R. de Baker, T. Barnes, & J. Beck (Eds.), *Proceedings of the 1st international conference on educational data mining* (pp. 8–17). Retrieved from http://www.educationaldatamiming.org/EDM2008/uploads/proc/1_Romero_3.pdf

Rudduck, J., Chaplain, R., & Wallace, G. (Eds.). (1996). *School improvement: What can pupils tell us?* London: Routledge.

Scheffel, M., & Drachsler, H. (2014). *Frame work of quality indicators.* Retrieved from http://www.laceproject.eu/deliverables/d3-1-quality-indicators.pdf

Scheffel, M., Drachsler, H., Stoyanov, S., & Specht, M. (2014). Quality indicators for learning analytics. *Journal of Educational Technology & Society, 17*(4), 117–132.

Scheffel, M., Niemann, K., Pardo, A., Leony, D., Friedrich, M., Schmidt, K., Wolpers, M., & Kloos, C. D. (2011). Usage pattern recognition in student activities (pp.341–355). In *Proceedings of EC-TEL'11,* Berlin, Heidelberg: Springer-Verlag.

Sciffer, S., & Shah, M. (2015). Widening the participation of disadvantaged students in engineering. *International Journal of Quality Assurance in Engineering and Technology Education (IJQAETE), 4*(1), 1–13.

Scott, G. (2005). *Accessing the student voice. Higher education innovation program and the collaboration and structural reform fund, Department of Education, Science and Training.* Canberra: Commonwealth of Australia.

Scott, G. (2008). *University student engagement and satisfaction with learning and teaching: Commissioned research and analysis report, review of higher education, DEEWR.* Canberra: Commonwealth of Australia.

Shah, M., Goode, E., West, S., & Clark, H. (2014). Widening student participation in higher education through online enabling education. *Widening Participation and Lifelong Learning, 16*(3), 36–57. doi:10.5456/WPLL.16.3.36

Shah, M., Lewis, I., & Fitzgerald, R. (2011). The renewal of quality assurance in Australian higher education: The challenge of balancing academic rigor, equity and quality outcomes. *Quality in Higher Education, 17*(3), 265–278.

Shah, M., & Nair, S. C. (2011). Building the plane while it's flying: Enhancing the missed opportunity for quality assurance and capacity-building in Australian private higher education. *European Journal of Higher Education, 1*(2–3), 261–273.

Shah, M., & Nair, S. C. (2013). Private for–profit higher education in Australia: Widening access and participation and opportunities for public-private collaboration. *Higher Education Research and Development (HERD), 32*(5), 820–832.

Sharma, B. R., & Bhaumik, P. K. (2013). Student engagement and its predictors: An exploratory study in an Indian business school. *Global Business Review, 14*(1), 25–42.

Shernoff, D. (2002). *Flow states and student engagement in the classroom.* Mill Valley, CA: American Sports Institute.

Shochet, I. M., Dadds, M. R., Ham, D., & Montague, R. (2006). School connectedness is an underemphasized parameter in adolescent mental health: Results of a community prediction study. *Journal of Clinical Child and Adolescent Psychology, 35*(2), 170–179.

Shum, S. B., & Ferguson, R. (2012). Social learning analytics. *Educational Technology & Society, 15*(3), 3–26.

Siemens, G. (2010). *What are learning analytics.* Retrieved from http://www.elearnspace.org/blog/2010/08/25/what-are-learning-analytics/

Siemens, G. (2012, April). Learning analytics: Envisioning a research discipline and a domain of practice. In *Proceedings of the 2nd International Conference on Learning Analytics and Knowledge* (pp. 4–8), New York, NY: ACM.

Siemens, G. (2013). Learning analytics: The emergence of a discipline. *American Behavioral Scientist, 57*(10), 1380–1400.

Siemens, G., & Long, P. (2011). Penetrating the fog: Analytics in learning and education. *EDUCAUSE Review, 46*(5), 30.

Sithole, A., Chiyaka, E. T., McCarthy, P., Mupinga, D. M., Bucklein, B. K., & Kibirige, J. (2017). Student attraction, persistence and retention in STEM programs: Successes and continuing challenges. *Higher Education Studies, 7*(1), 46.

Sizer, R. T. (1996). Dreams, interests, aspirations. *Journal of Research in Rural Education, 12*(3), 125–126.

Skinner, E. A., Wellborn, J. G., & Connell, J. P. (1990). What it takes to do well in school and whether I've got it: A process model of perceived control and children's engagement and achievement in school. *Journal of Educational Psychology, 82*(1), 22.

Smith, L. (2010, November). *StudyLink: A case study of an enabling program supporting the transition to the first year of university.* Paper presented at the 13th Pacific Rim First Year in Higher Education Conference, "Aspiration, access, achievement," Adelaide, Australia.

Smith, V. C., Lange, A., & Huston, D. R. (2012). Predictive modeling to forecast student outcomes and drive effective interventions in online community college courses. *Journal of Asynchronous Learning Networks, 16*(3), 51–61.

Stahl, G. (2009). *Studying virtual math teams.* New York, NY: Springer.

Stankov, L., Morony, S., & Lee, Y. P. (2014). Confidence: The best non-cognitive predictor of academic achievement? *Educational Psychology, 34*(1), 9–28. doi:10.1080/014 43410.2013.814194

Stoilescu, D., & McDougall, D. (2011). Gender digital divide and challenges in undergraduate computer science programs. *Canadian Journal of Education/Revue canadienne de l'éducation, 34*(1), 308–333. Retrieved from http://www.cje-rce.ca/index.php/cje-rce/article/viewFile/461/866

Stone, C., & O'Shea, S. E. (2013). Time, money, leisure and guilt-the gendered challenges of higher education for mature-age students. *Australian Journal of Adult Learning, 53,* 95–116.

Stone, G. (2014). Work all day, study at night: The interactive evening lecture to invigorate working students. *Accounting Education, 23*(1), 71–74.

Szulecka, T. K., Springett, N. R., & De Pauw, K. W. (1987). General health, psychiatric vulnerability and withdrawal from university in first-year undergraduates. *British Journal of Guidance and Counselling, 15*(1), 82–91. doi:10.1080/03069888708251646

Thomas, L. (2002). Widening participation in post-compulsory education. *Education & Training, 44*(4–5), 241–242.

Thomas, L. (2012). Building student engagement and belonging in higher education at a time of change. *Paul Hamlyn Foundation, 100.*

Thomas, L., & Jamieson-Ball, C. (2011). *Engaging students to improve student retention and success in higher education in Wales.* York: Higher Education Academy.

Tinto, V. (2012). Enhancing student success: Taking the classroom success seriously. *The International Journal of the First Year in Higher Education, 3*(1).

Todman, J., & Drysdale, E. (2004). Effects of qualitative differences in initial and subsequent computer experience on computer anxiety. *Computers in Human Behavior, 20*(5), 581–590. doi:10.1016/j.chb.2004.03.028

Tomaszewski, W., Perales, F., & Xiang, N. (2016). *Career guidance, school experiences and the university participation of young people from equity groups.* Perth: Curtin University.

Trewartha, R. (2008). Innovations in bridging and foundation education in a tertiary institution. *Australian Journal of Adult Learning, 48*(1), 30.

Upcraft, M. L., & Gardner, J. N. (1989). *The freshman year experience: Helping students survive and succeed in college.* San Francisco, CA: Jossey-Bass.

Verbert, K., Drachsler, H., Manouselis, N., Wolpers, M., Vuorikari, R., & Duval, E. (2011). Dataset-driven research for improving recommender systems for learning. In G. Siemens & D. Gasevic (Eds.), *Proceedings of the 1st LAK conference* (pp. 44–53). New York, NY: ACM.

Verbert, K., Manouselis, N., Drachsler, H., & Duval, E. (2012). Dataset-driven research to support learning and knowledge analytics. *Journal of Educational Technology & Society, 15*(3), 133–148.

Voelkl, K. E. (1995). School warmth, student participation, and achievement. *The Journal of Experimental Education, 63*(2), 127–138.

Walshe, J. (2009, June 13). Alarm as 'spoon-fed students' can't cope at college. *Irish Independent.*

Weiland, R., & Nowak, R. (1999). Academic preparation programs: A schema approach to learning in context. In K. Martin, N. Stanley, & N. Davison (Eds.), *Teaching in the disciplines/learning in context* (pp. 467–473). Perth: The University of Western Australia.

Whannell, P., & Whannell, R. (2013). Reducing the attrition of tertiary bridging students studying by distance: A practice report. In *Proceedings of the 1st Foundation and Bridging Educators New Zealand Conference (FABENZ 2012)* (pp. 26–37), National Centre for Tertiary Teaching Excellence.

Whannell, P., Whannell, R., & Allen, B. (2012). Investigating the influence of teacher strategies on academic self-efficacy and study behaviour of students in a tertiary bridging program. *Australian Journal of Adult Learning, 52*(1), 39–65. Retrieved from http://www.ajal.net.au/investigating-the-influence-of-teacher-strategies-on-academic-self-efficacy-and-study-behaviour-of-students-in-a-tertiary-bridging-program/

Whiteford, G., Shah, M., & Nair, S. C. (2013). Equity and excellence are not mutually exclusive: A discussion of academic standards in an era of widening participation. *Quality Assurance in Education, 21*(3), 299–310.

Willms, J. D. (2003). *Student engagement at school: A sense of belonging and participation.* Paris: Organisation for Economic Co-Operation and Development.

Wright, M. C., McKay, T., Hershock, C., Miller, K., & Tritz, J. (2014). Better than expected: Using learning analytics to promote student success in gateway science. *Change: The Magazine of Higher Learning, 46*(1), 28–34.

Yang, Y. F. (2011). Engaging students in an online situated language learning environment. *Computer Assisted Language Learning, 24*(2), 181–198.

Zepke, N. (2013). Student engagement: A complex business supporting the first year experience in tertiary education. *The International Journal of the First Year in Higher Education, 4*(2), 1.

CHAPTER 9

Triangulating Student Engagement with "Built & Bought" Learning Analytics

John Fritz and Robert Carpenter

1 Introduction

In social science research, the principle of triangulation broadly refers to using different methodologies to replicate—and thus validate—findings of any one method. The underlying premise is that any method, be it qualitative or quantitative, has inherent limitations or is subject to human error. But if you arrive at similar conclusions with multiple methods, you can generally have a higher degree of confidence that your results are sound, reliable, and (yes) even predictable. The term itself is taken from the practice of sailors to pinpoint their current location at sea by using the sun, moon, stars or fixed objects on the horizon as multiple points—and lines—of reference that converge at the sailor's eye on the ship.

While triangulation helps answer the question "where am I?" or "what have I found?" for the purpose of this chapter on learning analytics, we also want to use it as a broader metaphor to reflect on a context of uncertainty or imprecision it seeks to remedy. Admittedly, our perspective at a single institution, or the methods we use to clarify it, may be flawed, but we offer our perception of the current points of reference on the LA horizon, if only to provide context for our attempts to improve student success. In addition, triangulation typically involves multiple methods to interrogate a common dataset, to find that one fixed point where methods converge—or where they do not. By describing multiple projects and tools at our own and other institutions—each with different datasets representing different human subjects—we know we are not using triangulation in the most literal sense of the word.

1.1 Where Are We?

In 2017, the Gartner Hype Cycle[1] of higher education IT still placed learning analytics at the peak of expectations (Williams, 2017). A year earlier, however, Sharkey and Harfield (2016) disagreed, saying learning analytics had already slipped into the trough of disillusionment, and cited a new analytics angst described in the 2016 Campus Computing Survey of higher education Chief Information Officers (CIOs) (Green, 2016). With analytics frequently appearing on Educause's Top 10 IT issues for CIOs, this is another triangulation example of how key campus decision makers feel about this still maturing field.

From our perspective, learning analytics still tends to focus more on predictions than interventions, which is ironic given two of the most commonly-cited definitions of the field itself (*emphasis added*):

> [Learning analytics is]...the measurement, collection, analysis and reporting of data about *learners and their contexts*, for purposes of *understanding and optimizing learning and the environments* in which it occurs. (Society for Learning Analytics Research (SOLAR); Long & Siemens, 2011)

> At its core, learning analytics (LA) is the collection and analysis of usage data associated with student learning. The purpose of LA is to observe and understand learning behaviors *in order to enable appropriate interventions*. (Educause Learning Initiative (ELI); Brown, 2011)

Seven years later, one would be hard-pressed to find very much about reported intervention findings by scholars or practitioners in their respective publications, the *Journal of Learning Analytics* and *EDUCAUSE Review*. Those studies that do tend to be in such focused, discreet contexts, that the question of generalizability and scale is hard to ignore. Instead, we tend to find what might be broadly—and empathetically—described as perfecting predictions, perhaps at the expense of implementing good interventions. At some point, what do we do with what we think we know about our students improve learning, their term-to-term and persistence, and their eventual graduation? In short, assessment without action is of limited value.

To be clear, this is not a criticism of any one scholar or institution. Rather, we merely ask these questions as a good faith attempt to take a reading of where the LA field currently stands and to inform our own learning analytics initiatives. Understandably, few wish to state broad claims of fully understanding, let alone improving learning, but the relative lack of intervention design and evidence makes it challenging to replicate validate, and scale the potential impact of learning analytics.

Finally, during a recent keynote presentation at the Instructional Management Standards (IMS) Summit on Analytics, Vince Kellen (2017), Chief Information Officer at UC San Diego, rightly cautioned about the incredible complexity that is human learning, and by extension, those who would seek to do learning analytics. Consider the bullet points on his first slide, which is anything but a typical wall of numbers:

- Neurons in the brain: 10^{11}
- Synapses in the brain: 10^{14}
- Minutes in 10 billion years: 10^{16}
- Combinations of photos in a room of 200 people: 10^{60}
- Atoms in the universe: 10^{80}
- Maximum possible subsets of neurons in a brain: 10^{2048}

"The teaching and learning research space is much more complex than we realize," says Kellen, in describing the first of his "Seven Commandments of Learning Analytics"—*Cultivate Humility*. "Large jumps in teaching productivity akin to 20th century technology is not likely."

Indeed, consider for example what might seem like a straightforward exercise in triangulating college students' learning. If we observe that students who actually attend class earn higher final grades than course peers who do not, we could attempt to replicate this finding by observing different classes in different programs or even in different institutions. In this case, not only would we be increasing sample size, which could aid generalizability, but replication in more than one course, instructor or institution would also help control for any possible "instructor effect" or differences in discipline or teaching pedagogy (e.g., lecture, flipped, online/blended). Additionally, we might assume that "attendance" is a proxy for student engagement, but we might want to survey students directly to confirm this is the case or alternatively to develop alternate measures of engagement to determine whether attendance has an independent effect.

The challenge in studying student class attendance is truly understanding what we think we have measured. Is class attendance or engagement the same as student learning? With Kellen's caution in mind, and given some of these basic challenges in understanding something as complex as human learning, what does it mean for institutions to pursue learning analytics?

Institutions—and the field itself—may need to deploy multiple ways to triangulate student engagement to iteratively build a critical mass of learning analytics-based interventions and evidence. This chapter's contribution is to review the complementary findings of one institution's use of several "built and bought" learning analytics solutions and how we have translated some of them to interventions. We conclude with some cautionary notes for institutions who wish to invest time and resources in learning analytics, and for the field itself Before proceeding further, we want to attempt to define our key object of study: Engagement occurs when students actively participate in a formal or informal opportunities to know, understand or do something that they did not or could not before the opportunity itself. Admittedly, this responsibility for learning is a necessary, but insufficient condition to learn. But given the current state of research and practice, triangulating—or even "corralling" and "echo-locating"—student engagement as "responsibility for learning" may be the best we can do to scale interventions that improve student success.

In short, student engagement or responsibility for learning may only be a proxy for learning, but proxies are commonly used throughout the social sciences when the underlying variable of interest is difficult to observe. Indeed, as defined by the *Oxford English Dictionary*, a proxy is "the action of a substitute or deputy" or "agency of another"; from science and economics, "a variable that can be used as an indirect estimate of another variable with which it is correlated"; more generally "a property used as an estimate or indicator of another with which it is associated" ("proxy, n.," n.d.).

With all this in mind, we now turn to our own institution's attempt to do learning analytics.

2   Background

The University of Maryland, Baltimore County (UMBC) is a public research university in the mid-Atlantic United States. Total student enrollment is approximately 14,000 (11,000 undergraduate or bachelor's degree students, 3,000 graduate or master's & doctoral students). The most recent 6-year graduation rate (for new, full-time freshmen starting in Fall 2010) was 63%. By comparison, the U.S national average for public universities (for new, full-time freshmen starting in Fall 2009) is 59%.[2] In addition, the Blackboard learning management system (LMS) has been used since 2000 and overall adoption (95% of all students, 87% of all eligible instructors and 82% of all distinct course sections) is relatively high among Bb clients.

In 2006, as part of institutional efforts to improve student success—defined as term-to-term retention or persistence and eventual graduation—the institution developed its own data warehouse to facilitate analytics. Among other things, UMBC purchased iStrategy, a business intelligence software package, designed by a local company, to better understand its PeopleSoft student information system implemented in 2008. In 2010, Blackboard (Bb) acquired iStrategy, renaming it Blackboard Analytics, and developed a learning analytics solution—Bb Analytics for Learn—which UMBC helped influence and test. Early on, extensibility emerged as a key benefit as the institution was able to add and correlate multiple data sources, illustrated in Figure 9.1.

Over time, UMBC's data warehouse[3] has focused on four key functions: (1) data collection, (2) reporting, mostly through homegrown efforts, and more recently (3) analysis, including vendor solutions EAB, Civitas Illume, and Bb

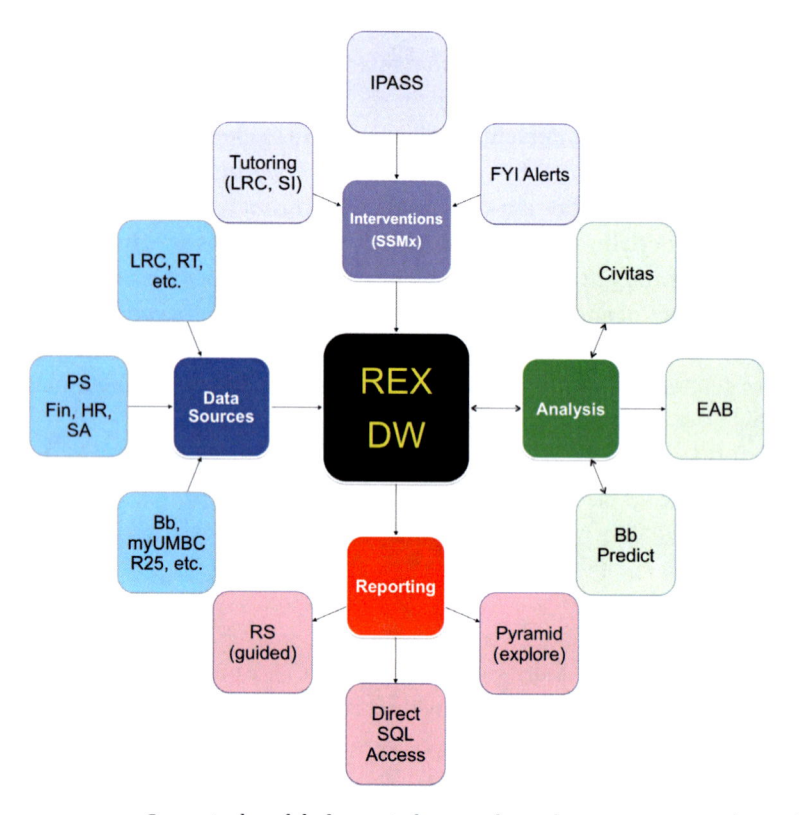

FIGURE 9.1   Conceptual model of UMBC's data warehouse known as report exchange (REX)

Predict, and (4) interventions, facilitated by the Student Success Matrix (SSMx) developed by the Predictive Analytics Research (PAR), recently acquired by Hobsons.

3   Lessons Learned

Admittedly, UMBC is flush with built and bought analytics tools and solutions, some of which we are still implementing and evaluating for continued use and sustained funding. However, some complementary findings are emerging as general lessons learned, including the following:

3.1   *Student LMS Activity as Proxy for Engagement during a Term—And Beyond*

Starting in 2007, UMBC's homegrown approach to learning analytics found that students earning a final grade of D or F used the Blackboard LMS about 40% less than students earning a C or higher (Fritz, 2011, 2013, 2016; Fritz &

Whitmer, 2017). The correlation has held true ever since and was complemented by an intriguing perspective on term-to-term retention and persistence provided through Bb Analytics for Learn (A4L):

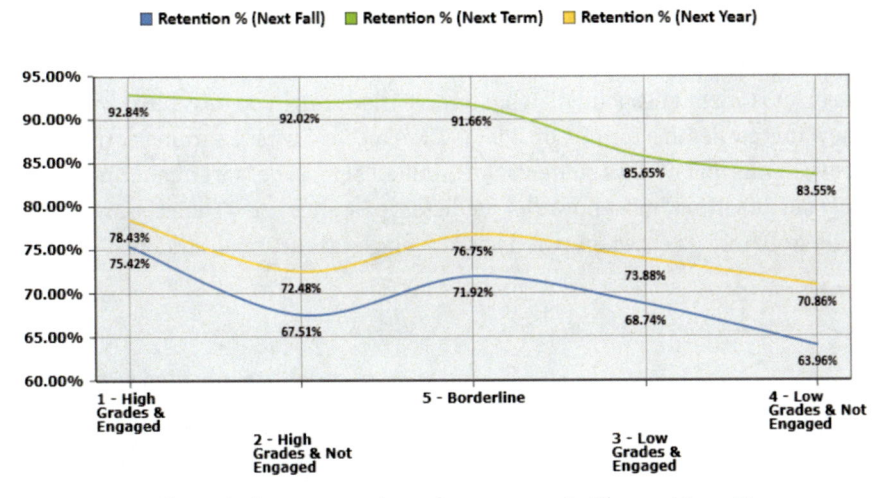

FIGURE 9.2   Fall 2013 freshmen & transfer student retention by Bb LMS risk profile

In Figure 9.2, notice how less academically successful but more engaged students (#3) are retained next year at slightly higher rates than more successful but less engaged peers (#2).[4] Who might we want to nudge in an effort to improve student success? There are tradeoffs for either group, but the reliability of the retention pattern prompts an important question: what, if anything, might we do with such information, to actually intervene? Consider also that the Education Advisory Board (EAB) found 43% of students who leave an institution do so with an institutional grade point average (GPA) between 2.0 and 3.0 on a 4.0 scale (Tyson, 2014). Finally, the institution's subsequent use of Civitas Learning has shown that student LMS use is consistently one of the most powerful predictors of student persistence from term to term.[5]

3.2   Direct Feedback to Students about Their LMS Activity Can Raise Awareness

Given the intriguing correlation between student LMS activity and grades, in 2008, the UMBC developed a feedback tool called Check My Activity (CMA) allowing students to compare how active they were relative to an anonymous summary of course peers.[6] More importantly, if a student's instructor used the LMS course site's online grade book, the CMA would allow students to compare how active they were to peers earning the same, higher or lower grade on any assignment. To date, slightly more than half of all students (54%) actually use the CMA, but those students that do are about 1.5 times more likely to earn a C or higher final grade and a 2.0 term GPA (Fritz, 2017).

Unfortunately, student use of the CMA may be an example of selection bias. Namely, engaged students may be more likely to seek or accept institutional feedback and resources than their disengaged peers. But if we accept LMS activity as a proxy for student engagement, what interventions might be possible if we could know this earlier in a term? Consider UMBC's recent Civitas Learning correlation between number of days students are enrolled before the start of a term—typically one of Civitas' most powerful predictors of student persistence—and these same students' LMS use compared to the average LMS use of all students.

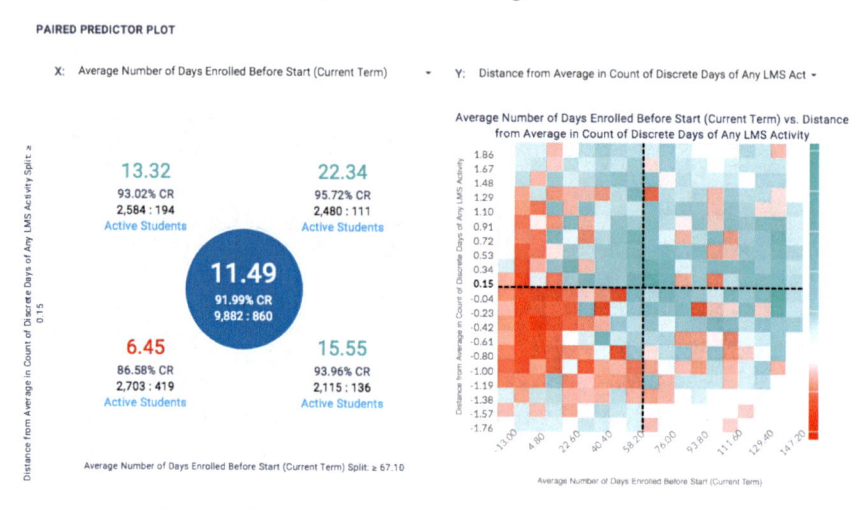

FIGURE 9.3   Fall 2017 freshmen & transfer persistence prediction by days enrolled & LMS use

In the left side of Figure 9.3, the overall predicted Continuation Rate (CR, the blue circle) is 91.9%, with 11.49 as the ratio of persisting students (9,882) to non-persisting students (860). But notice the heat-map clustering of students in the lower-left quadrant of on the right side panel of Figure 9.3. These are students who have not only enrolled close to the start of the term, but also have been relatively disengaged in the LMS in the past. This same pattern is consistent for many different student groups (e.g., race, gender, major, etc.). Given their disengagement before the term starts, should we be surprised that they are not as engaged during the term? Typically, cumulative GPA is of the most powerful predictors of future success, minimally defined as term-to-term persistence or retention. But like credits or final grades earned, institutions struggle to use these predictors to identify at-risk students early enough in the term intervene and change the predicted outcome. The challenge remains what can we do to engage these students? Perhaps identifying them earlier in the term is a start.

3.3   *Identifying and Intervening with at-risk Students Sooner Than Later*
One key assessment tool that might help is the online grade center, which
students have consistently identified as the most important LMS function
(Caruso & Salaway, 2007). Typically, UMBC has found that about 70% of all
courses use the grade center, which we have been promoting for years.

In Fall 17, UMBC validated its Fall 16 Blackboard Predict findings[7] against a
homegrown First Year Intervention (FYI) alert program, which asks faculty (at
midterm) to identify freshmen and transfer students at risk of earning a final
grade of D or F "if the semester were to end tomorrow" (https://lrc.umbc.edu/
alerts). While faculty FYI participation rates have varied over time, typically
about 55% of those who receive an FYI Alert earn a C or better final grade. We
compared Spring 17 Bb Predict *and* FYI results, to see if using both could help
us intervene with *any* at-risk undergraduates earlier in a term, when they have
more time to turn around poor performance.

As such, we had three primary goals:
– Validate Bb Predict against a homegrown intervention of 20 +years.
– Identify *any* at-risk undergraduates without increasing faculty workload.
– Intervene with students earlier in a term than in the past.
In Spring 17, we deepened this analysis to 10 high-enrollment "gateway"
courses with relatively high Bb usage and compared both Bb Predict and FYI
results for each. Among other things, we found Bb Predict does a better job of
predicting who will succeed, but the FYI program is better at predicting who
will fail. Using Bb Predict and FYI together was better than either approach
alone. Together, the use of the two systems would have reduced the number
of type II errors (students who would not have received an alert but failed)
and the number of type I errors (students who would have received an alert
but passed).

It is important to note that UMBC is intentionally *not* sharing Blackboard
Predict findings with students directly. We are even hesitant to share them
with faculty, lest they bias assessment of students too early in a term. Instead,
a university-wide Persistence Committee is using our Blackboard Predict and
other student success findings to more accurately target at-risk students for
existing nudge campaigns encouraging them to use proven help resources.

3.4   *Faculty LMS Course Design Could Be a Scalable Institutional*
       Intervention
If we accept student LMS activity as a proxy for engagement and that direct
feedback to students about their own LMS behavior—preferably earlier than
later—may help to raise their self-awareness, then what role might design of
LMS courses have on student use of the LMS tool? Learning analytics research
literature (Campbell, 2007; Dawson, McWilliam, & Tan, 2008; Fritz, 2013;

Macfadyen & Dawson, 2012; Whitmer, 2012) has identified three broad ways in which faculty use the LMS to design their courses:

1.   User & Content Management (e.g., enrollment, notes, syllabi, handouts, presentations)
2.   Interactive Tools (e.g., forums, chats, blogs, wikis, announcements)
3.   Assessment (e.g., practice quizzes, exams, electronic assignments, grade center use)

While most faculty use #1, and some use #2, far fewer actively use #3. However, intentional course design that leverages formative assessment can be one of the most impactful ways faculty can generate high student LMS use, time on task, engagement and responsibility for learning.

For example, UMBC has found that some faculty who use a little-known Blackboard function called adaptive release have seen dramatic increases in student engagement and final grades.[8] Specifically, adaptive release allows faculty to set pre-conditions that students must meet to access course content. These conditions include due dates and group membership, but the most powerful is grade on a prior assignment. Using adaptive release, instructors can create a syllabus quiz that students must take and pass before they can even see, let alone submit, the first assignment for credit.

In 2010, an adjunct economics instructor who had not seen very high student use of his LMS course redesigned his entire course around the adaptive release function. In addition to his course routinely becoming the institution's most active Blackboard course each term, his students consistently scored 20% higher on the department's common final exam compared to other sections of the same course. His students also went on to earn a half-letter grade higher in the next course that required his own, even though he did not teach the subsequent course. Other faculty using adaptive release saw similar gains in student engagement to create video-game like achievements or to regulate student access to Latin and Greek podcasts throughout the term—or their attempts to cram the podcasts at the end (Fritz, 2013; Fritz & Whitmer, 2017).

Unfortunately, UMBC faculty use of adaptive release is small, even though its impact can be great. For example, in Spring 2015, the institution found that on average, students accessed 86% of course content in Bb LMS courses using adaptive release vs. 53% of course content in LMS courses that did not use adaptive release. However, only 115 of 2,431 courses (4.7%) used adaptive release (see Figure 9.4). This provides poor incentives for faculty to develop LMS course sites: If they knew students would barely access half of their course content throughout the term, would this change how much time and effort they expended during the frantic two weeks before a term starts?

	Distinct Courses		% Items Accessed	
	Adaptive Release Rules	No Adaptive Release Rules	Adaptive Release Rules	No Adaptive Release Rules
College of Arts, Humanities and Social Sciences	80	1,407	80.0%	52.4%
College of Engineering and Information Technology	11	317	100.0%	54.3%
College of Natural and Mathematical Sciences	12	299	96.2%	56.9%
Division of Professional Studies		86		54.2%
Division of Student Affairs		37		59.3%
Division of Undergraduate Academic Affairs		50		60.1%
Provost / Academic Affairs		31		60.5%
School of Social Work	6	30	100.0%	51.7%
The Erickson School	4	29	100.0%	56.8%
No SIS College Mapped	2	30	66.7%	40.5%
Grand Totals	115	2,316	86.3%	53.6%

FIGURE 9.4   Spring 2015 LMS adaptive release use & percentage items accessed by students

Despite our mixed results with adaptive learning (e.g., compelling results, but relatively low faculty adoption), it has been encouraging to learn from other organizations and institutions. First, the IMS Global white paper, "From Adaptable to Adaptive: The Next Generation of Personalized Learning" (Edwards et al., 2017) not only provides examples from different institutions, but also provides a useful framework for different types of adaptive learning systems[9]:

– *Decision Tree*: "DT systems simply use a set of rules from a pre-prescribed set of content modules organized in pre-prescribed sets of assessments and answer banks. Using intervals of data and feedback, learner workflows are created and individualized work streams assigned throughout a set pace."
– *Rules Based*: "In RB, a particular learning path is predetermined by rule sets that can change for individual learners, and feedback is provided once a learning unit is concluded."
– *Machine Learning*: "Machine learning-based adaptive platforms are the most advanced method in which to establish a truly adaptive state. Machine learning uses techniques that are equivalent, pattern recognition, statistical modeling, predictive analytics. ML-based systems use programmed algorithms to make real-time predictions about a learner's mastery."
– *Advanced Algorithm*: "In AA systems, learning paths, feedback, and content are evaluated in real time by constantly analyzing data from the individual student and comparing it to other students exposed to the same or similar content. AA adaptive learning records and manages a huge amount data, tied to a learner profile, and records clickstreams, time intervals, assessment attempts and other transactional behavioral data."

From our perspective, two other institutions, Arizona State University and University of Central Florida, are doing exceptional work in scaling adaptive learning. For example, Dale Johnson (2018), Adaptive Program Manager at ASU—and one of the co-authors for the IMS white paper mentioned above—recently shared very compelling results from three large-scale adaptive learning pilots in different disciplines using different tools: College Algebra (ALEKS), Micro Economics (Cengage) and Introductory Biology (Cogbooks). His key point, which is hard to dispute, is that regardless of platform, adaptive learning works. This is another form of triangulating student engagement, albeit it at ASU.

In fact, the College Algebra initiative with ALEKS has been so effective (see Figure 9.5) that Johnson says ASU faculty eliminated remedial math altogether and now enroll admitted students directly into College Algebra—with a login to ALEKS for remediating any knowledge, skills, and abilities deficits.

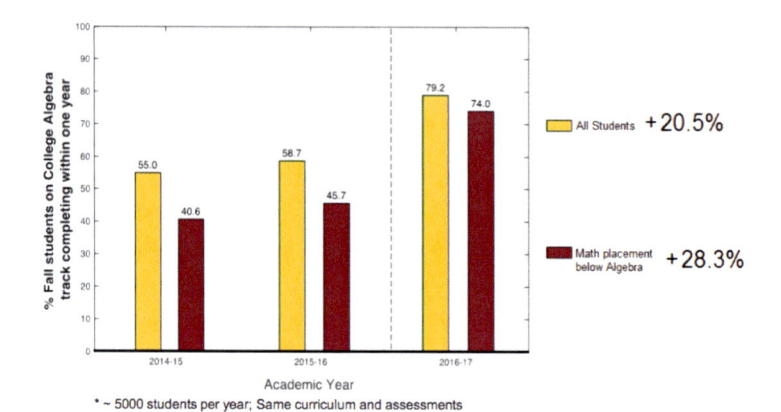

FIGURE 9.5   ASU's results with ALEKS in college algebra

Charles Dziuban and Patsy Moskal at the University of Central Florida (UCF) have long been leaders in online learning, with a particular knack for seeking out and understanding student attitudes and perceptions about asynchronous, blended and online learning (2015, 2007). In recent years, they've also developed, implemented and evaluated UCF's use of adaptive learning (2016) and partnered with other schools as well to understand how best to design adaptive learning courses (2017). In addition to compelling results we've come to expect from UCF, they've also incorporated their trademark focus on student perceptions as illustrated in Figure 9.6.

However, given the large amounts of real-time data generated by adaptive learning systems, Dziuban an Moskal (2016) also rightly explore the potential of predictive, adaptive analytics:

In addition to compelling results we've come to expect from UCF, they've also incorporated their trademark focus on student perceptions as illustrated in Dziuban, Moskal, and Hartman (2006, p. 6, Figure 9.1).

> [T]he massive amounts of data that are generated by adaptive platforms afford rich opportunities to engage faculty members and course developers in research on student learning and course design that can ultimately lead to greater levels of student success. One of the functions served by the grades assigned to students is to put a label on how much they did or did not learn. We can foresee a future where student learning can be both measured and assured, and where any and every student can legitimately earn an A.

4 Deep Dive: Validating a Nudge Intervention to Course Repeaters

Up to this point, we have focused on projects and methods that collectively paint a picture of undergraduate student engagement at UMBC. It may or may not resemble the student body at other institutions. But as we use learning analytics to understand our own students, and also learn from other institutions, it is informing our understanding of what any institution might do to help its students become more engaged and to take responsibility for their own learning. Towards this end, we offer a more detailed closing example of how we are currently thinking about moving beyond prediction to intervention.

4.1 Nudging Students to the Math Lab

With its orientation toward STEM fields, UMBC has a substantial enrollment in foundational math (here defined as College Algebra, Pre-calculus, Calculus I and II, and Applied Calculus). Foundational math presents challenges to student progression at many institutions and UMBC is no different. Between Fall 2009 to Spring 2016 over 23,000 students enrolled in foundational math courses. Over that period, approximately 36% of students enrolled in those courses received a grade lower than a "C."

Because math is an important course to progress in many popular majors and is a general education requirement, low success rates also lead to high course repeat rates. Nearly 300 students per term, 17%, or the equivalent of over seven sections of 40 students (our median class size) are repeaters. Senior leadership has made clear that higher success rates, without compromising rigor, is both an educational and a business imperative.

Unfortunately, success rates for repeaters are lower than for students making their first attempt. Approximately 45% of course repeaters fail to pass the class on a successive attempt. UMBC offers on-demand math tutoring, but utilization rates are low for both first time and course repeaters (approximately 11% for both groups).

Two questions became central to our efforts to improve student success in foundational math. Does the math tutoring we provide help? If so, can we use behavioral nudges to increase students' use of it?

Historically, we have measured the impact of the Math Lab by looking at the difference in success rates between students who used tutoring and students who did not. While recognizing this led to inconclusive results due to selection effects, we could not conduct random assignment in good conscience and the staff did not have the technical skills required to use statistical techniques that controlled for selection bias.

As part of UMBC's new strategic plan,[10] new staff and administrators brought more advanced techniques to analyze the impact of interventions like the Math Lab. This analytical effort combined information captured about student use of the Math Lab with information in our data warehouse. We then used a propensity score matching model to estimate the impact that math tutoring had on course repeaters in foundational math. Propensity score matching attempts to statistically replicate random assignment.

The results of the analysis were startling. Our estimates suggested a 17 percentage point increase in success rates (grades higher than "C") for students using math tutoring. The treatment effect for repeaters is approximately five times larger than that for students taking the class for the first time.

As math tutoring appears to help, we needed to construct a behavioral nudge to encourage students to use it. We decided to craft a message that used an empathetic tone ("math is hard for many people") that described how tutoring helps learning ("it makes study time more effective") emphasized its low cost ("it's free") and provided specific information about improved outcomes ("students who used the Math Lab were nearly 20% more likely to receive a passing grade"). This message was sent to all students repeating foundational math courses during the Fall 2017 semester (approximately 200 in all) during the first week of classes and during the sixth week of the term. Students who attended the Math Lab were sent an encouraging and congratulatory second message to reinforce their behavior ("you've made a good choice...keep going!")

We were surprised at the high "read rates" for these messages: approximately 60–70% of repeating students read the message. The highest read rate was exhibited by students receiving the congratulatory message. Struggling students most likely receive few positive institutional messages, and it may be that messages of this type are especially impactful.

Our preliminary results (constructed less than 30 days after the conclusion of the term) are interesting but must be interpreted with an appropriately high level of caution. We found that the nudge is associated with a large increase in the utilization rate of math tutoring: nearly 19% of students receiving the nudge used math tutoring, nearly doubling the longer-term average of 11%. For students who used math tutoring early (before the sixth week of the semester) there was an approximate 13 percentage point increase in their success rate (approximately a 25% change in success rates). When looking over the entire semester, however, the impact of the nudge is materially smaller, and very likely not statistically significant.

This pilot has certainly been successful as a proof of concept. Our efforts have brought together members from several different departments and divisions of the university. The costs of the intervention are largely those associated with setting up the analytical tools (message and messaging, data extraction, and the empirical model). Now that those start-up costs have been incurred, the costs of continuing the pilot are very low and we expect to continue it to build a larger sample to conduct additional analysis.

There is an important larger point that is not to be missed. Targeted messaging combined with analytics to identify pockets of at-risk students can be used to direct students to existing interventions. This type of intervention is scalable. Student support taking the form of tutoring or supplemental instruction, is also scalable at relatively low cost once analysis is used to identify courses where it is likely to have an impact.[11]

5 Conclusion

Given the current art and science of learning analytics, how might scholars and practitioners pursue and (ideally) scale the field's high goal of optimizing learning and enabling appropriate interventions? At least at the institutional level, the built and bought solutions and examples described in this chapter suggest the work will continue to be very iterative and ad hoc. Going forward, however, one hopes institutions—and the communities or vendors that support them the learning analytics field itself—might shift more time and effort from perfecting predictions to implementing, evaluating and disseminating reasonably good interventions. Unless or until we develop a critical mass of intervention design science and evidence of impact, the field may not bear the weight of its considerable hype and expectations.

Notes

1 https://www.gartner.com/technology/research/methodologies/hype-cycle.jsp
2 https://nces.ed.gov/fastfacts/display.asp?id=40
3 http://rex.umbc.edu/about
4 See time code 2:51 at http://screencast.com/t/mHuycLO6V for more years/
   semesters that illustrate the trend.
5 http://info.civitaslearning.com/community-insights-issue-2
6 For a brief demo, visit https://youtu.be/rpU1GdvS_yc
7 Specifically, in Fall 16, we found Bb Predict was 87% accurate in predicting C or better final grades by week 4. More info: https://doit.umbc.edu/news/?id=65634
8 https://doit.umbc.edu/itnm/practices/adaptive
9 By these definitions, our own use of Blackboard's Adaptive Release function would
   most likely fall into the "Rules Based" category.
10 http://planning.umbc.edu
11 A second pilot conducted during Fall 2017 that offered supplemental instruction
   in a social science course with low success rates had an estimated cost of approximately $14 per student.

References

Brown, M. (2011). *Learning analytics: The coming third wave (ELI brief)*. Retrieved
    from http://www.educause.edu/library/resources/learning-analytics-coming-
    third-wave

Campbell, J. (2007). *Utilizing student data within the course management system to
    determine undergraduate student academic success: An exploratory study*. Retrieved
    from http://proquest.umi.com/pqdweb?did=1417816411&Fmt=7&clientId=11430&R
    QT=309&VName=PQD

Caruso, J., & Salaway, G. (2007). *The ECAR study of undergraduate students and
    information technology, 2007 (Key findings)* (pp. 1–15). Retrieved from
    https://net.educause.edu/ir/library/pdf/ers0706/ekf0706.pdf

Dawson, S., McWilliam, E., & Tan, J. P. L. (2008). *Teaching smarter: How mining ICT data
    can inform and improve learning and teaching practice*. Paper presented at Ascilite
    Melbourne 2008. Retrieved from http://ascilite.org.au/conferences/melbourne08/
    procs/dawson.pdf

Dziuban, C., Howlin, C., Johnson, C., & Moskal, P. (2017, December 18). An adaptive
    learning partnership. *EDUCAUSE Review*. Retrieved from https://er.educause.edu/
    articles/2017/12/an-adaptive-learning-partnership

Dziuban, C., Moskal, P., Brophy, J., & Shea, P. (2007). Student satisfaction with asynchronous learning. *Journal of Asynchronous Learning Networks, 11*(1), 87–95. Retrieved from https://eric.ed.gov/?id=EJ842691

Dziuban, C., Moskal, P., & Hartman, J. (2006). Adapting to Learn, Learning to Adapt. *Educause Center for Applied Research Bulletin*, 1–13.

Dziuban, C., Moskal, P., & Hartman, J. (2016). *Adapting to learn, learning to adapt (Research bulletin)*. Louisville, CO: EDUCAUSE Center for Analysis and Research. Retrieved from https://library.educause.edu/resources/2016/9/adapting-to-learn-learning-to-adapt

Dziuban, C., Moskal, P., Thompson, J., Kramer, L., DeCantis, G., & Hermsdorfer, A. (2015). Student satisfaction with online learning: Is it a psychological contract? *Online Learning, 19*(2). Retrieved from https://eric.ed.gov/?id=EJ1062943

Edwards, M., Ford, C., Fritz, J., Johnson, D., Pugliese, L., & Birk. (2017). *From adaptive to adaptable: The next generation for personalized learning | IMS global learning consortium*. Retrieved from https://www.imsglobal.org/adaptive-adaptable-next-generation-personalized-learning

Fritz, J. (2011). Classroom walls that talk: Using online course activity data of successful students to raise self-awareness of underperforming peers. *The Internet and Higher Education, 14*(2), 89–97. doi:10.1016/j.iheduc.2010.07.007

Fritz, J. (2013). *Using analytics at UMBC: Encouraging student responsibility and identifying effective course designs (Research bulletin)* (p. 11). Louisville, CO: Educause Center for Applied Research. Retrieved from http://www.educause.edu/library/resources/using-analytics-umbc-encouraging-student-responsibility-and-identifying-effective-course-designs

Fritz, J. (2017). Using analytics to nudge student responsibility for learning. *New Directions for Higher Education, 2017*(179), 65–75. Retrieved from https://doi.org/10.1002/he.20244

Fritz, J., & Whitmer, J. (2017, July 17). Moving the heart and head: Implications for learning analytics research. *EDUCAUSE Review Online*. Retrieved from http://er.educause.edu/articles/2017/7/moving-the-heart-and-head-implications-for-learning-analytics-research

Fritz, J. L. (2016). *Using analytics to encourage student responsibility for learning and identify course designs that help* (Ph.D.). University of Maryland, Baltimore, MD. Retrieved from http://search.proquest.com.proxy-bc.researchport.umd.edu/pqdtlocal1005865/docview/1795528531/abstract/8BFCC74B55A94651PQ/1

Green, K. (2016). *The 2016 campus computing survey*. Retrieved from https://www.campuscomputing.net/content/2016/11/21/the-2016-campus-computing-survey

Johnson, D., Berg, K., De Gruyter, J., Vignare, K., Carter, D., Tesne, M., … O'Sullivan, P. (2018, January). *Go big: Early lessons from scaling adaptive courseware*. Retrieved from https://events.educause.edu/eli/annual-meeting/2018/agenda/sem03go-big-early-lessons-from-scaling-adaptive-courseware-separate-registration-is-required

Kellen, V. (2017, November). *Angst and expectations in learning analytics*. Keynote presented at the IMS Analytics Summit, Redmond, WA.

Long, P., & Siemens, G. (2011). *LAK '11: Proceedings of the 1st international conference on learning analytics and knowledge*. New York, NY: ACM. Retrieved from http://dl.acm.org/citation.cfm?id=2090116&preflayout=flat#abstract

Macfadyen, L. P., & Dawson, S. (2012). Numbers are not enough. Why e-learning analytics failed to inform an institutional strategic plan. *Journal of Educational Technology & Society, 15*(3), 149–163. Retrieved from http://www.ifets.info/journals/15_3/11.pdf

proxy, n. (n.d.). *OED online*. Oxford: Oxford University Press. Retrieved from http://www.oed.com/view/Entry/153573

Sharkey, M., & Harfield, T. (2016, November 23). Has analytics fallen into the trough of disillusionment? *EDUCAUSE Review Online*. Retrieved from https://er.educause.edu/blogs/2016/11/has-analytics-fallen-into-the-trough-of-disillusionment

Tyson, C. (2014, September 10). To maximize graduation rates, colleges should focus on middle-range students, research shows. *Inside Higher Education*. Retrieved from https://www.insidehighered.com/news/2014/09/10/maximize-graduation-rates-colleges-should-focus-middle-range-students-research-shows

Whitmer, J. (2012). *Logging on to improve achievement: Evaluating the relationship between use of the learning management system, student characteristics, and academic achievement in a hybrid large enrollment undergraduate course*. Retrieved from http://johnwhitmer.net/dissertation-study/

Williams, K. J. (2017). *Hype cycle for education, 2017*. Retrieved from https://www.gartner.com/doc/3769145/hype-cycle-education-

PART 4

Learning Analytics and Educational Research

∵

Implementation of a Learning Analytics System in a Productive Higher Education Environment

Clara Schumacher, Daniel Klasen and Dirk Ifenthaler

1 Introduction

Learning in higher education is increasingly supported through online learning environments allowing to track, analyze, and support learner behavior. A recent push toward implementing learning analytics systems in higher education institutions is well documented (Howell, Roberts, Seaman, & Gibson, 2018; Ifenthaler, 2017; Roberts, Howell, & Seaman, 2017). Learning Analytics use static and dynamic information about learners and learning environments, assessing, eliciting, and analyzing them, for real-time modeling, prediction, and optimization of learning processes, learning environments, and educational decision-making (Ifenthaler, 2015). Hence, learning analytics aim at better understanding and supporting student learning by offering personalized learning environments as well as providing just-in-time feedback (Gašević, Dawson, & Siemens, 2015). In times of growing and increasingly heterogeneous student cohorts, learning analytics are considered as effective means to early identify students at risk and thus reduce academic failure and attrition (Mah, 2016; Mah & Ifenthaler, 2018).

To meet these high expectations, learning analytics require a sound foundation in learning theory (Marzouk et al., 2016) and their implementation shall be aligned with technical possibilities. However, implementing learning analytics in organizations needs to be considered as an organizational change process and therefore requires all related stakeholders to be involved (Ifenthaler, 2017; Macfadyen & Dawson, 2012). Accordingly, implementing learning analytics in higher education institutions faces several challenges, such as:

a. students' willingness to reveal personal data (Ifenthaler & Schumacher, 2016; Pardo & Siemens, 2014; Slade & Prinsloo, 2013)

b. instructors' tasks to prepare a variety of learning materials and their potential lack of knowledge about analyses and the deduction of appropriate interventions (Greller & Drachsler, 2012; Gibson & Ifenthaler, 2017)

c.   the institutions' responsibility to make the resources available for integrating learning analytics into (existing) IT-infrastructure (Ifenthaler, 2017; Kevan & Ryan, 2016), and

d.   general challenges of institutional change (Buckingham Shum & McKay, 2018; Ifenthaler, 2017; Long & Siemens, 2011).

This chapter will introduce a decision-making process for identifying relevant learning analytics features based on empirical evidence and relating it to a feasibility analysis in terms of information technological costs as well as further organizational requirements. Further, the chapter reports an evaluation study of the implemented learning analytics system. The concluding section gives an outlook on further research needs and practical implications derived from this case study.

2   Implementing Learning Analytics in a Productive Higher Education Environment

2.1   *Pedagogical Perspective on Implementing Learning Analytics*

In contrast to big data related concepts in educational settings such as educational data mining (EDM) and academic analytics (AA), the primary focus of learning analytics is on being beneficiary for learners and educators by supporting and facilitating learning processes (Haythornthwaite, de Laat, & Dawson, 2013; Ifenthaler, 2015). One major aim of learning analytics is to provide personalized learning environments adapting to students' needs based among others on their previous interaction with the learning material and their learning progress (Sclater, Peasgood, & Mullan, 2016). Hence, the development of learning analytics system needs to go beyond technical issues. A strong foundation of learning analytics in learning theory as well as learners' and instructors' expectations supplemented with rigorous empirical evidence are the minimum requirements (Marzouk et al., 2016; Schumacher & Ifenthaler, 2018). For example, a study investigating students' expectations on features learning analytics systems could provide identified key features with regard to perceived learning support and students' willingness to use them (Schumacher & Ifenthaler, 2018). In this study, students perceived the highest learning support from features for self-assessments with immediate feedback ($M = 3.73$, $SD = .69$), learning recommendations for course completion ($M = 3.73$, $SD = .67$), and a timeline showing their current status towards learning objectives ($M = 3.63$, $SD = .76$).[1] Findings of this study also indicate that students' perceived learning support from a specific feature positively predicts their willingness to use it (Schumacher & Ifenthaler, 2018).

Clearly, learning analytics provide benefits for all involved stakeholders within the educational system. When focusing on the benefits directly related to learning and teaching process, the following benefits may be achieved (Ifenthaler & Widanapathirana, 2014):

– Teachers may analyze their teaching practices and increase the quality of teaching using a summative perspective after a semester. Using a real-time or formative perspective, they may be able to monitor students' learning progress and adapt their teaching according to students' needs (e.g., when they struggle with particular content or loss of motivation and attention). A predictive or prescriptive perspective of learning analytics may support them by identifying learners' at risk, planning upcoming interventions, or revising the curriculum based on learners' dispositions.

– For students, learning analytics may provide a summative understanding of their learning habits and help them to the possibility to compare their previously defined learning goals against their current outcomes. Real-time features may provide them with automated interventions as well as scaffolds and offer just-in-time feedback on their assessments. Predictive analytics features may allow students to optimize their learning paths and potentially increase their engagement.

Especially in higher education, students' capability to self-regulate their learning is considered as crucial for successful learning outcomes (Ifenthaler, 2012; Zimmerman, 1990). Learning analytics may provide helpful functionalities to support each phase of self-regulated learning. For example, (1) reminder for deadlines in the forethought phase, (2) just-in-time feedback on self-assessments, learning recommendations or suggestions of learning partners in the performance phase, (3) a timeline showing students' current status towards course objectives or a comparison with fellow students in the self-reflection phase (Schumacher & Ifenthaler, 2018).

To be capable to provide these benefits, learning analytics rely on a broad variety of data from several resources. Therefore, students need to reveal personal data, hence learning analytics are closely related to ethics and privacy issues (Pardo & Siemens, 2014; Prinsloo & Slade, 2017; Slade & Prinsloo, 2013; West, Huijser, & Heath, 2016). Students' acceptance of learning analytics systems and their willingness to use such systems depends on their perceived control over data, the transparency provided, and the perceived benefits (Ifenthaler & Schumacher, 2016; Roberts et al., 2017; Slade & Prinsloo, 2013).

Besides the above mentioned benefits, educators might fear extra workload when learning analytics are adopted by their institution (Macfadyen & Dawson, 2012). Reason may include the complexity of analyses of (big) educational data and the difficulty in understanding and interpreting the results of underlying algorithms which are often based on complex assumptions. As learning analytics aim at offering real-time feedback and even forecasts, these analyses need to be performed automatically on real-time data. Furthermore, working on big educational data differs from standard quantitative research methods by searching for usage patterns and generating hypothesis based on the data instead of defining hypotheses in advance and hence creating appropriate research set-ups (Gibson & Ifenthaler, 2017; Salganik, 2018). For example, algorithms are applied to reduce noise resulting in invalid results and to handle the high dimensionality of data in order to identify relevant attributes for the analyses (Costa, Fonseca, Santana, de Araújo, & Rego, 2017). To facilitate the understanding of analyses' results for non-professionals and to reveal behavioral patterns most commonly visualizations are generated such as radar plots, heat maps and bar charts (Greller & Drachsler, 2012; Liu et al., 2017). Nevertheless, to most educators the underlying assumptions of the analyses remain hidden and they hence have to rely on the automated outcome of the learning analytic system which might lead to hesitance to integrate the results into their educational practice (Howell et al., 2018). Furthermore, learning analytics are still deficient due to the incompleteness of data by only having insights into students' online user behavior and due to perpetual uncertainty which indicators are most efficient, thus educators have to critically weigh learning analytics suggestions (Greller & Drachsler, 2012). A recent study found that institutions besides technical requirements especially lack of specialists for implementing learning analytics in higher education institutions (Ifenthaler, 2017). Hence, the need to inform and train professionals in understanding but also in implementing learning analytics is vital for obtaining the above mentioned benefits (Gibson & Ifenthaler, 2017).

2.2　*Organizational Perspective on Implementing Learning Analytics*

In addition to the above described benefits for learning and teaching, leaning analytics have the potential to facilitate decision-making at the institutional level and provide insights into student attrition as well as to identify gaps in curricular planning (Arnold & Pistilli, 2012; Ifenthaler & Widanapathirana, 2014). *Institutional leaders* use summative learning analytics to optimise resource allocation to better support students' learning needs. Real-time learning analytics identify student attrition and track enrolment in study programmes and specific cohorts. Predictive learning analytics help institutions to detect gaps in institutional planning and forecast organisational processes and developments. Benefits for *governance* include the development of benchmarks for quality assurance, the collection of evidence for accreditation, and the supply of detailed information for policy makers.

However, are institutions and academics as well as administrative staff prepared for learning analytics? For example, the vast amount of available educational data calls for flexible data mining tools and new statistical methods including advanced machine learning algorithms (Ifenthaler & Widanapathirana, 2014). Further, institutions need to develop and implement interactive data visualisations which provide students, instructors, instructional designers, and administrators an overview of relevant information (Greller & Drachsler, 2012; Tempelaar, Rienties, & Giesbers, 2015).

The current state of implementation of learning analytics in higher education institutions may be a paradoxical exercise. On the one hand, world-class experts in data science, information systems, management, and education may be part of the institution. On the other hand, these experts may only have loose insights into the requirements of learning analytics when it comes to questions of implementation. Further, these experts may not be interested in facilitating change processes at their home institution. In order to overcome such institutional barriers, Buckingham Shum and McKay (2018) suggest serval organizational architectures including pros and cons: (a) The IT Service Center Model assumes that the learning analytics system is developed and implemented through IT services of the higher education instruction. The pros of this model are clearly on the technical side, as all systems (e.g., learning management system, data warehouse, student information system, etc.) are managed by this unit. Faculty may not have the opportunity to guide the development and implementation of the learning analytics system. In addition, an evidence-centred approach driven by academic faculty is unlikely. (b) The Faculty Academics Model assumes that academics conduct research and drive the implementation of a learning analytics system. Through evidence-centred research and development, immediate and robust findings are produced with regard to acceptance, effectiveness, and challenges involved when implementing learning analytics systems. (c) The Innovation Centre Model assumes an autonomous entity of the higher education institution which is well connected to faculty and administrative services. Partnerships among all stakeholders are vital for the success of this model. When overall accepted, this model combines the strengths of the afore mentioned models. The implemented learning analytics system introduced in this chapter followed the Faculty Academics Model, however, with a strong collaboration with the IT Service Centre of the university.

2.3 *Information Technological Perspective on Implementing Learning Analytics*

A standard infrastructure of a higher education institutions includes the following systems (see Figure 10.1): One system manages the student's semester

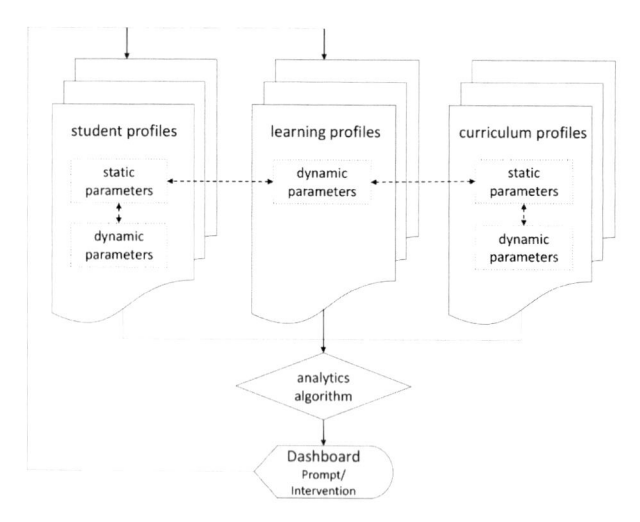

FIGURE 10.1   Student, learning, and curriculum profiles of the learning analytics framework
(adapted from Ifenthaler & Widanapathirana, 2014)

profile (e.g., courses, lectures), a second system manages the actual learning process within different courses (e.g., learning management system), and a third system is used to manage the curricular requirements (e.g., learning outcomes, corresponding materials).

These systems are deeply embedded into the university's infrastructure and often are not designed to reveal data for analytics. For accessing the necessary data, various connections to the university's legacy systems have to be established which are able to access the students' profiles, to capture the actual learning progresses and get access to curricula data. As these legacy systems are often based on various technologies, each connection has to be implemented as an individual project. Beside this technical effort, administrative effort with the operating university institution may not be underestimated (Buckingham Shum & McKay, 2018). In many cases, data of the source systems are managed in very specialized structures and may have to be revised and standardized before it can be used.

In addition to accessing the already existing data, many countries have strict privacy laws which complicate the capturing of additional data without a legal basis or an explicit agreement of the individual student. Students have to be able to determine for themselves, if and which personal data are collected. This personal data has to be handled very stringent, so that it can only be accessed by authorized persons (Ifenthaler & Schumacher, 2016). It is therefore recommended to keep the various types of data separated and link them via a secured identifier which reveals no conclusions about its source. A respective software solution has to be offered (Schön & Ifenthaler, 2018).

2.4 Conclusion for Implementing LeAP

The findings of students' willingness to use a certain learning analytics features and how they rate the perceived learning support were used as an empirical basis for selecting potential features to be implemented into the learning analytics system. The features were then categorized by experts (one from computer science and one from learning science), based on four aspects with a three points traffic light system from 1 (high effort/minor value) to 3 (minor effort/high value) and were multiplied to an overall prioritization value, similar to the risk index in a risk analysis matrix. The four aspects were (1) students' willingness to use the feature, (2) students' perceived learning support of a feature, (3) the technological effort of implementation, and (4) the organizational effort (e.g., data privacy issues). After ranking the features to their final prioritization value (see Table 10.1), the features were implemented from top to bottom. Beginning with a reminder for deadlines, self-assessments, and the course timeline which shows the current progress and goals. Unfortunately, the feature for providing feedback on assignments will cause considerable research and implementation effort and will be implemented at a later iteration of the learning analytics system.

3 Evaluation Study

3.1 Context and Research Questions

The implementation of the learning analytics system LeAP (learning analytics profiles) followed an evidence-centered design approach. Evaluation data were collected while implementing LeAP into the productive university systems as follows:

In the first semester, features were used which the university's learning management system could already provide to students, such as using a course structure view, transparent learning outcomes, and related materials. In addition, a variety of self-assessments were offered as well as the possibility to receive and give peer-feedback on project assignments. Furthermore, the material was supplemented by lecture recordings for each defined learning outcome. This initial level was used to identify the functionalities of the learning management system and the need to develop additional functionalities as well as to detect possibilities how to get access to learners' trace data. For evaluation purposes, a qualitative study approach was used focusing on the students' use of the learning management system, their perceived learning support, usability issues, as well as future features students would expect from an advanced learning management system.

TABLE 10.1   Decision matrix. The last column shows the final prioritization as product of the four aspects: students' willingness to use a feature, perceived learning support, technological effort of implementation and the organizational effort

Feature	Students' willingness to use a feature	Students' perceived learning support	Technological effort of implementation	Organizational effort	Prioritization
reminder for deadlines	3	2	3	3	54
self-assessments	3	3	2	2	36
timeline showing current status and goal	2	3	2	2	24
feedback on assignments	3	2	1	3	18
newsfeed with relevant news matching the learning content	2	1	2	3	12
time spent online	1	2	3	2	12
learning recommendations	3	3	1	1	9
rating scales for provided learning material	1	1	3	3	9
revision of former learning content	3	3	1	1	9
time needed to complete a task or read a text	1	1	3	2	6
comparison with fellow students	1	1	2	2	4
suggestion of learning partners	1	2	1	1	2
term scheduler, recommending relevant courses	2	1	1	1	2

In the following semester, the first version of the learning analytics system LeAP was implemented. LeAP offered reminders for deadlines, self-assessments, an overview about learning outcomes, and prompting functions. LeAP included a trace data feature for teachers/administrators which tracks students' online behavior. In order to meet data protection regulations and students' privacy perceptions, they may decide if their online behavior is (a) tracked anonymously without being linked to their pseudonym, (b) tracked and linked to their pseudonym, or (c) not tracked at all. For evaluation purposes, a quantitative study approach was used which was guided by the following hypotheses: It is assumed that students' prerequisites (current study grade (H1a), numbers of courses (H1b)), their perceived benefits from learning analytics (H2), and their interactions in the learning management system (number of interaction (H3a) and of completed self-assessments (H3b)) are related to their test performance.

In the following section the results from the qualitative study of the initial period of the implementation process and findings from the quantitative study will be presented.

4 Method

4.1 Participants and Design of the Qualitative Study

In the initial implementation period a qualitative interview study was conducted in order to obtain students' feedback on the improved offerings in the learning management system. In total, N_1 = 14 students (total participants in this course 117 students) participated in the study (9 female, 5 male) which were enrolled in the Bachelor's program of economic and business education at a European university. The interview duration was between 7.12 to 13.32 minutes with an average of 10.21 minutes (SD = 2.37).

4.2 Instruments of the Qualitative Study

Students were confronted with guiding questions concerning the usage of the learning management system, feedback on their perceived learning support, future features learning analytics system could provide, as well as usability issues. Examples of the guiding questions include "Which features in particular did you use?" and "What else could you think of the learning analytics system might provide to students to facilitate learning?"

4.3 Participants and Design of the Quantitative Study

In the following semester the pilot phase of the learning analytics system was accompanied by a quantitative online study with N_2 = 137 (105 female,

32 male) students participating. The average age of participants was 22.98 years (SD = 2.11). They were enrolled in the Bachelor's program of economic and business education at a European university. At the end of the semester students passed a written exam with an average percentage result of M = 79.3 (SD = 11.69) (max 100).

4.4   Instruments of the Quantitative Study

4.4.1   Learning Analytics Benefits Scale

The learning analytics benefits scale (LAB) assesses the benefits students perceive form learning analytics in terms of learning and more general support (Ifenthaler & Widanapathirana, 2014) (36 items; Cronbach's α = .938). Sample items of learning support are "The use of learning analytics would help me to compare my learning progress to that of my fellow students" or "The use of learning analytics would help to easier define my learning goals." Sample items for a more general support are "Using learning analytics allows teaching staff to better identify students at risk" or "Using learning analytics allows to better adapt courses to students' needs." All items were answered on a 5-point Likert scale, with 1 = strongly disagree to 5 = strongly agree.

4.4.2   Learning Analytics Acceptance Questionnaire

Based on the concepts of intended use and perceived usefulness of the technology acceptance model (Venkatesh, Morris, Davis, & Davis, 2003) this questionnaire focuses on students' intended use of learning analytics (LIU; 4 items; Cronbach's α = .957; sample item: "I think, learning analytics should also be offered in other courses.") and perceived usefulness (LPU; 5 items; Cronbach's α = .924; sample item: "Using learning analytics increased my performance"). All items were answered on a 5-point Likert scale, with 1 = strongly disagree to 5 = strongly agree.

4.4.3   Evaluation of LeAP

Students were asked about their perceived added value (1 item), their perceived data privacy (3 items; Cronbach's α = .904; sample item "I did not know who had access to my data"), and about their status of profile activation (1 item).

4.4.4   Final Exam

At the end of the semester students had to pass a final exam, consisting of 9 tasks (multiple-choice and text responses) designed for 90 minutes and a maximum possible score of 60 points.

4.4.5   Trace Data

If students agreed to activate their learning analytics profile the system tracks students' interactions within the piloted course such as resource usage or forum discussions. By generating a hash out of the user id the trace data could be integrated with the survey data by ensuring students' anonymity.

4.4.6   Demographic Data

Furthermore, students reported their demographic information, for example, age, course load, current GPA.

4.5   *Procedure*

For the qualitative study, students of the relevant class were invited to participate in an interview in June 2017. First, they received a short introduction about the interview situation and were then confronted with about 12 guiding questions which were adapted to the interview situation.

For the quantitative study, students of the relevant class were invited to participate at two measurement points at the beginning and at the end of the semester (autumn 2017). The first part included a knowledge test related to the course content including 10 multiple choice questions as well as student demographic data. The second part used the Motivated Strategies for Learning Questionnaire (MSLQ) (Pintrich, Smith, Garcia, & McKeachie, 1991), the knowledge test from the first measurement point, students' perceived difficulty of the class and confidence, perceived benefits and acceptance of learning analytics, and an evaluation of the particular system as well as the prompts students received during the semester. In addition to the survey data, students' online behavior was tracked with the LeAP trace data feature. The focus of this chapter will only include data from instruments which were described in more detail in Section 3.2.4.

4.5.1   Analysis

For the qualitative study, the audio recordings of all interviews were transcribed in text documents, using f4analysis – a software for qualitative data analysis – then the interviews were analyzed in terms of usage, perceived learning support, usability, and ideas on future features. Following a content sensitive qualitative research approach, both more frequent but also individual statements were taken into account. The statements of the interviewees were assigned in an iterative process to the prior categories.

For the quantitative study, the pseudonymized trace data from the learning management system were kept separately from the learning management systems database to increase data security. The survey data were also stored on a separate database. For analysis purposes, the trace data were aggregated with the survey data via a generated hash and analyzed using SPSS v.25.

5   Results

5.1   *Results of the Qualitative Study*

5.1.1   Usage of the New Functionalities

Almost all interviewees used at least the self-assessments and five respondents actively reported to have used the exercises with text-responses. Three participants (T7, T6, T5) reported that they primarily used the lecture recordings and rarely the self-assessments as they did not perceive it as necessary or did not realize early enough that it was offered for this course. One participant (T3) stated that he downloaded the lecture slides only and did not use any other material even though he recognized the potential support from it. Some students mentioned that they are not interested in further material or self-assessments on content which is not in particular relevant for the final exam, but they would prefer a specific training for mastering the exam (rehearsal). This was also highlighted by statements of three students that external links or additional resources were not considered necessary or not used due to a lack of time.

Lecture recordings were especially used by those who missed a class or decided not to participate in the lectures or (partly) for the preparation of the final exam. Two interviewees (T5, T10) reported that watching the lecture recordings was more helpful for their understanding "When using the lecture recordings, I have to admit that I took more notes and that it was even more helpful than participating in the class..." (interviewee T10). Furthermore, students emphasized the advantage of the lecture recordings in terms of flexibility of when to learn and to proceed in their individual pace.

In summary, the supplemented functionalities in the learning management system reached an overall acceptance by the students, especially self-assessments and lecture recordings. Two interviewees highlighted the enormous effort the teaching staff invested to offer further learning support and would prefer having this in other classes.

5.1.2   Perceived Learning Support

Students highly valued the possibilities to take self-assessments on each learning objective as this allowed a better understanding of what they should know and how potential tasks in the final exam could be like and most importantly supplemented their internal evaluation with external feedback on their performance. "In general, we are on our own and have to decide what might be relevant for the final exam, in this class the self-assessments were hints on what might be crucial to learn and to get feedback on how I am currently performing..." (interviewee T8). Half of the interviewed students even reported a higher motivation to learn for this particular class as they wanted to succeed in the self-assessments (T10), could flexibly listen to the lecture recordings (T9, T5) when they wanted, or felt to have more external support (T8).

As consistently working on learning material is associated with better learning outcome (Chen, Breslow, & DeBoer, 2018) one major aim of offering a variety of learning material to the learners is to encourage learners to follow up with course content timely. However, five interviewees reported that they did not start to learn earlier, however, eight students reported using the self-assessments during the semester for an early trial after "having read through the lecture slides," going deeper into detail when listening to the lecture recordings (T9), or at least being more online in this particular class. Three students indicated that they summarized the learning content already during the semester. In contrast to this, one interviewee (T7) stated that lecture recordings might even entrap to procrastinate instead of attending the class each week.

5.1.3 Students Feedback on Usability

All over, students preferred the clear structure of the course as each class was presented and supplemented by learning outcomes and related material such as self-assessments, lecture recordings and external resources (texts, library content, links, and videos). Students reported that they were able to find the necessary materials better and had a more detailed idea about the instructors' expectations on their knowledge. "I liked...that all material related to one topic was stored together and that I did not have to search for it...that it had a better structure...and easy to find..." (interviewee T6). However, two interviewees reported a difficulty to find the folder containing all reading material from the course. Four of the students who used the self-assessments asking for text responses reported that they did not receive the intended sample solution after submitting. However, one interviewee saw the advantage that she felt encouraged to check the lecture slides for the correct solution and another one perceived it a good occasion to think more about the solution.

5.1.4 Students Ideas for Future Features

Three students stated that they would like to compare their performance to their fellow students. Whereas, one student (T4) mentioned that this should be an optional function as it might not be motivating, and another interviewee thought that it might increase competitive pressure (T1). Furthermore, one student wanted to have a reminder function to get back on track and to learn more consistent during the semester (T6). Interviewee T4 would like to have a visualization of his learning progress. Another student wanted to receive a more detailed feedback on the performance on each learning outcome and on the self-assessments. Interviewee T1 raised concerns about the validity of automatic personalized feedback, as instead of having problems with a task a longer time on task might be due to external incidents.

5.2   Results of the Quantitative Study

5.2.1   Students' Evaluation of Learning Analytics

Regarding the evaluation of LeAP, students stated an average perceived added value of $M = 3.0$ ($SD = 1.16$). In terms of their privacy perceptions such as who has access to their data, how the data are processed, and where they are stored, students reported $M = 3.32$ ($SD = 1.07$). Furthermore, we asked which data tracking they allowed the system, more than half of the participants stated that they do not know any more (54.7%), 29.2% were active, 12.4% were anonym and a remaining 3.7% had an inactive profile. Regarding students' acceptance of learning analytics they rated the intended use of learning analytics systems with $M = 3.71$ ($SD = 1.02$) and their perceived usefulness was $M = 3.39$ ($SD = .89$). In terms of perceived benefits provided by learning analytics, students reported $M = 3.42$ ($SD = .55$).

5.2.2   Results from Trace Data Analyses

Fifty-seven students of the course activated their learning analytics profile, the average interaction per semester (number of clicks) was $M = 131.65$ ($SD = 86.83$) and in particular with self-assessments $M = 9.65$ ($SD = 18.15$).

Figure 10.2 provides an overview of students' use (all students with active or anonym learning analytics profile) of the LeAP system during the semester. The resources displayed are as follows: (a) *interaction* means general navigation through the learning management system not referring to any other resource; (b) *files* indicates if students accessed a stored file within the learning management system (e.g., lecture slides, PDF files); (c) *external resources* refers to students clicking on external links instructors provided (e.g., links to related websites, e-books); (d) *self-assessments* students' usage of self-assessments provided in the learning management system; (e) *forum* shows students' access of the forum in the learning management system. The chart shows an increase of interaction during the first four weeks of the semester, starting to decrease until week 7 followed by another peak in week 8 and 9 and receding till end of the semester. The lecture did not take place in week 5, 7, 8, and 9. The final exam was at the beginning of week 13. Two weeks before the exam interaction again increased (week 11 and 12).

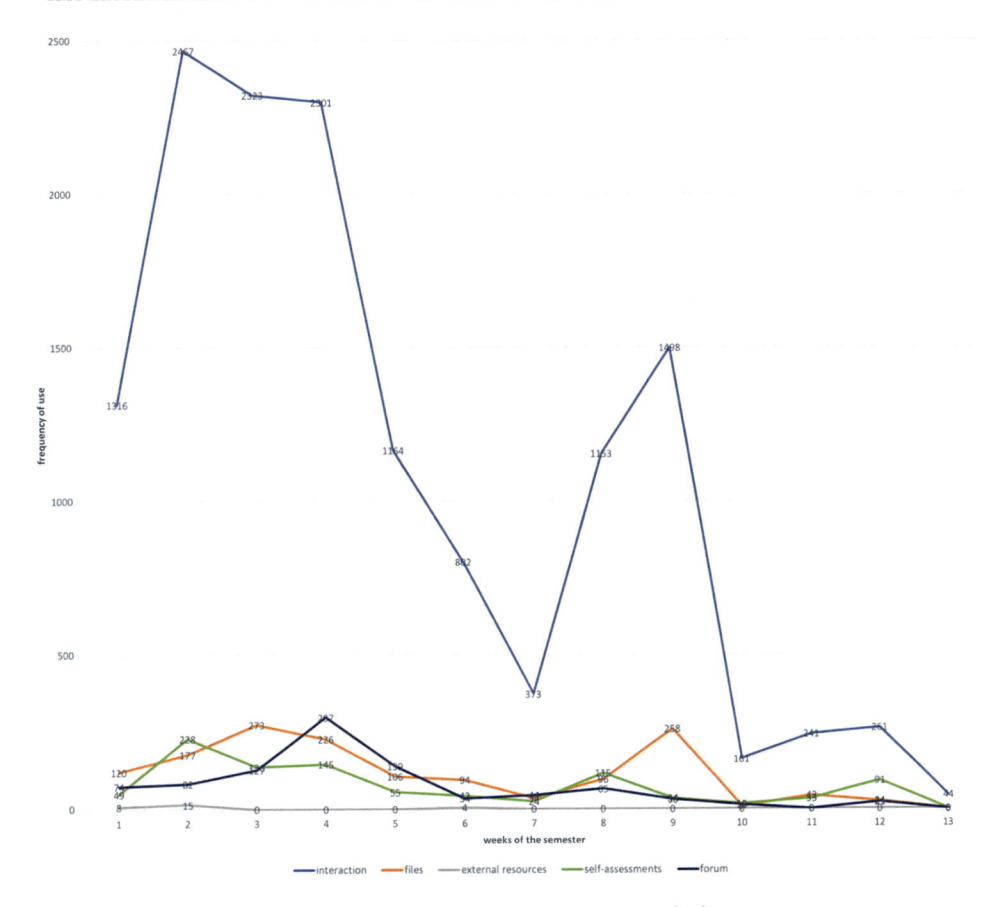

FIGURE 10.2 Students' frequency of use of the different resources in the learning management system for each week of the semester

5.2.3 Predicting Students' Test Performance with Learning Analytics

Linear regression analysis was used to determine whether students' prerequisites, the perceived learning analytics benefits, interaction with the learning management system and taken self-assessments were significant predictors of students' test performance. Students' current study grade ($\beta = -.389$, $t(41) = -2.793$, $p < .01$),[2] their interaction with the learning management system ($\beta = .364$, $t(41) = -2.2261$, $p < .05$), and with the self-assessments ($\beta = -.381$, $t(41) = -2.487$, $p < .05$) significantly predicted students' test performance. The final regression model explained a significant amount of variance in test performance, $\varnothing R^2 = .279$, $F(5,36) = 4.17$, $p < .01$. However, the number of courses during the semester and perceived learning analytics benefits were no significant predictors.

6   Discussion

Findings from the qualitative study highlighted students' perceived value of
self-assessments to receive feedback on their current progress and getting an
idea of the requirements of the course. Due to issues of the learning management system, students did not receive sample solutions of assessments with
text-responses. However, students coped with this issue in a positive way as
they thought in more detail about the solution or verified it by checking the
material again. Hence, offering self-assessments in learning analytics systems
can be considered as effective means to provide external feedback to learners
and supplementing internal monitoring processes (Butler & Winne, 1995). Nevertheless, further research should analyze students' dealing with and behavior
after receiving different forms of feedback (Chen et al., 2018). Another finding,
which needs to be considered in future studies is students' conception of only
focusing on rehearsing learning content and multiple-choice questions directly
linked to the final exam. Rehearsal is related to cognitive learning strategies
and associated with a more surfaced learning approach and not considered
as beneficiary for profound learning (Broadbent, 2017; Ifenthaler, Pirnay-
Dummer, & Seel, 2007). Students' expressions in the qualitative study that they
are not interested or do not have time to process additional external resources
such as websites related to course content or videos was also indicated by the
trace data showing virtually no interaction with external resources.

Lecture recordings aim at offering students the possibility to work on the
class content on their own pace, allowing more flexibility or review the material
again but might also lead to procrastination, lower lecture attendance, or impact
study performance (Bos, Groeneveld, van Bruggen, & Brand-Gruwel, 2016). In
our study, students also highlighted the flexibility and further they perceived a
better and more profound preparation of the learning content. Hence, lecture
recordings might support students' various needs such as revision or learning
on their own pace but further research is necessary as study results on learning
outcomes are diverse and depending on how students use the recorded lectures
(supplemental or solely) (Bos et al., 2016; Giannakos, Jaccheri, & Krogstie, 2016;
Leadbeater, Shuttleworth, Couperthwaite, & Nightingale, 2013).

Findings showed, that most students did not really allot their learning over
the whole semester, to increase students' motivation or self-regulated learning in general prompts and reminders are considered as promising means
(Bannert, 2009; Ifenthaler, 2012). Additionally, one student asked for reminders for more continuous learning.

Motivation is considered to be a vital source for successful learning processes (Cook & Artino Jr., 2016). Three students expressed they perceived a

higher motivation to learn in this particular course. Further research should investigate the relation of motivation and learning analytics in order to support and not impair students' motivation to learn.

As the findings of the qualitative study indicated different perceptions and preferences for customization of a dashboard (see also Roberts et al., 2017; Schumacher & Ifenthaler, 2018), this will be considered for future technical development of LeAP system to meet the expected high personalization.

Findings of the quantitative study indicate that trace data are related to students' learning outcome. However, it is not sufficient to quantify students' interactions with the learning management system as they can only be used limitedly for inferring the quality of learning or actionable interventions (Gašević et al., 2015). In order to produce benefits from learning analytics, the complexity of trace data and its relationship to learning design, social interactions, learner characteristics need to be considered.

However, findings also indicate that students' interaction with self-assessment resources show a negative impact on their final grade. One possible reason might be that weaker students tend to take more self-assessments than students who feel confident to pass the final exam. In the interviews and the prior study (Schumacher & Ifenthaler, 2018) students expressed a high perceived support through self-assessments especially to prepare for the final exam. A slight increase of tracked use of the self-assessments within the two weeks prior the final exam can be seen (Figure 10.3), however, a higher frequency of use would have been expected.

One major limitation was that in a course with 170 students only 57 enabled active tracking, the remaining 113 were anonym or did not allow any tracking at all. Hence, inferential statistical computing was limited to 42 students participating in the study and allowing an active tracking. Furthermore, the tracking of the trace data in this study are at an initial level and limited as this study was conducted within a face-to-face course supplemented with a learning management system implicating that learning takes place outside of the system. At that point of time, no distinct tracking of students' use of lecture recordings was feasible. In addition, our studies as well as the current system primarily focus on students' perspectives and was only available for one course. To attain a successful implementation of learning analytics within the institution the system as well as the research needs to include all relevant stakeholders and its' availability should be extended to other classes. Thus, besides generating benefits for students and hence resulting in an increase of their willingness to use the learning analytics system, benefits need to be extended for other stakeholders. Consequently, further research is necessary on perceptions of instructional staff and later on of administrative staff towards perceived usefulness and usability aspects of the learning analytics system (Roberts et al., 2017).

During this first pilot period, students were not used to learning analytics and only received few observable benefits from the LeAP system also indicated by the moderate results of the learning analytics benefit scale (M = 3.42; SD = .55) (5-point Likert-scale), the small number of students giving permission to be tracked actively, and low interaction in the learning management system. However, a previous study showed that students are more willing to share data if the system offers detailed feedback (Ifenthaler & Schumacher, 2016).

As the willingness to use learning analytics systems is the main prerequisite, voices of all stakeholders need to be integrated before an institution wide implementation (Kotter, 2007). Accordingly, putting a learning analytics system into practice is comparable to an organizational change process which makes it inevitable to prepare, inform, and guide the stakeholders to reduce uncertainty and resistance (Rogers, 1983). Users' perceived benefits need to exceed their perceived costs, such as extra workload, difficulties in using the system, uncertainty about the underlying algorithms, and their potential to support learning processes. Hence, increasing the willingness to implement and acceptance to use learning analytics could be realized by offering workshops addressing users' needs and barriers, pointing out the benefits, explaining the system and making users familiar with the functions by using them. Furthermore, findings of the quantitative study indicated that students were not sure about what happens with their personal data they revealed. Thus, to increase the (perceived) transparency and users' understanding, the learning analytics system could provide the possibility that students or educators can click on a result and get information about which data was used for it and the approach of the algorithm (Ifenthaler & Schumacher, 2016).

To get further insights into how students make use of a learning analytics system and how to better adapt the system to their needs upcoming studies might analyze patterns of usage behavior of students with better and weaker learning outcome (Liu et al., 2017) and to derive ideas of how to support both groups e.g. by prompting them to apply learning strategies.

In line with the qualitative and quantitative findings, we will offer students more elaborated learning analytics features including feedback about their progress and performance as well as improved prompting and reminder functionalities.

Hence, the next steps of the LeAP project are: (1) The implementation of a LeAP Cockpit displaying students' progress on each learning outcome, an overview about reminders concerning the course, and the possibility to decide if they want an active profile with all benefits or not (see Figure 10.3). (2) Evaluating the

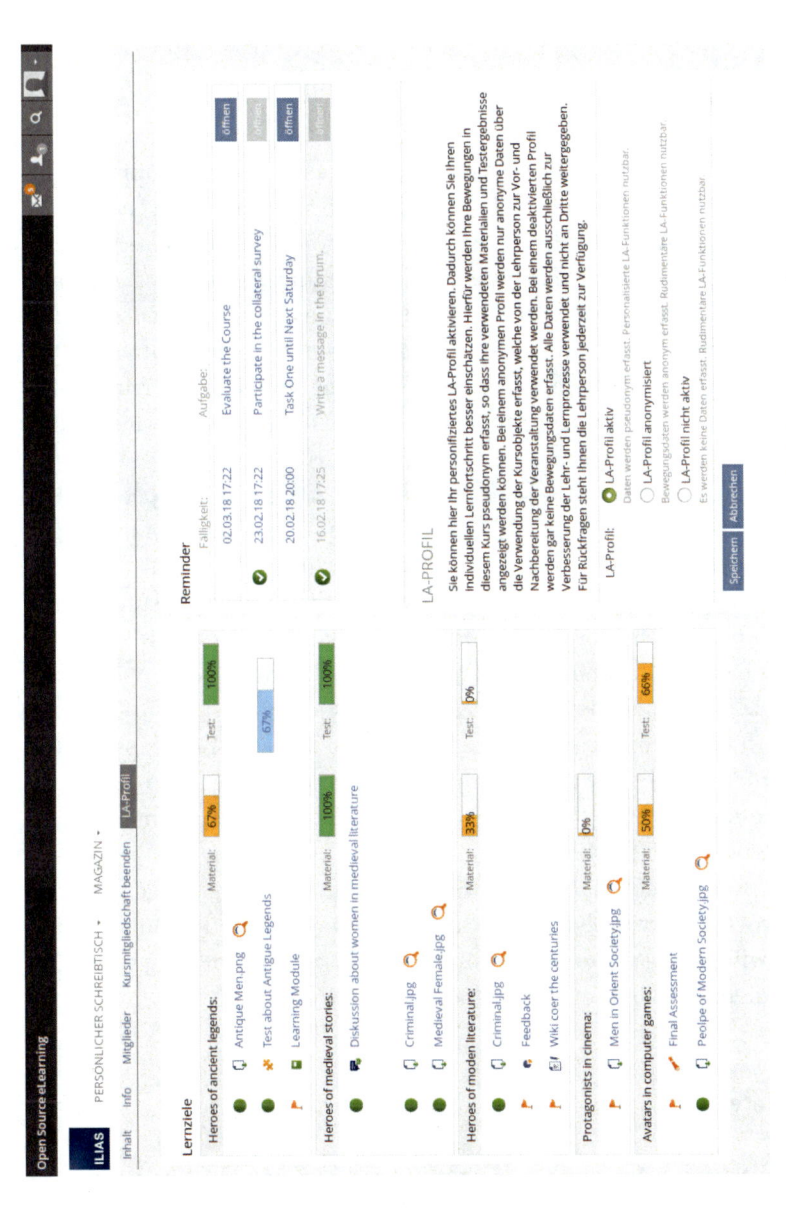

FIGURE 10.3 LeAP cockpit including learning outcomes and resources (on the left), information about reminders (top right) and students' possibility to decide about their anonymity (bottom right)

LeAP Cockpit in terms of students' usage by analyzing trace data and investigating students' feedback on it as well as their perceived benefits of the newly implemented features. (3) Offering the LeAP system to additional piloting classes.

7   Conclusion

Findings of the present studies indicate that students perceive support from learning analytics such as feedback on their progress and on what is expected from them or a higher flexibility due to the various learning materials provided. Furthermore, trace data was related to students' learning outcome (test performance). However, the relation of self-assessments and students' performance needs to be investigated further for example by contrasting the online behavior of better versus weaker performing students. Again it became obvious that students' privacy perceptions need to be considered when implementing learning analytics.

In order to meet the individual needs and achieve a better personalization of the learning environment, it may be useful to offer several learning opportunities to students, such as lecture recordings, additional resources, self-assessment with immediate feedback and further investigate students use by combining standard inventories on learner characteristics with trace data for further insights on potential factors influencing learning performance supported by learning analytics (Winne & Baker, 2013).

In sum, further empirical evidence is needed to meet the high expectations learning analytics are associated with. Rigorous research needs to go beyond technical questions by including concepts such as self-efficacy, interest, goal setting, metacognitive awareness or anxiety from learning theory.

In addition, interdisciplinary collaboration and a guided organizational change process are vital factors for successful implementation, high acceptance and willingness to use the learning analytics system providing benefits to all stakeholders within the higher education institution.

Notes

1 Items in this study were answered on a five-point Likert scale, with 1 = strongly disagree to 5 = strongly agree.
2 Due to the German grading system a negative correlation implies that a good GPA is related to a good grade in the final exam which in this study is expressed as a percentage.

References

Arnold, K. E., & Pistilli, M. D. (2012). *Course signals at Purdue: Using learning analytics to increase student success.* Paper presented at the LAK'12, Vancouver. Retrieved from https://www.itap.purdue.edu/learning/docs/research/Arnold_Pistilli-Purdue_University_Course_Signals-2012.pdf

Bannert, M. (2009). Promoting self-regulated learning through prompts. *Zeitschrift für Pädagogische Psychologie, 23*(2), 139–145.

Bos, N., Groeneveld, C., van Bruggen, J., & Brand-Gruwel, S. (2016). The use of recorded lectures in educatin and the impact on lecture attendance and exam performance. *British Journal of Educational Technology, 47*(5), 906–917. doi:10.1111/bjet.12300

Broadbent, J. (2017). Comparing online and blended learner's self-regulated learning strategies and academic performance. *Internet and Higher Education, 33,* 24–32. doi:10.1016/j.iheduc.2017.01.004

Buckingham Shum, S., & McKay, T. A. (2018). Architecting for learning analytics. Innovating for sustainable impact. *Educause Review, 53*(2), 25–37.

Butler, D. L., & Winne, P. H. (1995). Feedback and self-regulated learning: A theoretical synthesis. *Review of Educational Research, 65*(3), 245–281.

Chen, X., Breslow, L., & DeBoer, J. (2018). Analyzing productive learning behaviors for students using immediate corrective feedback in a blended learning environment. *Computers & Education, 117,* 59–74. doi:10.1016/j.compedu.2017.09.013

Cook, D. A., & Artino Jr., A. R. (2016). Motivation to learn: An overview of contemporary theories. *Medical Education, 50,* 997–1014.

Costa, E. B., Fonseca, B., Santana, M. A., de Araújo, F., & Rego, J. (2017). Evaluating the effectiveness of educational data mining techniques for early prediction of students' academic failure in introductory programming courses. *Computers in Human Behavior, 73,* 247–256. doi:10.1016/j.chb.2017.01.047

Gašević, D., Dawson, S., & Siemens, G. (2015). Let's not forget: Learning analytics are about learning. *TechTrends, 59*(1), 64–71. doi:10.1007/s11528-014-0822-x

Giannakos, M. N., Jaccheri, L., & Krogstie, J. (2016). Exploring the relationship between video lecture usage patterns and students' attitudes. *British Journal of Educational Psychology, 47*(6), 1259–1275. doi:10.1111/bjet.12313

Gibson, D. C., & Ifenthaler, D. (2017). Preparing the next generation of education researchers for big data in higher education. In K. Daniel (Ed.), *Big data and learning analytics: Current theory and practice in higher education* (pp. 29–42). Cham: Springer.

Greller, W., & Drachsler, H. (2012). Translating learning into numbers: A generic framework for learning analytics. *Educational Technolgy & Society, 15*(3), 42–57.

Haythornthwaite, C., de Laat, M., & Dawson, S. (2013). Introduction to the special issue on learning analytics. *American Behavioral Scientist, 57*(10), 1371–1379. doi:10.117/0002764213498850

Howell, J. A., Roberts, L. D., Seaman, K., & Gibson, D. C. (2018). Are we on our way to becoming a "helicopter university"? Academics' views on learning analytics. *Technology, Knowledge and Learning, 23*(1), 1–20. doi:10.1007/s10758-017-9329-9

Ifenthaler, D. (2012). Determining the effectiveness of prompts for self-regulated learning in problem-solving scenarios. *Journal of Educational Technology & Society, 15*(1), 38–52.

Ifenthaler, D. (2015). Learning analytics. In J. M. Spector (Ed.), *The Sage encyclopedia of educational technology* (Vol. 2, pp. 447–451). Los Angeles, CA: Sage Publications.

Ifenthaler, D. (2017). Are higher education institutions prepared for learning analytics? *TechTrends, 61*(4), 366–371. doi:10.1007/s11528-016-0154-0

Ifenthaler, D., Pirnay-Dummer, P., & Seel, N. M. (2007). The role of cognitive learning strategies and intellectual abilities in mental model building processes. *Technology, Instruction, Cognition & Learning, 5*(4), 353–366.

Ifenthaler, D., & Schumacher, C. (2016). Student perceptions of privacy principles for learning analytics. *Educational Technology Research and Development, 64*(5), 923–938. doi:10.1007/s11423-016-9477-y

Ifenthaler, D., & Widanapathirana, C. (2014). Development and validation of a learning analytics framework: Two case studies using support vector machines. *Technology, Knowledge and Learning, 19*(1–2), 221–240. doi:10.1007/s10758-014-9226-4

Kevan, J. M., & Ryan, P. R. (2016). Experience API: Flexible, decentralized and activity-centric data collection. *Technology, Knowledge and Learning, 21*(1), 143–149. doi:10.1007/s10758-015-9260-x

Kotter, J. P. (2007, January). Leading change: Why transformation efforts fail. *Havard Business Review*, pp. 96–103.

Leadbeater, W., Shuttleworth, T., Couperthwaite, J., & Nightingale, K. P. (2013). Evaluating the use and impact of lecture recordings in undergraduates: Evidence for distinct approaches by different groups of students. *Computers & Education, 61*, 185–192. doi:10.1016/j.compedu.2012.09.011

Liu, M., Kang, J., Zou, W., Lee, H., Pan, Z., & Corliss, S. (2017). Using data to understand how to better design adaptive learning. *Technology, Knowledge and Learning, 22*, 271–298. doi:10.1007/s10758-017-9326-z

Long, P., & Siemens, G. (2011). Penetrating the fog: Analytics in learning and education. *Educause Review, 46*(5), 31–40.

Macfadyen, L. P., & Dawson, S. (2012). Numbers are not enough. Why e-learning analytics failed to inform an institutional strategic plan. *Educational Technolgy & Society, 15*(3), 149–163.

Mah, D.-K. (2016). Learning analytics and digital badges: Potential impact on student retention in higher education. *Technology, Knowledge and Learning, 21*(3), 285–305.

Mah, D.-K., & Ifenthaler, D. (2018). Students' perceptions toward academic competencies: The case of German first-year students. *Issues in Educational Research, 28*(1), 120–137.

Marzouk, Z., Rakovic, M., Liaqat, A., Vytasek, J., Samadi, D., Stewart-Alonso, J., Ram, I., Woolosen, S., Winne, P. H., & Nesbit, J. C. (2016). What if learning analytics were based on learning science? *Australasian Journal of Educational Technology, 32*(6), 1–18. doi: 10.14742/ajet.3058

Pardo, A., & Siemens, G. (2014). Ethical and privacy principles for learning analytics. *British Journal of Educational Technology, 45*(3), 438–450.

Pintrich, P. R., Smith, D. A. F., Garcia, T., & McKeachie, W. J. (1991). *A manual for the use of the Motivated Strategies for Learning Questionnaire (MSLQ)*. Retrieved from https://files.eric.ed.gov/fulltext/ED338122.pdf

Prinsloo, P., & Slade, S. (2017). Ethics and learnig analytics: Charing the (un)charted. In C. Lang, G. Siemens, A. Wise, & D. Gašević (Eds.), *Handbook of learning analytics* (pp. 49–57). Retrieved from https://solaresearch.org/wp-content/uploads/2017/05/hla17.pdf

Roberts, L. D., Howell, J. A., & Seaman, K. (2017). Give me a customizable dashboard: Personalized learning analytics dashboards in higher education. *Technology, Knowledge and Learning, 22*, 317–333. doi:10.1007/s10758-017-9316-1

Rogers, E. M. (1983). *Diffusions of innovations* (3rd ed.). New York, NY: The Free Press.

Salganik, M. J. (2018). *Bit by bit: Social reserach in the digital age*. Princeton, NJ: Princeton University Press.

Sclater, N., Peasgood, A., & Mullan, J. (2016). *Learning analytics in higher education. A review of UK and international practice*. Retrieved from https://www.jisc.ac.uk/sites/default/files/learning-analytics-in-he-v3.pdf

Schön, D., & Ifenthaler, D. (2018). *Prompting in pseudonymised learning analytics. Implementing learner centric prompts in legacy systems with high privacy requirements*. Paper presented at the Computer Supported Education (CSEDU), Funchal.

Schumacher, C., & Ifenthaler, D. (2018). Features students really expect from learning analytics. *Computers in Human Behavior, 78*, 397–407. doi:10.1016/j.chb.2017.06.030

Slade, S., & Prinsloo, P. (2013). Learning analytics: Ethical issues and dilemmas. *American Behavioral Scientist, 57*(10), 1510–1529.

Tempelaar, D. T., Rienties, B., & Giesbers, B. (2015). In search for the most informative data for feedback generation: Learning analytics in data-rich context. *Computers in Human Behavior, 47*, 157–167. doi:10.1016/j.chb.2014.05.038

Venkatesh, V., Morris, M. G., Davis, G. B., & Davis, F. D. (2003). User acceptance of information technology: Toward a unified view. *Management Information Systems Quarterly, 27*(3), 425–478.

West, D., Huijser, H., & Heath, D. (2016). Putting an ethical lens on learning analytics. *Education Technology Research and Development, 64*(5), 903–922. doi:10.1007/s11423-016-9464-3

Winne, P. H., & Baker, R. S. J. D. (2013). The potentials of educational data mining for researching metacognition, motivation and self-regulated learning. *Journal of Educational Data Mining, 5*(1), 1–8.

Zimmerman, B. J. (1990). Self-regulated learning and academic achievement: An overview. *Educational Psychologist, 25*(1), 3–17.

CHAPTER 11

Discourse Analysis Visualization Based on Community of Inquiry Framework

Masanori Yamada, Yoshiko Goda, Kosuke Kaneko, Junko Handa and Yumi Ishige

1 Introduction

In the age of technological innovation, Computer-Supported Collaborative Learning (CSCL) is one of the powerful platforms available to support collaborative work. However, there are several challenges in the implementation of collaborative learning in educational settings, such as the comprehension of a collaborative learning situation. Learning analytics on collaborative learning seems to be powerful method to analyze a collaborative learning situation, and give feedback to teachers for the improvement and support of the collaborative learning. In order to do so, appropriate CSCL design and analysis should be investigated based on theories focusing on human relationship formation.

The background of CSCL is based in socio-constructivist pedagogical theory, which posits that knowledge should be constructed and re-constructed through interaction between learners, or between learners and artifacts (Scardamalia & Bereiter, 1993). In order to support collaborative work via CSCL, it is important to consider how one may enhance the interaction between learners who work collaboratively in a virtual setting when designing CSCL environments. The advancement of information technology allows us to understand collaboration situation, context, and level, and visualize this information. Mochizuki et al. (2006) developed the visualization tool "i-Bee" that visualizes activities and features words in a bulletin board system. Mochizuki et al. (2006) indicated that the visualization of the relationships between featured words and discourse activities promotes the learners' reflection on their collaborative learning. Oshima et al. (2012) developed and evaluated the effects of the social networking analysis (SNA) tool "KBDeX" that visualizes the discourse in collaborative learning on Knowledge Forum. KBDeX allows teachers to understand the process and discourse situation, using visualization technology based on social networking analysis. SNA is one of the most useful tools to visualize discourse on CSCL environments (Lee & Tan, 2017).

The Community of Inquiry (CoI) framework is one of the useful frameworks for the evaluation of learning activities and behaviors in learning communities in collaborative learning analytics. This study aims to evaluate the effects of the visualization for CSCL based on social presence in order to contribute to the enhancement of learning motivation and achievement in support of collaborative learning programs.

2   Community of Inquiry Framework

Garrison and Anderson (2003) constructed a CoI framework in which teachers and learners interact via text-based, online communication. The CoI framework consists of three elements: social presence, cognitive presence, and teaching presence. Social presence is defined as "the ability of participants to identify with the community, communicate purposefully in a trusting environment, and develop inter-personal relationships by way of projecting their individual personalities" (Garrison & Anderson, 2003). Social presence is regarded as a necessary element for creating a secure environment for interpersonal communication in order to foster an open environment that is conducive to discussion. Shea and Bidjerano (2009) suggest that social presence is fundamental factor in predicting the level of cognitive behaviors, that high cognitive learners treated low cognitive learners by responding to them using social presence. Cognitive presence is defined as "a vital element in critical thinking, a process and outcome that is frequently presented as the ostensible goal of all higher education" (Garrison et al., 2000). Teaching presence is defined as the design, facilitation, and direction of cognition and social processes for the purpose of realizing personally meaningful and educationally worthwhile learning outcomes (Gunawardena & Zittle, 1997). Integrating the three presences above for learning environment design promotes CoI (Shea et al., 2010), as doing so promotes metacognition for collaborative learning (Akyol & Garrison, 2012) and learning performance (Yamada & Kitamura, 2011; Goda & Yamada, 2012). Several studies have tried to design and develop a CSCL system that is either based on CoI or that comprises CoI components (e.g., Yamada et al., 2016a). The present study aims to evaluate social presence visualization, which is based on the "Social Presence" CoI element.

Enhancing social presence is effective not only in promoting learning satisfaction (Gunawardena & Zittle, 1997), but also in the promotion of cognitive learning behavior (Shea & Bidjerano, 2009). In order to enhance social presence, a reflective system in which learners monitor and adjust the current degree of social presence is needed (Yamada & Goda, 2012); because social presence is an unconscious feature, learners are not always engaged in collaborative learning with the consciousness of social presence. Social perspectives (e.g., self-introduction, saying thank you/good-bye, and referring to other opinions), which are formed in collaboration, are difficult features to support using groupware (Phielix et al., 2010). Several researchers tackled this challenge by using visualization. Mochizuki et al. (2007) developed and evaluated a visualization system called "ProBo Portable" which visualizes the situation and progress of each group member's task on a mobile phone. Visualization seems to be effective in the enhancement of social presence through monitoring learners' social presence level. This research reveals that the visualization of situation and progress in collaborative circumstances is effective as a reflective feature in monitoring each other and in enhancing the learning community.

3 System Used in This Study

Integrated computer-supported collaborative learning system "C4" (Yamada et al., 2016a, 2016b) was used in this study. This system was developed as a Moodle plugin (Version 2.8.X, 2.9.X, 3.1.X). This system consists of two parts: One is social presence visualization, and other is the function for social and

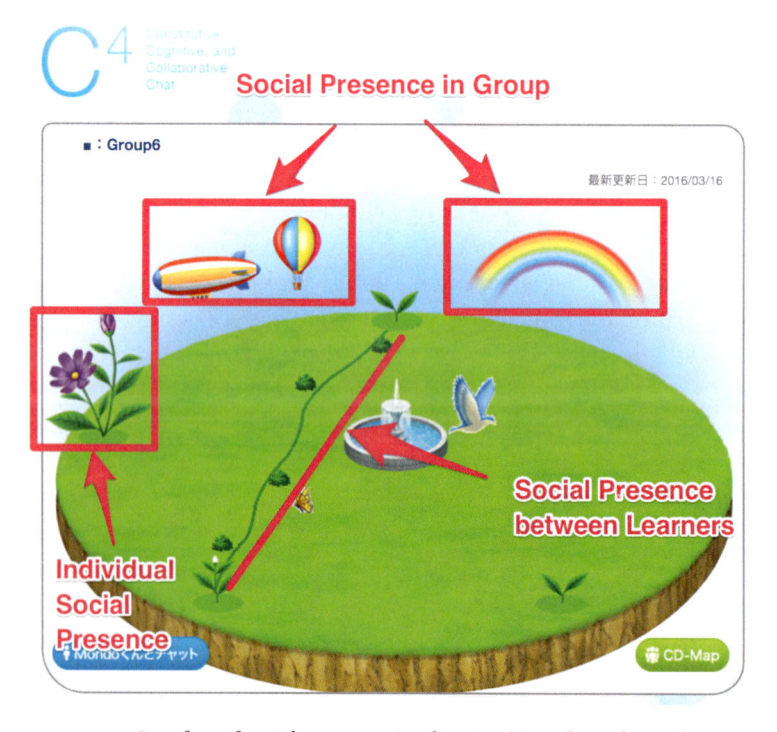

FIGURE 11.1   Interface of social presence visualization (Yamada et al., 2016)

cognitive communication, the "CD-Map." Figures 11.1 and 11.2 show the interfaces of the social presence visualization. The system stores every comment written by each user into a chat group thread and calculates the three types of Social Presence Scores: (a): Score of a user in a group, (b): Score of a user's reply to another user; and (c): Score of a whole group. The calculation of score (a) is based on every comment written by a user in a chat group thread. The calculation of score (b) is based on every reply made by one user in response to the comment of another user. For the calculation of score (b), the visualization system collects the data of the user name that sent the messages as variable name "MENTION." That is, the phrase "Reply Symbol" that is used in Table 11.1 refers to a kind of symbol that appears in the text when a user replies to another user's comment in the proposed system. Only when the symbol appears in the text is the first value in the score set as 1; otherwise, the value is 0. The calculations of score (c) are based on every comment written by every user in a chat group.

The proposed system has a national language processing (NLP) module for analyzing the text written by each user as a comment in a chat group. The core part of the system is implemented using PHP so that the system can be easily implemented to cooperate with Moodle which is developed in PHP. Only the module is implemented using Python because Python has many helpful libraries that support NLP. "Stanford CoreNLP" (Manning et al., 2014), a popular NLP library for analyzing documents written in English, is used in the module for the text analysis. The procedure that is used to calculate the Social Presence Scores starts with the core system's passing of one text written by a user into the

FIGURE 11.2   The interface of the change of social presence visualization

module, which is followed by the module's calculation of the Social Presence Score of the text. After this score is calculated, the score is returned to the core system. The returned score is expressed as a 19-value sequence (social presence and mention) of 0s or 1s, separated with commas, e.g., 0,1,0,0,1,0,0,0,0,0,0,0,0, 0,0,0,1,1,1. A value of 1 is set on the bit flag only when the text contains a factor related to each category supporting the Social Presence Theory. Otherwise, 0 is set on the bit flag. The 17 categories of Social Presence are listed in Table 11.1. The core system repeats the pass-and-receive process until every comment in a chat group is checked. After the process, the system adds up every returned score and presents the Social Presence Scores. The NLP module analyzes the texts by using rule-based procedures. Table 11.1 presents the rules that determine whether or not the text contains a factor that supports each category. The use of "Feature Word" in Table 11.1 shows that a text contains a feature word that supports the categories. The feature words were extracted in the pre-process phase from several sample chat data, which had 3,570 comments in 10 groups, and were also extracted from the WordNet database (Miller, 1995). The use of "Feature Phrase" in Table 11.1 refers to a certain phrase that frequently appears in a text supporting the categories. The phrases are selected based on the experiences of an expert who researches Social Presence by investigating phrase patterns of the sample chat data. Different from the case of the "Feature Word," the module checks the dependencies of each word on constructing the phrase. The feature words introduced in the previous section are extracted based on two types of methods: (a): The Statistical Method and (b): The Word-Net database. Method (a) uses the term frequency-inverse document frequency (tf–idf) method, which is one of the more popular statistical methods to extract feature words in documents. The feature words were extracted from the sample chat data containing 3,570 comments from 10 groups composed of university students. Every comment in the sample data has the Social Presence Score evaluated by several experts. For example, 0,1,0,0,0,0,0,0,0,0,0,0,0,1,0,0,0,1, 0,1 is the same format of the score returned from the module. In this research, the extracted feature words for a certain category show that the word appears 6 times in a text supporting the category in the whole document and appears less than 70 % of the time in texts throughout the entire document. A total of 345 words were extracted by the statistical method. However, several extracted words were removed by the experts because these words were influenced by the topic of the sample data.

Figure 11.3 shows the interface of the "CD-Map." After learners click the chat module link in the course, learners can move to the social presence visualization page displayed in Figure 11.1. When learners click the "CD-Map" button, learners can move to the CD-Map shown in Figure 11.3. The CD-Map consists of

TABLE 11.1   Social presence indicators and rule-based procedures for text analysis for social presence (Yamada et al., 2016)

Category	Indicator	Rule-based procedure
Affective	Expressing emotions	an Emoticon appears in a text
		a Feature Word appears in a text
	Use of humor	a Feature Word appears in a text,
		a Feature Phrase appears in a text
	Self-disclosure	a Feature Word appears in a text,
		a Feature Phrase appears in a text
	Use of unconventional expressions to express emotion	a Feature Word appears in a text, an Additional Feature Word appears in a text
	Expressing value	a Feature Word appears in a text
Open communication	Continuing a thread	a Reply Symbol appears over 2 times in group chats
	Quoting from other's messages	the Same Comment in the past 20 comments
	Referring explicitly to others' messages	a Feature Phrase appears in a text
	Asking questions	a Question Mark appears in a text
	Complimenting or expressing appreciation	a Feature Word appears in a text
	Expressing agreement	a Feature Word appears in a Positive sentence, a Feature Word of disagreement appears in a Negative sentence, an Additional Feature Phrase appears in a text
	Expressing disagreement	a Feature Word appears in a Positive sentence, a Feature Word of agreement appears in Negative sentence
	Personal advice	a Feature Word appears in a Positive sentence.
Cohesive	Vocatives	Mr./Ms. attached to a Named Entry of a Person appears in a text, a Reply Symbol appears in a text

(*cont.*)

TABLE 11.1 Social presence indicators and rule-based procedures for text analysis for social presence (Yamada et al., 2016) *(cont.)*

Category	Indicator	Rule-based procedure
	Addresses or refers to the group using inclusive Pronouns	The Feature Words, "we," "our," "us," "they," "their" and "them" appear in a text
	Phatic conversation, salutations, and greetings	a Feature Word appears in a text, the phrase of "how are you" appears in a text
	Course reflection	a Feature Word appears in a Positive sentence

two functions; chat and concept map. The chat function allows learners to post their messages using emoticons and share files. Learners can mark other posts as a "favorite" by pushing the "like" button. In the concept map, leaners can click and drag a posting object in the chat area to the concept map area, and then show relationships between postings using arrow lines. The concept map function as a group cognitive tool allows learners to index the information on the concept map, and thus is effective on the improvement of group memory (Hoppe & Gaßner, 2002). The researchers indicated that the system used in this research may be effective in enhancing social presence and improving discussion quality (Yamada et al., 2016).

4   Method

4.1   *Subject and Procedure*

Fifty-nine sophomores registering for one of the computer-assisted language learning (CALL) classes for English as a foreign language (EFL) participated in this research. The course was a one-credit mandatory class and consisted of fifteen 90-minute lessons. The students were from the Department of Architecture at a national university in Japan. These students had the minimal computer skills and knowledge (such as keyboard typing) required to participate. The average TOEIC-IP score was 470 from scores ranging from 270 to 680. Each lesson usually consisted of two parts, dictation and self-paced drill and practice e-learning.

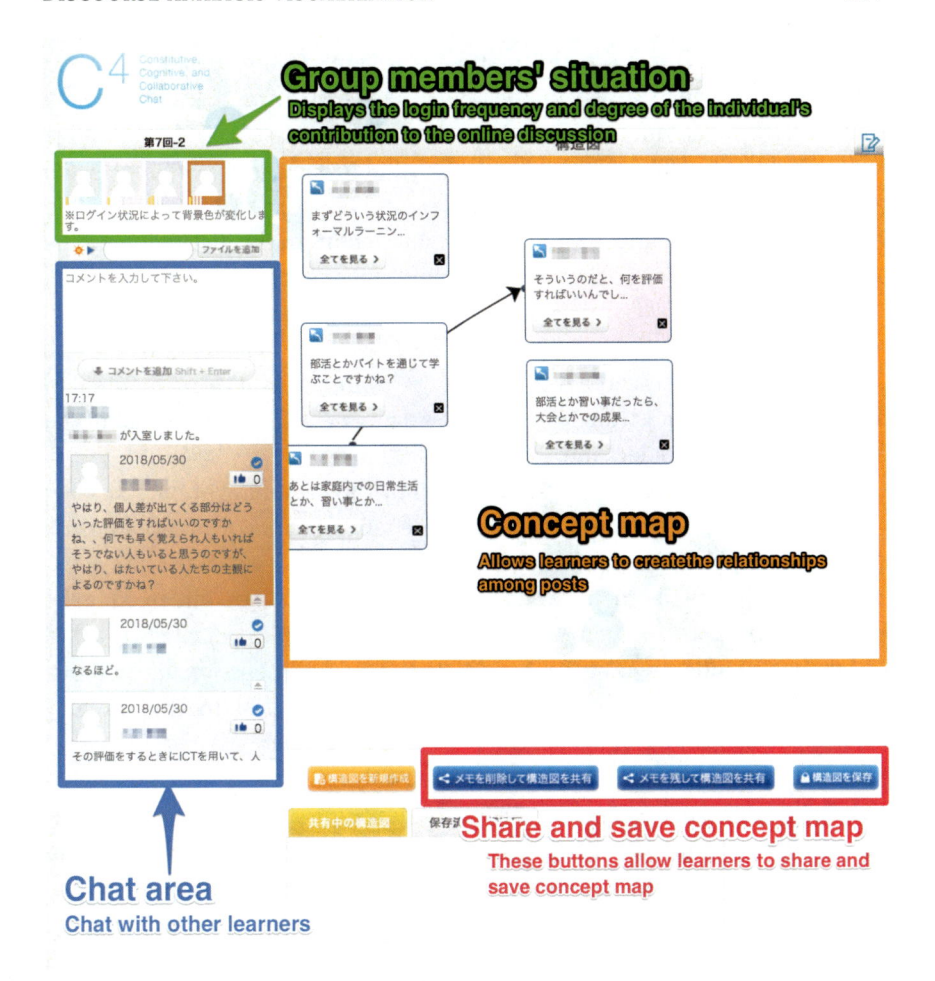

FIGURE 11.3   Interface of chat, concept map and member's login time display (Yamada et al., 2016a)

In this research, a project-based learning (PBL) activity was included in the usual classes in a month that included a winter vacation. The detailed PBL design is shown in Table 11.2. The PBL activity was counted as 10% of the final grade. The online discussion activities gave students additional opportunities to practice their English communication skills in and out of class.

The discussion topic, "The country that you want to live in," was selected, and students' interest in enhancing motivation, being engaged, and relating previous knowledge and/or experiences to the topic were considered. Students were required to set task schedules, and do division of labor. All students were required to participate in all activities and all conversation and discussion took place with the chat function of the C4 system. Each group consisted of three or four students. Students were randomly assigned to each group. Students were required to submit the information matrix (see Table 11.3) that described the viewpoints and evaluation of the country and report on the discussion theme of the PBL class 1 through the learning management system.

During the two-week winter vacation, students researched the information required to complete the assigned PBL class 1 tasks (see Table 11.4). In the PBL class 2, utilizing the research results from the group, students were required to discuss the topic. They were instructed to select one country at the end of the discussion as a group decision.

The students had to submit a final report by the beginning of the PBL class 3 to sum up the group discussion and provide rationales and evidence for their decision. Using the students' final reports, the class reflection on the PBL activities was led by the instructor. Then, finally, the students were directed to take Questionnaire 2.

Among 59 students, 52 students participated in the discussion and submissions, but three students out of 52 students did not take post questionnaire.

4.2 Data Collection

The CoI questionnaire, perceived contribution (one question), and the perceived effects of the visualization interface (two questions) survey was conducted at the end of the class two weeks later, in order to measure CoI level and learning behavior. The CoI survey according to Swan et al. (2008), displayed in Table 11.5, consists of 34 five-point Likert scale items, but this study used 21 items for the investigation of social and cognitive presences, because the instructor did not attend the online discussion. Students were also required to answer the perception of their individual contributions to their collaborative tasks in numeral format (min 0 to max 100), and provide a reason. This score is set as the dependent variable for the evaluation of this system. We set two questions regarding the perceived effects of the visualization interface as follows; Q1. The interface allowed me to understand the degree of the group activity level easily, Q2. This interface was intuitive for me to understand the degree of the group activity level.

All postings were categorized in cognitive presence following cognitive presence indicator displayed in Table 11.6. Two researchers categorized all postings using cognitive presence indicator through the discussion. If a posting contained one of the cognitive presence item, s/he set "1," if not "0." Each learner's score of cognitive presence was calculated by counting.

TABLE 11.2 Activities for project based learning (PBL)

Date	Activity	Highlighted instruction
PBL Class 1, 19-Dec-17	Questionnaire 1 (10)*	
	Practice Using C4 System (10) Instruction of PBL (5) Group Discussion to Share the Roles in a Group and Assign Tasks during the break (45)	-"Suppose we have to move to a country outside of Japan. If you had to live in another country for 10 years, which country would your group choose to live in? Choose one country, and identify your reasons for choosing that country at the end of the project."
		-Today, first, please download the "PBL1_CountrytoLive.xls" and decide on a group leader and a clerical officer for your group.
		Then, please identify, at most, four candidate countries and at least 10 items to research in your group. Then, decide who will be in charge of what with the "Task-Management" sheet of the file. The clerical officer should fill in the sheet based on the group discussion.
		-After that, please use the C4's "Project Management" function to plan your work by the next class. Please refer to the "Manual for Project Management" downloadable from the top of this page.
		-During the winter vacation, please research the assigned tasks in the group, fill your research results in the downloaded file, and upload it through the C4 system by the beginning of the next class, January 9th.
		-The group leader should check the task progress of the group members. Then, if necessary, please send other members reminders to push them to complete the tasks by the due date.

(cont.)

TABLE 11.2 Activities for project based learning (PBL) (cont.)

Date	Activity	Highlighted instruction
PBL Class 2, 09-Jan-18	Submission of PBL Assigned-Task List by Clerical Officer (5)	Clerical Officer, please add your group number at the end of the file before submitting the file. e.g., PBL1_CountrytoLive_AssignedTasks_Group2
	Submission of PBL Individual Research Results by Everyone before the Class	Please submit the excel file filling in the research results on the assigned items here.
	Submission of PBL Organized Results in Group (5)	Clerical Officer, please submit the organized results of the group here before today's discussion.
	Group Discussion on the Discussion Topic with the Organized Research Results as Evidence (60)	
PBL Class 3, 16-Jan-18	Submission of Final Report by Everyone before the Class	Please choose one country best to live in for the group. Then, please discuss the reasons why the country is the best to live in, including the progress of the group discussion. At last, please add your personal opinion. For example, you totally agree with the group selection, or you partially disagree with other members. You can justify your opinion illustrating the supporting evidence and/or rationales.
	Reflection of PBL in the Class (20)	
	Questionnaire 2 (10)	

* Allocated time in minutes.

TABLE 11.3   Part of task assignment matrix form

Research items	Description	Country 1	Country 2	Country 3	Country 4
E.g. Educational Level	*Check world ranking for higher education	John	Sam	Alex	Alen
1					
2					

5   Results

Forty-nine students out of 52 students answered the CoI questionnaire. First, the group effects were analyzed for further research. The scores of the social and cognitive presences were calculated by sum-up. Table 11.7 shows the descriptive data.

Three kinds of scores for the dependent variable "perceived contribution" were calculated in order to consider the group effects on individual perception of this system; Interclass correlation coefficients (ICC1, and ICC2), and design effect. If these three scores satisfy the criteria (that is, ICC1 is over 0.1, ICC2 is over 0.7, and design effect is over 2), multilevel analysis should be employed in order to investigate the group effect on individual perception. From the results of the calculation, all scores did not meet the criteria (ICC1: 0.005, n.s, Design effect: 1.013, ICC2: 0.017); these results indicated that group effects on individual perception were slight, and multilevel analysis is not appropriate for the data in this study.

In order to investigate the effects of this system, the relationship among the perceived effects of the interface, social and cognitive presence, and perceived contribution was investigated using sequential equation modeling (SEM). Figure 11.4 shows the results. Model fitting parameters (CFI, TLI, RMSEA, χ^2) are acceptable for validity (CFI = 1.000, TLI = 1.049, RMSEA = 0.000, $\chi^2(14)$ =11.35, p = 0.656). All relationships between the variables are positive. The results indicated that the perceived effects of the visualization interface enhanced the utterance of, and perception of social presence. The ease with which the degree of the group activity level was understood enhanced the perceived social presence, and intuitiveness of the interface to understand the degree of the group activity level enhanced the utterance of social presence. The utterance of social presence increased the utterance of cognitive presence, and the

TABLE 11.4   Sample of group research results (authors did not modify wrong spelling)

	Research Items	Description	Country 1	Country 2	Country 3	Country 4
			America(California states)	Germany	Spain	Canada
1	Living Level	*Check world ranking for higher living level	Student A: America is one of the highest quality of life countries, but in America it is differs from state to state. California is too.	Student B: Germany is one of the highest quality of life countries. Source:(http://info-graphic.me/life/3793)	Student C: The 17th place of world.	Student D: Canada is one of the highest quality countries.
2	Facilities for travel	*Check facilities for travel	Student A: They are using cars.	Student B: In Germany, there are many buses, subways and trains, so facilities for travel are good. Source:(http://www.hankyu-travel.com/guide/germany/traffic.php)	Student C: They are moving by subways and trains.	Student D: Canada is too large, so travelers should move by cars.
3	Language	*Check language of the mother country	Student A: They are using English.	Student B: The mother tongue of Germany is German.	Student C: it is Spanish.	Student D: They use English.
4	Climate	*Check climate	Student A: Is famous place is Hollywood country BeverlHills.	Student B: The climate of Germany is cold. Source:(http://www.hankyu-travel.com/guide/germany/country.php)	Student C: Mediterranean climate in this country.	Student D: Canada is too large, so it is diferrent from states to states.

(cont.)

TABLE 11.4   Sample of group research results (authors did not modify wrong spelling) *(cont.)*

	Research Items	Description	Country 1	Country 2	Country 3	Country 4
5	Commodity price	*Check commodity price	Student A: They are using top.	Student B: Commodity prices in Germany are about the same as Japan. Source:(https://www.compathy.net/magazine/2016/07/13/german-cost/)	Student C: Japan and equality or,a little,the top.	Student D: Japan and equality or,a little the top.
6	Population	*Check the number of people without nationality in the country	Student A: The number of people without nationality in the country is higher.	Student B: The number of people without nationality in the country is higher.	Student C: The number of people without nationality in the country is higher.	Student D: The number of people without nationality in the country is higher.
7	Indigenous products	*Check indigenous products	Student A: The famous place is Hollywood and Beverly Hills.	Student B: German indigenous products are beer and sausage.	Student C: Spanish indigenous products are Cheese.	Student D: Canadian local specialties are maple syrup.80% of maple syrup from all over the world is made in Canada.

(cont.)

TABLE 11.4   Sample of group research results (authors did not modify wrong spelling) *(cont.)*

Research Items	Description	Country 1	Country 2	Country 3	Country 4
8 Race	*Check race	Student A: They are using are 16.2%.	Student B: The main race in Germany is German. Source:(http://www.hankyu-travel. com/guide/germany/country.php)	Student C: The main race in Spain is Spanish.	Student D: A European Caucasian is 76.7% for 2011 years according to natural census,and a black people is 2.9%,and indigenous people are 4.3%,and others including Latin America and Asia are 16.2%.
9 Creed	*Check creed		Student B: The main religion in Germany is Christianity. Source:(http://www.hankyu-travel. com/guide/germany/country.php)	Student C: These people are Christian Catholic.	Student D: A Christian commands majority(77%) according to natural census in 2001. Though a breakdown is Anglo-America area, there is most Catholic with 43.2%.

(cont.)

Research Items	Description	Country 1	Country 2	Country 3	Country 4
					Next protestant,29.2%,the Great Orthodox Church and eastern several Catholic society are 1.6%.Muslem 2% and yahud 1.1% and Buddhist 1.0% and a Hindu follower 1.0% and a Skih are 0.9%. Irreligion is 16.5%.
10 Crime	*Check world ranking for the number of criminals	Student A:	Student B: Percentage of criminal population is higher than Japan.	Student C: They are 2,030,000cases.	
11 Hours of sleep	*Check world ranking for higher sleep level	Student A: Americans are sleeping the second longest time in the world.	Student B: The average of sleep time in Germany is longer than Japan	Student C:3 rank.	

TABLE 11.5   Community of inquiry instrument (Swan et al., 2008)

#	Category	Item
1	Teaching	The instructor clearly communicated important course topics
2	presence	The instructor clearly communicated important course goals
3		The instructor provided clear instructions on how to participate in course learning activities.
4		The instructor clearly communicated important due dates/time frames for learning activities.
5		The instructor was helpful in identifying areas of agreement and disagreement on course topics that helped me to learn.
6		The instructor was helpful in guiding the class towards understanding course topics in a way that helped me clarify my thinking
7		The instructor helped to keep course participants engaged and participating in productive dialogue.
8		The instructor helped keep the course participants on task in a way that helped me to learn.
9		The instructor encouraged course participants to explore new concepts in this course.
10		Instructor actions reinforced the development of a sense of community among course participants.
11		The instructor helped to focus discussion on relevant issues in a way that helped me to learn.
12		The instructor provided feedback that helped me understand my strengths and weaknesses relative to the course's goals and objectives.
13		The instructor provided feedback in a timely fashion.
14	Social presence	Getting to know other course participants gave me a sense of belonging in the course.
15		I was able to form distinct impressions of some course participants.
16		Online or web-based communication is an excellent medium for social interaction.
17		I felt comfortable conversing through the online medium.
18		I felt comfortable participating in the course discussions.
19		I felt comfortable interacting with other course participants.

(cont.)

TABLE 11.5 Community of inquiry instrument (Swan et al., 2008) *(cont.)*

#	Category	Item
20		I felt comfortable disagreeing with other course participants while still maintaining a sense of trust.
21		I felt that my point of view was acknowledged by other course participants.
22		Online discussions help me to develop a sense of collaboration.
23	Cognitive	Problems posed increased my interest in course issues.
24	presence	Course activities piqued my curiosity.
25		I felt motivated to explore content related questions.
26		I utilized a variety of information sources to explore problems posed in this course
27		Brainstorming and finding relevant information helped me resolve content related questions.
28		Online discussions were valuable in helping me appreciate different perspectives.
29		Combining new information helped me answer questions raised in course activities.
30		Learning activities helped me construct explanations/solutions.
31		Reflection on course content and discussions helped me understand fundamental concepts in this class.
32		I can describe ways to test and apply the knowledge created in this course.
33		I have developed solutions to course problems that can be applied in practice.
34		I can apply the knowledge created in this course to my work or other non-class related activities.

perceived contribution to group work directly. Perceived social presence was the centrally-mediated element of the promotion of group work contribution. Perceived social presence promoted the perception of the contribution to group work, as well as perceived cognitive presence strongly. Learners who rated their perceived contribution to group work by a score of over 50 were typically required to integrate the members' opinions in a group or were required to lead a discussion or report on the discussion. In these cases, these learners tended to decide the roles for group work and assumed roles such as the group leader.

TABLE 11.6   Indicators of cognitive presence (Shea et al., 2010)

Phase	Indicator	Description
Triggering event	Evocative (Inductive)	Recognize problem
		Puzzlement
Exploration	Inquisitive (Divergent)	Divergence
		Information exchange
		Suggestions
		Brainstorming
		Intuitive leaps
Integration	Tentative (Convergent)	Convergence
		Synthesis
		Solutions
Resolution	Committed (Deductive)	Apply
		Test
		Defend

TABLE 11.7   The descriptive data of the social and cognitive presences, the perception of
contribution to the collaborative task, and perceived effects of the visualization
interface

Questionnaire	Mean	SD
Perceived social presence (9–45)	26.63	5.87
Perceived cognitive presence (12–60)	33.94	7.73
Number of utterance	11.78	9.42
Utterance of social presence	15.78	13.12
Utterance of cognitive presence	4.08	4.09
Perceived contribution (0–100)	41.78	22.41
Interface Q1	3.43	1.46
Interface Q2	3.43	1.44

6   Discussion

The results indicated that social presence visualization was effective in the
enhancement of social presence directly, and cognitive presence and perceived
contribution indirectly. These results were supported by previous research

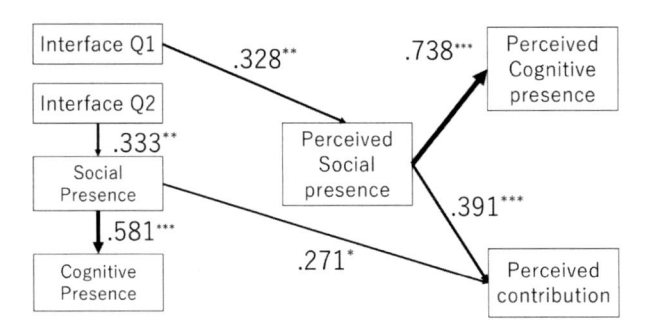

FIGURE 11.4 The results of sequential equation modeling for the relationships among social, cognitive, and perceived contribution

such as Shea and Bidjerano (2009). Social presence is a fundamental element in the enhancement of cognitive learning behavior (Garrison & Anderson, 2003; Shea & Bidjerano, 2009). The results of this research also promoted cognitive learning behaviors and awareness. The system, in particular visualization, can support the important perception for collaborative tasks. Social presence visualization seems to have reflective features to understand individual and group activity level. However, it seems that the perceived effects of the interface depended on the learners, that is, the standard deviation of the rates was slightly high (Q1: Ave. 3.43, SD. 1.46, Q2: Ave. 3.43, SD. 1.44). In dialogue, several groups noticed the change of the interface displayed in Figure 11.3, but there were also groups that were not aware of the change of the interface.

The relationship between perceived cognitive presence and the sense of contribution was not confirmed in this study. The 22 learners who rated their degree of contribution as 50 points stated that the reason for doing so was because they were required to integrate the group members' opinions and the information about their tasks. These activities are related with cognitive presence and cognitive learning behaviors. There seem to be two possible reasons; one is that students were not engaged in deep discussion. Analyzing dialogues, students tended to decide the division of labor, and share and integrate the learning outcomes that each group member accomplished; however, they did not suggest the project work direction and critical viewpoints, or ask questions about the learning outcomes achieved by other members on this system. In that situation, students seemed to have fewer opportunities to consider their learning outcomes critically; therefore, students faced difficulty in recognizing other members' contribution to self-tasks. The second possibility is that the system used in this research analyzed the utterances about the decision process of the role as social presence. Division of labor is one of the social processes in group work. The learners were required to decide the tasks and roles of each member, considering the social relationships. The utterance of this process contained words that were analyzed as social presence utterance by this system.

7   Conclusion and Future Research

The research aimed to investigate the effects of the collaboration visualization system on collaborative activities and awareness, based on the CoI framework. The results revealed that the interface can enhance the collaboration based on CoI, and perception of the contribution to group work. However, the results also indicated that the effects of the interface depended on the learners' perception, and cognitive learning behaviors and awareness did not have relationships with the perception of the contribution.

Future research requires the following points to be addressed. One is to modify the algorism to visualize the social presence. Social process in collaborative learning also contains cognitive learning behaviors such as information integration. The algorism should be analyzing the utterances of cognitive learning behaviors.

Second is to analyze the utterance about the division of labor. Division of labor is one of the social processes in collaborative learning, but several important utterances (e.g., "I will be engaged in group learning," "You should be group leader") were not analyzed by this system. Such a process is important for the analysis of collaboration. In future research, the function that analyzes the utterance about division of labor should be developed.

The last point is to investigate the effects of the modified visualization on collaborative learning activities and awareness, using more datasets. In this research, 49 datasets were used for the investigation. Group effects should be confirmed, although this research did not find any group effects. Future research requires the analysis of more datasets.

Acknowledgement

This study is supported by JSPS Grant-in-aid for Scientific research (JP16H03080, JP17K18659), QR Tsubasa program at Kyushu University.

References

Akyol, Z., & Garrison, D. R. (2012). Assessing metacognition in an online community of inquiry. *Internet Higher Education, 14*, 183–190.

Garrison, D. R., & Anderson, T. (2003). *E-learning in the 21st century: A framework for research and practice*. London: RoutledgeFalmer.

Garrison, D. R., Anderson, T., & Archer, W. (2000). Critical inquiry in a text-based environment: Computer conferencing in higher education. *Internet and Higher Education, 2*(2–3), 87–105.

Goda, Y., & Yamada, M. (2012). Application of CoI to design CSCL for EFL online asynchronous discussion. In Z. Akyol & D. R. Garrison (Eds.), *Educational community of inquiry: Theoretical framework, research and practice* (pp. 295–316). Hershey, PA: IGI Global.

Gunawardena, C. N., & Zittle, F. J. (1997). Social presence as a predictor of satisfaction within a computer-mediated conferencing environment. *American Journal of Distance Education, 11*(3), 8–26.

Hoppe, U. H., & Gaßner, K. (2002). Integrating collaborative concept mapping tools with group memory and retrieval functions. In *CSCL 2002 Proceedings of the Conference on Computer Support for Collaborative Learning* (pp. 716–725).

Lee, A. V. Y., & Tan, S. C. (2017). Temporal analytics with discourse analysis: Tracing ideas and impact on communal discourse. In *Proceedings of Learning Analytics and Knowledge 2017* (pp.120–127).

Manning, C. D., Surdeanu, M., Bauer, J., Finkel, J., Bethard, S. J., & McClosky, D. (2014). The Stanford CoreNLP natural language processing toolkit. In *Proceedings of the 52nd Annual Meeting of the Association for Computational Linguistics, System Demonstrations* (pp. 55–60).

Miller, G. A. (1995). WordNet: A lexical database for English. *Communications of the ACM, 38*(11), 39–41.

Mochizuki, T., Kato, H., Fujitani, S., Yaegashi, K., Hisamatsu, S., Nagata, T., Nakahara, J., Nishimori, T., & Suzuki, M. (2006). Promotion of self-assessment for learners in online discussion using the visualization software. In N. Lambropoulos & P. Zaphiris (Eds.), *User-centered design of online learning communities* (pp.365–386). London: Idea Publishing.

Mochizuki, T., Kato, H., Yaegashi, K., Nishimori, T., Nagamori, Y., & Fujita, S. (2007). ProBoPortable: Does the cellular phone software promote emergent division of labor in project-based learning?. In *CSCL 2007 Proceedings in the 8th International Conference on Computer-Supported Collaborative Learning* (pp. 516–518).

Oshima, J., Oshima, R., & Matsuzawa, Y. (2012). Knowledge building discourse explorer: A social network analysis application for knowledge building discourse. *Educational Technology Research & Development, 60*(5), 903–921.

Phielix, C., Prins, F. J., & Kirschner, P. A. (2010). Group awareness of social and cognitive behavior in a CSCL environment. In *ICLS 2010 Proceedings of the 9th International Conference of the Learning Sciences* (Vol. 1, pp. 230–237).

Scardamalia, M., & Bereiter, C. (1993). Technologies for knowledge-building discourse. *Communication of the ACM, 36*(5), 37–41.

Shea, P., & Bidjerano, T. (2009). Community of inquiry as a theoretical framework to faster epistemic engagement and cognitive presence in online education. *Computers and Education, 52*(3), 543–553.

Shea, P., Hayes, S., Vickers, J., Gozza-Cohen, M., Uzuner, S., Mehta, R., Valchova, A., & Rangan, P. (2010). A re-examination of the community of inquiry framework: Social network and content analysis. *Internet and Higher Education, 13*, 10–21.

Swan, K., Shea, P., Richardson, J., Ice, P., Garrison, D. R., Cleveland-Innes, M., & Arbaugh, J. B. (2008). Validating a measurement tool of presence in online communities of inquiry. *E-Mentor, 2*, 1–12.

Yamada, M., & Goda, Y. (2012). Application of social presence principles to CSCL design for quality interactions. In J. Jia (Ed.), *Educational stages and interactive learning: From kindergarten to workplace training* (pp. 31–48). Hershey, PA: IGI Global.

Yamada, M., Goda, Y., Matsukawa, H., Hata, K., & Yasunami, S. (2016a). A computer-supported collaborative learning design for quality interaction. *IEEE Multimedia, 23*, 48–59.

Yamada, M., Kaneko, K., & Goda, Y. (2016b). Social presence visualizer: Development of the collaboration facilitation module on CSCL. *Communications in Computer and Information Science, 647*, 174–189.

Yamada, M., & Kitamura, S. (2011). The role of social presence in interactive learning with social software. *Social Media Tools and Platforms in Learning Environments*, 325–335.

CHAPTER 12

Learning Support Systems Based on Cohesive Learning Analytics

Fumiya Okubo, Masanori Yamada, Misato Oi, Atsushi Shimada,
Yuta Taniguchi and Shin'ichi Konomi

1 Introduction

E-learning systems have become indispensable in educational institutions (Alsabawy, Cater-Steel, & Soar, 2013). The Learning Management System (LMS), the Course Management System (CMS), or the Virtual Learning Environment (VLE), is one such e-learning system and it is widely accepted in higher education (Islam, 2015). LMSs are used for facilitating e-learning. The LMS process is used to store and disseminate educational material and to support administration and communication associated with teaching and learning (McGill & Klobas, 2009). Ubiquitous technology is effective in enhancing the effects of the LMS and VLE on learning performance (Yin et al., 2015; Yamada et al., 2016). By using logs stored in the server, information technologies allow instructors to understand student learning behaviors. By using various data from sources such as the logs, learning analytics research contributes to the clarification and improvement of education and the learning environment (e.g., Ifenthalar, 2015; Ogata et al., 2015).

To support student learning, revealing its patterns by using learning analytics methods might be useful. For example, Oi and her colleagues (Oi et al., 2015; Oi, Okubo, Shimada, Yin, & Ogata, 2015; Oi, Yamada, Okubo, Shimada, & Ogata, 2017) investigated the relationship between the use of e-books outside the classroom and academic achievement. They categorized e-book logs from the e-book delivery system as follows: If a log was recorded before a class session in which the same e-book was used as the textbook, it was labeled a preview log, and if after, a review log.

As pointed out by Ausubel (1960) in his classical study, if a student gains knowledge of the contents of a course by performing a preview, it may help the student's learning in the classroom by acting as an advance organizer. Performing a review may facilitate memory consolidation by working as a rehearsal of the contents of the course. The main findings are as follows: (1) The preview is more deeply related with academic achievement than the review (Oi, Okubo et al., 2015), (2) high achievers may actively link related e-books and their pages with a preview and a review (Oi, Yin et al., 2015), and (3) relatively low achievers attempted to perform previews, but they tended to give up easily (Oi et al., 2017).

These results suggest that previews may be effective for higher academic achievement, and in indicating some issues, such as, revealing why low achievers gave up on their review and how to help them start their preview and review processes. In Sections 3.2 and 3.4, we will introduce possible solutions.

The e-book log also provides useful information by which to predict a learner's psychological state such. One common issue under discussion is how psychological variables affect learning performance within the learning environment using ICT (Greene & Azevedo, 2010). Psychometric data as well as learning logs should be collected, in order to analyze learners' behaviors in order to achieve effective learning support. Particularly helpful would be introducing learning styles, such as self-regulated learning (SRL) (Roll & Winne, 2015).

Yamada et al. (2015) indicate that self-efficacy, one element of SRL, had a significant correlation with learning behaviors, such as highlighting and annotation. Yamada et al. (2017b) further suggested that the use of cognitive learning strategies, such as annotation, as well as giving appropriate time for reading learning materials, play important roles in enhancing SRL awareness. Yamada et al. (2017a) also indicated that awareness of self-efficacy, intrinsic value, and cognitive learning strategies had a significant correlation with the frequency of out-of-class activities, submission times of reports, and learning performance. Moreover, they found that the relationship between SRL awareness and out-of-class activities such as, reading activities and bookmarking, had a significant correlation with SRL awareness.

Due to the high adoption of LMSs that promote the massive store of learning data, as well as the analyses of this data, the findings mentioned above could bring us insights into student activity and indicators of teaching quality. In the following section, we introduce an integrated ubiquitous learning platform, "M2B (Mitsuba)," in order to improve learning and teaching based on learning analytics.

2   M2B: Learning Support and an Analytic Platform

M2B consists of a common learning management system (Moodle), an e-portfolio system (Mahara), and an e-book system (BookRoll) (Ogata et al., 2017). Moodle is mainly used by teachers to manage student attendance, provide quizzes, and receive reports. Both teachers and students use Mahara for keeping notes in e-portfolios. BookRoll enables students to browse e-book materials before, during, and after lectures, anywhere and anytime, using their PC or smartphones. All user actions performed on the e-book system, such as page flips and opening material, are recorded in the learning logs and automatically sent to the university's database. The e-book system provides additional functions of bookmarking, highlighting, annotating, and searching. By the end of April, 2017, approximately 45,000,000 logs were collected from approximately 20,000 students. Analyses of educational big data from M2B showed progress in the students' understanding of activities. In the next section, we introduce M2B plug-ins based on the learning analytics methods used to enhance learning performance.

3   Learning Support Systems Based on Cohesive Learning Analytics

3.1   *A Visualization Tool to Overview Learning Activities through a Course*

Many kinds of logs of students' learning activities are stored in the M2B system. For teachers to utilize these learning logs and improve their teaching in their classes, specific purposes should be used to visualize the logs. Here, we consider a system of visualization in order to understand an overview of student learning activities during a course.

At Kyushu University, the training of students and the evaluation of student learning both inside and outside the classroom are regarded as important issues. In order to analyze and visualize the many kinds of logs from this point of view, we select nine major learning activities, and evaluate them by individual students, using a scale of 0 to 5 points for each week of the course. A vector of these nine evaluations is called an Active Learner Point (ALP). The nine selected learning activities and the method for evaluating them are summarized in Table 12.1. We note that

- The logs of attendance, quizzes, reports, and course views are stored in Moodle.
- The logs of slide views, markers, memos and actions are stored in BookRoll. Here, the item "slide views" is calculated by the total time of slide views outside of class.
- The logs of word counts in journal are stored in Mahara.

The logs of the number of course views, total time of slide views, number of markers, number of actions, and word count in a journal are evaluated relatively in a course. For example, the top 10% of students who are most active in their learning activities obtain a score of 5.

TABLE 12.1   Criteria for active learner point (ALP)

Activities	5	4	3	2	1	0
Attendance	Attendance		Being late			absence
Quiz	Above 80%	Above 60%	Above 40%	Above 20%	Above 10%	Otherwise
Report	Submission		Late submission			No submission
Course Views	Upper 10%	Upper 20%	Upper 30%	Upper 40%	Upper 50%	Otherwise
Slide Views	Upper 10%	Upper 20%	Upper 30%	Upper 40%	Upper 50%	Otherwise
Markers	Upper 10%	Upper 20%	Upper 30%	Upper 40%	Upper 50%	Otherwise
Memos	Upper 10%	Upper 20%	Upper 30%	Upper 40%	Upper 50%	Otherwise
Actions	Upper 10%	Upper 20%	Upper 30%	Upper 40%	Upper 50%	Otherwise
Word Count	Upper 10%	Upper 20%	Upper 30%	Upper 40%	Upper 50%	Otherwise

The ALPs of students represent their activeness for learning in the course. Therefore, the ALP can also be useful for predicting students' performance, an important issue in the research field of educational data mining (Baradwaj & Pal, 2011). Our research group showed that the students' final grades (Okubo et al., 2017a, Okubo et al., 2017b) and quiz scores (Okubo et al., 2018) could be predicted, using the ALP and Recurrent Neural Network.

For visualizing an overview of students' learning activities using ALP, we have developed a system called the Active Learner Dashboard, which consists of three functions. Each function enables teachers and students to know the learning expectations in the course. Here, we explain the implementation of the system and its details. The Active Learner Dashboard is implemented as the set of "block" type plugins in Moodle. The "block" type plugins are always displayed in the sidebar during the course as simple "block display" mode (see Figure 12.1).

The advantage of this display mode is that when teachers and students access the course, they can readily view their teaching and learning situations, respectively, at a glance. By clicking the "View" button, a "detailed" mode of

FIGURE 12.1   Block display of the active learner dashboard

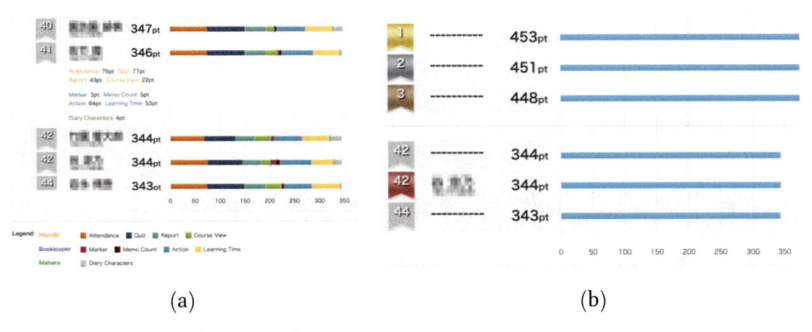

(a)   (b)

FIGURE 12.2   Active learner ranking

each function is displayed. Figure 12.2 shows the detailed displays of the Active Learner Ranking for teachers (a) and for students (b).

This function displays the ranking of each student according to the sum of the ALP that they have acquired so far in the course. In order to maintain student privacy, we have different contents for teachers and students. For teachers, the breakdown of points obtained for each item in the ALP is displayed. For students, their own total points and rank are displayed, along with the top three students.

Figure 12.3 gives a detailed display of the Active Learner Process (a) and the teacher's Active Learner Distribution (b) for teachers. The Active Learner Process shows a transition in the average value of ALPs each week as a red line in the graph. A breakdown of the ALP is displayed by mouse-over. By selecting each learning activity, the rate of achievement is displayed in a bar graph. The Active Learner Distribution shows the distribution of students, categorizing them into specified numbers of levels based on their ALPs for each week. By using these functions, teachers can see how the activity of their class changes week to week.

We asked 77 students attending the "Introduction to Pedagogy" course that opened the first semester in 2016, to use the system of Active Learner Ranking and then we gave them the following questionnaire:
(1)   Were you concerned about your ranking in the Active Learner Ranking?
(2)   Did you reflect on your learning awareness by using the Active Learner Ranking?

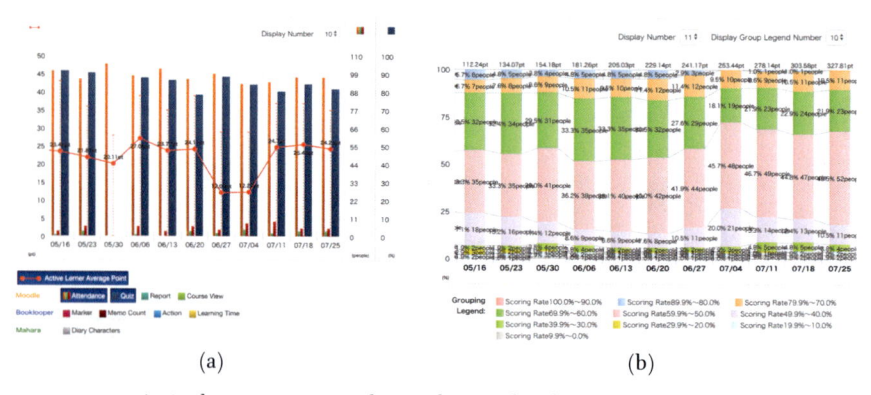

FIGURE 12.3   Active learner process and active learner distribution

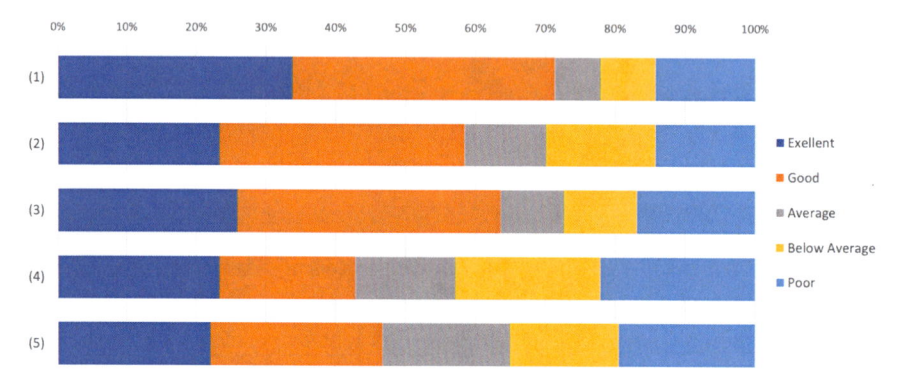

FIGURE 12.4   Summary of students' answers regarding active learner ranking

(3)   Did you care about the learning activities of other students due to the Active Learner Ranking?

(4)   Did competition awareness increase due to the Active Learner Ranking?

(5)   Did you actively learn in this course due to the Active Learner Ranking?

The responses are summarized in Figure 12.4. We can see that approximately 60% of the students were concerned about their Active Learner Ranking, they reviewed their learning awareness, and they were conscious of other students' learning activities due to the system. On the other hand, students who said that the competition awareness increased or that they learned actively in the course was less than 50%.

These results imply that the system of Active Learner Ranking is effective for changing student learning awareness, however it does not reach the same effectiveness in the actual change in student learning activities. For this reason, it seems necessary to consider a system that responds to each student individually according to their situation.

3.2 *Automatic Summarization of Learning Materials for Enhanced Preview*

When discussing enhancements to the learning processes, it is often argued that studying in advance of class is very important to enable students to understand the narrative of the class, become familiar with important keywords, and discover new terms and concepts. Ausubel (1960) emphasized the importance of providing preview information to be studied in advance.

In addition, Beichner (1995) reported that adequate preparation prior to lectures leads to improved student performance. In universities, students are often asked to prepare for their next class by reading a textbook or previewing material. Hereafter, we use the term "preview" to denote any form of studying and/or reading material provided in advance by a teacher.

The proposed automatic summarization system was designed to produce a set of lecture slides that contain text explanations, as well as various types of visual content, including images, tables, and mathematical formulas. The purpose of slide summarization is to maximize the importance of the content using a selection of subset pages under a given condition (in this case, browsing time). The most important pages must be selected without losing the overall narrative of the lecture. In the proposed system, we assume that the narrative of the original lecture material consists of a sequence of important keywords. Moreover, we assume that important pages exhibit the following characteristics:

- Sufficient content to be worth browsing,
- Unique content,
- Keywords that appear frequently in a page,
- Keywords that rarely appear throughout the set of pages.

Based on the first assumption, the system selects pages containing figures and/ or tables that support the reader's understanding of the content. Based on the second assumption, the system removes redundant content, such as animations. Based on the third and fourth assumptions, the system locates important keywords that appear frequently in a given page, but rarely appear throughout the total set of pages. These characteristics are analyzed using a combination of image and text processing.

Figure 12.5 shows an overview of the proposed approach. First, a set of slide pages, *S*, are analyzed to extract important visual and textual features from each page. In terms of visual importance, how much text and how many figures, formulations, or other objects are contained in each slide is estimated using a background subtraction tool, and an inter-frame difference tool. In addition, word importance is measured using the TF-IDF (term frequency–inverse document frequency) method (Salton, 1988; Wu, 2008). Meanwhile, a

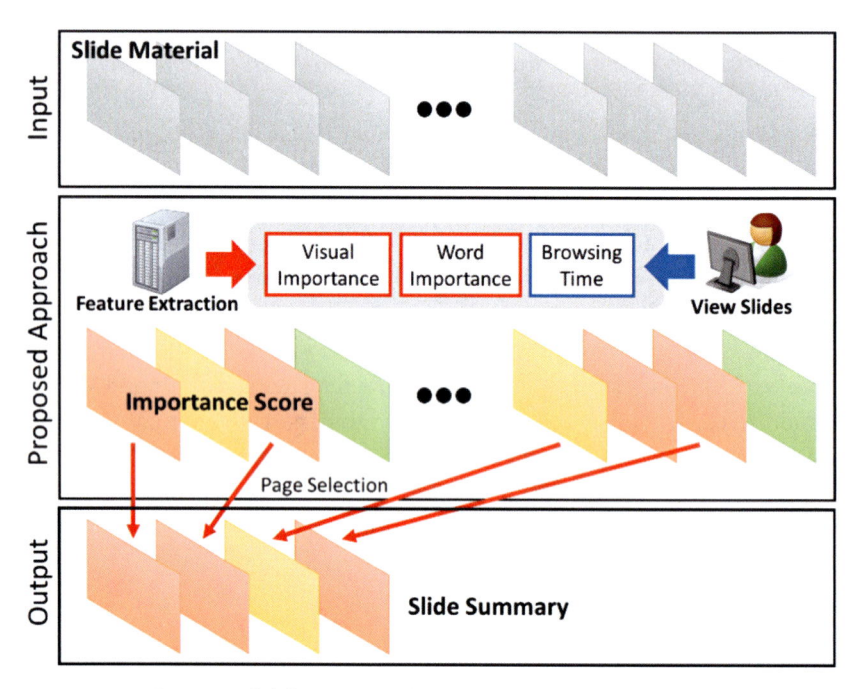

FIGURE 12.5   Overview of slide summarization

teacher estimates the time that students need to spend studying each slide. Then these visual, textual, and temporal features are combined to predict an importance score $I(S_i)$ for each slide page, where S_i indicates the page number of the set of slide pages, S. Finally, an optimal subset $\hat{S}$ is selected, whereby the importance score is maximized for a given preview time. For more details, refer to Shimada (2017).

We investigated the effectiveness of the proposed approach in a series of information science courses over three weeks. In total, 372 first-year students, including both art and science students, attended the classes, which began in April, 2015. All students brought their own laptops to class every week. Each week, students were asked to preview material in preparation for the next lecture. We prepared three sets of summarized slides (short, medium, and long versions), in addition to the complete set of slides. Figure 12.6 displays the full set of slide pages from the third week, along with the summarization results.

The four sets of slides outlined above were given to four student groups using an e-book system (Yin, 2014). This system enables us to collect browsing logs for each set of slide pages to confirm whether a student actually previewed the material within the specified period (the week preceding the lecture). Therefore, we can classify the students into five groups, including those who

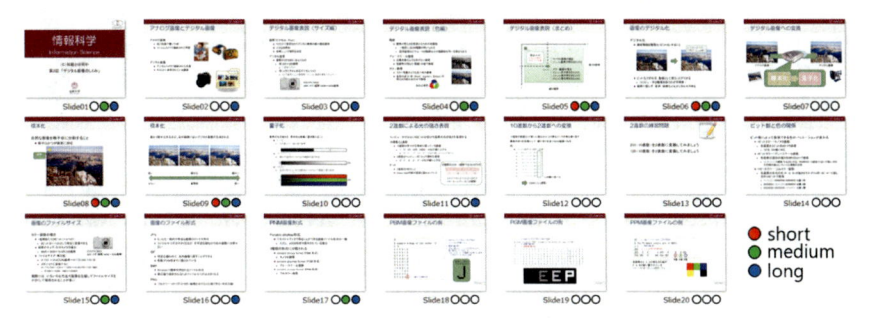

FIGURE 12.6   Examples of selected pages

TABLE 12.2   Number of students who browsed the slides

	Short	Medium	Long	All	None
1st week	44	39	40	92	157
2nd week	40	30	33	111	124
3rd week	43	42	51	105	100

did not preview the slides. Table 12.2 shows the number of students in each group.

We compared the quiz scores among the five groups:
- Short: students who previewed the short set of summarized slides
- Medium: students who previewed the medium set of summarized slides
- Long: students who previewed the long set of summarized slides
- All: students who previewed the original set of slides
- None: students who did not preview any slides.

We then conducted t-tests to compare all possible pairings of the groups. We compared the groups who previewed the three summarized slide sets with those who previewed all the slides. We also compared the groups who previewed sets of slides with the group who did not preview any slides. Figure 12.7 shows the average score for each group.

The average scores for groups that previewed the various sets of slides (short, medium, long, and all) exceeded those of the group that did not preview the slides (none). With regard to the first week, the contents of the slides were not complex, so there was little difference in the quiz scores. The contents of the slides became more difficult as the lecture series proceeded, and therefore, the differences between the scores increased over the second and third weeks.

The most important point to note (and our major argument), is that the summarized slide sets did not have a negative effect on the quiz scores. This is supported by the fact that the null hypotheses between the summarized slides and all the slides were not rejected. Instead, previewing the short and medium sets of summarized slides improved the students' quiz scores compared with previewing the full set of slides (all).

From these results, we can see that the proposed method for summarizing the slides is very effective. In addition, students who previewed the medium set of summarized slides obtained the best scores in all of the quizzes. Note that this summarized slide set was given to a different group each week. This is a very interesting result, and is closely related to the achievement ratios obtained in previewing the slides.

Figure 12.8 shows the achievement ratio for each slide set in each week. With regard to the second week, almost 90% of students previewed their slide sets, regardless of the length of the set. However, in the cases of the first and third weeks, achievement ratios clearly decreased as the number of slide pages and the estimated preview time increased (see Table 12.1). Almost one-half of all students who were given all the slides abandoned their preview early in the process. We concluded that too much material caused a decrease in the students' attention spans. Therefore, it is important to make a summary set of slides for preview by students.

3.3 Real-Time Analysis to Understand Students' Behaviors during a Class

There are roughly three types of feedback loops in terms of their frequency: yearly, weekly and real-time. A typical example of a yearly (or term-by-term)

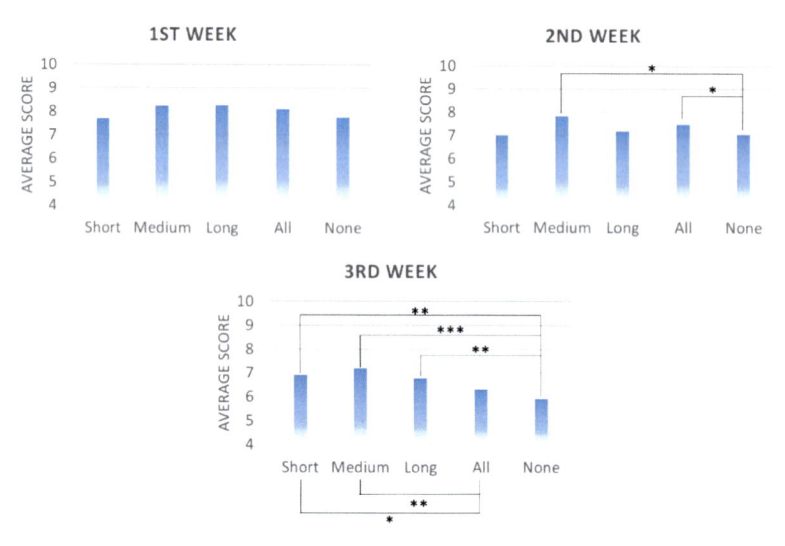

FIGURE 12.7   Average quiz scores (*P < 0.05, **P < 0.01, ***P < 0.001)

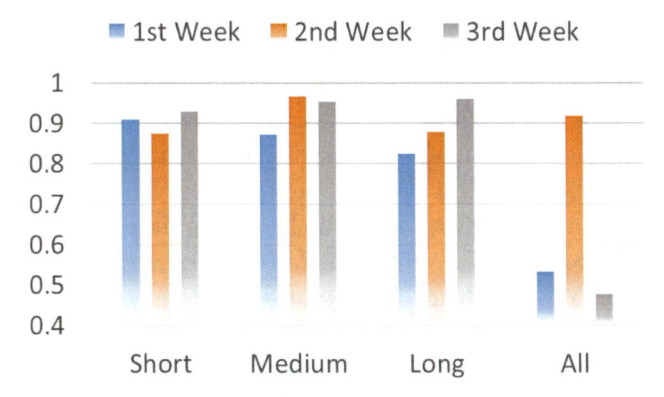

FIGURE 12.8   Achievement ratios: percentages of students who previewed more than 80% of slide pages

feedback loop, is the assessment and improvement of education. Student grades, examination results, class questionnaires, and so on, are typically analyzed and evaluated (Mouri, 2016; Okubo, 2016). The yearly feedback loop is designed so that the results will be delivered the following year (or term). Students and teachers will not directly receive the feedback results.

A weekly feedback loop can recommend related material based on student status determined using the prediction of academic performance through the analysis of the learning logs, such as attendance reports and quiz results (Shimada, 2016). In contrast to the yearly feedback loop, the analysis results are directly fed back to the students and teachers.

The main difference between a weekly and a real-time feedback loop is that the results can be fed back to the students and teachers in the classroom during a lecture. The teacher can monitor what students are doing (e.g., whether students are following the explanation or whether they are doing something unrelated to the lecture). Based on this timely feedback, a teacher can easily control the speed of the lecture, take more or less time for exercises, or make other adjustments.

Our study has focused on feedback and specifically, how to feedback efficient information to the on-site classrooms during lectures. The aim of this research is to realize real-time feedback, which has not often been discussed with respect to the on-site environment. Our target is on-site classrooms where teachers give lectures and a large group of students are listening to the teacher's explanation, participating in exercises, etc. In such a large classroom, it is not easy for teachers to grasp each student's behavior and activities.

We utilize an e-Learning system and an e-Book system to collect real-time data regarding learning activities during the lectures. We have developed two main feedback systems. One is useful for the teacher prior to beginning the lecture. This system provides summary reports of the previews of given materials and quiz results. Using the preview achievement graph, the teacher is able to check which pages were well previewed and which pages were not. Additionally, the teacher can check which quizzes were difficult for students, and the suggested pages that should be explained in the lecture to aid students. The other is the real-time analytics graphs, which are helpful for the teacher to control his/her lecture speed. The system collects e-Book logs operated by students sequentially, and performs analytics in real-time on how many students are following the teacher's explanation.

In Figure 12.9, we present an example case study which was applied to a lecture in our university. The time line is divided into two parts: before starting a class and during a class. During the previous lecture, the teacher gave students some preview materials that were automatically generated by the summarization technique (Shimada, 2017). Students previewed the given materials before the class and the operation logs recorded during the previews were collected in the system. Before the class started, students answered the quiz questions and the results were collected in the server.

Just before the lecture started, our system analyzed the learning logs to create a summary report containing previews of the achievement and quiz results. Additionally, the system provided information regarding important pages that should be explained well in the lecture. For example, should the teacher focus on pages that are related to the quiz questions, especially those that have led to

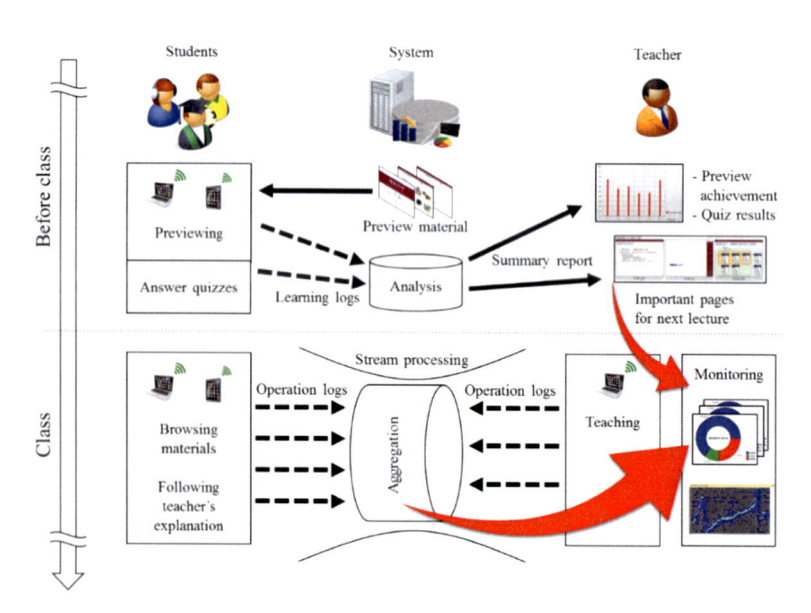

FIGURE 12.9   A case study of lecture support

lower quiz scores? Our system analyzed in advance the relationship between quiz statements and their related pages in the lecture material.

During the lecture, the teacher explained the content of the materials and students browsed the materials on their lap-tops. In our university, students are asked to open and browse the same page as the teacher, and to highlight or add notes on the important points. During the lecture, learning logs were sequentially collected and stored. The analysis results were immediately visualized on the web interface, as shown in Figure 12.10, and updated every minute. Therefore, the teacher was able to monitor the latest student activity. The visualization included real-time information regarding how many students were following the lecture, how many students were browsing previous pages, etc. The teacher adaptively controlled the speed of the lecture according to what he/she was learning about the students. For example, if many students were not following the lecture and were still on previous page, the teacher slowed down the lecture. For detailed information about implementation, refer to Shimada (2017b).

We investigated the effectiveness of the proposed system in two classes at Kyushu University, Japan. One was the control group (N = 58), without the system. The other was the experimental group (N = 157), using the system. The contents of two lectures were completely the same. The class was designed to provide an introduction to information and communication technology in a number of disciplines. First-year students, including both arts and science students, attended the class, which began in October, 2016. All of the students brought their own laptops to class. The lecture was given by the same teacher, using the same materials.

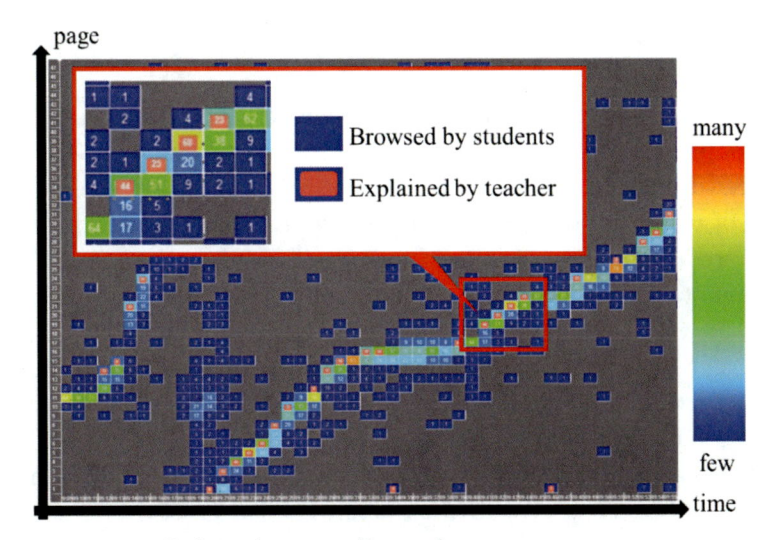

FIGURE 12.10   Real-time heat map of browsed pages

The analyses of the preview status and the quiz scores were performed just before the lecture started. The system reported that most students answered two of eleven questions incorrectly. The pages related to the quizzes were shown on the display and the teacher confirmed them. The teacher spent considerable time on the explanation of these pages. In fact, the page was opened by the teacher for three minutes in the experimental group, meanwhile, one minute for the control group. We analyzed the number of bookmarks, highlights and notes on the two pages, where the teacher emphasized the explanation. In the experimental group, about 61% of students used those functions. On the other hand, only 53% of the students in the control group used the functions.

When the teacher gave the lecture to students in the experimental group, he monitored the display on which real-time analysis results were shown. He controlled the speed of lecture to allow students to catch up as much as possible. We evaluated the synchronization of the classroom; how many students opened the pages explained by the teacher. We counted the numbers minute-by-minute after setting a suitable delay.

Table 12.3 shows the ratio of synchronization of each group. For example, if we set the allowable delay to three minutes (i.e., if students opened the same page with the teacher within the three-minute delay), the synchronization ratio of the experimental group was 0.7661. The score was significantly different from the score of the control group. In other allowable delay settings, the synchronization ratios of the experimental groups were higher than those of the control group. We consider that such high synchronization was realized by the lecture speed control through the real-time feedback of classroom activities.

3.4   Learning Journal Analysis toward Teaching Analysis

3.4.1   Introduction

The practice of reflection is regarded as an important skill in higher education (Hatton & Smith, 1995). Reflection helps students see their learning activities objectively and deepen their understanding. Reflective writing is a representative activity of reflection. Through journal writing, students reflect on their process of learning and reconstruct the knowledge learned in the class. This allows students to see different aspects of learning activities and discover meaningful knowledge from it.

In reflective writing, it is common for students to record what they learn, what they wonder, and any other details regarding positive and negative perceptions of their learning experience. Therefore, from the viewpoint of learning analytics, researchers analyzed students' journals for automatic evaluation of the engagement in reflective activities (Chen, Yu, Zhang, & Yu, 2016) and

TABLE 12.3   Synchronization ratio of each group in three minutes of allowable delay

	Control	Experimental	p-Value
1 min.	0.4275	0.5174	0.0403[*]
3 min.	0.6598	0.7661	0.0033[**]
5 min.	0.7508	0.8599	0.0014[**]

[*]$p<0.05$, [**]$p<0.01$

for measuring student's emotion (Nwanganga, Aguiar, Ambrose, Goodrich, & Chawla, 2015) by text mining techniques.

While writing is very helpful for enhancing student learning, from the teacher's perspective, student journal writing is also useful for improving teaching. In a classroom, teaching and learning are very closely connected and thus, a student's negative experience could be caused by the teacher's technique or learning materials. Therefore, student journals are considered full of resources that enable teachers to objectively view their own teaching.

However, because of time constraints, it is challenging for teachers to grasp all useful information found in the journals. Reading journals is extremely time-consuming, and teachers may not be able to understand every journal, especially in the case of a large class. Therefore, computational assistance is crucial to a full utilization of student journals.

To this end, we consider two types of approaches: the method that supports teachers in reading journals and the automatic analysis method. The former gives us greater flexibility of analysis with a moderate amount of time required, and the latter provides easier understanding with less time for analysis. Neither way can fit every teacher's needs every time, so we need to appropriately combine both approaches.

In this article, we describe our proposed methods for both approaches based on *weekly keywords*. First, as the former approach, we describe a Web-based interactive reporting tool (Taniguchi, Okubo, Shimada, & Konomi, 2017), which makes it possible for teachers to explore student journal writings without losing important details. Second, we describe a method based on the latter approach that automatically extracts what students mention and how they think about them in their journals (Taniguchi, Suehiro, Shimada, & Ogata, 2017). As a case study last year, we applied our method on the journals for the course, "Information Science," held for the first-grade students during the first semester 2016 at Kyushu University. We discuss the results in the rest of this section.

During our research, *weekly keywords* played an important role. Since our aim is to improve teaching, we want to understand what course-related topics were commonly discussed in the students' journals writings. For the purpose, it is useful to measure how much each term used in journal writings is related to course contents. We assume that different topics are taught every week, and that students are told to write a reflection for each individual week. With this assumption, we can expect that the words related to the weekly topics will basically appear only in the journals for that particular week. Thus, using the week-specific nouns (*weekly keywords*) we can find the journal entries which are strongly related to the corresponding weekly topics.

Our method is based on the TF-IDF term-weighting measure (Salton & Buckley, 1988). The TF-IDF value of a word is defined as the product of term frequency (TF) and inverse document frequency (IDF). Since the IDF measures the document-specificity of words in a document set, we can measure the week-specificity by considering concatenated journal entries for a particular week as a single document. Table 12.4 shows extracted weekly keywords, where only the top ten words given the highest TF-IDF scores are shown. Comparing the keywords with actual topics, we can see that many keywords specific to course contents were successfully extracted.

We proposed a web-based interactive reporting tool for journal entries, which provides weekly keyword-based navigation of journal entries and summary plots of word usage patterns. The graphical user interface, shown in Figure 12.11, displays weekly keywords as entry points of journal exploration. The keywords are shown in ranked tables for each week according to their TF-IDF values, and allow to see how the usage of words varies from week to week.

In addition to that, there are also three interactive features. The first feature is a pop-up sentence view. When we hold the cursor over a word in the table, a popup appears and shows all the sentences containing the selected word in the corresponding week. This is helpful for us to understand in what context and how the word is used in real sentences.

The second feature is word highlighting, which emphasizes all occurrences of a highlighted word across the ranking tables. Since the ranking table shows the relative importance in a particular week, this feature makes it possible to see how the usage pattern of the word changes through a semester.

The last feature is grouping adjectives and verbs by their polarity, based on a dictionary. We can toggle the feature, and get positive and negative words in ranking tables colored with green and red colors, respectively. This is helpful in order to quickly assess journal contents from a sentimental point of view. Similar to this feature, we also show two types of plots in Figure 12.12. These

TABLE 12.4   Example results of weekly keywords extraction. Weekly keywords are extracted from the journal entries for the course "information science." From the 1st week to the 14th, actual topics taught in classes and extracted weekly keywords are listed. We can see topic-related words were extracted and general words were eliminated successfully

Week	Actual topics	Extracted weekly keywords
1	Positioning the lecture	Internet, orientation, university, search, binary, remaining, system, method, life, study
2	Introduction to information science	Morse code, signal, topic, quiz, homework, Japanese, thought, English, remaining, like
3	Information quantity and entropy	code, entropy, prefix, encoding, average, word, combine, length, symbol, multiple
4	Entropy	entropy, mutual, expectation, value, quantity, log, computation, with, information, condition
5	Channel coding	correction, error, automated, detection, Hamming, distance, communication, encoding, doodlebug's pit, example
6	Cryptography, computer science	cipher, encryption, key, Caesar, mod, public, RSA, secret, decryption, high school
7	Computation, algorithm, time complexity	coin, Euclid, mutual division, balance scale, fake, algorithm, method, mathematics, GCD, rectangle
8	Midterm exam	exam, midterm, one question, perfect score, final, right answer, question, miss, two questions, effect
9	Stack and queue, bubble sort	notation, Polish, queue, stack, infix, sort, order, bubble, principle, first
10	Heap sort, merge sort	sort, heap sort, merge, tree, binary, comparison, algorithm, binary tree, drawback, practice
11	Bucket sort, binary search	sort, bucket, search, binary, search, binary, dictionary, Google, comparison, heap sort
12	Digital images	image, app, install, usage, download, exercise, Irfanview, rose, file, organism
13	Image processing, character recognition	image, recognition, processing, next week, letter, unistroke, edge, final, report, single stroke
14	Final exam	exam, final, small, perfect score, report, first semester, two questions, three questions, plan, final

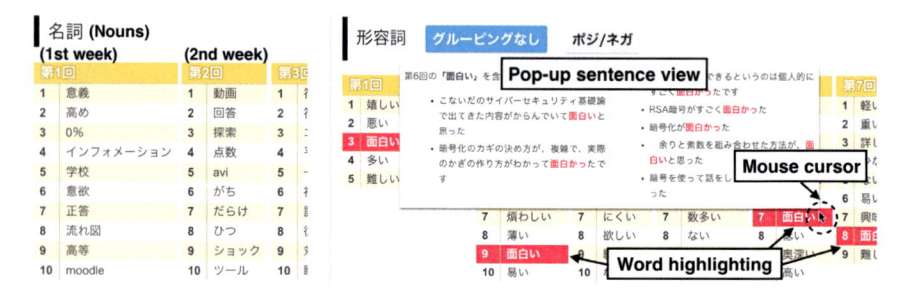

FIGURE 12.11   The second section of the reporting tool showing weekly keyword rankings. On the left, rankings of noun keywords for the first three weeks are shown. Additional dynamic features are shown on the right

charts make it possible for teachers to track the temporal changes in adjectival word usage, which in turn helps them identify topics interesting or difficult for students.

According to a short survey about our tool, responding teachers believed our tool does make it easier to read journals and identify any difficulties with their students.

When reading journal entries to acquire the students' impressions, adjectives are the most descriptive words. Since adjectives modifying nouns is universal, we can find them by considering their co-occurrences (Schütze & Pedersen, 1994) with nouns in journal writings. Based on this idea, we proposed a method to find students' impressions in pairs of weekly keywords and their associated adjectives.

We considered the co-occurrences within a sliding window and used Normalized Point-Wise Mutual Information (NPMI) (Bouma, 2009) to quantify the degree of association between two words. Briefly speaking, NPMI tells us about the dependency that occurs between two words just as a correlation coefficient does.

Furthermore, for easy understanding, we employed Nonnegative Matrix Factorization (NMF) as proposed in (Sra & Dhillon, 2006) to extract the collective impressions. NMF is a low-rank matrix approximation similar to a principal component analysis, and allows us to obtain a reduced matrix representation of relationships. We apply NMF to a modified NPMI matrix, whose elements are scaled so that the matrix contains only positive values. In order to automatically determine an optimal value for a parameter of ranks, we employed the stability analysis-based method proposed in Greene, O'Callaghan, and Cunningham (2014).

Table 12.5 shows an example list of weekly keywords most strongly associated with the adjective "difficult," and the list of adjectives most strongly

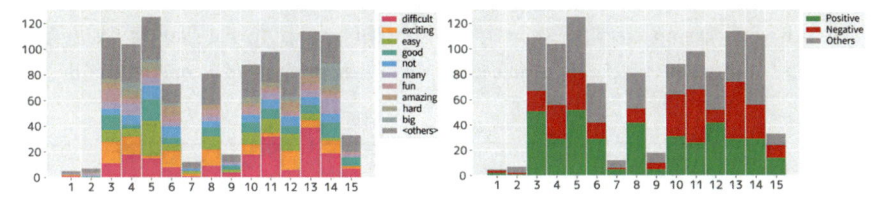

FIGURE 12.12   The third section of the interactive reporting tool shows temporal changes
in adjective word usage. The frequencies of individual words are shown as
a stacked bar chart on the left. The same for three groups of words, *positive*,
negative, and *other*, is shown on the right

associated with the weekly keyword, "cipher." From the table, we can see what
weekly topics are frequently mentioned in the student journals when students
were writing about something *difficult* for them, and students had *troublesome*
feelings regarding "ciphers."

Table 12.6 shows an example result of abstraction of impressions by NMF.
For example, the first group can be interpreted as the impression relevant to
understanding concepts, and they are strongly associated with cryptography,
algorithms, and information theory. In this example, we can interpret the
result as the difficulty of these course topics were most important to many
students compared to other topics. Such abstracted view of learning journals helps us to collectively understand the impressions of course contents.

In this chapter, we discussed the analysis of students' reflective writings for
teaching analysis. We described two examples of analysis adopting different
approaches. We designed and implemented a web-based user interface for
exploring student learning journals interactively, which facilitated reading the

TABLE 12.5   Example lists of strongly associated words for the words "difficult" and "cipher."
For the word "difficult," the most strongly associated weekly keywords are shown.
For the word "cipher," in turn, the most strongly associated adjectives are shown.
We can see what topics are considered difficult by students and how students
feel about cipher from the lists

Target	Associated weekly keywords/adjectives
"difficult"	Irfanview (0.379), exercise (0.271), Japanese (0.227), infix (0.217), notation (0.199), Caesar (0.193), merge (0.117), comparison (0.117), encoding (0.117), code (0.100)
"cipher"	troublesome (0.247), detailed (0.208), fun (0.118), good (0.117), amazing (0.111), easy (0.088), interesting (0.068), difficult (0.022)

TABLE 12.6   An example result of impression abstraction by NMF. In this example, we
             obtained four groups of adjectives. We can see every group is composed fairly
             differently

ID	Descriptive adjectives
1	difficult, easy, fun, troublesome, interesting, difficult, interesting, new, amazing, few
2	heavy, light, easy, interesting, few, involved, interesting, long, difficult, difficult
3	many, difficult, smart, big, well, difficult, interesting, rare, short, right
4	good, regretful, amazing, interesting, detailed, wonderful, happy, casual, terrible, near

entries. The other proposal is a method that automatically extracts students'
impressions and abstract them for collective understanding. In future work,
we can consider more extended analysis of journal writings, for example, for
comparative analysis of different teachers. We can extract class-specific keywords and compare various teaching styles of teachers, which leads to learning
journal-based teaching analysis.

3.5   *Learner-Centric Notification Based on Learning Analytics*

Next we discuss learner-centric notification mechanisms for learning analytics
platforms based on our experiences with M2B, a campus-wide platform at Kyushu
University. We argue for the use of commodity devices, such as smartphones,
smart watches, personal computers, cameras, low-cost eye trackers, microphones
and IoT appliances, so as to complement conventional online learning logs with
the rich environmental, social, and physiological contextual data.

Assessment of learning in open-ended environments often focuses on learning processes and as such, quantifying learning outcomes may be difficult.
Researchers have explored the potential of multimodal learning analytics to
capture and analyze learning processes in project-based learning (Worsley,
2012) and other open-ended learning contexts (Blikstein, 2013). More recently,
Worsley and Blikstein analyzed learning in a hands-on engineering design
context, using speech, gesture, and electro-dermal activity data (Worsley &
Blikstein, 2015). Oshima, Oshima, and Matsuzawa (2012) developed and
evaluated the Knowledge Building Discourse Explorer, which captures and
visualizes collaborative learning processes based on social network analysis

techniques. However, their research narrowly focuses on dialogue rather than overall knowledge building processes.

Some learning analytics projects have explored proactive capabilities of data-driven environments based on prediction (Okubo et al., 2017b) and mobile alerts (Straumsheim, 2013), although they do not fully respond to the dynamic contexts of learners. Context-responsive notifications have been used to provide personalized feedback regarding energy consumption (Igarashi et al., 2016) and safety (Sasao et al., 2017). However, they do not explicitly support learning processes.

3.5.1   Designing Learner-Centric Notifications

In order to support learners effectively, we considered a co-design process of notification, in which teachers and learners design mobile and wearable notification tools together to enhance the everyday lives of learners with relevant learning opportunities. Moreover, as students use mobile and wearable devices to access pervasive learning opportunities, the system continuously generates various sensor data to enrich learning analytics. This allows for incremental optimization of notification mechanisms based on machine learning techniques.

We imagine that the co-design process of notifications can make learning *adaptable* to personal goals and visions. This can help go beyond the limits of adaptive learning systems that rely on data about what happened in the past. As multimodal notifications can be developed in co-design workshops involving different stakeholders (Sasao et al., 2017), we opt for an approach that encourages teachers and students to design notifications in face-to-face settings or by using asynchronous collaboration tools.

3.5.2   Smart Delivery of Notifications

In order for notification environments to be successful, systems should be able to trigger the right notifications at the right time in the right place in the right way, and assure the quality of contextual learning experiences in everyday life settings. We can extend and integrate existing mobile and situated crowdsourcing techniques (Goncalves et al., 2017), as well as machine learning approaches, to predict the right context that would trigger notifications to learners.

Delivering notifications in the right way requires the appropriate presentation of notifications for different learners in different contexts. This would involve using not only visual, auditory and textual alerts, but also ambient displays. Moreover, systems could notify teachers who have the skill to present the notifications to their students effectively. As participatory sensing expands, the potential of pervasive sensing, participatory actuation, or participatory presentation of notifications in particular, can expand pervasive learning in everyday contexts.

4   Conclusion

In this chapter, we introduced the tools for supporting learning and teaching with the utilization of the learning logs that are stored in the integrated learning support system, M2B. The system was developed to enhance learning awareness and performance both inside and outside the classroom consistently, based on the fundamental investigation of the relationships between learning behavior data, self-regulated learning theory, and learning patterns outside the classroom that promotes learning student academic achievement.

For grasping an overview of learning activities through a course, we introduced the Active Learner Dashboard that enables teachers and students to understand the learning situation in the course. From the user questionnaire, we found that this tool is effective for changing the student's learning awareness, however, a system that responds to each student individually is considered necessary. For this reason, we conducted an automatic summarization of learning materials to promote previewing and real-time analysis to understand students' behaviors during class time, as well as a learning journal analysis to learn students' situations of learning and self-reflection after a class. The tools and analysis that match the learning situation have positive effects on the improvement of the learning environment and students' learning performance.

Finally, we discussed learner-centric notification mechanisms for learning analytics platforms. Providing timely feedback of knowledge obtained through learning analytics to students and teachers with appropriate designs and triggers is a further important task to be investigated in the future, as suggested by our research.

Acknowledgements

This work was partially supported by JST PRESTO Grant Number JPMJPR1505, "Research and Development on Fundamental and Utilization Technologies for Social Big Data" (178A03), the Commissioned Research of National Institute of Information and Communications Technology (NICT), and Kyushu University Interdisciplinary Programs in Education and Projects in Research Development, Japan.

References

Alsabawy, A. Y., Cater-Steel, A., & Soar, J. (2013). IT infrastructure services as a requirement for e-learning system success. *Computers & Education, 69*, 431–451. Retrieved from https://doi.org/10.1016/j.compedu.2013.07.035

Ausubel, D. P. (1960). The use of advance organizers in the learning and retention of meaningful verbal material. *Journal of Educational Psychology, 51*(5), 267–272. doi:10.1037/h0046669

Baradwaj, B., & Pal, S. (2011). Mining educational data to analyze student's performance. *International Journal of Advanced Computer Science and Applications, 6*(2), 63–69.

Beichner, R. J. (1995). Improving the effectiveness of large-attendance lectures with animation-rich lecture notes. *AAPT Announcer, 20*, 917.

Blikstein, P. (2013). Multimodal learning analytics. In *Proceedings of the 3rd International Conference on Learning Analytics and Knowledge* (pp. 102–106).

Bouma, G. (2009). Normalized (pointwise) mutual information in collocation extraction. In C. Chiarcos, R. E. de Castilho, & M. Stede (Eds.), *Proceedings of GSCL Conference* (pp. 31–40). Potsdam: Narr Verlag.

Chen, Y., Yu, B., Zhang, X., & Yu, Y. (2016, April 25–29). Topic modeling for evaluating students' reflective writing: A case study of pre-service teachers' journals. In *Proceedings of the 6th International Conference on Learning Analytics & Knowledge Conference* (pp. 1–5), Edinburgh, UK.

Goncalves, J., Hosio, S., Vukovic, M., & Konomi, S. (2017). Mobile and situated crowdsourcing. *International Journal of Human-Computer Studies, 102*, 1–3.

Greene, D., O'Callaghan, D., & Cunningham, P. (2014). How many topics? Stability analysis for topic models. In A. M. Jorge, L. Torgo, P. B. Brazdil, R. Camacho, & J. Gama (Eds.), *Joint European Conference on Machine Learning and Knowledge Discovery in Databases* (pp. 498–513). Heidelberg: Springer.

Hatton, N., & Smith, D. (1995). Reflection in teacher education: Towards definition and implementation. *Teaching and Teacher Education, 11*(1), 33–49.

Ifenthaler, D. (2015). Learning analytics. In J. M. Spector (Ed.), *The Sage encyclopedia of educational technology* (pp. 447–451). Thousand Oaks, CA: Sage Publications.

Igarashi, M., Shimada, A., Nagahara, H., & Taniguchi, R. (2016). *Evaluation of effectiveness and acceptability of personalized feedback for efficient energy usage.* Paper presented at Proceedings of the 11th International Workshop on Information Search, Integration, and Personalization (ISIP 2016).

Islam, A. K. M. N. (2015). E-learning system use and its outcomes: Moderating role of perceived compatibility. *Telematics and Informatics, 33*(1), 48–55. doi:10.1016/j.tele.2015.06.010

Lockyer, L., Heathcote, E., & Dawson, S. (2013). Informing pedagogical action. *American Behavioral Scientist, 57*(10), 1439–1459. Retrieved from https://doi.org/10.1177/0002764213479367

McGill, T. J., & Klobas, J. E. (2009). A task–technology fit view of learning management system impact. *Computers & Education, 52*(2), 496–508. Retrieved from https://doi.org/10.1016/j.compedu.2008.10.002

Mouri, K., Okubo, F., Shimada, A., & Ogata, H. (2016). Bayesian network for predicting students' final grade using e-book logs in university education. In *Proceedings of the 16th IEEE International Conference on Advanced Learning Technologies* (pp. 85–89).

Nwanganga, F., Aguiar, E., Ambrose, G. A., Goodrich, V., & Chawla, N. V. (2015). Qualitatively exploring electronic portfolios: A text mining approach to measuring student emotion as an early warning indicator. In *Proceedings of the 5th International Conference on Learning Analytics & Knowledge* (pp. 422–423).

Ogata, H., Taniguchi, Y., Suehiro, D., Shimada, A., Oi, M., Okubo, F., Yamada, M., & Kojima, K. (2017). M2B system: A digital learning platform for traditional classrooms in university. In *Practitioner Track Proceedings of the 7th International Learning Analytics & Knowledge Conference* (pp. 154–161).

Oi, M., Okubo, F., Shimada, A., Yin, C., & Ogata, H. (2015a). Analysis of preview and review patterns in undergraduates' e-book logs. In *Proceedings of the 23rd International Conference on Computers in Education* (pp. 166–171).

Oi, M., Yamada, M., Okubo, F., Shimada, A., & Ogata, H. (2017). Finding traces of high and low achievers by analyzing undergraduates' e-book logs. In *Joint Proceedings of the 6th Multimodal Learning Analytics Workshop and the 2nd Cross-LAK Workshop (MMLA-CrossLAK)* (pp. 15–22).

Oi, M., Yin, C., Okubo, F., Shimada, A., Kojima, K., Yamada, M., & Ogata, H. (2015b). Analysis of links among e-books in undergraduates' e-book logs. In *Proceedings of Workshop of the 23rd International Conference on Computers in Education* (pp. 665–669).

Okubo, F., Hirokawa, S., Oi, M., Shimada, A., Kojima, K., Yamada, M., & Ogata, H. (2016). Learning activity features of high performance students. In *Proceedings of the 1st International Workshop on Learning Analytics across Physical and Digital Spaces* (pp.28–33).

Okubo, F., Yamashita, T., Shimada, A., & Konomi, S. (2017a). Students' performance prediction using data of multiple courses by recurrent neural network. In *Proceedings of the 25th International Conference on Computers in Education* (pp. 439–444).

Okubo, F., Yamashita, T., Shimada, A., & Ogata, H. (2017b). A neural network approach for students' performance prediction. In *Proceedings of the 7th International Learning Analytics & Knowledge Conference* (pp. 598–599).

Okubo, F., Yamashita, T., Shimada, A., Taniguchi, Y., & Konomi, S. (2018). On the prediction of students' quiz score by recurrent neural network. In *Proceedings of the 2nd Multimodal Learning Analytics across (Physical and Digital) Spaces Workshop (CrossMMLA2018)*.

Oshima, J., Oshima, R., & Matsuzawa, Y. (2012). Knowledge building discourse explorer: A social network analysis application for knowledge building discourse. *Educational Technology Research & Development, 60*(5), 903–921.

Salton, G., & Buckley, C. (1988). Term-weighting approaches in automatic text retrieval. *Information Processing & Management, 24*(5), 513–523.

Sasao, T., Konomi, S., Kostakos, V., Kuribayashi, K., & Goncalves, J. (2017). Community reminder: Participatory contextual reminder environments for local communities. *International Journal of Human-Computer Studies, 102*, 41–53.

Schütze, H., & Pedersen, J. O. (1997). A cooccurrence-based thesaurus and two applications to information retrieval. *Information Processing & Management, 33*(3), 307–318.

Shimada, A., & Konomi, K. (2017). A lecture supporting system based on real-time learning analytics. In *Proceedings of the 14th International Conference on Cognition and Exploratory Learning in the Digital Age* (pp. 197–204).

Shimada, A., Okubo, F., Yin, C., & Ogata, H. (2016). Automatic generation of personalized review materials based on across-learning-system analysis. In *Proceedings of the 1st International Workshop on Learning Analytics across Physical and Digital Spaces* (pp. 22–27).

Shimada, A., Okubo, F., Yin, C., & Ogata, H. (2017). Automatic summarization of lecture slides for enhanced student preview: Technical report and user study. *IEEE Transactions on Learning Technologies, 11*(2), 165–178.

Sra, S., & Dhillon, I. S. (2006). Generalized nonnegative matrix approximations with Bregman divergences. In Y. Weiss, B. Scholkopf, & J. Platt (Eds.), *Advances in neural information processing systems* (Vol. 18, pp. 283–290). Cambridge, MA: MIT Press.

Straumsheim, C. (2013). Before the fact. *Inside Higher Ed.* Retrieved June 24, 2017, from https://www.insidehighered.com/news/2013/10/18/u-kentucky-hopes-boost-student-retention-prescriptive-analytics

Taniguchi, Y., Okubo, F., Shimada, A., & Konomi, S. (2017). Exploring students' learning journals with web-based interactive report tool. In *Proceedings of the 14th International Conference on Cognition and Exploratory Learning in the Digital Age* (pp. 251–254).

Taniguchi, Y., Suehiro, D., Shimada, A., & Ogata, H. (2017). Revealing hidden impression topics in students' journals based on nonnegative matrix factorization. In *Proceedings of IEEE 17th International Conference on Advanced Learning Technologies* (pp. 298–300).

Yamada, M., Oi, M., & Konomi, S. (2017a). Are learning logs related to procrastination? From the viewpoint of self-regulated learning. In *Proceedings of 14th International Conference on Cognition and Exploratory Learning in Digital Age* (pp. 3–10).

Yamada, M., Okubo, F., Oi, M., Shimada, A., Kojima, K., & Ogata, H. (2016). Learning analytics in ubiquitous learning environments: Self-regulated learning perspective. In *Proceedings of the 24th International Conference on Computers in Education* (pp. 306–314).

Yamada, M., Shimada, A., Okubo, F., Oi, M., Kojima, K., & Ogata, H. (2017b). Learning analytics of the relationships among self-regulated learning, learning behaviors, and learning performance. *Research and Practice in Technology Enhanced Learning, 12,* 13. doi:10.1186/s41039-017-0053-9

Worsley, M. (2012). Multimodal learning analytics: Enabling the future of learning through multimodal data analysis and interfaces. In *Proceedings of the International Conference on Multimodal Inter-faces (ICMI 2012)* (pp. 353–356).

Worsley, M., & Blikstein, P. (2015). Leveraging multimodal learning analytics to differentiate student learning strategies. In *Proceedings of the 5th International Conference on Learning Analytics and Knowledge* (pp. 360–367).

Wu, H., Luk, R., Wong, K., & Kwok, K. (2008). Interpreting TF-IDF term weights as making relevance decisions. *ACM Transactions on Information Systems, 26*(3), 1–37.

CHAPTER 13

The Learning Analytics and Flipped PBL for Tool-Design Learning

Il-Hyun Jo

1 Tools and Problems

1.1 Tool-Mediated Problem Solving in Nature

Life's primary problem for all living beings is to live each day in a way to avoid dying. It is true that every living organism will try to solve this problem by any means possible with the highest level of motivation. Some are successful, some are not. The factors that make the difference are given to the organisms by chance. Lucky individuals born in a good healthy and a strong body have a greater chance to survive than its weaker competitors. Whenever a living environment changes, it is noted that associated life-death factors and survival criteria also change, even by chance. A balance between the stronger and the weaker breaks down, and a new criteria sets in. The stronger entity in the previous environment may become the weaker in the new environment and, now, their chance to survive diminishes. The general rule to test who survives and who perishes is not the strength of the individual, but the fit of the individual to the environment.

The mechanism of solution generation to the life-death problem takes a long time across generations. Lucky individuals who fit to the new environment are likely to successfully survive and produce more off-springs. The mean attributes shift to the fit due to the regression effect. The problem solver is not individual but species specific. This problem-solving method of survival of the fittest is based on randomness mechanisms; natural environmental change and individual attribute distribution follow the rule of probability. None of these two factors, such as an individual's innate attributes and nature's random variations, can be controlled by the individual or species. Their destiny is under the dictator, the chance.

The kinds of evolutionary biological solutions generated to the life-death problems are diverse. When climate changes and gets drier, tall trees diminish and short grasses dominate the environment. This new environment brings in novel problems to a hominid who lives on the fruits on top of the trees. The evolutionary solutions to this problem are many. His taste preference can change from fruits to grass. His body size can get smaller to consume less fruits, and climb to smaller fruits hanging in higher branches. He can also grow thick hairs to move and survive in a remote terrain, which is richer in fruits but colder in weather. These solutions are different in many ways. However, they are equivalently good since they have worked for the entity to survive.

This random problem-solving mechanism in the nature results in biological diversity. One problem can be solved by many equivalently effective solutions. This is called as "equifinality of solutions." The system related concept of equifinality reflects the reality that there are usually several acceptable ways to accomplish the same end (Bertalanffy, 1972). The equifinal problem-solving mechanism always brings diversity in the world. This problem-solving mechanism in the nature does not need the design of the designer-creator. The only factors needed are randomness and life-death tests against individuals. It takes long time to generate a solution and sacrifice of millions of individual lives who are not lucky enough.

Human is the only species that uses different solutions to solve the problem; such as with tool mediation. Tools are defined as artifacts that mediate human activity to the problems of life. They are artifacts, and thus are subjects of design by their creators. They are mediators but not actors, and thus, without human actors, they do not generate values but stay as things. With the tools, human actor's problem-solving activities can be effectively facilitated. By chance and long time, the hominid in the African savanna has evolved for the plasticity of the brain, freed hands by upright walking, and opposable thumbs. The brain's logical and sign processing capacity, and opposable hand's gripping and object operation capability put together, are the rare combinatory conditions for the design to develop, and use tools. We are creatures by nature's random mutations and subjects of tests of the survival of the fittest, but at the same time, we are creators of tools that mediate us to become the fittest species on the earth. With tools, we can effectively resist the tyranny of nature, and create artificial environment, the civilization.

There are two kinds of tools as what they mediate us with; utilizing the physical and mental competencies. A physical tool mediates human activity by extending our physical competencies, such as a Hunting tomahawk mediates a hunter to catch wild boars that are faster and stronger than the hunter. His hunger problems can be effectively solved by the mediation of the tomahawk. The mental tool mediates the human activity by extending his mental competencies. The CAD system mediates an architect to build structurally complex buildings. His engineering problem can be effectively solved by the mediation of the CAD and the use of mathematics.

1.2   *Tool-Induced Problems in Civilized Society*

The development of a creature by natural selection takes a long time to evolve to adapt to nature. However, creature by design takes a short time to be created to meet the human's needs. In addition, the same human needs can be met by equifinality, many equivalently effective solutions to a problem. As a result, the number and kind of the tools used increase rapidly. Tools have evolved from simple to complex by design activity.

1.2.1   Evolution of Tools

There are four mechanisms in tool evolution; derivation, specialization, complication, and hybridization.

Derivation: A tool derives creation of other tools. A knife derives a sheath, and whetstone. Addition derives subtraction, and multiplication. A tool mediates a problem, and also generates more problems that users have never dreamed of before.

Specialization: A general-purpose tool evolves into many specialized tools. My mother used a kitchen knife. With it she cut vegetables, skinned apples, minced garlics, and fileted sushi out of a whole fish. My wife uses 17 knives all specialized for a specific purpose. As a result, a number of tools increases and each requires learning time to internalize.

Complication: Tools designed for different purposes are integrated into a single system tool as its parts. Part tools are associated into tool system (Heidegger, 1996). The parts in a tool system interact each other to perform novel functions that each tool could not do. For example, an automobile, mathematical formula, and instruction are examples of complex tool systems. Complexity is defined as the number of the components and the degree of interactions among them. As the number of the components of a product increases, the complexity of the product increases linearly. As the degree of interactions increases, the complexity of the product increases exponentially. For example, to supply its self-driving cars to users, Google needs diverse knowledge components such as mechanics, electronics, AI, and ergonomics, etc. These knowledge components should interact interdependently for the safe and reliable operation of the car. If the number of components is 10, the possible degree of component interactions is 45 ($=10*8/2$). As the number of components doubles (20), the degree of interaction increases greater than triples in number (190). To be and stay as a competitive duck in the pond, employees should be specialized in focal components, and should be effective collaborators for the interactions with colleagues from diverse specialties.

Hybridization: Different modes of tool presence emerges into a hybridized form. The physical and mental tools put together and creates a novel

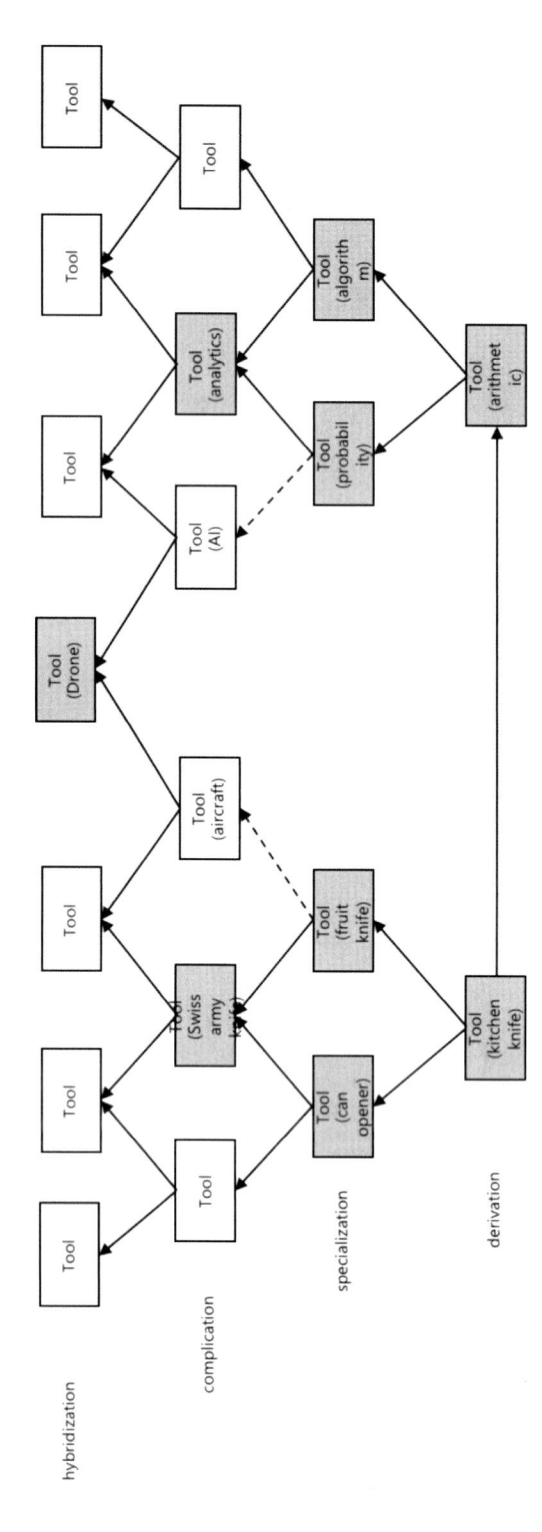

FIGURE 13.1   Evolutionary tree of tools

function that hybridized tools only can generate. The iconic technology of the 4th industrial revolution is hybridization of analog and digital technologies. Robots with AI, drones, self-driving car, 3-D printers are examples of tool hybridization. The artificial Cogitans embodied in artificial Extensa creates intelligent tools that think and act on their own. It is a tool that is most complex in structure and most simple to use. In its ultimate evolutionary stage, the use of instruction, as a tool for learning, should also be hybridized.

1.2.2   Tool-Use Problems

Today, more problems can be solved by a tool system, which is combination of tools as parts that are seen as interdependently operating. Computers, cars, instructions are all considered a complex tool system. As the result, the civilization is filled with a complex system of tools. This creates novel problems; too many tools to learn to use.

When we create a tool, its mode of presence is a Thing. Only when, by learning, mastered by the user, the tool functions as mediator that helps us solve problems in the world, which can be natural or artificial. Its mode of presence becomes an embodied type of Equipment. A hammer becomes an extended arm. A mathematical algorithm becomes his 'natural' way of thinking only when we learn to use it without friction. Once internalized by tool use learning, a tool disappears from user's consciousness and becomes his extension, physical or mental. In this way, no efforts, no cognitive loads are required when using the tool once equipped. The tool-use problem is the gap between Equipment and Thing. This gap is not of the tool but of user's learning to use it. To solve the problem, the users should learn to master the tool as mediator. Today there are so many tools and so less time to learn them.

From instructional design perspective, there two types of problems to solve; well-structured and ill-structured. The well-structured problems are defined as a problem for which the existing state and desired state are clearly identified, and the methods to reach the desired state are fairly obvious. The tool-use problem is an example of a well-structured problem. The target tool is present in its concrete form and observable function, and the gap between the existing state as a novice user, and a desired state as an expert user can be clearly identified. The problem, the gap between existing state and desired state can be analyzed objectively. For a well-structured problem in a tool-use situation, an instruction can be designed to fill the gap by practices. The Evaluation of the instruction is based on the degree of how much the gap is eliminated as result of the instructions.

1.2.3   Tool-Design Problems

Once internalized, a tool is ready to function as mediator to problems. When the tool breaks down or malfunctions, it becomes visible and shows its presence to the user. It now is an object of a design activity. It can be repaired to make it as it was. It can be totally redesigned to create novel tool. However, when it breaks down, the user recognizes the tool as a Thing again. Now, it is the time for a design activity to begin. The user himself or more skillful professional designer repairs it.

User designs tools based on his hands-on experience in using them. The user design activity is amateurish, voluntary, and no instruction is required. In the early evolutionary stages of tool design, tools are mostly designed by the user himself. My mother designed her kitchen knife on sketch book and our neighbor blacksmith made it for her as she designed it. In pre-industrialized society, master users are often the designers, or even makers of their own tools.

The professional designers design tools for others. Professional design activity requires knowledge, skills, and attitude learned through years of instructions. Today where most tools are specialized and complex, most of the tools are designed by professional designers. Automation and intellectualization of tools make the tool-use easier and tool-design more difficult. I use the Hyundai, iPhone, Google, and R packages, but I do not design them. My Hyundai car has an automatic gear, which is easier to use than manual gear that my older car is equipped with at the time. But the internal mechanism of automatic gear is too complex for me to understand its mechanical operations. The tools are too specialized, complex, and hybridized, which is highly knowledge and skills intensive human activity. I could fix the simple problems of my older car. I now go to a repair shop if my car breaks down. I know it is better not to open the hood. It only will make problems more complicated.

Ill-structured problems are defined as problem for in which its existing state and the desired state are unclear and, hence, the methods of reaching the desired state cannot be found, but only emerging during problem solving activity. The tool-design problems are examples of ill-structured problems. Designers can analyze an existing state, but they do not have idea or image of the desired state. You want to design 2019 model of Ferrari because you feel some upgrades are needed in 2018 model. Until you complete your design, however, there is no 2019 model in the world yet. Your ill-structured design problem can only be solved when you create a novel tool that never existed.

We become professional designers of some sorts for living in this world, which is filled with complex tool systems. I earn my income by designing instructions to pay for products and services designed by paid professional designers that I never met. In this way, without becoming effective designers of some use values, we may not solve our life-death problems in this civilized world.

1.3   *Primacy of Tool-Design Instruction in Information Society*

In general, as user interface gets simpler, and automation advances, the internal structure and process of the product gets more complex. Today, the world is getting both simpler and more complex. For users, it is getting simpler. One click to buy a product on the Internet is enough to have your merchandise thereby shipped to your home. Sitting in a seat and saying "home" is enough to bring yourself home in a car equipped with a GPS system and voice activation controls. In this simple user's world, you do whatever you want, while you have enough income to do these commands. You do not have a lot of problems and headaches. Thus, what you have to do is continue enjoying your simple user's life. For the designers, however, the world is getting more complex. To provide painless one-click online marketing such as what is available on Amazon and Netflix, to run a Google self-driving car in the traffic of Seoul, the system inside of the service and product should be very, very complex. To design complex tools, multidisciplinary knowledge and skills, collaborative generations and tests of mockup solutions, and self-regulated learning for novel information are required.

In this world, you are living as both the user and the designer. You are like a duck. As a consumer, you are calm on the surface, but, as supplier, you should be always paddling like the dickens underwater. You are a mechanical engineer working for Google car division. You have to be busily paddling all the time. You buy a kindle e-book from Amazon to read for your vacation. You are calm on the Amazon's intuitive interface. You do not have to intentionally learn to be calm. But you have to learn to paddle. If you want to swim faster than other ducks, you have to learn to become much more, such as being efficient and faster at managing your job.

2   Tool-Induced Problems and Instruction

2.1   *Instruction as Tool for Learning*

The concept of Random natural learning is suitable for biologically primary learning. For tools that are designed and created, and not evolved with us in the nature, we do not have biologically inherited readiness to learn them in a natural way. These tool learning problems should also be solved by using specialized tool, instruction. We design instructions and use them for learning physical and mental tools such as hammer, car, mathematics, signs, and cetera. Remember. We are a tool-making species.

Instruction is a also considered a tool. As other tools have, instruction has evolved from simple to complex to hybrid. The expert hog hunter gives a simple instruction regarding how to chase a herd of hogs by telling and drawing on the dirt. Today's instruction is composed of diverse elements that are systemically interacting with each other toward the instructional goals. Elements include: textbooks, video clips, computer games, test instruments, and instructors guide, etc. Instructional 'systems' design (ISD) focus is on how to design instructional system as a tool for target learning goals.

The creative design approach combines analytical and systems thinking with human factors in instructional design to create and take advantage of opportunities to serve tool-users or the society in general. The most pervasive assumption of instructional design is that different learning outcomes necessitate different conditions of learning (Gagne, 1980). Tool-use learning and tool-design learning are different purpose or raison d'etre of instruction, the learning outcomes. For different tools, different instructions are necessary to be designed. The instruction for tool-use problems should be different from instruction for tool-design problems, just like the instruction for math problems should be different from the instruction for health problems. Another assumption of instructional design is that different learning outcomes are hierarchically interdependent. For example, the instruction for rule-application differs from that for problem-solving. However, a rule-application instruction should be offered before problem solving instruction, because rule-application is a prerequisite knowledge to problem-solving competency.

2.2 *Instruction for Tool-Use*

Roughly speaking, the instruction for certain learning outcomes should be designed to provide learners similar experience to learned performance with practice and feedback. For reading performance, the learners should read. For programing performance, the learners should write programs. For driving performance, the learners should drive in a safe, controlled manner, and have given them feedback. The general instructional procedure includes iterations of presentation-practice-feedback-test-revision process until the objective "goal" is achieved. The direct instruction of expert in using the tool is a most efficient and effective way to learn to use tools. When your destination is identified, you don't have to find the route on your own trial and error. Instead, you may simply ask the local people which way to go, and follow as he instructs. The instructional design for well-structured problem solving begins with the identification of instructional objectives, the defined structure and apparent certainty of outcome. It is a neat, tidy, easy to teach and efficient way to examine instructional design. The ADDIE model is a representative instructional design model for well-structured tool-use problems. It is suitable for situations where the 'need' is given.

For instruction for well-defined tool-use problems, the structured instructional techniques can be used. The most typical technique to use is the Gagne's Nine Events of Instruction model (Gagne, 1980). The nine events are; (1) Gain attention: e.g. present a good problem, a new situation, use a multimedia advertisement, and ask questions. This helps to ground the lesson, and to motivate, (2) Describe the goal: e.g. state what students will be able to accomplish and how they will be able to use the knowledge, and give a demonstration if appropriate. This allows students to frame information, i.e. treat it better. (3) Stimulate recall of prior knowledge: e.g. remind the student of prior knowledge relevant to the current lesson (facts, rules, procedures or skills). This shows how knowledge is connected, provide the student with a framework that helps learning and remembering. Tests can be included. (4) Present the material to be learned: e.g. text, graphics, simulations, figures, pictures, sound, etc. This chunks learned information into manageable granularity (avoid memory overload, recall information). (5) Provide guidance for learning: e.g. presentation of content is different from the instructions on how to learn. This uses of different channel, (6) Elicit performance "practice:" let the learner do something with the newly acquired behavior, practice skills or apply knowledge. (7) Provide informative feedback: show the correctness of the trainee's response, analyze the learner's behavior, present a good (step-by-step) solution of the problem, (8) Assess performance test, if the lesson has been learned. Also give sometimes a general progress information or report as feedback, and (9) Enhance retention and transfer: e.g. inform the learner about similar problem situations, provide additional practice. Put the learner in a transfer situation. Let the learner review the lesson.

2.3   *Instruction for Tool-Design*

2.3.1   Design as Ill-Structure Problem Solving

The essence of design is the creation of tools for the utility, comfort, and advancement of mankind. In other words, a designed tool is 'reified intention.' The outcome of this intention can be a kitchen knife, self-driving car, or other types of instruction. In fact, all activities directed towards the materialization of an intent can be described as a form of a design.

Design is a human activity in which there is no clearly defined goal or objective, but instead an ill-defined awareness that a change of a tool is needed. Ill-structured problems are defined as a problem for in which its existing state and the desired state are unclear and, hence, methods of reaching the desired state cannot be found but are emerging. Thus, a design activity is a kind of an ill-structured problem solving task. Designers involved in such activity often refer to their task as ill-structured problem-solving (Boradkar, 2010). If a well-structured problem solving is like trip to an identified destination, then an ill-structured problem solving is like adventure to an unknown utopia. We feel that we have to explore, but do not know where and how to get there because no one has been there and can instruct us on how to achieve this goal.

Ill-structured design problem solving process is composed of 4 steps (Holt et al., 1985):

1. The design begins with a vaguely felt need of individuals. Individual differences in perceptions, values, and premises that are culturally and professionally biased, are a true source of creativity in setting the felt need to the agree-upon design objectives. This stage is critical since accepting the objectives may well result in misdirected efforts carried out with great competence.

2. Individuals generate mockups or notional systems to discover new possibilities for satisfying that need. The individual's will to succeed, relevant prior knowledge and skills, learning skills to fill the gaps of knowledge, and communication skills influence to give structure, content, and form of the mockups.

3. Notional system is then compared with the real world, providing a formal vehicle for debate to enable potential changes to be defined. The free and open communication between participants can be distorted by vested interest and inequalities of power in this case.

4. Assuming that the participants can agree on some directions of change, then a new version of a mockup is constructed, to be again compared with the real world, and so the learning process proceeds. The test criteria is socially constructed to the social interests of potential users.

2.3.2   Design Process as Learning

The design process is also a learning and an understanding process. The design process involves individual learning, team mockup generation, and test of the mockup in larger community of expert designers. The biases and distortions among the participants are a source of true creativity. The increased understanding and insight emerges from this cyclic pattern of imagining and locating in the real world. Design too is concerned with things that might be, but only if they satisfy the test of the world. Things that ought to be come from things that might be, as tested against reality.

In contrast, well-structured problems have only one 'the' solution, which can be found by an analysis of the problem itself. No external information, knowledge, skills, discussions and attitude influence the generation of the solution, which stands alone objectively. The creative solution can be generated by open and free group discussion, but cannot excel the solution by one genius providing feedback for this process.

Human factors such as distorted communication, power, anxiety, and negotiations should be combined with analytical systemic and human behavioral components, for it is then that a true picture of design profession emerges for the intending designers. The social quality of the designer's work is rooted in the quality of learning throughout the design process. It is clear that developing such a system would need to involve a team of experts. The process of design is inherently an interdisciplinary process, and it is typically conducted in cross-functional teams (Holt, Radcliffe, & Schoorl, 1985).

Design is an intelligent activity; the quality and range of ideas depends on the generation of images, prototypes of potential solutions. Design is a knowing activity; knowledge necessary to validate ideas must be acquired from many sources. Notably, for this reason, design is a social activity; for the designer's reason for existence is the creation of a social utility.

These conditions of the ill-structured problem solving design brings in learning for a tool-design. In contrast, a well-structured problem solving process is likely to restrict the designer rather than enhance his abilities. Its "fix-it" mentality concerning itself with solving well-structured rather than exploiting learning opportunities does not demand new insights, nor does it offer new opportunities, but may in effect be accomplished by routine and does not constitute a tool design. There are prerequisites to design as ill-structured problem-solving; the self-regulated will to succeed in the problem solving, the relevant knowledge, learning skills to fill the gaps of knowledge, sufficient experience, and the further communication of skills.

Ill-structured problem solving processes involve designer competency as inductive and deductive thinking, creative or divergent thinking and critical and divergent thinking. The recognition that a well-structured problem solving is applicable to only a certain class of problems is important to an understanding of the design process. Checkland (1999) suggests that a well-structured problem is a special case of the core general ill-structured problem. A well-structured problem is suitable for situations where the 'need' is given; ill-structured problem solving or design allows for completely unexpected answer to emerge. In a real design situation, target problems are situated somewhere between the two extreme states.

3   Flipped PBL for Tool-Design Instruction

3.1   *PBL*

3.1.1   Background and Process

PBL, problem-based learning, is an instruction to learn about a subject through the experience of solving an open-ended ill-structured problem. This includes knowledge acquisition, enhanced group collaboration and communication. The process works and allows for learners to develop skills used for their future practice. It enhances critical appraisal, literature retrieval and encourages ongoing learning within a team environment. The PBL process involves working in a small group of learners. Each student takes on a role within the group that may be formal or informal and the role often alternates among the learners. It is focused on the student's reflection and reasoning to construct their own learning.

To enumerate, the Maastricht seven-jump process involves clarifying terms, defining problem(s), brainstorming, structuring and hypothesis, learning objectives, independent study and synthesis. In short, this process is able to help the overall process, as it is identifying what they already know, what they need to know, and how and where to access new information that may lead to the resolution of the problem. The role of the instructor is to facilitate learning by supporting, guiding, and monitoring the learning process of the learner. The tutor aims to build student's confidence when addressing problems, while also expanding their understanding. This process is based on constructivism. The PBL represents a paradigm shift from a traditional teaching and learning philosophy, which is more often lecture-based. The constructs for teaching PBL are very different from traditional classroom or lecture teaching and often requires more preparation time and resources to support a small group learning.

3.1.2   Expectations and Advantages

PBL uses an authentic, complex problem as the impetus for learning and fosters the acquisition of domain knowledge, problem solving and collaboration skills, and self-regulatory learning capacity all together in this process. This approach emphasizes the student's active role in constructing knowledge and student's actively engaging in inquiry and problem solving, typically in a collaborative framework. Learning is anchored to real-world or authentic contexts for the benefit of the learners. In sum, the PBL process is a classroom mirror image of real world ill-structured problem solving processes such as with tool-design.

In this process, the students are allowed and facilitated to solve ill-structured design problems, such as medical prescriptions, auto design, policy design, and research design which are few examples.

There are several advantages of the utilization of the PBL. One advantage is that it is student-focused, which allows for increased active learning and better understanding and retention of knowledge. It also helps to develop life skills that are applicable to many domains. It can be used to enhance content knowledge while simultaneously fostering the development of communication, problem-solving, critical thinking, collaboration, and self-directed learning skills for the student learner. The use of the PBL may position students to optimally function using real-world experiences to enhance learning. By harnessing collective group intellect, differing perspectives may offer different perceptions and solutions to a problem. Ill-structured problems have many equifinal solutions which should be designed based on knowledge, skills, and attitudes and should be tested by other people and ready to be revised at any time for better learning opportunities. The process is a real, deductive, and functioning knowledge-based solutions process.

3.1.3   Conditions and Limitations

According to Wood (2003), the major disadvantage to this process involves the utilization of resources and tutor facilitation. It requires more staff to take an active role in facilitation and group-led discussion and some educators find PBL facilitation difficult and frustrating to use. It is resource-intensive because it requires more physical space and more accessible computer resources to accommodate simultaneous smaller group-learning teams. Students also report uncertainty in this learning arena with the possility of information overload and are unable to determine how much study time is required for this system, and the relevance of the information available. Students may not have access to instructors who serve as the inspirational role models that the traditional curriculum offers. Although students generally like and gain greater ability to solve real-life problems in problem-based learning courses, instructors of the methodology must often invest more time to assess student learning and prepare course materials, as compared to direct instructions and traditional instruction means testing.

Student readiness is a critical premise of PBL. The typical medical students are highly motivated in both professionally and academically concepts, have clear professional career orientation, and exhibit maturity. They also are exposed to real problems in real world situation as they advance to become interns and residents in the hospitals. These learner characteristics are not common in most typical college students. The qualified students for the PBL should be equipped with a minimum of prerequisite knowledge, skills, and self-regulation for active and self-directed learning to solve ill-structured problems. Certainly active problem solving is useful as learners become more competent, and are better able to deal with their working memory limitations (Sweller, 2006). But early in the learning process, these learners may find it difficult to process a large amount of information in a short time. Thus the rigors of active problem solving in this case may become an issue for the student novices. Once learners gain expertise the scaffolding inherent in problem-based learning, the process helps learners avoid these issues. Also critical is the use of the instructor's coaching and tutoring skills. The instructors have to change their traditional teaching methodologies in order to incorporate a problem-based system for learning. Their task is to question the student's knowledge, as well as beliefs, and give only hints to correct their mistakes and guide the students in their research. All of these features of problem-based learning may be foreign to some instructors; hence they find it difficult to alter their past habits of instruction for student learning.

These conditions are prerequisites of the PBL system of learning. If we meet the prerequisite conditions, the PBL can be a solution to higher education.

3.1.4 Ecological Context

The PBL's birth place is a medical school where real problems (patients to be healed), learning resources (medical apparatus, clinical records, expensive instruments and facilities, etc.), instructors with clinical expertise, and highly motivated students are a rich environment of usage for the PBL. These luxuries are not typically available to a regular college classroom. Adaptation to the ecological differences for regular colleges requires the use of non-traditional solutions such as technology.

Student readiness: Typical medical students are highly motivated in both professionally and academically, have clear professional career orientation, and exhibit a high level of maturity. They also are exposed to real problems in the real world situations as they advance interns and residents in the hospitals. These learner characteristics are not common in the typical college students.

In sum, the use of the PBL in regular colleges do not have access to the PBL-friendly learning environment in those cases. Without taking care of these challenges systematically, a wide dissemination of the use of the PBL across the college campuses may be impractical. A redesign of the PBL to adopt to general HE context by augmenting with flipped learning and by intellectualizing with learning analytics is necessitated in this case for successful use of this system.

3.2   *Flipped Learning as Augmentation to PBL*

The flipped learning approach is a new way of promoting and supporting active learning (Jensen et al., 2015), in which the in-person classroom lectures are "flipped" with other learning activities at home. This approach offers one possible solution as a way to realize the student-centered pedagogy and the benefits of active learning, which primarily focuses on bringing activities, promoting student engagement in class, and encapsulating the idea of "learning-by-doing" in the pedagogy (Wong & Cheung, 2015). Such inverted classrooms are motivated by many factors, including devoting class time toward encouraging critical thinking and student collaboration, supporting different student learning styles, and addressing the needs of the students who have grown up with online media technology.

Flipped classrooms also redefine in-class activities. The in-class lessons accompanying flipped classroom may include activity learning to engage students in the content. The class activities may vary but may include in-depth laboratory experiments, debate or speech presentation, current event discussions, and peer reviewing, which are typical methods of an in-class PBL session. Because these types of active learning scenarios allow for a type of highly differentiated instruction, more time can be spent in class on higher-order thinking skills such as problem-finding, collaboration, design and problem solving as students tackle difficult problems, working in groups, pursuing research, and constructing knowledge with the help of their instructor and peers. Flipped classrooms have been implemented in both schools and colleges and been found to have varying differences in the method of implementation. The instructor's interaction with students in a flipped classroom can be more personalized and less didactic, and the students are actively involved in knowledge acquisition and construction as they participate in and evaluate their learning (Abeysekera & Dawson, 2015).

With the use of flipped learning (FL), the technologically augmented pedagogy that blends digital self-paced learning prior to face-to-face analog classroom activities, is emerging as a compromise of the effectiveness-efficiency dilemma of the PBL. The FL's technological feature contributes to the logistic factor of the PBL by allowing access to and management of large number of students to pre-study material, which provides an opportunity to enhance the individual's self-paced learning. This "anytime and anywhere" pedagogical feature of the FL will help learners to prepare themselves to cognitively demanding PBL sessions coming forth. If learners achieve equipment of mastery learning of pre-study material, the PBL-based large scale instructional innovation should be facilitated.

Flipped learning can also be enrichment of the PBL when adapted in higher education. In HE, as compared to medical school, has advantages in diversity in the kinds of problems and domain knowledge of domain knowledge and in the scalability of technology-based learning. The university as its name implies is comprised of universal types of problems, and ideas from diverse disciplines. The university is truly a melting pot with social and natural sciences, management, humanities, engineering, and arts.

Designing tools are used for almost every problem in the society, which can be solved by the use of multi-disciplinary teams in the university level of teaching. In terms of a disciplinary diversity, the university has more advantages than medical schools. In terms of technological aspects of flipped learning, the university has great advantages than medical schools with small class sizes.

The Flipped PBL is a student-driven, group-centered instructional process. The student's active learning and interactions to each other are indicators of the success of this system. To effectively facilitate students, the instructor should be informed student's activities. Without the monitoring and assessing of the dynamic process of Flipped PBL, the instructors are not able to help individual students and to coach group activities.

4   Intellectualization of Flipped PBL by Learning Analytics

4.1   *Premises of Flipped PBL*
The critical premise of flipped learning is to make sure that the learners master prerequisites of face-to-face session during the online pre-study. By allowing more study time for individuals falling short of the requirements for the face to face sessions, learners can make themselves, at least theoretically, become equipped with enough skills and knowledge for the following interactive instructional phase such as problem-based learning activities. In reality, however, instructors often get into trouble when they discover large variances from the learners in the degree of readiness of the prerequisites for this system. And without detailed information of individual learner's learning behaviors and her psychological dynamics underlying the behaviors, instructors may not be able to provide remedial individualized instruction and to construct collaborative teams with maximum diversity and productivity, which are critical success factors in the use of highly interactive team-based learning such as the PBL. Accessing to the online pre-study material is a necessary condition, but not a sufficient condition for mastery learning of the prerequisite knowledge and skills for the use of the PBL. Systematic learning assurance initiatives should be established in this case.

4.2   *Learning Analytics for In-Individual Pre-Study*

One way to resolve this issue is through learning analytics, which often refers to the collection, analysis, and reporting of data about learners in their learning context using the techniques of data mining (Ali et al., 2012). The learning analytics provides a possible new way of looking into these data resources, and is an emerging research area in educational technology to assist formative assessment (Kumar et al., 2015). The lack of student monitoring capabilities in online education represents both a potential pitfall and a promising design opportunity for the developers. In the current online systems, instructors are unable to observe students during instruction and thus have no means to verify whether students paid attention to the lesson, understood the material, or even watch the lecture at all in this case.

Its contributions to the flipped PBL can be categorized in temporal and pedagogical dimensions. In temporal dimension, the LA may contribute before, during, and after the PBL sessions. During the pre-PBL online session, the use of learning analytics can help the individual students learning behavior by providing feedback to himself and instructor using dashboard, for example. The Individual's self-regulatory and reflective behavior can be improved by the dashboard. Instructors can provide a nudge and help, online o face-to-face, to help equip students with prerequisite knowledge and skills, which should contribute an effective PBL. During the in-PBL, a face-to-face session can be assisted by the LMS. In the HE, the LMS is a widely used commodity to help online communication and resource sharing. More students are using online features of individual communication with colleague students and instructors and TAs in LMS even in majorly face-to-face classes. With every type of click and reference to this system, the student learning types are recorded as digital footprints and are used as data for learning analytics. Thus, the LA for a face-to-face PBL session may provide useful information to instructor to better facilitate group activities and help individuals in need face-to-face. Also, post-PBL, the LA can help the instructor or instructional designer to conduct a formative evaluation of the initial design of flipped PBL. This may serve as an evolutionary mechanism for the evolution of a flipped PBL. As a useful tool, the evolution of flipped PBL will result in further specialization, complication, and hybridization of the flipped PBL in the HE ecology.

In a pedagogical dimension, the LA may contribute to an instructor or instructional designer by providing assessment and treatment information. An assessment is useful for understanding students. The treatment is for intervention based on the assessment. The dashboard can be used either for an assessment or for a treatment. The dashboard for the learner is used for an assessment and treatment. By the same token, the dashboard for the instructor is used for an assessment. The treatment is designed by the instructor based on the assessment. The instructor is the actor and the learning analytics is a tool. The LA used as a tool should not replace human actors such as instructor, student, but mediate or nudge them to facilitate learning. The learning analytics can augment flipped PBL in several ways. First, it helps student self-regulate. With the LA, students are able to see their statistics, data, etc. They receive the personalized feedback through visualizations, so that they can reflect about their own learning and they can take actions on the pre-study material prior to in-class PBL session. Second, it provides augmented information for instructors. Instructors can know the general tendencies about the students, and know the specific problems of each student, etc. before the face to face lesson, so instructors can adapt the face to face lesson to be more effective based on the data provided by the LA. Third, the LA can be used for the evaluation of materials, students and the learning process. Based on these evaluations, different actions can be taken to improve the course for future editions. (Martínez, Merino, Valiente, Kloos, Díaz, & Ruiz, 2015).

Another problem that was not solved yet is the instructor's lack of coaching skills. The coaching primarily requires an understanding of the learners and their learning activities, to create a supportive learning environment that encourages active participation by all members and continuously monitors the quality of learning (Savin-Baden M. Berkshire, England: Open University Press; 2003. Facilitating problem-based learning: illuminating perspectives). In this way, lLearning is central to effective coaching: coaches facilitate the learning process (The psychology of coaching, mentoring and learning). In the PBL, there are two kinds of learners; student-learners who learn from instructional material, and instructor-learners who learn from the student-learner's learning.

4.3   *Expected Benefits of Flipped PBL by Learning Analytics*

The Flipped PBL is complex and hybridized tool system. It is composed of digital and analog components. The degree of blending in the FL can be physical, chemical, and organic. The physical blending, putting digital learning first before analog class, is the lowest level of blending. Additionally, there is no functional interdependence between the two parts. The chemical blending creates a unique instructional effect that none of the two elements independently provides. The digital learning and analog instruction complement each other compensating each other's weaknesses and appropriating strengths. The organic blending, which is the highest level of blending, allows interactions and feedback between the two elements, and evolves as learning environments and learner needs change. To develop a physical FL to organic FL, communication and feedback mechanism, or intelligent nerve system, should be installed for use in the instructional system. Instructional analytics may serve as the nerve system in the flipped PBL.

By utilizing learning analytics for intellectualization of the flipped PBL, instructors and instructional designers can catch four birds at the same time.

Bird one: the assurance of learning in a pre-study online *before* PBL. As an ill-structured design problem, the PBL requires the learner's prior knowledge on the domain knowledge, communication, self-regulation, and problem itself. The FL is providing the opportunity for learning, and the LA can assess how much learning is actually realized from the opportunity. Since the pre-study process is online, we can utilize the advancement of the LA.

Bird two: the assessment of learners for a custom instruction *during* the PBL. During the PBL face-to-face session, the instructors need to know the individual's value, perspective, learning characteristics, and network position in the team. In this instance, the instructors who are trained as a researcher in their PhD program are not expert coaches for collaborative work with open and free atmosphere with just-in-time nudge as necessary. Their role is not sage on the stage but guided by the side use of instruction. As discussed previously, creative and quality solutions to ill-structured problems grows in a free and open atmosphere of the collaboration group. If the instructor behaves as the authoritative sages typically do, distortion of communication, student's anxiety and fear will be resolved. But by providing the student information to the instructors, they can provide informed facilitation to the collaboration process as guide.

Bird three: the analysis of big data for revision of instructions *after* the PBL for the next semester. According to the process of ill-structured problem-solving, there is no final or ultimate final solution, but continually evolving solutions in the PBL. Once semester the is over, the instructor and instructional designer could be able to reflect upon the information based on the learning analytics and conduct formative evaluation for revision of the whole Flipped PBL process and redesign it for next semester. The student's viewing and clicking behavior with online material, their social and discursive online interactions data during pre-study are useful data to identify the needy individuals in the process and team dynamics of the groups.

Bird four: the evidence-based decision making by the management of the institutions are facilitated by the academic analytics. The previous analysis is focused on the within-class analytics. For the management aspect, the between-class analytics can support their decisions in strategic decisions to support the classrooms in many ways. For example, the class size, instructor's tenure and PBL training, discipline- and gender-interaction effect to PBL vs.

direct instruction, etc., can be analyzed and provided to the management. This institutional data can be open to the public to enhance the opportunity for accountability and transparency of the institution.

5   Conclusion

5.1   *Summary*

The concept of learning is a leverage effect to relate to life's problem solving activities. We design tools to solve our problems, and the tools have evolved into diversity through the derivation, specialization, complication, and hybridization of its usage. Tools are many in the kinds of tools available to the user, and it can be difficult to learn to use these implements, which creates novel problems, tool-use problems. The recent progress in automation and intellectualization of tools alleviate the tool-use problems. In contrast, the need for the ill-structured tool-design problem solving capacity development has been escalated. The tool-design capability including problem-solving skills, domain knowledge, collaboration and communication skills are on the top priority instructional goals of today's higher education. The instructional tools designed to solve ill-structured tool-design problem solving capacity is the use of the PBL. The ecological context of the PBL's birthplace, medical school classroom, is different from that of the general university with larger and diverse participants than medical schools. Thus the adaptation of the PBL is necessary. The flipped learning and learning analytics, are useful as learning tools in recent technological innovations, such as in the large-scale learning environment. The flipped learning can help students prepare themselves with prerequisite knowledge, self-regulation and collaboration skills while using in-individual online sessions. The learning analytics can help the instructors to monitor and assess the students by analytics information, and help to make the students ready to provide enhanced learning opportunities prior to in-class session. The learning analytics model that refers to the flipped PBL instruction and helps to mediate instructors should be developed and investigated in the future.

5.2   *Implications of Flipped PBL Referred LA*

There are practical and theoretical implications of learning analytics for flipped PBL.

Practical implications: the mass-customization of the PBL to the context of the large general universities for both effectiveness and efficiency of the tool-design instruction, accountability of the HE instruction by the evidence-based decision making, one-source-multi-use of small granularity learning data up to learner, instruction, and institutional level analytics. Research implications: emerging ID, PBL, referenced LA, systemic integration of intra-class instructional analytics and inter-class academic analytics, theoretical perspective for LA as mediator to instructor, institution-wide data collection and analytics research opportunity for enhancing student learning.

5.3   *Future Research*

The allowance of the instructor and the learner's user-design activity of a pre-designed LA: the LA is seen instructor's tool to mediate his instructional problem solving. As a tool, the PBL is not one but many tools used through specialization, complication, and a hybridization process. As a tool user and prime actor of the activity, the user of the tool should be allowed to user-design the instrument for enhanced learning opportunities.

The specialization of the LA to diverse instructional models: institution-wide redesign of LA should be done by a professional designer of Instructional Analytics. I coined this new term to emphasize the coupling of Instruction and Learning Analytics. Beyond posteriori reference, the learning analytics should be designed in parallel with instructional design.

The LA is a tool for instructor. It can be a concept called Thing or an Equipment. The interface design and instruction to use the LA based on the needs of instructors should be systematically studied. The LA is tool designed to mediate the success of an instruction. Thus the LA model designer should refer to the instructional design. As the field of learning analytics evolves, the need to align both analytic approaches and outputs with a conceptual frame of reference and educational context has been acknowledged (Lockyer, Heathcote, & Dawson, 2013). This is a loaded research question that should be pursued in the future.

References

Abeysekera, L., & Dawson, P. (2015). Motivation and cognitive load in the flipped classroom: Definition, rationale and a call for research. *Higher Education Research & Development, 34*(1), 1–14.

Ali, L., Hatala, M., Gašević, D., & Jovanović, J. (2012). A qualitative evaluation of evolution of a learning analytics tool. *Computers & Education, 58*(1), 470–489.

Boradkar, P. (2010). Design as problem solving. In R. Frodeman, J. T. Klein, & C. Mitcham (Eds.), *The Oxford handbook of interdisciplinarity* (pp. 273–287). Oxford: Oxford University Press.

Checkland, P. (1999). Systems thinking. In W. J. Currie & B. Galliers (Eds.), *Rethinking management information systems* (pp. 45–56). Oxford: Oxford University Press.

Evensen, D. H., & Hmelo-Silver, C. E. (2000). *Problem-based learning: A research perspective on learning interactions.* New York, NY: Routledge.

Gagne, R. M. (1980). *The conditions of learning.* New York, NY: Holt, Rineheart & Winston.

Heidegger, M. (1996). *Being and time: A translation of Sein und Zeit.* New York, NY: SUNY Press.

Herreid, C. F., & Schiller, N. A. (2013). Case studies and the flipped classroom. *Journal of College Science Teaching, 42*(5), 62–66.

Holt, J. E., Radcliffe, D. F., & Schoorl, D. (1985). Design or problem solving: A critical choice for the engineering profession. *Design Studies, 6*(2), 107–110.

Jensen, J. L., Kummer, T. A., & Godoy, P. D. D. M. (2015). Improvements from a flipped classroom may simply be the fruits of active learning. *CBE-Life Sciences Education, 14*(1), ar5.

Jonassen, D. H. (2000). Toward a design theory of problem solving. *Educational Technology Research and Development, 48*(4), 63–85.

Kumar, V. S., Somasundaram, T. S., Boulanger, D., Seanosky, J., & Vilela, M. F. (2015). Big data learning analytics: A new perspective. In *Ubiquitous learning environments and technologies.* Berlin: Springer.

Law, H. (2010). Coaching relationships and ethical practice. In S. Palmer, A. McDowall, S. Palmer, & A. McDowall (Eds.), *The coaching relationship: Putting people first* (pp. 182–202). New York, NY: Routledge.

Lockyer, L., Heathcote, E., & Dawson, S. (2013). Informing pedagogical action: Aligning learning analytics with learning design. *American Behavioral Scientist, 57*(10), 1439–1459.

Martínez, D. R., Merino, P. J. M., Valiente, J. A. R., Kloos, C. D., Díaz, H. J. P., & Ruiz, J. S. (2015). Combining learning analytics and the flipped classroom in a MOOC of maths. In *CHANGEE/WAPLA/HybridEd@EC-TEL* (pp. 71–79).

Sweller, J. (2006). The worked example effect and human cognition. *Learning and Instruction, 16*(2), 165–169.

Von Bertalanffy, L. (1972). The history and status of general systems theory. *Academy of Management Journal, 15*(4), 407–426.

Wood, D. (2003). ABC of learning and teaching in medicine: Problem based learning. *British Medical Journal, 326,* 328–330.

CHAPTER 14

Learning Analytics Cockpit for MOOC Platforms

Karin Maier, Philipp Leitner and Martin Ebner

1 Introduction

Data Mining has become an omnipresent concept and it seems every research field benefits from the application of its algorithms and tools. The field of education is no exception here. The ubiquitous learning environment, computers, mobile devices, learning management systems (LMS), any cloud system—they all are connected via the Internet, leave us the by-product of captured, explicit data rather than ephemeral impressions of the learning process, which needs further processing and interpretation (Siemens & Long, 2011).

Siemens and Long (2011) predicted that big data and analytics will be major factors influencing the higher education sector. In this intersection of various academic fields, for example education, psychology, pedagogy, statistics, machine learning, and computer science a term was coined: Learning Analytics (Dawson et al., 2014).

Mentioned first in the Horizon Report 2012 (Johnson, Adams, & Cummins, 2012), it is variously defined amongst others as "the measurement, collection, analysis and reporting of data about learners and their contexts for purposes of understanding and optimizing learning and the environments in which it occurs" (Siemens, 2011). Or "learning analytics is about collecting traces that learners leave behind and using those traces to improve learning" (Duval, 2012).

Another relatively new concept in the field of education are Massive Open Online Courses. They can be considered as one of the emerging online environments. The growth of interest in this area attracts researchers to examine the data available from the vast repositories (Khalil & Ebner, 2016). In these learning environments adequate tools to gather, process, and visualize are needed to support the learners and provide teachers with insights and feedback rather than leaving uninterpreted data dumps to the researchers and administrators of such MOOCs.

Despite being a young research area, Learning Analytics is an actively researched one and involves development, use, and integration of new processes and tools. The aim is to extract information from educational data to support education-related decision making to improve the performance of

© KONINKLIJKE BRILL NV, LEIDEN, 2019 | DOI: 10.1163/9789004399273_014 teaching and learning of individual students and of teachers (Leitner et al., 2017).

Two underlying principles drive the field of learning analytics research—to understand and to optimize learning itself, and the learning environments in which learning occurs. Whereas the prediction of learning success was an early research goal, recent advances return to improve domain knowledge to increase the quality of the available learning analytic tools (Dragan et al., 2017). Educational theory and advanced machine learning methods are building blocks for modelling behaviour, cognitive, and social processes within the learning process (Schwendimann et al., 2016).

In Leitner et al. (2017) the stakeholders of this learning process have been categorized into three types: Researchers/Administrators, Learners, and Teachers. Each group has their own motivation and interest using learning analytics, though these are not mutually exclusive, neither are the benefits these groups can draw from.

The idea of using the gained knowledge to improve the underlying learning environment, "closing the feedback loop" (Clow, 2012), is very intuitive and was picked up by Khalil and Ebner (2015) who introduced a learning analytics life cycle, depicted in Figure 14.1.

In this cycle, the learners produce data when acting in their learning environment. This representation of learning is stored as massive datasets and as Big Data. In the next step, Analytics are needed to interpret these traces of learners' behaviour. Based upon those results it is possible to act upon and optimize the learning environment. In the middle of this, the tools for learning analytics are set. When the goal is to design and implement a learning analytics tool, none of those aspects can be neglected.

At an early stage of design for a learning analytics prototype one has to look at what has already been done, what worked, and what did not. Ebner et al. (2015) suggest seven features of smart learning analytics:

- Learning Awareness: Learners should be informed about their state and process in the learning process by the tool.
- Privacy Awareness: Data confidentiality must be considered from all stakeholders to be able to trust the tool.
- Time Awareness: Learning does not happen at one specific point in time, smart tools need to provide temporal information about the learning process.
- Visual Feedback: Smart tools can visualize highly complex coherences in an easy and understandable fashion.
- Pedagogical Intervention: Educators have to know how to react/interact with the provided information by the tool.

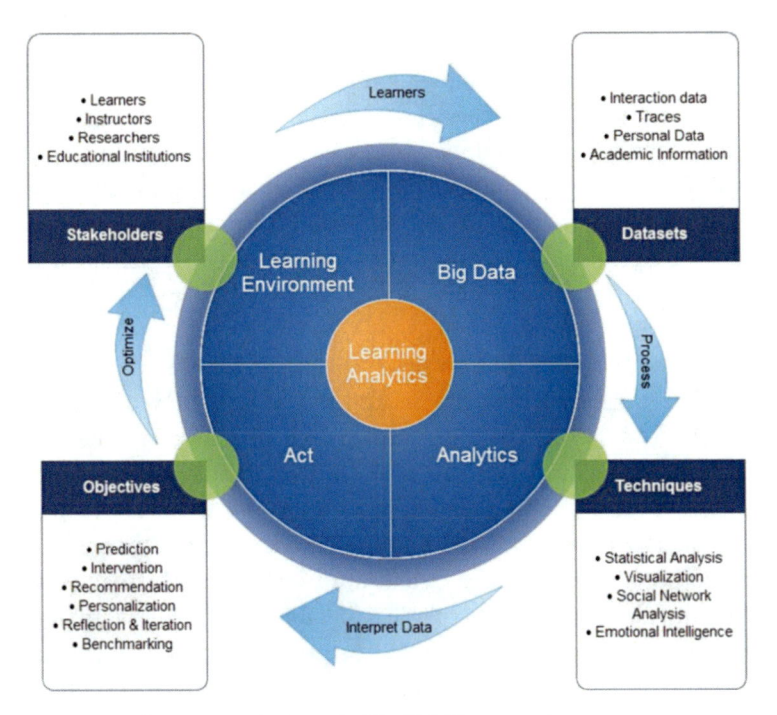

FIGURE 14.1   Learning analytics cycle (Khalil & Ebner, 2015)

- Big Data Centralism: Produced learning data should be aggregated centrally and reliably.
- Knowledge Structure Acquisition: New knowledge arising from the tool should be brought into the feedback loop to enhance the tool as well.

With these guidelines and lessons learned in mind this research work aims to provide a proof-of-concept implementation of a learning analytics tool, a Learning Analysis Cockpit subsequently called *LA Cockpit*. Analysing the available datasets generated from MOOCs requires the definition of metrics. These define the core of the learning analytics tool. Further, the metrics are needed to structure the aggregated data into a representation easy usable for visualization. The integration into a learning management system requires a certain modular structure as well as a level of configurability. The prototype should be easily integrated and extendible for further research.

2   Research Design

In our research study we are strongly following the approach of information systems prototyping. According to Alavi (1984) as well as Larsen (1986) prototyping is based on four steps: identifying basic requirements, development of a working prototype, implementation and usage, and revision. Therefore, we identified adminstrators' requirements according to a Learning Analytics Dashboard and developed a first working system (Nunamaker & Chen, 1990). The following chapters will describe the concept, design, and implementation of the cockpit in more detail. After the final implementation, we observed the usage through administrators and did some workshops with them to refine our prototype.

2.1   *Concept and Design of the Cockpit*

The developed Learning Analytics (LA) Cockpit should be deployed as plugin for the MOOC platform iMooX (https://imoox.at), which is based on the popular learning management system Moodle (https://moodle.org/). Derived from discussions with involved stakeholders, administrators, and researchers administering the MOOC platform, the tool should take care of data aggregation, logging, and provide interactive visualizations whilst still be seamlessly integrable into the platform. The modular expandability, high configurability, and customization options of the Open Source prototype is able to guarantee further use and development. Therefore, the following features are defined beforehand:

- The *LA Cockpit* must be provided as plugin for Moodle for easy maintenance and upgrade.
- It should be reliable for scheduled data aggregation and processing in the background.
- There must be a unit-tested data aggregation.
- Modular and configurable system design is also a precondition.
- The Dashboard design is choose for a flexible customization.
- Finally, an interactive visual representation of aggregated data should be possible.

2.2   *Concept*

The *LA Cockpit* prototype should be integrable into the MOOC platform (Moodle) as easily as possible, guaranteeing maintainability as well as extendibility. Based on the requirements the prototype has been divided into the following main components: the data aggregation, metrics to identify the key aspects of the *LA Cockpit,* and subsequently the visualization of the key figures in a dashboard layout.

1.   Data Aggregation: The *LA Cockpit* needs to gather its datasets from the platform database's tables. Moodle stores and projects the user activity and system events in different tables. Regular and scheduled data

aggregation can be done with Moodle's scheduled tasks which are essentially cronjobs run from the LMS instance itself. Plugins can add their own tasks to that, the prototype adds its cronjob for daily data aggregation.

2. Metrics: The prototype focuses on a minimal group of stakeholders, namely administrators and researchers. 'How active are users on the platform?' or 'Is the quiz used at all?'—These and similar questions arise and can be answered in a clear and simple way. The main motivation for the *LA Cockpit* metrics is to define key aspects on how to measure the learners' level of engagement. Most of the learning management systems, including Moodle, record learners' activities by gathering information about events and storing them in exhaustive log tables. Processing them into a higher level of abstraction improves insight into the learning process. (Munoz-Merino et al., 2013). The learner's behaviour can be separated into different categories directly related to the offered activities in the courses of the MOOC. In the prototype, we focus on a global abstraction level—aggregating key aspects platform wide and propose three basic metrics.
   - M1: Logins over time
   - M2: Quiz Statistics
   - M3: Forum Post Frequency

The data aggregation will happen daily, even if the visualization might provide a weekly time frame. One of the requirements was reliability and with daily aggregation as cronjob we can guarantee an efficient and detailed logging process. Distinct user information is not logged, only aggregated numbers are part of the metrics. Further, all log files are deleted in a pre-defined time interval to comply with privacy regulations. Privacy and ethics are a delicate topic when applying learning analytics in MOOCs and as all data are user-related it has to be handled with confidentiality and cautiousness (Pardo & Siemens, 2014).

2.3 *Design Reflections*

The features agreed on in the concept require the *LA Cockpit* to provide a high-level overview of available metrics as well as the filter or customization options. A dashboard design will provide a familiar environment. Each metric is a small piece of grouped information visualized via a chart and each chart is encapsulated into a widget (Taraghi et al., 2011). Widgets must consist of a header, filter-area, and the chart canvas itself and be susceptible to customization, resizing, and dragging on the dashboard. This allows better user experience and focus on certain parts of the visualized data and metrics.

The user can arrange each widget to their preferences, resizing, and dragging several of those widgets on the dashboard might lead to overlap between them. Therefore, the *LA Cockpit* constrains resizing and hiding essential information behind another widget by snapping back to allowed size or position. Movement of the labox containers is constrained to the left and right of the current available page size of the Moodle theme from iMooX to prevent horizontal scrolling. The bottom resizes dynamically with the drag of a widget. That way the dashboard is kept uncluttered whilst still being dynamic in arrangement of the widgets

2.4 Use Cases

A typical user session with the *LA Cockpit* can consist of various actions. In this section we created the most important use cases:

- Log in to the system: Moodle itself requires a login, the credential upon login is checked. If the capabilities are present, they will see a link to the plugin in the side navigation tree in the Administration Block. The prototype *LA Cockpit* is only accessible for users with the administrator role.
- Redirect to dashboard: A click upon that navigation item redirects to a new page, the dashboard layout. Header and footer of the original Moodle theme are kept, all other navigation elements are hidden.
- Displayed widgets: The state, the plugin exited last session, is recovered, all widgets and their filter preferences present in the database are loaded. The current available data in the plugin's tables is loaded.
- Change: Adding or deleting widgets with the provided menu options. Filter data with provided filter options.
- Session: Logging out from the user or a time out by the system guarantees no access to unauthorized users.

3 Implementation

3.1 Overall Architecture

The easiest way to provide new functionality while still guaranteeing maintainability for Moodle is by writing plugins. There are many predefined types available; it was decided to implement a local plugin. This type features the most freedom for developers, as it imposes no restrictions on structure, design, and capabilities.

Structurally, a Moodle plugin is a folder of PHP scripts (as well as CSS, JavaScript, etc. if necessary). Moodle core communicates with the plugin by looking for particular entry points, often defined in the file lib.php within the plugin.

3.2   *Widgets Implementation*

Each widget of the *LA Cockpit* holds one of the visualizations of the metrics M1 to M3. They all share a common structure but need different charting options (chart type, axes, titles). An abstract factory design pattern allows efficient creation of widgets with guaranteed common functionality in the abstract functions and different concrete implementations (Figure 14.2).

The abstract class chart.php holds member variables for id, canvas id, xpos, ypos, height, width, dataset, labelset, and additional charting options such as chart title and the corresponding getter functions. Further its constructor construct (id, type, xpos, ypos, width, height) and functions to display and render the widgets with Moodle's integrated module, and functions to setup the HTML elements of a widget labox.

The class chartfactory.php has a function constructAllFromDbase(), called from index.php upon start of the plugin. All widgets displayed on the dashboard are queried from the *LA Cockpit* table dashboard. The factory call then creates the corresponding widget type.

Each widget prepares a HTML5 canvas element for the visualization, the chart itself is provided by the Chart.js library. The basic structure of such a chart.is the same for each type of visualization, together with the factory design pattern it is possible to configure each chart to its displayed data.

The array data consists of labels and datasets. With the options array it is possible to configure a variety of display options such as axes, labels, titles or tooltips. *LA Cockpit* makes heavy use of this configuration to dynamically add content and styling options to each widget.

Adhering to this structure by initially creating only a basic chart and adding further options with JavaScript dynamically later, the extendibility of the prototype is guaranteed.

Adding new widgets (and therefore metrics) to the core of the prototype is simple, because the basic building blocks stay the same and only the separate visualization properties need to be set.

3.3   *Cockpit Interaction*

After the *LA Cockpit* dashboard loads, all the displayed chart data is up-dated with AJAX requests. There are no multiple page reloads necessary to visualize the widgets.

In more detail, upon redirect to the *LA Cockpit* index page, the dashboard layout is set up. The plugin checks in its dashboard table which widgets are presented. For each of those, the chart factory creates the labox container and its header-, filter- and chart elements and uses Moodle's renderer to display the widgets. The display method calls the corresponding JavaScript functions for

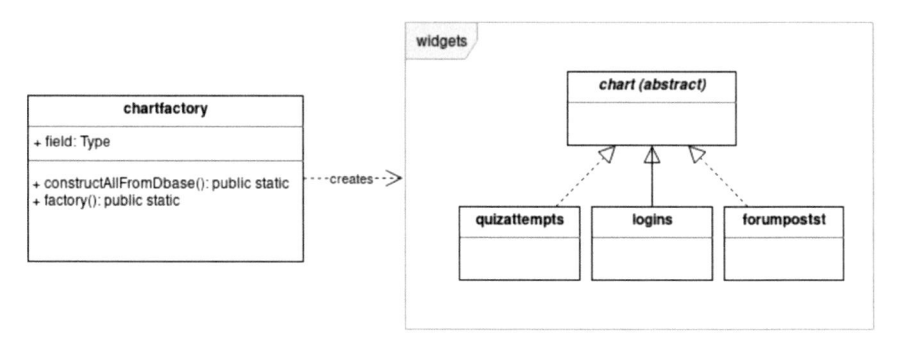

FIGURE 14.2   UML of abstract factory pattern for chart.php

the filter and chart elements, which in turn use the provided AJAX functionality to fetch the chart data from the corresponding tables.

For a better overview of the widget's dynamic loading process the sequence diagram (Figure 14.3) lists the involved server and client files and the AJAX requests in between them.

4   Discussion

In general, it can be pointed out that the visualizations of the metrics help to get a first impression of the online courses. This impression is used to look for a conspicuousness of a specific course. Normally courses behave rather typical—for example on Monday most of the learners log on and getting fewer along the course time period. Most of the learners never do a post in a forum and most of the posters not more than two postings. There are already a number of studies carrying out the drop-out-problem (Khalil & Ebner, 2014) or addressing the less interaction (Lackner et al., 2016).

With the help of this metrics it can be seen very fast if a MOOC behaves like other ones. On the other side if a didactical measure is taken this can lead to a non-typical graph. For example, in the publication of Khalil et al. (2017) the use of Gamification-elements within MOOCs is described and that the number of done quizzes increase von week 1 to week 2. Similar effects can be seen by the use of Open Badges as certification (Kopp & Ebner, 2017).

Figure 14.4 presents the widget for the timespan of one of our MOOCs, the SIMOOC with over 1300 participants. It started at the 9th October 2017 and the duration was 8 weeks. Whereby, every week a module is made accessible to the participants of the course. The basic metric of the *logins over time* shows the number of distinct successful logged in events of the system. The visualization for M1 is a line chart, due to its temporal character; this metric is

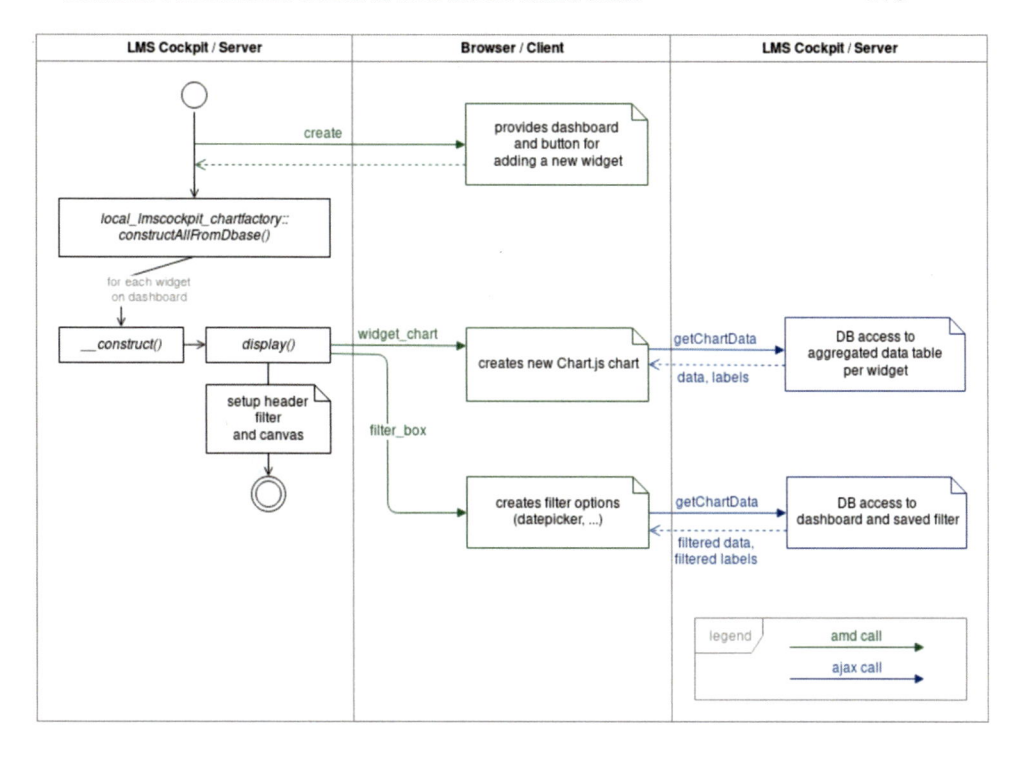

FIGURE 14.3   Sequence diagram of widget creation

filterable per time frame. The line chart presents that more people are active at the beginning of each week when a new section was made accessible and decreases drastically until the end. Additionally, it shows the overall activity for the participants decrease over the duration of the course.

The next metric of the prototype represents the activity in forums (M3). It counts the number of users per number of forum posts and forums are attributed to a course. Whereby, a course can contain more than one forum. The cron task daily aggregates the distribution per course without direct attribution to individual users. The information is filterable per course which allows side-by-side comparison in a doughnut chart.

Figure 14.5 presents the comparison of the forum post frequency between three different MOOCs. It can be seen that the MOOC "Das Internet in meinem Unterricht" holds much more postings as the other ones. Furthermore, there are more learners posting more than 2 postings than in a typical MOOC. If a closer look is done, it can be pointed out that in this MOOC the teachers used the forum intensively for an exchange between learners and prompted them to talk about their personal experiences in different school situations. This leads to many personal statements and discussions and must be seen as a didactical measurement.

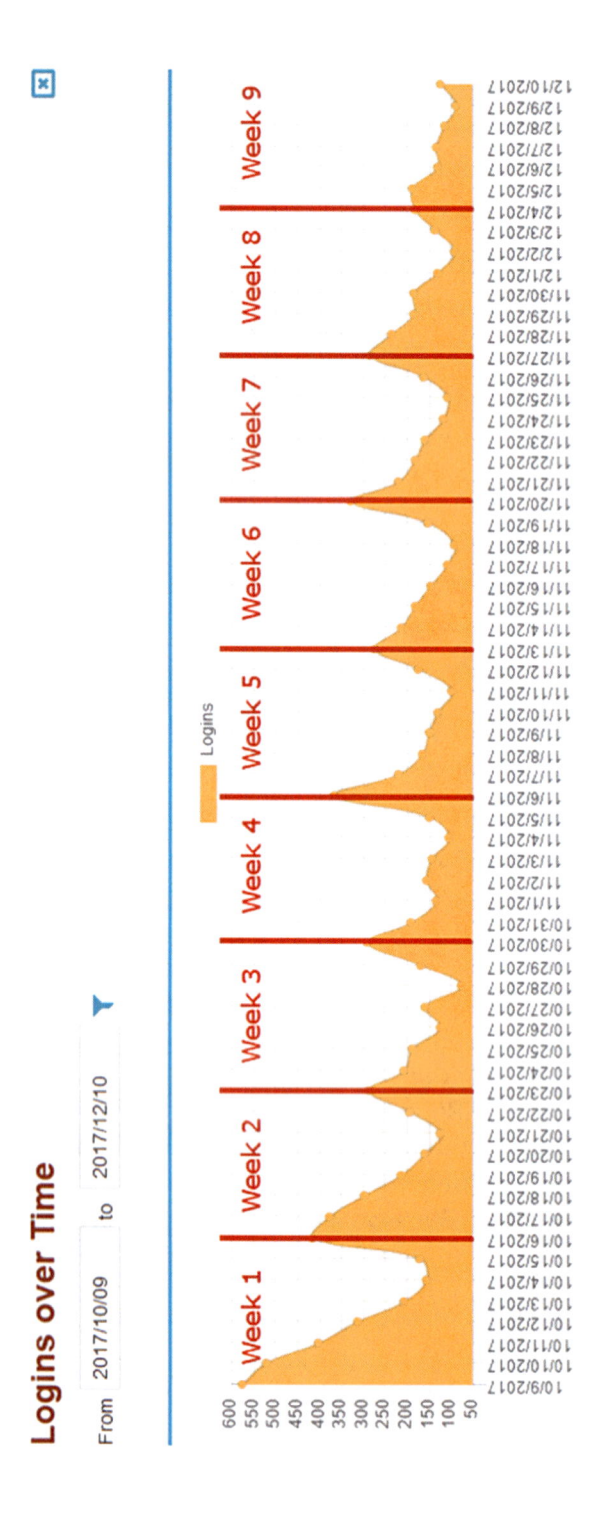

FIGURE 14.4   Widget for logins over time with filter set for the duration of the s1MOOC

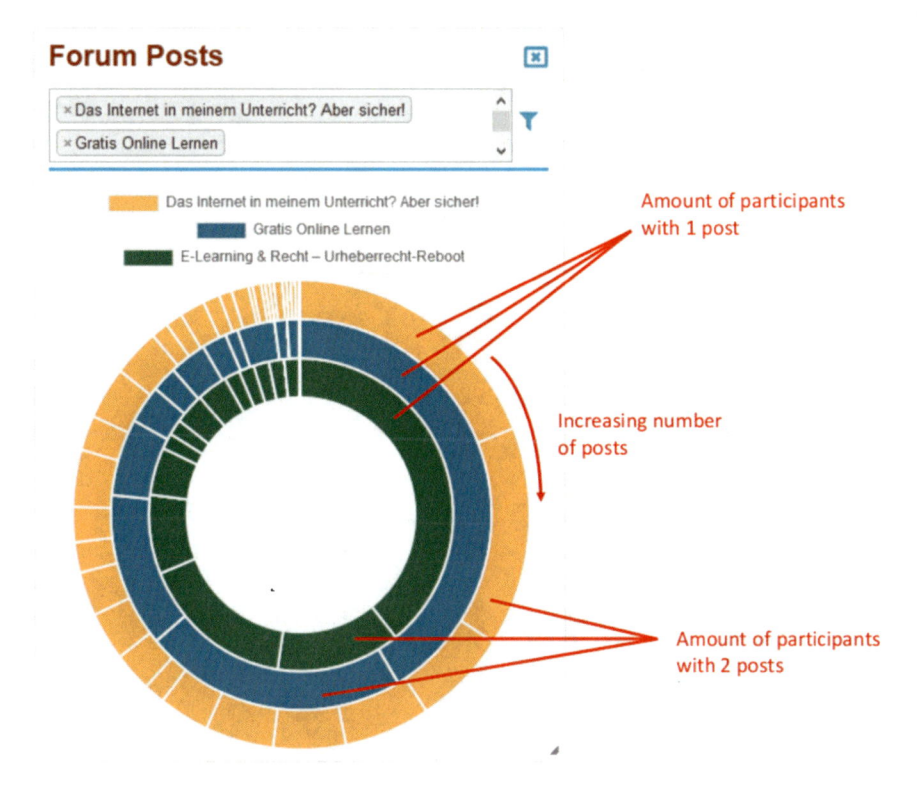

FIGURE 14.5   Widget with the comparison of the post frequency between three different
MOOCS

The last metric (M2) is about quiz statistics. Quizzes are often part of a course and require the learner to participate and finish them successfully. LA Cockpit daily aggregates the state the learners are in, for each quiz from the table quiz and quiz attempts. The count of users per quiz for the states of finished and in process are visualized in a stacked bar chart.

In Figure 14.6 there are some quizzes, which are dramatically different to the rest and provide a high finishing rate. Looking a little bit closer, it can be seen that those quizzes are part of MOOCS with obligatory exams. In other words those quizzes are mandatory for a higher number of students. Therefore, this leads to the statement that the use of MOOCS within a curriculum leads to a higher commitment of the learners.

Finally, it can be seen that the visualization of the metrics should lead to a final report for teachers as well as administrators. Teachers will need that to get an information about how their course performed, to see how learners engaged with their learning contents, and if there are problems occurring or vice versa a didactical approach works quite well. Administrators can see

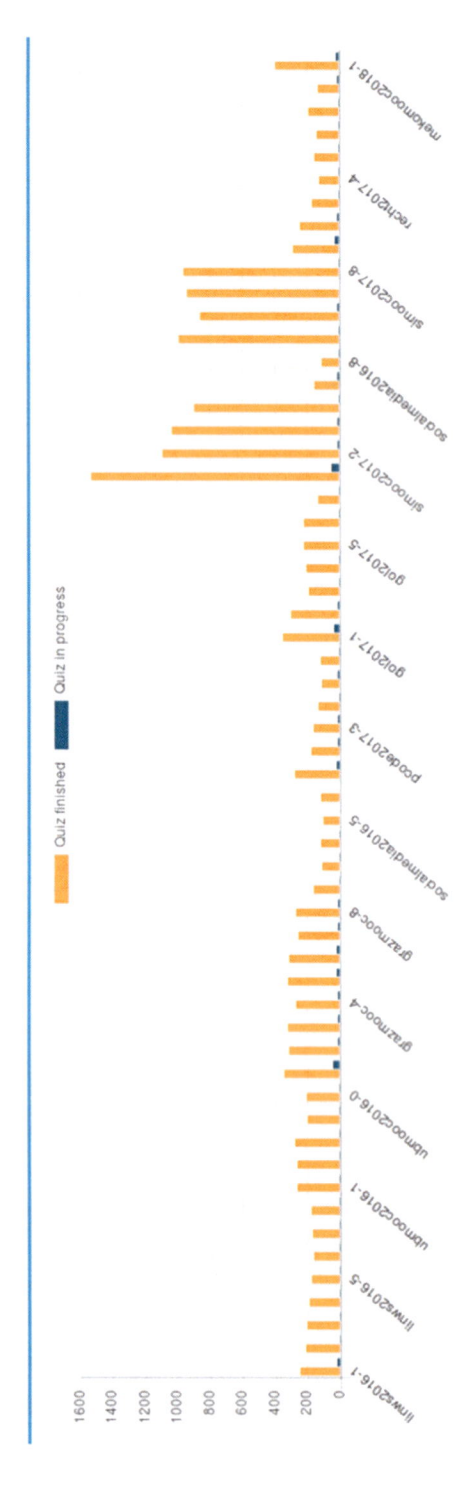

FIGURE 14.6   Widget for quiz attempts, which opposes users with state *in progress* to state *finished*

if a course behaves normal or un-normal. They can learn which didactical approaches are of interest for forthcoming MOOCs and which should not be used anymore. This report will be one of the next steps for the dashboard.

5 Conclusion

The Open Source learning management system Moodle provides a suitable environment to deploy a working prototype of a learning analytics plugin. In the context of MOOCs and the target user group of the tool it is very important to carefully choose the data, which should be aggregated and displayed. Learning Analytics uses a set of tools and the focus was not only about what to visualize but also how to visualize aggregated data.

The visualizations of the metrics are dynamic, interactive, and allow the user to quickly see coherences from big datasets otherwise not graspable. The research work shows that even in a prototype such as the *LA Cockpit* appealing visualizations are a key component when transferring statistical information and transferring learning analytics knowledge.

The promising feedback for the *LA Cockpit* will hopefully foster further learning analytics with this tool. The prototype, crafted with extensibility in mind, should allow further quantifiable insight in the learner's behaviour and process of learning with MOOCs on the iMooX platform.

The *LA Cockpit* shows that even a small set of stakeholders and users benefit from applying basic learning analytics. Data visualization of customized metrics allows interpretation of data coherences otherwise not accessible in an efficient and user-friendly way.

The prototype is an extendible and configurable base, therefore it is simple to add further learning analytics capabilities. These additional metrics can cover a wide range of activities. Courses that offer video lectures can provide motivation for aggregating key aspects such as "number of video lessons watched."

More filter options breaking the aggregated data from a system-wide down to course-wide level will further improve the user experience of *LA Cockpit*.

Extending the metrics will also be one of the most promising next steps for the *LA Cockpit*. Changing the granularity of displayed data gives the stakeholders additional insight in the learners' behaviour in the context of the iMooX platform.

Future features of the *LA Cockpit* should not only close the feedback loop to help learners in their learning process. On one hand, comparison to average scores might provide an incentive to the learner and help them successfully complete their MOOCs. On the other, the provided learning material in MOOCs as part of the learning process can benefit from optimization due to learning analytics. Well-documented and interactive learning material encourages learner activity as well.

References

Alavi, M. (1984). An assessment of the prototyping approach to information systems development. *Communications of the ACM, 27*(6), 556–563.

Clow, D. (2012). The learning analytics cycle: Closing the loop effectively. In *Proceedings of the 2nd International Conference on Learning Analytics and Knowledge.* doi: 10.1145/2330601.2330636

Dawson, S., Gasevic, D., Siemens, G., & Joksimovic, S. (2014). Current state and future trends: A citation network analysis of the learning analytics field. In *Proceedings of the Fourth International Conference on Learning Analytics and Knowledge.* doi: 10.1145/2567574.2567585

Dragan, G., Jelena, J., Abelardo, P., & Shane, D. (2017). Detecting learning strategies with analytics: Links with self-reported measures and academic performance. *Journal of Learning Analytics, 4*(2), 113–128. doi: 10.18608/jla.2017. 42.10

Duval, E. (2012). *Learning analytics and educational data mining.* Retrieved from https://erikduval.wordpress.com/2012/01/30/learning-analytics-and-educational-data-mining/

Ebner, M., Taraghi, B., Saranti, A., & Schön, S. (2015). Seven features of smart learning analytics: Lessons learned from four years of research with learning analytics. *eLearning Papers, 40,* 51–55.

Elias, T. (2011). *Learning analytics: The definitions, the processes, and the potential.*

Johnson, L., Adams, S., & Cummins, M. (2012). *The NMC horizon report: 2012 higher education edition.* Retrieved from https://www.learntechlib.org/p/48964

Khalil, H., & Ebner, M. (2014). MOOCs completion rates and possible methods to improve retention: A literature review. In *Proceedings of World Conference on Educational Multimedia, Hypermedia and Telecommunications 2014* (pp. 1236–1244), Chesapeake, VA: AACE.

Khalil, M., & Ebner, M. (2015). Learning analytics: Principles and constraints. In *Proceedings of ED-Media 2015 Conference.*

Khalil, M., & Ebner, M. (2016). When learning analytics meets MOOCS: A review on IMOOX case studies. In *Innovations for Community Services, 16th International Conference.* doi: 10.1007/978-3-319-49466-1 1

Khalil, M., Ebner, M., & Admiraal, W. (2017). How can gamification improve MOOC students engagement? In *Proceedings of the European Conference on Game Based Learning* (pp. 819–828), Graz, Austria.

Kopp, M., & Ebner, M. (2017). La certificación de los MOOC. Ventajas, desafíos y experiencias prácticas. *Revista española de pedagogía, 75*(266), 83–100.

Lackner, E., Khalil, M., & Ebner, M. (2016). How to foster forum discussions within MOOCs: A case study. *International Journal of Academic Research in Education, 2*(2), 113. doi: 10.17985/ijare.31432

Larson, O. (1986). Information systems prototyping. In *Proceedings Interez HP 3000 Conference* (pp. 351–364). Retrieved from http://www.openmpe.com/cslproceed/HPIX86/P351.pdf

Leitner, P., Khalil, M., & Ebner, M. (2017). Learning analytics in higher education: A literature review. In A. Peña-Ayala (Ed.), *Learning analytics: Fundaments, applications, and trends* (pp. 1–23). doi: 10.1007/978-3-319-52977-6

Munoz-Merino, P., Ruiperez Valiente, J., & Kloos Delgado, C. (2013). Inferring higher level learning information from low level data for the Khan Academy platform. In *Proceedings of the Third International Conference on Learning Analytics and Knowledge.* doi: 10.1145/2460296.2460318

Nunamaker Jr., J. F., Chen, M., & Purdin, T. D. (1990). Systems development in information systems research. *Journal of Management Information Systems, 7*(3), 89–106.

Pardo, A., & Siemens, G. (2014). Ethical and privacy principles for learning analytics. *British Journal of Educational Technology.* doi: 10.1111/bjet.12152

Schwendimann, B. A., Rodriguez-Triana, M. J., Vozniuk, A., Prieto, L. P., Boroujeni, M. S., Holzer, A., Gillet, D., & Dillenbourg, P. (2016). Understanding learning at a glance: An overview of learning dashboard studies. In *Proceedings of the Sixth International Conference on Learning Analytics & Knowledge.* doi: 10.1145/2883851.2883930

Siemens, G. (2011). *Learning and academic analytics.* Retrieved from http://www.learninganalytics.net/?p=131

Siemens, G., & Long, P. (2011). Penetrating the fog: Analytics in learning and education. *EDUCAUSE Review, 46*(5). doi: 10.17471/2499-4324/195

Taraghi, B., Altmann, T., & Ebner, M. (2011, July 12–14). *The world of widgets: An important step towards a personalized learning environment.* Paper presented at Proceedings of the PLE Conference.